New Public Governance, the Third Sector and Co-Production

Edited by Victor Pestoff, Taco Brandsen and Bram Verschuere

Routledge
Taylor & Francis Group
NEW YORK   LONDON

First published 2012
by Routledge
711 Third Avenue, New York, NY 10017

Simultaneously published in the UK
by Routledge
2 Park Square, Milton Park, Abingdon, Oxfordshire OX14 4RN

First issued in paperback 2015

*Routledge is an imprint of the Taylor & Francis Group,
an informa business*

Typeset in Sabon by IBT Global.

Library of Congress Cataloging-in-Publication Data
   New public governance, the third sector and co-production / edited by Victor Pestoff, Taco Brandsen, and Bram Verschuere.
      p. cm. — (Routledge critical studies in public management ; 7)
   Includes bibliographical references and index.
   1.   Public administration.   2.   Nonprofit organizations.   3.   Public-private sector cooperation.   4.   Social participation.   I. Pestoff, Victor Alexis. II. Brandsen, Taco. III. Verschuere, Bram, 1977–
   JF1351.N46 2011
   338.6'3—dc23
   2011023968

ISBN 13: 978-1-138-95207-2 (pbk)
ISBN 13: 978-0-415-89713-6 (hbk)

Contents

PART II
How Does Co-Production Work?

PART III
How Does Co-Management Work?

Tables

Figures

Foreword

Elinor Ostrom

This book, edited by Professors Pestoff, Brandsen and Verschuere, is a major step forward in the integration of the concept of co-production with other key concepts used in policy analysis, including the third sector, housing cooperatives, information sciences and a wide variety of public policy problems. They draw on research that has been conducted in many countries in Europe, including Germany, Italy, Norway and Sweden. This volume marks the beginning of a new era when co-production is viewed as an important process that can increase the benefits to citizens as well as to public officials trying to improve the quality of public services without major increases in costs.

Co-production describes processes through which diverse inputs are contributed by individuals and organizations that are not part of an official government agency primarily responsible for producing a particular public good or service. When parents allocate time watching children at play in a day care center, supervising high school students at a sports event or working with a group doing their math homework, they are "co-producing" education with the public staff hired by a school to train and watch children enrolled in public schools. Further, educational achievements cannot be obtained without the co-production of the students.

The term "co-production" originated in an effort to understand some of the empirical findings obtained in a series of studies of urban policing in a diversity of U.S. urban areas (Parks et al., 1981). Responses by citizens to surveys administered in studies of similar neighborhoods served by small- to medium-sized police departments compared to very large departments differed strongly in regard to the level of trust that citizens had in a department. This was in turn affected by the size of the department. Citizens living in small cities were more likely to know some of the officers, to report suspicious events rapidly, and to evaluate police responses positively (Ostrom and Parks, 1999). In some of the neighborhoods served by large cities, residents did not know the police serving their area (largely because police officers rotated service areas every twenty-eight days). They were unwilling to report suspicious events. In fact, we were frequently told that a respondent served by large departments would not call the police for anything other than a major crime in their home. There was a sense that they might be hassled if they called the police.

We tried to make sense of the findings that the cost of policing was less in small- to medium-sized departments, while the results in terms of crime rate, citizen evaluation of police and other factors showed that they were more effective. We did not think it was simply that the police were more effective. We had the sense from talking with citizens that they were more involved. After struggling with it, we finally decided to use the term "co-production" to reflect the fact that in many of these smaller units, the police were not the only producers of safety. Citizens were actively co-producing much of the safety in the neighborhood by watching children walking home from school, by noticing that there was a light on in someone's home and a strange car parked in front when they were known to be on vacation and by gathering together in various ways to enjoy coffee together on outdoor porches in front of their homes. In general, citizens served by small- to medium-sized departments felt responsible for what was occurring in their neighborhood. After struggling to develop the concept, we developed still further more theoretical discussions of it. We then realized that it related to schools and many other services, including health and neighborhood upkeep (see McGinnis, 1999).

In this book, the authors have first reviewed the basic meaning of co-production and some of the debates that have ensued over the concept since our first development of it in the 1970s. What is encouraging is that new examples of co-production have been described in countries across the world.

In the second part of the book, the question "how does co-production work?" is addressed. Here the concept of volunteering that has a long tradition in the United States is discussed as one of the important mechanisms for achieving co-production. Network structure in public education and other services is another mechanism. The authors are careful to indicate repeatedly that co-production is not a panacea. There are efforts made to increase the voice and activities of citizens that fail. When these efforts do involve citizens in a productive way, however, outcomes are much more positive and costs are less.

The authors then contrast co-production with "co-management." Obviously, processes that enhance co-management get citizens into the decision-making arena for some of the day-to-day management decisions related to local governments, public housing or other activities. As co-managers, they may not *produce* services but do provide their voice in how services are produced and evaluated.

In the last section, the authors focus on service quality, accountability and democracy as potential effects of co-production. By engaging in careful empirical work of alternatives in the field, such as the difference in service quality obtained in co-produced child care versus municipally produced child care, scholars are digging into alternative ways of sharing production processes, including privatization as well as voluntary associations. By identifying co-production as a core element of new public governance, Victor Pestoff provides a cogent overview of new conceptions of governance that do not view the state as the sole actor in governance processes.

The depth of analysis and breadth of application of the chapters in this book will enable scholars, public officials and citizens to gain better insight about complex processes of governments. Yes, co-production is a key concept of new approaches. It is excellent to have a book that covers the breadth and depth that the authors of this book have achieved. As someone involved in the early struggle to understand co-production, I have benefited greatly from the work presented in this volume.

REFERENCES

McGinnis, M., ed. 1999. *Polycentricity and Local Public Economies: Readings from the Workshop in Political Theory and Policy Analysis*. Ann Arbor: University of Michigan Press.

Ostrom, E., and R. B. Parks. 1999. Neither Gargantua nor the land of Lilliputs: Conjectures on mixed systems of metropolitan organization. In M. McGinnis, ed., *Polycentricity and Local Public Economies: Readings from the Workshop in Political Theory and policy analysis*. Ann Arbor: University of Michigan Press, pp. 284–305.

Parks, R., P. Baker, L. Kiser, R. Oakerson, E. Ostrom, V. Ostrom, S. Percy, M. Vandivort, G. Whitaker, and R. Wilson. 1981. Consumers as coproducers of public services: Some economic and institutional considerations. *Policy Studies Journal* 9 (7): 1001–1011.

1 Co-Production as a Maturing Concept

Taco Brandsen, Victor Pestoff and Bram Verschuere

INTRODUCTION

The concept of co-production has been around for decades, but in recent years it has experienced a revival. Public management research in a variety of disciplines has paid increasing attention to the role of citizens and the third sector in the provision of public services. The growth of interest in co-production during the past ten years provides important insights into, and at the same time poses important challenges for, public management.

Following previous work in this field, particularly in the tradition of Ostrom, we will define co-production as

> the mix of activities that both public service agents and citizens contribute to the provision of public services. The former are involved as professionals, or "regular producers," while "citizen production" is based on voluntary efforts by individuals and groups to enhance the quality and/or quantity of the services they use. (Parks et al., 1981)

This understanding has been referred to as a possible bridge over the great academic divide between the consumption and provision of public services (Ostrom, 1999). More recently, exploring co-production has become increasingly topical for a broad range of academics with a focus on, and/or practitioners working with, public services and management. These include the issues of the nature of co-production (Alford, 2002); how co-production has developed in recent decades (Pestoff and Brandsen, 2006); the relationship between individual and group participation in the provision of public services (Bovaird and Löffler, 2003); how co-production can contribute to the development of service quality in public services (Bouchard et al., 2006); how it can promote participative democracy (Ostrom, 2000; Fung, 2004); and how ownership and institutional set-ups are related to co-production (Vamstad, 2007; Pestoff, 2009).

However, although there is a growing body of work describing, or claiming to describe, co-production, we still lack a comprehensive theoretical and systematic empirically orientated understanding of what happens when citizens and/or the third sector are drawn into public service provision and of the various aspects of co-production. This book takes a step forward in developing a better understanding of this phenomenon.

BACKGROUND

Co-production can potentially be traced to various traditions, which will be addressed in the various chapters of this volume. Here we will specifically refer to the 2009 Nobel Laureate in Economics, Elinor Ostrom (Ostrom 1999). In the early 1970s, she and her colleagues studied urban reform in major cities in the United States (Ostrom, 1975). After completing their research on urban services and summarizing their results, they concluded that most public services are not delivered by a single public authority, but rather by several different actors, both public and private. Moreover, many public services depend heavily on the contribution of time and effort by the same people who consume these services, that is, the clients and citizens.

They coined the term *co-production* to describe the potential relationship that could exist between "regular producers," such as street-level police, schoolteachers or health workers, and their "clients," who want to be transformed by the services into safer, better educated and/or healthier people. It later spread to Europe, Asia, Australia and elsewhere and is now used by researchers in many parts of the world to analyze citizen participation in the provision of publicly financed services, regardless of the provider. This is of course not to say that there was no empirical or theoretical work on the issue prior to the concept of co-production. Indeed, many studies focusing on citizen participation have addressed it, albeit with different terms and with a different focus. What is new is that it is addressed as a cross-cutting phenomenon in the context of public management research.

In this sense, research on the topic came together at the beginning of the new century, in networks that were assembled around the study of nonprofit or third sector organization in the public sector. In particular, much of the work focusing on co-production as a cross-cutting phenomenon came together under the auspices of the European Group for Public Administration (EGPA) and the International Research Society for Public Management (IRSPM). Several conference papers presented at the annual sessions of the EGPA's third sector study group and at third sector panels of the IRSPM focused on various aspects of co-production. This has led to the further refinement of the concept. In particular, it led to the distinction between the original concept of co-production, which focuses on the relationship between individual citizens and producers, and "co-management," which centers on relationships at the organizational level (see Brandsen and Pestoff, 2006). Both are addressed in this volume.

In 2006, the *Public Management Review* published a special issue (volume 8 number 4) on co-production, called *Co-Production. The Third*

Sector and the Delivery of Public Services. It was later reprinted by Routledge and made available in paperback (Pestoff and Brandsen, 2006). This book is a second collection that aims to go further by systematizing the growing body of academic papers and reports that focus on various aspects of co-production and its potential contribution to new public governance (Osborne, 2010).

FOCUS OF THIS BOOK

This book addresses the nexus of issues and disciplines interested in co-production, and through them it makes a contribution to public management research. The concept of co-production sits at the crossroads of a number of disciplines—including business administration, policy studies, political science, public management, sociology and third sector studies. They all have important perspectives on this topic, and all of them are important for the development of public management and public services. Bringing them together in this volume both allows for comparing and contrasting these different perspectives and for potential theoretical collaboration and development.

More particularly, this volume addresses the following concerns:

- *Conceptual issues*: What is the nature of co-production, and what different conceptualizations exist, especially in the context of public management?
- *Empirical issues*: How does co-production in public service delivery work in practice? Is it as successful as some of its proponents have claimed? Given that we know how it works in practice, can co-production contribute to improved quality in public services?
- *Comparative issues*: How does the practice of co-production differ between countries and sectors?
- *Methodological issues*: What methods and theoretical approaches are most suitable for the examination of the topic?

CONTENTS

In this collection, we bring together a wide range of authors. Inevitably, we have had to strike a balance between capturing the diversity of approaches that exist in the field and achieving a systematic framework for the study of the concept.

The first part of the book addresses the question "what is co-production" and discusses the concept of co-production theoretically. In Chapter 2, Pestoff argues that co-production is the mix of public service agents and citizens who contribute to the provision of a public service.

This chapter addresses some crucial conceptual issues for co-production, including definitions and level of analysis; relations between the professional staff and their clients; motives for citizens to engage in co-production and collective action; and co-production as individual acts, collective action or both, and so on.

In Chapter 3, Bovaird and Loffler argue that user and community co-production can be conceptualized as a movement from "public services FOR the public" toward "public services BY the public" within the framework of a public sector that represents the public interest and publicly valued outcomes, not simply the interests of public service "consumers." However, it is not a panacea for all public sector issues, as the case studies clearly demonstrate. They show that, while co-production can achieve major improvements in outcomes and service quality and also cost savings, it is not resource-free. Co-production may be "value for money," but it usually cannot produce value *without* money.

In Chapter 4, Ewert and Evers argue that co-production lacks a fixed meaning, both on the level of interactions between organizations and the level of providing services to users. Different meanings unfold once one looks at the impact of narratives, such as consumerism, managerialism or participatory governance. Together with the traditions of state welfare, they simultaneously influence the modes and meanings of co-production in personal services. The example of modern health care systems in Germany shows that uncertainty and ambiguity is normal rather than an exception when it comes to defining co-production. Role expectations, such as the "expert-patient" or the "citizen-consumer," may have a liberating potential, but likewise they can marginalize crucial issues, such as trust and the need for protection. Moreover, user organizations face challenges in their roles beyond helping users to cope with making as good a choice as possible with some models of co-production.

In Chapter 5 by Vaillancourt, the participation of the third sector in the development of public policy in Canada is examined on two levels: the Canadian federal state level, and the provincial state level (Quebec). He concludes that third sector participation in public policy can take two forms: co-production, or the participation in the application of policy, and co-construction, or the participation in the design of policy. From this conceptual angle, two federal and six provincial policy initiatives are analysed and compared.

Ackerman discusses co-production and co-governance in terms of accountability in Chapter 6. Through an exploration of case studies from a wide variety of contexts (Brazil, Mexico, United States and India) and policy areas (poverty reduction, infrastructure provision, school reform, electoral administration and police reform), his chapter shows that state reformers should move beyond strategies based on "exit" and even "voice" to establish spaces of full "co-governance" with society. Instead of sending sections of the state off to society, Ackerman argues that it is often more fruitful to invite society into the inner chambers of the state, in order to strengthen government accountability.

The second and third parts of the book contain chapters on the practice of two related concepts: co-production and co-management. In both parts, chapters deal with the question "how do co-production and/or co-management work?"

Cahn and Gray note in Chapter 7 that citizen co-production in the advancement of public goods and services has a rich history in the United States. The concept embraces a wide range of volunteering, but it also can lay claim to distinctive progeny stemming from the civil rights movement and the Johnson administration's war on poverty. The statutory mandate "maximum feasible participation" in the Economic Opportunity Act of 1964 sought to enfranchise the poor with both a voice and a role in the implementation of the programs initiated as part of that effort. The chapter provides numerous examples of co-production generated by TimeBanking. The TimeBank movement developed its own version of co-production as a catalytic vehicle that takes "maximum feasible participation" as a source of citizen empowerment to a new level.

Porter's work in Chapter 8 demonstrates advantages of applying the concept of co-production to a specific government service, basic education. The co-production function for education services combines input from students, teachers, parents and community institutions. Input from these regular and consumer producers are required in some cases and are discretionary or contingent in others. At the student-teacher nexus, co-production is required. No learning can take place without voluntary, active involvement by a student. In addition, a large body of research has found that parents, student peers and community institutions contribute vital, but contingent, input. His chapter explores how the presence of these network structures constrains organizational arrangements used to coordinate and administer the co-production of education services.

Brandsen and Helderman note in Chapter 9 that co-production in housing could be of crucial importance, since housing is an area in which the involvement of citizens in the provision of services has the potential to enrich individual lifestyles, local communities and the organizations providing housing, regardless of whether they are public or private for-profit or nonprofit. However, in current housing markets, housing tends to be purely individual, either self-organized (through home ownership) or collectively managed (through social housing). The chapter explores the conditions under which co-production in this area could be successful as an alternative model. The analysis is based on empirical fieldwork carried out among German housing cooperatives. As it turns out, successful co-production depends primarily on the long-term maintenance of group boundaries and specific trajectories of organizational development. Established public and nonprofit housing providers could play a crucial role in fostering co-production by providing essential support to groups of citizens.

In Chapter 10, Meijer discusses the meaning of co-production in an information age. The core of his message is that technology is able to facilitate new practices of co-production: costs of large scale and dispersed action can be lowered, and new media can make co-production more "social" and "playful." The essential question, however, is what these changes mean for government. Meijer argues that in the information age, government needs to reassess the need, opportunities and forms of co-production. New connections between government and citizens can be developed, but the challenge remains to develop forms of co-production that appeal to citizens' motives to co-produce.

Brown and her colleagues in Chapter 11 maintain that while governments are engaged in developing social policy responses to address wicked issues, such as poverty, homelessness, drug addiction and crime, long-term resolution of these issues has remained elusive. Joint action and partnership between government and the community sector, such as co-management, is seen as a way of harnessing productive capability and innovative capacity of both these sectors to resolve these complex problems. However, models for actually undertaking this joint action are not well understood and have not been fully developed or evaluated. Their chapter examines new approaches to resolving the wicked issue of homelessness. It analyses a new horizontal "hub-based" model of service delivery that seeks to integrate actors across many different service areas and organizations. The role of the third sector in co-managing public services is examined through the in-depth case studies, and the results are presented together with an assessment of how co-management can contribute to service quality and service management in public services.

In Chapter 12, Schlappa discusses three cases of urban regeneration in which third sector organizations (TSOs) are engaged. Two cases are examples of co-management, where staff members of local development partnerships (LDPs) produce new services in collaboration with third sector organizations. In the third case, the local development partnership contracts and commissions services with third sector organizations, a practice that does not leave much scope for real collaboration. The analysis shows that co-management can occur in very different institutional contexts, and that TSOs and LDPs can both derive significant benefits from co-managing the development and delivery of new services. A number of variables can be identified that support the co-management process, specifically in urban regeneration contexts. These include a high degree of organizational flexibility in participating organizations; workers who share responsibility together for the provision of a new service; and senior managers who are able to navigate regulatory, institutional and political barriers that stand in the way of collaborative cross-organizational working.

Dezeure and De Rynck examine citizen participation in the realm of local service delivery in Chapter 13, addressing two fundamental questions: How does local government cope with the private initiatives set up by groups of citizens in several policy domains over time? And do these arrangements evolve to governance in terms of co-management or partnerships? They address these questions by merging two distinct strands of research—the theory of local participation and studies of local governance—and conduct an empirical analysis based on in-depth cases in several policy domains in the city of Ghent (Belgium). The main conclusion is that each nonprofit organization has its own story and line of development over time, embedded in its own institutional setting and mixed with the different balance between rules-in-form and rules-in-use. The findings underline the fact that local government is interfering in ongoing particular processes as they attempt to "manage" and "get a grip" on the citizen organizations. Over time, "particular" organizations are losing their autonomy, although they do not always perceive it that way, as some very government-like instruments tend to have a very governance-like impact in daily practice.

Freise discusses thirteen case studies of communal regulation partnerships in the field of traffic safety in North Rhine-Westphalia (Germany) in Chapter 14. He questions whether these partnerships can be considered as examples of co-production, and which strategies and methods these partnerships develop. But perhaps more importantly, Freise addresses the question of whether regulation partnerships between municipal police departments and civil society organizations increase input and output legitimacy, or whether they are an imposed cooperation from top down with the purpose of a democratic window dressing instead.

In Chapter 15, Tsukamoto examines the potential and limitations of nonprofit governmental partnerships for promoting citizen engagement in Japan. Increasing attention is paid to the involvement of nonprofit organizations in the provision of public services and to their partnership with local governments. Under local partnership frameworks, local nonprofit organizations become providers of services in different fields. They are also expected to promote civic engagement and to improve the quality of services. However, current public service reforms are primarily market driven by a New Public Management regime, through the introduction of the "Designated Manager" system. This subjects them to "institutional isomorphic" pressure. Tsukamoto's chapter examines the potential of local nonprofits to actively promote civic participation as co-production and to manage their interorganizational relationships with local governments.

In the fourth part of the book, we take a look at what effects co-production may yield. In several chapters, the effects of co-production on issues such as service quality, accountability and democracy are addressed.

Chapter 16 by Vamstad presents results from a study of service quality in co-produced child care in Swedish parent cooperatives. The results are compared to those of municipal child care, where there is little participation by the users of the services. The parent cooperative and the municipal child care represent two different schools of thought with regard to service quality. The municipal services have a strong tradition of professionalism, in which user participation is not allowed to interfere with the qualified work performed by trained professionals. The parent cooperatives have another tradition, in which service quality is developed in a dialogue between users and staff while they co-produce the services together. The former tradition is the dominant one in the Swedish welfare state, and this chapter provides a historical background to both professionalism and co-production in Sweden. The main conclusion of the chapter is that service quality is better in the parent cooperative child care, in spite of the widespread assumption in Sweden that service quality is close to synonymous with professionalism.

Calabrò notes in Chapter 17 that the privatization process has characterized and changed the public sector in many European countries in recent decades. However, it often ended with inefficiencies in public services, especially due to the incompleteness of privatization processes that usually resulted with providers still controlled by the state. In this debate, co-production of public services and goods seems to be a reasonable alternative to partial privatization processes. Stemming from different theoretical perspectives, the chapter highlights some problematic issues related to the lack of accountability characterizing many public service providers and suggests some main reasons in favor of co-production as a reasonable alternative. Through a multiple case study analysis, this chapter gives some insights into the Italian and the Norwegian situations. In spite of their institutional differences, the ministries are still the major owners of service providers in both countries and a common pattern appears to exist in relation to accountability problems. Finally, the chapter concludes that co-production provides a reasonable alternative for improving accountability to citizens and to cope with the problematic issues generated by partial privatization processes in such widely different contexts.

Vancoppenolle and Verschuere address the question whether co-management, conceptualized in Chapter 18 as the involvement of private organizations in public service provision, is threatening public accountability. Evidence collected from a case study of Flemish child care shows that the service delivery in Flemish child care is dysfunctional in at least two ways. First, the search process of parents for child care is very complex and difficult. Second, service providers do not always adhere to the admission policy regulations that apply when they decide to accept a child in their facility. It is argued that these problems at least partly stem from the complexity of the network of Flemish child care, characterized by many actors with multiple and fragmented accountability relations.

In Chapter 19, Pestoff shows that New Public Governance (NPG) puts much greater emphasis on citizen participation and third sector provision of social services than either traditional public administration or New Public Management. Co-production is a core element of NPG that promotes the mix of public service agents and citizens who contribute to the provision of a public service. However, client participation and influence in public services vary greatly and can range from manipulation to client control. This chapter explores the implications of two comparative studies of parent participation in preschool services in Europe. The first notes that co-production involves different dimensions: economic, social, political and service-specific participation. The second observes that citizen participation clearly varies between different providers of social services, as too does client and staff influence. This empirical overview concludes that some third sector providers can facilitate greater citizen participation, while a "glass ceiling" for participation exists in municipal and for-profit preschool services. These findings can contribute to a better understanding of the emerging paradigm of New Public Governance.

To *conclude* the book, Chapter 20 by Brandsen, Verschuere and Pestoff aims to draw together the main insights emerging from this collection and to raise some issues for further discussion and research.

REFERENCES

Alford, J. 2002. Why do public sector clients co-produce? Towards a contingency theory. *Administration & Society* 34 (1): 32–56.

Bovaird, T., and E. Löffler. 2003. Understanding public management and governance. In T. Bovaird and E. Löffler, eds., *Public Management & Governance*. London: Routledge.

Brandsen, T., and V. Pestoff. 2006. Co-production, the third sector and the delivery of public services: An introduction. *Public Management Review* 8 (4): 493–501.

Fung, A. 2004. *Empowered Participation: Reinventing Urban Democracy*. Princeton, NJ: Princeton University Press.

Osborne, S. P., ed. 2010. *The New Public Governance? New Perspectives on the Theory and Practice of Public Governance*. New York: Routledge.

Ostrom, E. 1975. *The Delivery of Urban Services: Outcomes of Change*. Beverly Hills, CA: Sage.

Ostrom, E. 1990. *Governing the Commons: The Evolution of Institutions for Collective Action*. Cambridge, UK: Cambridge University Press.

Ostrom, E. 1999. Crossing the Great Divide. Co-production, Synergy and Development. In M. D. McGinnes, ed., *Polycentric Governance and Development: Reading from the Workshop in Political Theory and Policy Analysis*. Ann Arbor: University of Michigan Press.

Ostrom, E. 2000. Crowding out Citizenship. *Scandinavian Political Studies* 23 (1): 1–16.

Ostrom, E. 2009. *Nobel Prize Lecture*. www.nobelprize.org.

Parks, R. B., P. C. Baker, L. Kiser, R. Oakerson, E. Ostrom, V. Ostrom, S. L. Percy, M. B. Vandivort, G. P. Whitaker, and R. Wilson. 1981. Consumers as co-producers of public services: Some institutional and economic considerations. *Policy Studies Journal* 9(7): 1001–1011.

Pestoff, V. 2009. *A Democratic Architecture for the Welfare State*. London: Routledge.

Pestoff, V., and T. Brandsen. 2006. Special issue, *Public Management Review: The Third Sector and the Delivery of Public Services* 8(4).

Vamstad, J. 2007. *Governing Welfare: the Third Sector and the Challenges to the Swedish Welfare State*. Östersund: Mid-Sweden University.

Part I
What Is Co-Production?

Conceptual and Theoretical Perspectives

2 Co-Production and Third Sector Social Services in Europe
Some Crucial Conceptual Issues

Victor Pestoff

Today, many European governments are searching for new ways to involve their citizens in the provision and governance of publicly financed social services. At a general level, the reasons are similar throughout Europe. First is the challenge of an aging population; second is the growing democracy deficit at all levels, local, regional, national and European; and third is the semipermanent austerity in public finances, made more acute by the recent global economic crisis. The response to these three challenges will, of course, vary between countries and across sectors of service provision, but some general trends are nevertheless observable. First is the promotion of greater volunteering. Second is the growth of new and different ways to involve users of social services as co-producers of their own and others' services. Third is the spread of new techniques of co-management and co-governance of social services, where the third sector plays a more prominent role in various European countries. Fourth is the development of user councils or other forms of functional representation at the local level to engage users in a dialogue about public services and to facilitate user participation in the provision and governance of such services. Taken together, they represent a major social innovation in the provision of public services and imply a different relationship for the third sector vis-à-vis the state.

Nobel laureate Elinor Ostrom and her colleagues analyzed the role of citizens in the provision of public services in terms of co-production (Parks et al., 1981). However, citizens in today's advanced welfare states have several different roles that represent diverse aspects of postmodern life. To name just a few, they are workers or salaried employees usually for eight hours a day, five days per week, for most of their life; they are family members, with a variety of roles and responsibilities that typically shift over time, circumstances and their life-cycle; they are taxpayers who contribute financially to the provision of public services; they are consumers who purchase various goods and services on the market;

they are clients who expect services from the public sector, and given increasing privatization of public service provision, even from private and third sector providers of publicly financed services; they are members of two or more voluntary organizations, perhaps active in some and inactive in others; they are voters who participate in elections every second to fifth year, depending on the country and support or reject the policies of the sitting government; they are active in various sports or other leisure activities, cultural or religious groups, and so on. Sometimes these roles complement each other, but sometimes they can come into conflict with each other. Moreover, sometimes citizens play these roles as individuals, but other times they do so in close collaboration with others, that is, in informal groups or in various voluntary organizations.

More important, given major social changes in Europe and Scandinavia, particularly with the growth of the welfare state at the end of World War II, the very state they interact with has also changed significantly. In the immediate post-WWII period, they faced a rapidly expanding, yet basically traditional public administration, with its hierarchical chain of command, where citizens were primarily viewed as passive clients of mostly public services. Later, with the spread of neoliberalism and introduction of New Public Management, they were expected to become active consumers and exercise more choice between various providers of publicly financed services, be they public or private for-profit or nonprofit. Here, the market replaced the state as the main governing mechanism for the expression of citizens' preferences. More recently, the spread of network society (Hartley, 2005) and New Public Governance (Osborne, 2006; Osborne, 2009) implies a more plural and pluralist model of governance and provision of welfare services, based on public-private networks, where citizens now have even more active roles as co-producers of some or many of the services they expect, demand or even depend on to fulfill a variety of their most important roles.

Thus, both the shifting roles that citizens play in their daily life and the changing context within which they play them place complex demands on the concepts and methods needed to study and understand such far-reaching changes. It is necessary to explore both individual and collective aspects of such changing roles for citizens. First, as individual clients, consumers and co-producers of publicly financed services, how do they interact with the public sector, market and third sector to express and satisfy their needs and promote their interests? Second, as members of third sector organizations, particularly of service organizations, how do they best promote their needs and interests to obtain the services they and others like them not only need, but may depend entirely on? How can they become active in and contribute to the provision of crucial services they are dependent on?

The relationship between co-production and New Public Governance is explored in Chapter 19 of this volume. This chapter focuses on co-production, particularly of enduring social services. What is co-production, and what are the crucial conceptual issues for better understanding its contribution to the provision of public services? This chapter proposes to explore these questions.

CO-PRODUCTION: SOME CRUCIAL CONCEPTUAL ISSUES

There are several crucial conceptual issues related to the growing international academic interest in co-production that need to be explored in order to make them more visible. Doing so can contribute greater clarity and understanding to the academic and practitioner debate about this important social phenomenon, but this is certainly not the last word on such important topics. The issues discussed in this chapter include: definitions of co-production and levels of analysis; relations between the professional service providers and their clients; who becomes a co-producer; citizens' motives for becoming involved in the co-production of social services; citizens' motives for engaging in collective action for social services; co-production as individual acts, collective action or both. Each of them is explored briefly.

As noted earlier, citizens have many different roles in postmodern societies. They are voters, taxpayers, employees, members of voluntary associations, family members, consumers of private goods and services, users or clients of public services and so on. I will, as far as possible, retain the original term employed by various authors concerning their role as consumers, clients and users when discussing co-production; but I shall refer to citizens as clients of public services more generally (compare Alford, 2009). However, this varied usage should not detract from their basic rights and responsibilities as citizens.

DEFINITIONS OF CO-PRODUCTION AND LEVELS OF ANALYSIS

Definitions of co-production range from "the mix of public service agents and citizens who contribute to the provision of public services" to "a partnership between citizens and public service providers." Differences between them can express cultural differences, differences of focus or both. They can also express different levels of analysis. We will contrast a few of them, as there seems to be some notable discrepancy between the American, British, Canadian and European usage of the term co-production. The concept of co-production was originally developed by Elinor Ostrom and the Workshop in Political Theory and Policy Analysis at Indiana University during the 1970s to describe and delimit the involvement of ordinary citizens in the production of public services. They struggled with the dominant theories of urban governance, whose underlying policies recommended massive centralization of public services, but they found no support for the claims of the benefits of large bureaucracies. They also realized that the production of services, in contrast to goods, was difficult without the active participation of those receiving the service. Thus, they developed the term *co-production* to describe the potential relationship that could exist between the "regular producer" (street-level police officers, schoolteachers or health workers) and their clients, who want to be transformed by the service into safer, better-educated or healthier people (see Parks et al., 1981).

Initially, co-production had a clear focus on the role of individuals or groups of citizens in the production of public services, although their involvement also had some ramifications for both the meso- and macrolevels of society. Co-production is, therefore, noted by the mix of activities that both public service agents and citizens contribute to the provision of public services. The former are involved as professionals or "regular producers," whereas "citizen production" is based on voluntary efforts of individuals or groups to enhance the quality and quantity or both of services they receive (Parks et al., 1981).

Bovaird proposed another definition of co-production: "User and community co-production is the provision of services through regular, long-term relationships between professionalized service providers (in any sector) and service users and or other members of the community, where all parties make substantial resource contributions" (2007, 847). This definition focuses not only on users, but also includes volunteers and community groups as co-producers, recognizing that each of these groups can have a quite different relationship to public sector organizations. However, Alford (2009) clearly distinguishes between volunteering and co-production. Citizens contribute resources when they volunteer, but do not personally consume the services provided, whereas co-producers both contribute resources and consume the services provided. Nevertheless, by including a temporal aspect in his definition, Bovaird appears to exclude more mundane acts of co-production, such as using postal codes, filing tax returns and so on.

Furthermore, the British Cabinet Office views co-production as a partnership between citizens and public service providers to achieve a valued outcome (Horne and Shirley, 2009). Co-production is essential for meeting a number of growing social challenges that neither the government nor citizens have the necessary resources to solve on their own. But, it seems legitimate to ask whether co-production is just another example of "old wine in new bottles," or perhaps just more neoliberal hype designed to roll back the state and promote more volunteering? However, the British Cabinet Office argued that this clearly was not the case because co-production comprises an approach that was distinct from other traditional responses, such as volunteerism, managerialism or paternalism (ibid.). Whether this still holds true after the 2010 parliamentary election and the big budget cuts that the new coalition announced in the fall of 2010 remains to be seen.

As already noted, the term co-production has also been used to analyze the role of voluntary and community organizations (VCOs) in the provision of public services in the United Kingdom (Osborne and McLaughlin, 2004). However, it is sometimes contrasted with co-management or coordination between the public and third sectors in providing some public services, and with co-governance (ibid.) or co-construction as it is often called in Canada and Latin America. Such a multilevel perspective provides a more nuanced understanding than a singular focus on co-production at the individual level or using the same term for various levels. However, co-production in the UK context also appears to imply a more limited service delivery role for VCOs, that is, they are simply service agents or providers. By contrast, co-management refers to a broader role for VCOs in local service management, while co-governance refers to the role of VCOs in policy formulation and community governance. The latter is best illustrated by the Voluntary Sector Compact(s), at both the national and local levels and local strategic partnerships designed to promote local regeneration in the United Kingdom (ibid.). However, in Canada, Vaillancourt (2009) distinguishes between only two levels, co-production and co-construction, where the latter closely corresponds to co-governance. See also his chapter in this book (Chapter 5).

Co-production has also recently been introduced to the continental European discussion, where it refers to the growing direct and organized involvement of citizens in the production of their own social services (Pestoff, 1998, 2006; Vamstad, 2007). The continental perspective seems to adhere more to the US than to UK usage of the term co-production. For example, parents can participate in the co-production of child care, both individually and collectively through parent associations or cooperative preschool services in France, Germany and Sweden. We also find ample evidence of co-management and co-governance of public services in many European countries. Several of the chapters in this volume will address various aspects of these phenomena.

So the term co-production has been used in different contexts and for different phenomena, however, these differences are not always made clear (Brandsen and Pestoff, 2006). Sometimes co-production is used as a general term to cover many different types of citizen participation in public service provision, and it also includes various ways citizens and/or the third sector participate both in policy making and policy implementation. Other times, it seems to focus on a different level or phenomena that involve citizen or third sector participation, or both, in policy making and/or public service delivery. It is necessary to keep these differences in mind for the sake of clarity. So co-production can refer both to direct citizen participation in the delivery of a publicly financed service, at the site of service delivery, as well as to group provision of such services.

Co-production at the site of service provision is nevertheless different from the mesolevel phenomenon of co-management, where the third sector participates alongside other public and private actors in managing the growing complexity of delivery of diverse publicly financed services, without any direct citizen or user participation. The growing mix and diversity of service providers not only implies greater opportunities for citizen involvement in the provision of publicly financed services, but it also becomes necessary to manage and govern this growing diversity. Co-management, therefore, refers to the growing diversity or hybridization of providers of welfare services, typically found in situations where different nonprofit and for-profit organizations participate in the provision of publicly financed services (Brandsen, 2004). Elsewhere, this has been referred to as the "growing welfare mix" (Evers and Laville, 2005).

It is worth noting that both co-production and co-management take place on the output or implementation side of the political system, once a public policy has been determined. Co-governance, on the other hand, is usually found on the input side and involves the third sector and other private actors in the determination of public policy for a given sector. Co-governance refers to attempts to manage this growing diversity in a more democratic fashion, through the creation of citywide, provincial and/or national bodies, where various providers are represented and given both a voice and a vote in developing and deciding the future of a sector, that is, in its governance. The appropriate site for co-governance structures will depend, of course, on constitutional differences between various welfare states.

So, in addition to serving as a general term for citizen and/or third sector participation in many kinds of public service, co-production can also be distinguished from co-management and co-governance. Thus, we will employ the following terminology to distinguish between these phenomena.

- *Co-production*, in the more restricted use of the term, refers to an arrangement where citizens produce their own services, at least in part. The latter could also refer to alternative service delivery by citizens, with or without direct state involvement, but with public financing and regulation (Brandsen & Pestoff, 2006). Such financing can either be in the form of a direct public subsidy, service vouchers or preferential tax rules for nonprofit organizations.
- *Co-management* refers to an arrangement, in which the third sector, along with public agencies and for-profit actors, delivers services in collaboration with other actors.
- *Co-governance* refers to an arrangement in which the third sector, along with public agencies and for-profit actors, participates in decision making and the planning of public services. This is often called co-construction in Canada and Latin America (Vaillancourt, 2009).

However, it should be noted that these three concepts are not mutually exclusive. We can expect to find different patterns of cooperation between the public and third sector, both in different service sectors and in different countries. Thus, there may be co-production in one service sector but not another in the same country. For example, there may be co-production in preschool services, but not in elder care. There may be co-production in one service sector in one country, but not in another country. So you can find associative and cooperative preschool services in France, Germany and Sweden, but not in Italy. Or there may be both co-production and co-management in one sector and country, but not in another. Thus, you can find both co-production and co-management in preschool services in France and Germany, but only co-production in Sweden.

The remainder of this chapter will primarily focus on co-production in the form of individual and collective participation in the provision of publicly financed social services, while co-management and co-governance will not feature in the following discussion. Therefore, this chapter will adopt a more generic definition of co-production as "the mix of public service agents and citizens who contribute to the provision of public services," while keeping in mind the variation in the definitions and levels of analysis noted earlier. However, some of the other chapters in this volume will illustrate the mix or overlap of co-production and co-management, or of co-management and co-governance.

RELATIONS BETWEEN THE PROFESSIONAL
SERVICE PROVIDERS AND THEIR CLIENTS

Co-production clearly implies different kinds of relationships between professional service providers and their clients. In some cases, both parties are physically present, and the production and delivery of the service are absolutely *inseparable*. But there is also a time dimension or aspect involved, and many services are based on one time or ad hoc meetings between service professionals and their clients, whereas others can involve repeated meetings and a more long-term relationship between them. Most social services are long-term and involve repeated interactions between the professional staff and their clients. In addition to such temporal aspects, at least three different types of kinds of relations that exist between the professional staff and their clients are found in the literature on co-production, that is, interdependence, supplementary and complementary.

When an organization cannot produce the service without some customer input, they are considered *interdependent*. Examples of this are found in various types of educational or vocational training programs for the long-term unemployed (Alford, 2002, 2009). The customer or client can also be a *supplement*, or substitute, for the professional service provider, at least in some activities. Examples of this include properly filling in postal codes on letters and accurately filing tax forms in a timely fashion. However, this depends both on the clients' willingness and ability to do so. It can be facilitated by the design of the tasks clients are expected to perform and the motives used to facilitate client co-production (ibid.).

Client inputs can also *complement* the tasks performed by the professional staff. Here, the professional staff continue to perform all the key or core activities of the organization, while the clients perform some secondary or peripheral tasks. Parent participation in cooperative or associative preschool services provides a good example of such a complementary relationship. The staff has full pedagogical responsibility for the content and development of the preschool services, while parents are normally in charge of the maintenance, management, bookkeeping and sometimes even cooking at a preschool facility (Pestoff, 2006, 2008). Such a clear division of labor in a complementary co-production situation helps to avoid or at least to mitigate some potential conflicts of interest between the staff and their clients.

Some public services that feature in the literature on co-production will be used in the following sections to explore the combination of individual acts and collective action, but they also illustrate clear patterns of collaboration between the staff and their clients in terms of co-production. They are the services of neighborhood safety and security, public health services for people with special diseases and elementary school services. In all these cases, we find close collaboration and interdependence between the public sector professionals and ordinary citizens who want to benefit from greater individual and collective safety in the neighborhoods where they live (US), support and understanding from public health authorities (Sweden) and greater cooperation and understanding between local schools and parents to promote good elementary education (UK and US). In most instances, citizens perform a variety of tasks that could not be performed by the local police, local health authorities or local school authorities. This includes marking their possessions, installing burglar alarms and keeping an eye out for strangers; monitoring their blood sugar, taking their insulin shots, eating the right foods and getting exercise; or arranging fund-raising events for their son or daughter's local elementary school, planning social events for their class and supporting the teachers. Clearly, public sector clients in no way substitute the activities of professionals; rather, they complement them.

Also in cases where private nonprofit actors provide services, we find close collaboration between the professional staff and their clients. Preschool services from parent associations, initiatives or cooperatives (France, Germany and Sweden), as well as preventative and long-term health care and medical services (Japan), comprise examples of the third sector directly providing services, with considerable public funding, that are separate and somehow different from public services, because they rely on active client participation in the provision of these services. However, at the microlevel or site of preschool service provision, the parents' role is normally limited to performing complementary tasks, such as the management and maintenance of the facility, rather than the core pedagogical ones. Similarly, members of the medical co-ops in Japan perform tasks that could not be performed by professional staff, such as monitoring their own diet, exercise and lifestyle habits and discussing them together with other members (Pestoff, 2008). So, parents and patients are not supplementing or replacing the professional staff in their core activities at preschool facilities or hospitals, rather they are complementing them.

WHO PARTICIPATES IN CO-PRODUCTION: THE BENEFICIARIES, FAMILY MEMBERS, AND OTHERS?

It is necessary to have a realistic assessment of the range of diverse interests and varying motives for engaging in co-production from the perspective of various stakeholders, that is, the municipal authorities, professional staff and users/citizens. The authorities and staff will have various economic, political and professional motives, such as lower costs, higher quality service and more legitimacy. Citizens' motives are based on economic, social, political and quality considerations. It is also important to understand these differences and try to bridge the gap between them in order for co-production to be sustainable. In particular, this becomes crucial when co-production is based on enduring social services that require repeated and frequent interaction between the professional staff and users/consumers, often on a daily basis. This is impossible without a dialogue between them, something that can help both these groups to mutually adjust their expectations of each other and of the service provided in a way beneficial for both groups (Hirschman, 1970). Such a dialogue also reduces the transaction costs for providing the services, compared to other ways of providing them that do not require a continuous dialogue between the providers and clients of a welfare service. Such a dialogue can become institutionalized in a third sector organization.

We also need to ask who participates in the co-production of enduring social services. Is it the direct beneficiaries of the services or someone else? It is important to realize that the participants in and beneficiaries of co-production are not necessarily the same person. If they are not, then we need to ask whether they are family members, relatives, friends or neighbors? In publicly financed social services, particularly of the enduring type, the participants in co-producing a service are not always identical with the subject of the service or the beneficiaries. Who participates and who benefits depends, at least to some degree, on the type of service provided.

In elementary education, for example, parents can participate actively in co-producing local public and private education services for their children. They can join a local parent-teacher organization and become active in it, or they can help to form or join a local organization for providing alternative services to public schools. Such schools may be based on an alternative pedagogy or promote faith-based education. Only after a certain age does the focus shift from parental participation and support for the benefit of their children to the individual pupil herself or himself. Already by the time they reach junior high and certainly by the time they are in high school, the pupils are expected to assume greater individual responsibility for their own lives, including their education and to participate actively in the learning processes.

While it is natural to assume that parents will contribute their time, effort and money to co-produce good quality education for their children up to a certain age, beyond that age, young adults will be expected to fend more and more for themselves. By the time they reach adulthood, it is safe to assume that they themselves will bear the primary burden for their education and other important aspects of their life, with or without their parents' continued support. Similarly, with health and medical care, age is an important factor in determining who participates in the co-production of publicly financed health and medical care and who benefits from it.

Thus, certain enduring social services will be more closely associated with people other than the immediate beneficiaries participating in the co-production of these social services, while other services will be more clearly noted for the participation of the individual beneficiary herself or himself, rather than their loved ones. In the case of preschool services, elementary education, handicap care and elder care, we can expect a high degree of participation by someone other than the main beneficiary, probably a family member, relative, friend or neighbor. In the case of junior-high and high school education, housing, and preventative and long-term health care, we can expect a greater incidence of individual participation and responsibility, or perhaps a lack thereof. This suggests the lack of a clear division between individual and family participation in co-production of enduring social services.

Rather, there appears to be a shifting level of participation depending on an individual's situation, progress in their life cycle and so on. Given these shifting circumstances, it is therefore natural for parents or other loved ones to participate in the co-production of social services in some situations, such as when the main recipient is a minor or incapacitated; while in other circumstances it is much more likely that the participant and beneficiary will be the same person.

Thus, our understanding of co-production should not be limited solely to the active participation of the main beneficiaries themselves. It should also include the active participation of family members when circumstances warrant it. In this fashion, we can avoid the risk of over-emphasizing individual participation or only considering spontaneous ad hoc participation at the expense of organized collective participation in the co-production of publicly financed social services.

WHY DO CITIZENS BECOME INVOLVED IN
THE CO-PRODUCTION OF SOCIAL SERVICES?

Alford (2009) compares the engagement of public sector clients in using postal codes, long-term unemployment training and filing their tax returns in Australia, the United Kingdom and the United States. He notes that it is usually assumed that most individuals' cost-benefit analysis will lead them to seek only extrinsic self-interest rewards. However, he argues that different motives exist for co-production in different contexts. The more public the value consumed by clients, the more complex the motivations for them to co-produce. He notes that "eliciting co-production is a matter of heightening the value that clients receive from the services by making more explicit their non-material aspects through intrinsic rewards, solidarity incentives or normative appeal" (ibid., 187). He concludes that intrinsic rewards can also be powerful motivators, because people are not solely motivated by self-interest but also by social values. The latter includes the enjoyment associated with interacting with other people, gaining their approval or avoiding their disapproval. Normative purposes are also important for motivating co-production, including values such as participation, influence and democracy. Thus, there are three types of motivation—intrinsic, social and normative—in addition to material rewards that can elicit co-production. In order to prompt clients to co-produce, an organization must offer them something of material, social or normative value (ibid.).

In her seminal article on co-production, "Crossing the Great Divide" (1999), Ostrom compares the conditions for co-production in two developing countries, that is, condominial water systems in suburban areas in Brazil and elementary education in Nigeria. In the latter, she notes that villagers were actively engaged in several community projects, including building roads and the maintenance of school buildings. However, she documents the detrimental effects of centralization and frequent changes in government policy concerning primary education. She compared four villages, two where parents valued education highly and focused on primary education, with good results in terms of pupils passing their final exams (85 percent). In two other villages, parents valued education less and contributed very little to the local primary schools. Without parental support, the teachers were incapacitated and demoralized, and the children only obtained a scattered education, if any at all. She concludes that when co-production is discouraged by taking over schools that villagers had perceived as their own, by creating chaotic changes in who is responsible for financing them, by top-down command administration and so on, only the most determined citizens will persist in co-production activities (ibid, 357).

Exploring citizen involvement in the co-production of social services further, we need to consider the two related issues of the ease of involvement and the motivation of individuals to participate in the co-production of social services. How easy is it for citizens to get involved in the provision of social services, and why do they become active participants in the service provision process? The ease or facility of citizens becoming involved will depend on several things, such as the distance to the service provider, the information available to citizens about the service and its provision and more. They are related to the time and effort required for citizens to become involved and might therefore be seen as the transaction costs of participation. If and when opportunities exist for motivated citizens to participate actively in the co-production of a social service, lowering the transaction costs will make it easier for them to do so. However, the greater the effort required of citizens to become involved, the less likely they will do so. Citizens' motivation to become involved as a co-producer will, in turn, depend on the importance or salience of the service provided. Is it an important service for them, their family, loved ones, a relative, a friend, or not? This will reflect how the service affects them, their life and life chances. Does it make a direct impact on their life or life chances, or does it only have an indirect effect? If and when a person feels that a service is important to them or their loved ones or vital to their life chances, they will be more highly motivated to get involved in the co-production of social services.

It is, therefore, necessary to make a distinction between enduring and non-enduring social services. Many social services belong to the former category and therefore, have an immediate impact on the life, life chances and quality of life of the people receiving them. The importance and impact of such services guarantees high client interest in the development of such services, especially in service quality. Enduring social services include: child care or preschool services, basic and higher education, elder care, handicap care and housing, as well as preventive and long-term health care. Users of such services are locked into them for a longer period of time and can therefore not normally rely on exit to provide them with influence or redress. The transaction costs of exit are often prohibitive (Pestoff, 1998), so voice, rather than exit, provides clients with influence and redress (ibid.).

Both these central dimensions of co-production, the ease or facility of involvement and the salience of the service for individual citizens, can be seen as a continuum, ranging from low to high or less to greater. However, for the sake of simplicity, they can also be divided into two categories, low and high or less and greater. When we combine these two dimensions, it results in a classical fourfold table with the following patterns of citizen involvement in co-production, as seen in Figure 2.1.

Combining these two dimensions helps us to identify two types of service providers as well as their clients, who range from passive clients to active co-producers. In between, there are active consumers and ad hoc participants. In non-participatory modes of service provision, where the hurdles to participation are high and the ease of participation is low, we can either expect to find active consumers or passive clients. The former

Ease and Salience:	Low	High
Greater	Active consumer	Active co-producer
Less	Passive client	Ad hoc participant

Figure 2.1   Citizen involvement in social service co-production: ease and salience.

are the ideal type for New Public Management, while the latter are the typical mode associated with traditional public administration. However, in more participatory forms of service provision, where client participation is encouraged, facilitated or even maybe required, we can expect to find both active co-producers and ad hoc participants. The former are the ideal type for New Public Governance (NPG), while the latter may sometimes participate in important matters. Thus, by combining ease of participation with the salience of the service we get a more mixed or nuanced picture of client motivation than if we only considered one dimension at a time.

It is important, however, to understand that citizen involvement is more than just a question of facilitating greater citizen participation or developing techniques to motivate them. It is a combination of the ease of involvement and individual motivation. In other words, citizens are not like a jack-in-the-box, just waiting for someone to push a lever or remove a latch that will immediately release their energies and result in their engagement in social service co-production. They need to be motivated to do so, but the greater the effort required of them to overcome hurdles to participation, the greater their motivation must be. However, the greater the effort required of them in order to become involved in co-producing a public service, the more a service provided by a public agency must be both relevant and salient for them personally. Thus, less ease of involvement may thwart greater citizen participation, even in highly salient services, thereby limiting their participation to ad hoc, spontaneous and individual involvement. However, many public and for-profit services appear to hinder client participation, as seen in Chapter 19.

THE COOPERATIVE GAMBIT: WHY DO CITIZENS ENGAGE IN COLLECTIVE ACTION?

A cooperative gambit is the willingness of individuals to sacrifice their short-term personal interest for the sake of the long-term individual and group benefits stemming from collective action. A social cooperative or social enterprise can create trust that helps to surmount the limits of the short-term personal interest of group members. This encourages them to contribute their time, effort and other resources to achieve the fruits of their collective efforts that can't be achieved by isolated individuals. Of course, not everyone is willing to participate in collective action, but there are enough of them to make it worth considering why they do. Extensive research in experimental psychology repeatedly and clearly shows that in real world collective action situations, there are two other types of norm-using players in addition to rational egoists (Ostrom, 2000). The first group is the "conditional cooperators," who are willing to initiate or join collective action when they estimate that others will reciprocate, and they will continue such actions as long as others demonstrate similar behavior. The second group of cooperators are called "willing punishers." They rely more heavily on social control as the basis for collective action. However, research shows that many people combine both these traits. Both groups are prone to pursue the cooperative gambit, especially when certain institutional forms exist.

Ostrom also develops six design principles for the emergence of self-organizing collective action (ibid.). Several of them are relevant for understanding collective action, but only two of them will be considered here. The first is setting clear group boundaries to determine who uses a resource or service and who does not. The second principle concerns the right of members to influence decisions concerning the management of a resource or service, that is, they are self-governing groups. Thus, in addition to trust as a basis for a cooperative gambit, a social cooperative or social enterprise created to provide a particular service for its members must establish clear boundaries, and they must be able to influence decisions through internal democratic channels. These two aspects are, of course, mutually reinforcing and, taken together, they help to make a cooperative gambit more viable. Thus, Ostrom's research establishes that the rate of contribution to a public good is affected by various contextual factors and that these design principles make self-organized collective action more robust.

Olsen (1965) discusses the failure of large groups to form voluntary organizations in the pursuit of public interest. This is primarily due to the costs of collective action and problems of "free riding." However, a small scale group or organization allows individual members to survey and control the efforts and contributions of others, thereby avoiding or limiting problems of "free-riding." Olsen refers to "the privileged position of small groups" and argues that they are subject to the second logic of collective action (ibid.). Thus, it is easier for small groups to organize themselves than larger ones due to social controls. These two phenomena, the cooperative gambit and small group control, help to explain the growth and success of co-production and third sector provision of public services in Europe.

The cooperative gambit not only represents a "quantum leap" in terms of the presumed maximization of individual short-term utilities. It also recognizes that individuals have different dispositions toward cooperation. Some people appear more willingly disposed to cooperate than others. Moreover, it also suggests that "methodological individualism" is not only biased toward short-term utility maximizing individuals, but it also ignores, or perhaps even denies, the existence of other dispositions, such as "conditional cooperators" and "willing punishers." So there is no longer any viable reason for maintaining this negative stance toward cooperation between rational actors, beyond ideology. Thus, collective action is not only possible when "selective incentives" are present, as Olsen argued, but also when enabling institutions help to remove the hurdles facing "conditional cooperators" and "willing punishers." However, Ostrom warns that external rules and monitoring can also crowd out cooperative behavior (Ostrom, 2000).

Individual and collective self-regarding activities are not necessarily the same thing, nor can they easily be equated with each other, because they imply different social mechanisms. Moreover, collective interaction between the members of small self-help groups is very different from the general phenomenon of collective action. Collective self-help efforts differ from other forms of collective action primarily in terms of the proximity and the durability of the activities for providing such social services. There is a growing number of "watchdog" or advocacy groups in the United States without local or regional branches (Skocpol, 2002). Rather, they have distant national "check-book" membership that does not involve (daily) local grassroots collective interactions with other members. Parallel with this is the spread of "required" volunteering, where schools or employers require that their students or employees volunteer so many hours per month or year in order to gain or retain their status as a student or employee (Hustinx, 2010). Thus, much of the local interaction necessary for creating and maintaining social capital is lost in twenty-first-century voluntary organizations.

Self-help groups, on the other hand, rely heavily on close personal ties that remain stable for a long period of time. In collective self-help activities, clients contribute their time, effort and money for the co-production of social services for themselves, but they do it together with others and for others who are in a similar situation. The repeated face-to-face interactions of small self-help groups not only contribute to the creation of social capital, but they also promote solidarity and support for others in a similar situation and facilitate the mutual reinforcement of their individual goal(s). There are both individual and collective benefits found in collective self-help efforts that are not available to the single or solo individual volunteer. Thus, compared to the macro social trends toward "checkbook" memberships and "required" volunteering, the development at the microlevel of collective self-help groups that co-produce publicly financed social services is all the more interesting and important. However, given the dominant emphasis on methodological individualism, very little empirical research exists in this area, except for the pioneering work of Ostrom (2000). Therefore, this should be an area of priority in future research to better understand collective participation in the co-production of publicly financed social services.

As already noted, the pursuit of self-interest can either be individual or collective. In the latter, there is an element of common benefit that is not found in the former. Collective action and, even more, collective interaction have the ability to transform the pursuit of self-interest into something more than the sum of individual self-interest. It makes possible the achievement of common goals that would otherwise be impossible for isolated, unorganized individuals. Such goals can include good quality elementary education, good quality preschool services, good quality health care, elder care and so on, at a reasonable cost to individuals and society. The pursuit of collective self-interest also has the potential added value of promoting the participation of the clients and staff in the provision of publicly financed services in a way and to an extent that neither public nor private for-profit services can under current circumstances. Neither the individual pursuit of self-interest in the provision of social services nor the public provision of such services can alone achieve this result. Only greater collective client participation in the co-production of publicly financed social services and greater third sector provision of such services can achieve this collective result.

Collective action can help solve some social and personal dilemmas created either by the lack of some important social services on the market or by the variable quality of such services provided by the state. The lack of good quality child care services is a prime example in many countries today. The local authorities don't provide them, or enough of them, and the market simply prices them out of reach of most citizens. Thus, many families struggle to combine their professional career demands with family needs, particularly for high quality child care. Therefore, many of them reason that if they don't join hands with other like-minded people to form an association and provide the service themselves, then it simply won't be available to them. If the market cannot provide an adequate amount of the service at affordable prices for most citizens or if the quality of standardized public services is not acceptable to some citizens, they can join hands to form an association to provide it for themselves and others who lack such services. Thus, without collective action, a particular service wouldn't be made readily available, or it wouldn't be available in the quality desired by some groups. Therefore, in spite of well-known hurdles to collective action (Olsen, 1965), without engaging in it, no suitable child care service will be provided for a number of concerned families. However, government understanding of this dilemma and acceptance of third sector alternatives may also prove crucial for success.

The development of alternative preschool services in Sweden provides a case in hand (Pestoff, 1998). Well-educated parents wanted something more from public day care services in the 1970s than the municipalities could provide with their highly standardized services. Parents wanted more pedagogical content in the child care activities and tried to gain more influence on the development of these services, but they soon hit the "glass ceiling" that limits client participation in public services in Sweden. So they joined forces with alternative child care educators, who were inspired by special pedagogical programs, such as Montessori, Waldorf, Reggio-Emilia and so on, to provide an alternative to the municipal day care services. After a long struggle, these services finally gained public recognition in the mid-1970s and could, therefore, qualify for a public subsidy similar to that received by the municipal providers. They were also set up as parent co-ops with a work obligation. Here, better quality played an important role in motivating parents to engage not only in co-production, but also in collective action.

A decade later, when growing popular demand for child care services far exceeded public provision of it, combined with unrelenting public criticism over the shortage of good quality child care services, the government conceded again. It granted small groups of parents the right to form parent co-ops in order to provide child care for themselves and others. They too received public subsidies on par with support for municipal day care services. This was particularly urgent in a time of constantly expanding new suburbs in the three major urban areas, where no municipal day care services yet existed. However, without child care, women could not return to their jobs after maternity leave. So, many of them had to choose between continuing to work or having children, but at the price of sacrificing their careers. This didn't fit well with the growing ranks of two income families that was rapidly becoming the norm in Sweden. Here we find a good example of how a lack of public services promoted not only engagement in co-production, but also in collective action in order to provide it. (See Vamstad in Chapter 16 for more details.)

Finally, when the first neoliberal government took the reins of Swedish government in the early 1990s, it removed the final vestiges of public restrictions on the forms of providing child care services. Any type of provider could now compete for public funds to provide preschool services in Sweden, including not only private for-profit firms, but also worker co-op preschool services. Some municipalities actively pursue a policy of encouraging the staff to take over municipal services and turn them into worker co-ops. This, of course, proved popular among the staff.

It is important to realize that co-production can involve both the participation of the direct beneficiaries of social services as well as their family members. It is also important to understand how the lack of available services can motivate and promote collective action, but how dependent it is on the government's understanding of the problem and its acceptance of third sector alternatives, if not its sympathy and support. Without removing the restrictions of public financing laws for day care services, the expansion of co-production and collective action in preschool services simply would not have been possible. Without doing so, the public monopoly would have remained intact, and the market would have been seen as the only alternative to public provision of day care services. There is nevertheless a difference between understanding and acceptance, and sympathy and support. Small parent co-ops can remain isolated islands of co-production, without participating in co-management or co-governance.

CO-PRODUCTION: INDIVIDUAL ACTS, COLLECTIVE ACTION OR BOTH?

It is often argued that the analysis of co-production needs to distinguish between individual acts and collective action and focus on one or the other. Are we mainly interested in individual or collective participation in the provision of public services? While this distinction may sometimes seem relevant or even a necessary part of a research design, in the field there is often a mix of both of them in the same service delivery. Let's look, therefore, at the options available in terms of co-production. They are:

- *Individual acts of co-production* that involve ad hoc, spontaneous or informal acts done in public or at home. However, sometimes they are perceived as a necessary part of the service or even a mandatory activity expected of all citizens. The use of postal codes on letters and filing individual tax returns illustrates this type of co-production (Alford, 2002). Alford explores how to engage clients as co-producers of these public services (2009). Yet, given their low salience, few would expect them to elicit any collective action.
- *Collective acts of co-production* that involve formally organized and institutionalized activities done together with others. They often concern the provision of enduring social services previously discussed. Such services produced by a small group at the microlevel often imply more collective interaction than collective action, which can promote the development of social capital, mutualism and reciprocity (Pestoff, 2006).
- A *mix of both individual and collective action*. Many acts of co-production combine both individual and collective action(s), often in a repeated fashion for a long time. This mix of individual and collective action is highly relevant when it comes to social services, particularly enduring social services. So the relevant question is not only how to elicit greater individual client co-production, but also how to facilitate more collective action in public service provision and a greater mix of both.

Five examples will be employed here to illustrate the potential mix of individual and collective action(s) in the co-production of public services. Here we will take some known examples from the literature on co-production, such as services for neighborhood security in the United States, preschool services in Europe, diabetes in Sweden, cooperative health and medical care in Japan and elementary education in the United Kingdom, the United States and elsewhere.

Exploring the first case, individual residents in the United States can make personal efforts in collaboration with the police to promote greater neighborhood security. If individuals mark their most valuable belongings, this will help the police to trace any stolen items, and if they install a security system, this will help deter or thwart burglary. Citizens can also join together to collectively form a "neighborhood watch" in order to survey the neighborhood for strangers and intruders and then contact the police as soon as unwanted people are sighted nearby. In addition, the police can arrange classes and seminars for groups of interested neighbors on how to best protect themselves and their property. In this fashion, individual and collective action(s) come together to promote both greater individual and collective security in a neighborhood (Parks et al., 1981).

Turning to the second case in Europe, individual parents can encourage and help their children to learn as much as possible at preschool. They can read to them, tell them stories, as well as help them learn to draw, paint, read, spell, tell time and use numbers. They can also join together to form a parent association, or co-op, to provide preschool services when such services are not readily available in their local neighborhood or when the services are deemed of inferior quality. In this fashion, both their individual and collective efforts can promote a better start in life for their children (Pestoff, 1998, 2006, 2008; Vamstad, 2007).

Turning to the third case in Sweden, individuals with diabetes can regularly monitor their blood sugar, take their insulin shots, eat the right foods and get lots of exercise to avoid deteriorating health from diabetes. They can also engage in collective action to support, encourage and enable other people in a similar life situation. They can form a diabetes association to promote both individual action to deal with the symptoms of diabetes and collective action to promote the situation of people with diabetes in general. Such an association can demand making insulin shots available free of charge, arranging training courses and seminars to disseminate information, both to people with diabetes, to the public at large and to professionals about the situation of people with diabetes (Soderholm-Werko, 2008). Again, we see that there is no clear separation between individual and collective actions, although they may involve different or separate activities.

The fourth case focuses on cooperative health and medical care in Japan, where individual members of the health care co-ops are encouraged to join a heath care *han*, or a small discussion group of eight to ten people. They individually monitor their blood pressure, test their urine for the salt content and make some other health tests. They meet regularly to discuss how these basic facts are related to their health and lifestyle, how much they exercise and how best to maintain their health. In addition, members of these health care co-ops are represented on the board of local co-op hospitals, making them multistakeholder bodies (Kurimoto, 2005; see also Pestoff, 2008). Here again we find a combination of individual acts and collective action in promoting health care in Japan.

Finally, parents' support is also important in elementary education in most countries, and they can play both an individual and a collective role in co-producing it. Here we will briefly consider the example of the United Kingdom and the United States. At the individual level, they can help and support their children with their homework and/or to remind them to do it. At the collective level, parents can join a local branch parent-teacher association (PTA) or an equivalent local parent-teacher organization (PTO). In the United Kingdom, the National Coalition of Parent Teacher Associations (NCPTA) represents over 13,000 local PTAs across England, Wales and Northern Ireland. Its purpose is to advance education by encouraging the fullest cooperation between home and school, education authorities, central government and all other interested parties. In the United States, the PTA is a national association with 23,000 local branches in most school districts around the country. It is composed of parents, teachers and staff that intend to facilitate parental participation in public and private schools.

A local PTA or PTO serves as an advisory board for an exchange of ideas, as well as engaging in fund-raising activities for local schools. Such events include a variety of activities: fairs, discos and dances, quiz nights, auctions, coffee mornings, barbecues, cake or bake sales, book sales, carnivals and so on, to help raise money for the local school. Parents can volunteer in several different roles They can either become active in the local PTA/PTO board; spend time in the classroom during school hours, either as a "room mother" who assumes responsibility for arranging holiday parties and social events, or as a "teacher's aide." The latter can be assigned to any class in the elementary school where there is a special need for tutoring and assistance that goes beyond the current capacity of teachers or due to staff shortages.

Thus, we find a number of individual and collective actors working together to co-produce elementary education in the United Kingdom, the United States and elsewhere. They include not only individual parents in their role as parents at home, but also parents as members of a local PTA branch or local parent club, parents as room mothers or teachers aides at school and sometimes even the children themselves, if they participate in a homework club. So, not only is there a mix of actors playing different roles at different times, but also a mix of individual and collective action to co-produce elementary education.

SUMMARY AND CONCLUSIONS: CRUCIAL CONCEPTUAL ISSUES

In sum, this chapter explored several crucial conceptual issues related to co-production, given the central importance attached to it by recent analysis of the change in the delivery of public services and public governance. Various definitions of co-production were considered and a generic one, stemming from the early writings of Ostrom and her colleagues was adopted. It focuses on the mix of activities that both public service agents and citizens contribute to the provision of public services. The former are involved as professionals or "regular producers," while "citizen production" is based on voluntary efforts by individuals or groups to enhance the quality and/or quantity of services they use.

We also considered the relevance of different levels of analysis and distinguished between co-production, co-management and co-governance. We pursued our inquiry into the relations between the professional staff and their clients and noted that they can be interdependent, supplementary or complementary. We then distinguished between co-production by the clients themselves and their family members. We noted that both the ease of participation and the salience of the service for the individual and/or their family were important for better understanding of why citizens become involved in co-producing social services. It was argued that enduring social services have a greater salience than non-enduring services, given the impact such services have on their life and life chances, as well as that of their family and loved ones.

Then we briefly introduced the idea of a cooperative gambit and explored differences between collective action in general and collective interaction in small self-help groups. We illustrated the necessity to engage in collective action in order to get access to better quality child care services in Sweden in the 1970s and to get access to any child care at all in many new suburban areas in the 1980s. We then turned our attention to whether co-production only comprises individual acts, collective action or both, and found several examples of a mixed pattern of involvement in the co-production of publicly funded social services both in different sectors and nations. Thus, we end up with an expanded definition of co-production for the social services that includes both individual and collective participation, both beneficiary and family member participation and both public and third sector provision of social services, given that the latter receives substantial public funding.

REFERENCES

Alford, J. 2002. Why do public sector clients co-produce? Towards a contingency theory. *Administration & Society* 34 (1): 32–56.

Alford, J. 2009. *Engaging Public Sector Clients: From Service Delivery to Co-production*; Houndmills, UK: Palgrave Macmillan.

Bovaird, T. 2007. Beyond engagement and participation: User and community co-production of public services. *Public Administration Review* 67 (5): 846–860.

Brandsen, T. 2004. *Quasi-Market Governance: An Anatomy of Innovation*. The Hague: Lemma.

Brandsen, T., and V. Pestoff. 2006. Co-production, the third sector and the delivery of public services: An introduction. *Public Management Review* 8 (4): 493–501.

Evers, A. & J-L. Laville (eds). 2005. *The Third Sector in Europe*. Cheltenham, UK & Northampton, MA, USA: Edgar Elger.

Hartley, J. 2005. Innovation in governance and public services: Past and present. *Public Money & Management* 25 (1): 27–34.

Hirschman, A. 1970. *Exit, Voice and Loyalty: Responses to Decline in the Performance of Firms, Organizations and States.* Cambridge, MA: Harvard University Press.

Horne, M., and T. Shirley. 2009. *Co-production in public services: A new partnership with citizens*; Cabinet Office, the Strategy Unit. London: Her Majesty's Government.

Hustinx, L. 2010. *New Forms of Volunteering in Europe: Toward a Late Modern Re-Construction of a Dwindling Phenomenon.* Istanbul: ISTR Conference paper.

Kurimoto, A. 2005. What can co-operative health and social care offer? In C. Tsuzuki et al., eds., *The Emergence of Global Citizenship: Utopian Ideas, Cooperative Movements and the Third Sector.* Tokyo: Robert Owens Society of Japan.

Olsen, M. 1965. *The Logic of Collective Action.* Cambridge, MA: Harvard University Press.

Osborne, S. 2006. The New Public Governance. *Public Management Review* 8 (3): 377–387.

Osborne, S. P. ed. 2009. *The New Public Governance? Emerging Perspectives on the Theory and Practice of Public Governance.* London: Routledge.

Osborne, S, and K. McLaughlin. 2004. The cross-cutting review of the voluntary sector. What next for local government voluntary sector relationships. *Regional Studies* 38 (5): 573–582.

Ostrom, E. 1999. Crossing the great divide: Co-production, synergy, and development. In M.D. McGinnis, ed., *Polycentric Governance and Development: Readings from the Workshop in Political Theory and Policy Analysis.* Ann Arbor: University of Michigan Press.

Ostrom, E. 2000. Collective action and the evolution of social norms. *Journal of Economic Perspectives* 14 (3): 137–158.

Parks, R. B., P. Baker, L. Kiser, R. Oakerson, E. Ostrom, V. Ostrom, S. Percy, M. Vandivort, G. Whitaker, and R. Wilson. 1981. Consumers as co-producers of public services: Some economic and institutional considerations. *Policy Studies Journal* 9 (7): 1001–1011.

Pestoff, V. 1998. *Beyond the Market and State: Civil Democracy and Social Enterprises in a Welfare Society.* Aldershot, UK: Ashgate.

Pestoff, V. 2006. Citizens as co-producers of welfare services: Preschool services in eight European countries. *Public Management Review* 8 (4): 503–520.

Pestoff, V. 2008. *A Democratic Architecture for the Welfare State: Promoting Citizen Participation, The Third Sector and Co-Production.* London: Routledge.

Pestoff, V. 2010. *The Role of Volunteering and Co-Production in the Provision of Social Services in Europe.* Istanbul: ISTR Conference paper.

Skocpol, T. 2002. United States: From membership to advocacy. In R. Putnam, ed., *Democracies in Flux: Evolution of Social Capital in Contemporary Society.* Oxford, UK: Oxford University Press.

Soderholm-Werko, S. 2008. *Patient Patients? Achieving Patient Empowerment through Active Participation, Increasing Knowledge and Organization.* Doctoral Thesis, School of Business, Stockholm.

Vaillancourt, Y. 2009. Social economy in the co-construction of public policy. *Annals of Public and Cooperative Economics* 80 (2): 275–313.

Vamstad, J. 2007. *Governing Welfare: The Third Sector and the Challenges to the Swedish Welfare State.* Doctoral Thesis, Östersund.

3 From Engagement to Co-Production

How Users and Communities Contribute to Public Services

Tony Bovaird and Elke Löffler

INTRODUCTION

Not so long ago—in the 1980s—public services were essentially seen as activities that professionals did to, or for, members of the public to achieve results "in the public interest." Much has changed since then. We now believe that public services should be designed to bring about "outcomes," not just "results," and that these outcomes should, in large measure, correspond to those that service users and citizens see as valuable, not simply those that are seen as valuable by politicians, service managers and professionals. From being a kind of "marketeering" heresy in the 1980s, such views are now largely shared across most stakeholders involved in public services. This has, indeed, been a kind of revolution—"public services for the public."

However, as with all revolutions, this has satisfied neither the revolutionaries nor those who were meant to benefit from the changed world that was created through this process. The public has continually revised its expectations upward—and is therefore still not satisfied with the public services that are being offered. The revolutionaries have also upped their demands—now there is widespread talk of "public services BY the public." This is the stage on which co-production is now strutting its stuff. The co-production movement is partly a harking back to some of the philosophical roots of public service: "To everyone according to their needs, from everyone according to their ability." It is also partly a recognition of the limits of the state: "It takes a village to raise a child." But it is, above all, a recognition that "we are all in this together"—state and civil society must work together if those outcomes are to be achieved that most people identify with a good society—"If you want to walk fast, travel alone: if you want to walk far, travel together."

In this chapter, we explore the ways in which this movement can be conceptualized as a shift from "public services FOR the public" toward "public services BY the public," within the framework of a public sector that continues to represent the public interest, not simply the interests of "consumers" of public services.

DEFINITIONS AND CHARACTERISTICS

The National Endowment for Science Technology and the Arts (NESTA) argues that co-production offers a different vision for public services, built on the principles of reciprocity and mutuality, and they suggest a working definition as follows: "Co-production means delivering public services in an equal and reciprocal relationship between professionals, people using services, their families and their neighbors. Where activities are co-produced in this way, both services and neighborhoods become far more effective agents of change" (2001, 4). This definition makes clear that co-production is a genuinely joint activity between professionals and the public—and that the public concerned is wider than simply service users. However, it is still service-oriented and it insists on an "equal and reciprocal relationship," conditions that have rarely been encountered in the sphere of public services.

We, therefore, take a slightly different stance, defining user and community co-production of public services as: "the public sector harnessing the assets and resources of users and communities to achieve better outcomes or lower costs" (Governance International, 2011). This again emphasizes reciprocity, but less firmly anchored to "equality" in the relationship, and it directly focuses on the achievement of "better outcomes" or "lower costs," rather than simply services.

This definition also differs from that used earlier by Bovaird (and used by several authors in this book): "User and community co-production can be defined as the provision of services through regular, long-term relationships between professionalized service providers (in any sector) and service users or other members of the community, where all parties make substantial resource contributions" (2007, 847). Our more recent definition focuses on outcomes, not services, and does not require a long-term relationship between the co-producing parties.

All of these definitions have at their core a vision of service users and the communities in which they live that is different from the traditional view of the public as "passive." We now realize that service users:

- are essential to making a service actually work by going along with its requirements ("users as critical success factors")
- know things that many professionals don't know ("users as thinking people")
- have time and energy that they are willing to put into helping others ("users as resources")
- have diverse capabilities that make them potentially valuable contributors to their communities, not simply supplicants asking the public sector to make good some perceived "deficit" they have ("users as asset-holders")
- can promote the value of the public services they receive, so that other citizens are more likely to work closely with those services and agree to their funding ("users as legitimators and testimonial providers")

- can engage in *collaborative rather than paternalistic relationships* with staff, with other service users and with other members of the public

THE GENESIS OF USER AND COMMUNITY CO-PRODUCTION OF PUBLIC SERVICES

The term "co-production" has been in use for over thirty years, both in public and private sectors. By the 1980s, the limitations of traditional "provider-centric" models of the welfare state had become obvious. One reaction was to give a larger role to *customer service*, including user research, quality assurance and user choice between providers, while a very different response was to promote *competition* between providers for contracts commissioned by public agencies (Gunn, 1988; Pollitt, 1990; Hood, 1991; Barzelay, 2001). The role given to service users and communities varied greatly in these initiatives but continued to be decided mainly by managers and professionals, as they debated where to work on the Arnstein (1971) "ladder of participation."

However, this conception of the role of service users became challenged as underambitious in both private sector (Zeleny, 1978; Lovelock and Young, 1979) and public sector (Whitaker, 1980; Sharp, 1980; Parks et al., 1981; Warren et al., 1982; Brudney and England, 1983; Percy, 1984). Indeed, it was quickly realized that user and community co-production already had a long history, for example, in citizen militias, jurors and volunteer fire fighters. Particularly influential was Normann (1984), who suggested that in service systems, the client appears twice, once as a customer and again as part of the service delivery system. Sometimes, service professionals "do the service for the customer" (for example, a surgeon performs an operation on a patient), which Normann labels the "relieving logic." However, service professionals often play solely an "enabling" role, so the client actually performs the service task (e.g., a student finds appropriate material and writes an essay on a topic). The private sector had been quick to see this potential for co-production (e.g., self-service supermarkets or bank cash withdrawal machines). In a world of increasingly competent service users, Normann predicted that enabling relationships would become more prominent and that "relievers" would experience tough competition from "enablers."

By the 1990s the "enabling" logic of provision was well established in parts of the private sector (Wikström, 1996; Ramirez, 1999)—not only in service delivery but also in service design and testing, for example, of computer software (although the users of prematurely released software that, unwillingly, find and report glitches, are not necessarily very impressed by this shunting of software development costs). Since that time, there has been an explosion of interest in "co-creation" of value by service users— most famously in the case of Apple's iPhone and iPad, where millions of applications have already been developed (and marketed) by their users.

In the United States, collaboration between users and collaboration within communities to improve outcomes became key themes of the communitarian movement (Etzioni, 1995), which favors direct forms of participation in socially valuable activities (such as self-help groups and social support networks). While many of these approaches did highlight how self-help and self-organizing could complement publicly provided services, they were often rather "state-free" in their emphasis. However, analysis of social capital (Putnam, 2000) highlighted that co-production is often most common in countries with large welfare states, so that one is not necessarily a substitute for the other. In other fields, the narratives differed between authors: while advocates of asset-based community development (Kretzmann and McKnight, 1993) drew attention to the widespread role of community groups in the self-management of community centers, play areas and sports facilities, they often neglected to point out that many of these facilities had been funded initially from the public purse.

A decade ago, Kelly and colleagues (2002) noted a reawakening of interest in co-production in UK public services, and the Lyons inquiry into local government functions and financing in the United Kingdom suggested a major future role for co-production (Lyons, 2006). Further impetus in the United Kingdom was given by a cabinet office report on co-production (Horne and Shirley, 2009) and from Local Authorities Research Council Initiative (Löffler, 2010).

Following the 2008 global recession, many governments have instigated major cuts in public sector spending, which has triggered renewed interest in co-production as a way of reducing the costs of services or even rescuing services that might otherwise be entirely cut. However, there has been little evidence to date on which types of co-production are fully *substitutive* (replacing government inputs by inputs from users and communities), as opposed to *additive* (adding user and/or community inputs to professional inputs or introducing professional support to previous individual self-help or community self-organizing). This distinction becomes critical to public agencies that need to achieve major cuts in spending—co-production that simply increases the cost-effectiveness of outcomes but requires higher investment (at least initially) is less attractive in these circumstances.

DIFFERENT ELEMENTS OF CO-PRODUCTION IN SERVICES MANAGEMENT

Taken together, these references from recent literature in Europe and the United States illustrate that the concept of co-production is now relevant not only to the service delivery phase of services management (where it was first discovered in the 1970s) but can extend across all phases. Indeed, it is clear that the different usages of the term "co-production" in the previous section do not always refer to the same thing. We can distinguish a wide range of service activities that have each been identified as "co-production" by different authors:

- *Co-planning of policy*—for example, deliberative participation, *Planning for Real, Open Space*
- *Co-design of services*—for example, user consultation, *Service Design Labs*
- *Co-prioritization services*—for example, individual budgets, *Community Chests,* participatory budgeting
- *Co-financing services*—for example, fundraising, charges, agreement to tax increases
- *Co-managing services*—for example, leisure center trusts, community management of public assets, school parent-governors
- *Co-delivery of services*—for example, peer support groups (e.g., expert patients), nurse-family partnerships, meals-on-wheels, neighborhood watch
- *Co-assessment* (including co-monitoring and co-evaluation) of services—for example, tenant inspectors, user online ratings, participatory village appraisal

The distinction of these different service functions in this way allows us to identify a wide range of different approaches to "co-production." In services where we are talking about just one of these co-producing approaches, it makes sense to say so directly and not to use a generic term such as "co-production," which is not widely used and is often misunderstood.

However, there may appear to be a downside to this disaggregation of services management. The range of functions outlined here is so wide that most services are likely to have some element of co-production to them. This begs the question: what services are *not* "co-produced"? We approach the answer to this question by observing that, in general, the UK approach to public management in the past decade has increasingly distinguished "service commissioning" from "service provision" (Bovaird, Dickinsen, and Allen, 2011). In this distinction, all the previously mentioned functions, with the exception of managing and delivering the service, are included as "commissioning." Consequently, we would suggest that full co-production of services only occur where they are *both* co-commissioned and co-provided (see Table 3.1).

Table 3.1   The Typology of Co-Commissioned and Co-Provided Services

		Level of user and community involvement in commissioning of services	
		Low	*High*
Level of user and community involvement in the *provision* of services	*Low*	Traditional services	Co-commissioned services
	High	Co-provided services	Fully co-produced services

Source: Boviard and Loefler, 2011.

UNBUNDLING SERVICES TO IDENTIFY
POTENTIAL CO-PRODUCTION ACTIVITIES

One of the most important analytical phenomena over recent decades in the study of services has been their "unbundling" into their constituent parts to understand the "architecture" by means of basic activities that are combined to result in the service outputs. The most famous approach to this was the value chain analysis of Porter (1985). As shown in Figure 3.1, this allows us to distinguish "primary" and "support" activities in the production process of a public service organization, where primary activities are those that are performed sequentially in order to make a good quality service available, and "support" activities are those that are needed to ensure that all of the primary activities are undertaken properly.

The version of the value chain in Figure 3.1 differs significantly from that suggested by Porter, both because it is specifically designed to apply to a service (rather than a manufactured good in Porter's case) and because all of the activities are seen to be potentially "co-produced" by users and their communities. This possibility was not even hinted at by Porter in his original analysis, although more recently he has suggested ways in which organizations can work with other stakeholders, including those in the community, to create shared value (Porter and Kramer, 2011). While some of these co-produced activities may be less likely than others (e.g., only specialists among users are likely to be capable of co-design of much of service technology, and few will wish to engage in co-leadership of the organization), they are all plausible in certain circumstances.

Figure 3.1 also shows that the value chain of a public service organization is embedded within a wider "value system," consisting of both its "upstream" supply chain of activities (which may or may not be "co-produced" in similar ways) and its "downstream" customer value chains, in which customers themselves produce value through the ways in which they use the service to improve their quality of life. This can occur, for example, through users exploring new uses of a service (e.g., using telecare technology, such as webcams meant for security purposes, to send video messages to their families over the Internet) or new ways in which a service can be speeded up (e.g., through getting users to self-diagnose or self-administer medication).

These customer value chains can, in turn, lead to further value added for other citizens, as shown in Figure 3.2. Here, the ways in which the users benefit directly from the service provide further benefits:

- for their families, careers (formal and informal) and friends
- for other users, who can learn how to make better use of the service through this example
- for other citizens who may need the service in the future and who can now see that it is available and is likely to work for them also

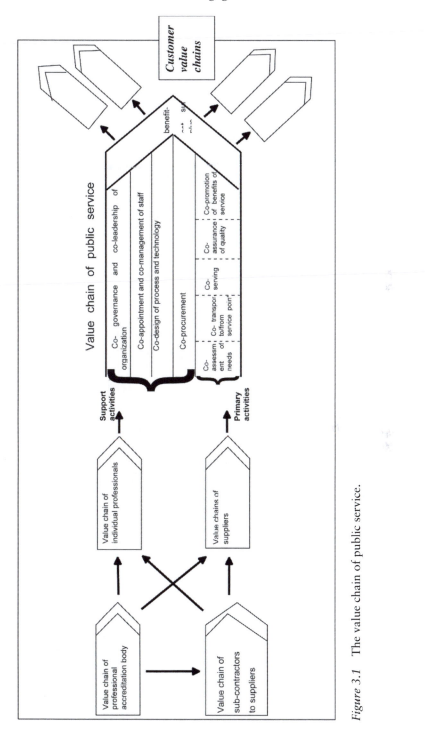

Figure 3.1 The value chain of public service.

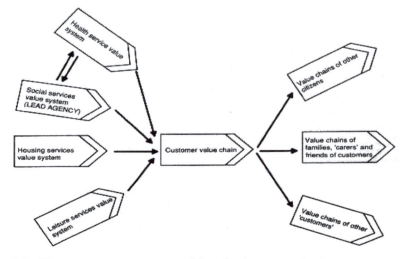

Figure 3.2   How consumers can create public value in a co-production system.

Figure 3.2 also illustrates that each customer may internalize and integrate the benefits from several different service value chains, thus providing synergy from the services. Moreover, this process of integration is likely to speak to their own circumstances and needs, resulting in holistic benefits for them, which would unlikely be achieved without their full involvement in the process.

CO-PRODUCTION AND PUBLIC VALUE

These analyses of co-production in the value chain and in the value system of which it is a part require a definition of "value." Moore suggests that "public value" can be conceptualized "partly in terms of the satisfaction of individuals who [enjoy desirable outcomes] and partly in terms of the satisfactions of citizens who have seen a collective need, fashioned a public response to that need, and thereby participated in the construction of a community . . . " (1995, 47). While helpful, this remains rather vague and difficult to operationalize. We suggest that "value-added" in the public sector typically has several dimensions:

- user value
- value to wider groups (such as family or friends of service users, or individuals who are indirectly affected)
- social value (creation of social cohesion or support for social interaction)
- environmental value (ensuring environmental sustainability of all policies)

- political value (support to democratic process, e.g., through co-planning of services with users and other stakeholders)

In the private sector, "value" has traditionally referred to the first two items, the set of benefits to the firm's end users and the returns to one particular "wider group," namely, its shareholders. However, nowadays there are also pressures for "corporate social responsibility," which bring the other dimensions of value into play even in the private sector. For public and third sector organizations, it is likely that all of these elements of public value are important—and often user value may be outweighed by the other elements. This provides a key insight to the motivations that may lie behind co-production. Purely selfish motivation on the part of users may explain their willingness to co-produce in order to ensure high levels of user value. However, users may also be encouraged to play an active role in the service in order to increase other elements of value, for example, environmentally conscious users may be active in the service planning, design and delivery in order to ensure that its carbon footprint is minimized; while community-conscious users may wish to push the design and management of the service toward goals that emphasize social inclusion and the spreading of benefits across the widest possible range of local community members.

In order to operationalize this model of public value creation, a project has recently been initiated in England, as part of the Total Place initiative launched by central government in 2009 to 2010, to construct a model of the drivers of public outcomes. The Total Place initiative in Birmingham, as in the other twelve pilots in England, explored the implications of harnessing all the public sector expenditure available in a council area in pursuit of the key priorities that the public sector has for that area. The Birmingham pilot went further—it proposed a model of the impacts on public outcomes, across Birmingham as a whole, of both public spending programs and citizen self-organizing and co-production activities. An outline of the model is shown in Figure 3.3 (from Bovaird, 2010). Data on citizen inputs, whether on self-organizing or co-production activities, are particularly sparse at the moment—using this model is likely to stimulate renewed effort to pick up these costs of public services, which are met by citizens and therefore largely unrecorded.

A key aspect of the model-building process will be bringing together the results into a "policy simulator," which will allow policy makers to ask what the predicted effects on outcomes are likely to be at city level when variations are made to spending, inputs (whether from public sector or through citizen inputs into co-production or self-organizing activities) or quality of service. The simulator will also be used to do sensitivity tests to demonstrate the effects on predicted social, economic and environmental outcomes of different assumptions about those relationships for which no data is currently available—thus demonstrating which of these relationships appear the most critical to priority outcomes. This will give an indication

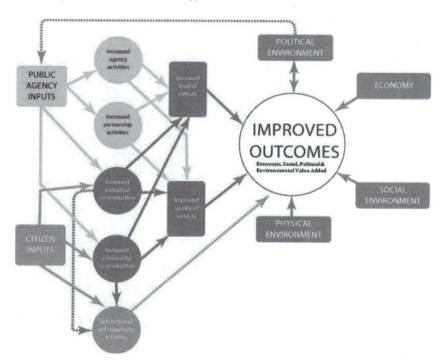

Figure 3.3   Birmingham model of public outcomes.

of which relationships in the model should be given particular attention, for example, by gathering some relevant data. It is intended that the simulator will be used with the Birmingham partners in the development of their citywide programs and budgets for 2012 to 2013.

CO-PRODUCTION: FROM PREVENTION
THROUGH "TREATMENT" TO "RECOVERY"

One of the most topical arenas in which co-production is currently being debated throughout most Organisation for Economic Co-operation and Development countries is in relation to the "prevention versus treatment" choice in many public services. In fact, this fundamental issue is common to most public services, in that the need for a service can often be reduced by early intervention. The full set of issues involved actually is quite complex and involves the set of interrelationships between prevention, detection, treatment, rehabilitation and improving the functioning of those people who have the condition or who experience the problem. In Figure 3.4, we set out one possible way of conceptualizing these very different pathways to improved quality of life outcomes.

In recent years, there has been considerable attention paid to the potential of co-production in the pathways to outcomes that operate through the prevention route. For example, NESTA (2011) reports that evaluations of the Local Area Coordination scheme in Australia estimate the cost of services for people benefiting from the scheme is about 35 percent lower than average social care costs, and the Nurse Family Partnership scheme in the United States provides savings, by the time the child is four years of age, of between $2.50 and $5.70 in preventative costs across criminal justice, education, welfare and health, for every $1 invested by the program (with further savings up to age 15).

Nevertheless, co-production can actually occur on any of the pathways in Figure 3.4. For example, the "rehabilitation" pathway can be delivered through approaches such as "expert patients," where users can manage their own conditions. Similarly, peer support can help to change user behavior toward their own functioning (e.g., peers can work with people suffering from back pain to show them effective ways in which they can take their minds off their condition, or at least be less bothered by it, when it is becomes particularly painful). The analysis in Figure 3.4 suggests that behavior change is a key element to some of the pathways shown—and is particularly likely to be important along the prevention pathway. Behavior change requires, by definition, a key contribution by the citizens involved, and so it involves co-production. Moreover, in this illustration, the behavior change of the citizens is modeled as being driven, at least partly, by those who are "influencers" of their own behavior, and so ties together user and community co-production. Nevertheless, the basic lesson illustrated in Figure 3.4 is that neither behavior change nor co-production more generally are likely to be restricted to "prevention" pathways to outcomes.

BARRIERS TO CO-PRODUCTION

Research has shown that powerful cultural and systemic barriers exist, which prevent co-production from breaking into the mainstream and from being scaled more widely in public services. NESTA (2011) has summarized these barriers as:

- *Funding and commissioning barriers:* while funders and commissioners tend to look for achievement of specific objectives and narrow performance indicators generated from a narrow range of anticipated activities, co-production often encompasses a broad range of activities to deliver outcomes—although this may be partly tackled through outcomes-based commissioning.
- *Difficulties in generating evidence of value for people, professionals, funders and auditors:* co-produced services often incur costs in one

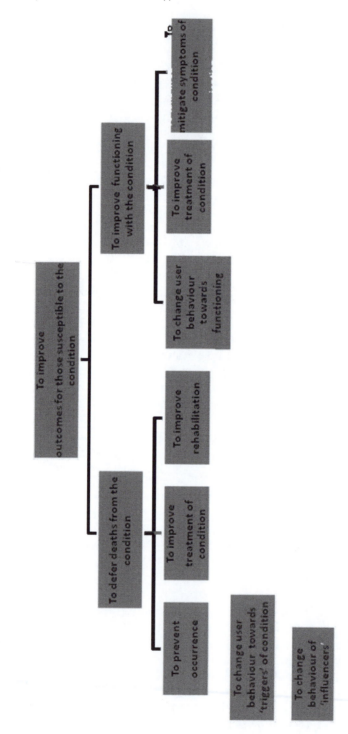

Figure 3.4   "Prevention" or "treatment"? Mapping potential pathways to improved outcomes.

service but benefits in others; moreover, their effects are often long term and complex. New ways to account for value in accounting and performance management systems, and of building a business case that convinces key stakeholders, may be needed if the potential contribution of co-production is to be fully appreciated.

- *Need to develop the professional skills to mainstream co-production:* co-production requires new skills, including being able to see and harness the assets that people have, making room for people to develop for themselves, and using a wide variety of methods for working with people rather than processing them. This is likely to require changes to the way professionals are trained, recruited, developed and performance managed.

To these barriers, we can add:

- *Risk aversion:* co-production is still seen as highly risky by many politicians, managers and professionals, as the behavior of the co-producing users and citizens is less understood and seen as more unpredictable than that of more passive users. However, it needs to be recognized that existing services also carry substantial risk, often only sketchily understood by the public sector, which calls in question whether some of the presumptions of increased risk through co-production have any substance.
- *Political and professional reluctance to lose status and "control":* not only are the skills lacking inside public service organizations to move to co-production, sometimes the willingness is missing also, particularly where it is seen as ceding status and "control" (Shakespeare, 2000). Where this is a factor, a culture shift may be needed to give co-production any chance of success, not just retraining or new performance indicators.

For all the interest since the early 1980s in user and community co-production of public services, there are still few examples of co-production being mainstreamed and taken to scale across public services. Moreover, as NESTA (2011) notes, evidence is still weak on how this might best be done—that is, by growing successful co-production initiatives, whether in the same organization but in other services, or in the same service but across other organizations and geographical areas. Part of this problem may be that the previously mentioned barriers are still very large in many organizations. However, it may also be that the very newness of the approach (at least, as seen by many staff) may simply mean that there is not yet a portfolio of tools for ensuring that it is more widely understood and tried out. Consequently, there is still little evidence as to whether co-production can deliver savings, better outcomes or build social capital when applied at scale.

Table 3.2   Barriers to Co-Production and "Big Society" Initiatives

Barriers to co-production	UK government initiatives under "Big Society"
Funding and commissioning barriers	Big Society Bank Forthcoming White Paper on Public Sector Reform "Community budgeting" or "Place-based budgeting" Local integrated services Transition funding for third sector organisations Suggested minimum levels of commissioning from third sector organizations (in the Green Paper on Commissioning)
Difficulties in generating evidence of value for people, professionals, funders and auditors	Building a business case for co-production (HELP project funded by Department of Health) Social rate of return analysis (being developed by new economics foundation, with Her Majesty's Treasury report)
Need to develop the professional skills to mainstream co-production	No current initiatives
Risk aversion	Encouraging public sector workers to form social enterprises and mutuals
Political and professional reluctance to lose status and "control"	Forthcoming White Paper on Public Sector Reform Encouraging public sector workers to form social enterprises and mutuals
Lack of power (and powers) of users and local communities	Community right to buy/and community right to challenge (Localism Bill) Referenda
Lack of capacity of users and local communities	Green Paper on Giving Big Society Bank Transition funding for third sector organisations
Lack of mechanisms that users and local communities can use	Green Paper on Commissioning and Third Sector Community organisers Participatory budgeting User ratings of services (especially online)
Lack of motivation or self-confidence on part of users and local communities	National Citizen Service Community organisers

Source: Boviard and Loefler, 2011.

GOVERNMENT INITIATIVES UNDER THE "BIG SOCIETY"

In Table 3.2, we set out how the barriers identified in the previous section are being tackled by initiatives in the current UK government's "Big Society" approach. As can be seen, some of the barriers are being given much more attention than others. It seems likely that some of the barriers that are hardly being tackled may be particularly important and may therefore circumvent the government's intentions—that applies in particular to the need for developing the professional skills to mainstream co-production and to political and professional reluctance to lose status and "control."

SOME CO-PRODUCTION CASE STUDIES

In this section we illustrate the points made in this chapter through a number of brief UK case studies that cover the different elements of co-production—co-planning, co-design, co-prioritization, co-financing, co-management, co-delivery and co-assessment.

In each case, we classify the case study by level of co-production (full or partial); the degree of outcome orientation; aspects of public value; whether it involves prevention, treatment, rehabilitation or improved functioning; barriers overcome; and whether it has been taken to scale.

Co-Planning: The Rural Community Trust in Caterham, Surrey

In 1990, the army declared redundant a barracks of attractive and well-constructed buildings on a large site in the middle of the small village of Caterham in Surrey, within commuting distance from London. After active lobbying by local residents, the site was declared a conservation area in 1995, which stopped the clearance of the barracks and their proposed replacement by an estate of private large detached houses. An "urban village" development has subsequently taken place with 400 houses and apartments, some business premises and community facilities (Bovaird, 2006). The site developers, admittedly under pressure from local politicians and residents, agreed to work closely with the community in planning the development. "Planning for Real" exercises involved a high proportion of villagers, facilitated by a major London community planning practice, and the Village won an Urban Design Award in 1996.

When planning permission for the redevelopment was granted in 1998, the developers paid £2.5m under a section 106 agreement to the newly formed Caterham Barracks Community Trust, with members from the surrounding community, including one local politician. Its chief executive was an ex-councilor personally involved in the original lobbying for the conservation area. The trust has used its funds to establish a community theater group, craft workshops, sports teams and many other activities, in line with the priorities expressed by local residents who were board members, appealing to different age groups and different tastes. It has also ensured that the developer's proposals for the site have been compatible with its overall character and that they have provided affordable housing, investment in a cricket pitch and alternative vehicle parking for nearby residents. Targeting young people in particular, the trust built a high-quality indoor skate park, which quickly notched up 5,000 members, up to 570 users per week and a turnover of more than £100,000 p.a. (Moran, 2002). The Community Trust came to play a major role in the co-production of a higher quality of life, not only in its own neighborhood but in the wider village and surrounding district, emphasizing partnership between the local community (and its various associations), with the developer, the planning authorities and the local public service providers. Co-production is central to this model—the investment decisions have been planned with the community itself and all the facilities funded by the trust are managed by groups within the local community.

Table 3.3   The Rural Community Trust in Caterham, Surrey

Case study	The rural community trust in Caterham, Surrey
Level of co-production	Initially, high at co-planning stage, eventually high at co-prioritization and co-management stages
Degree of outcome orientation	Quite high: "Planning for Real" exercise gave vision of final "master plan" for village
Aspects of public value involved	High on user, social and environmental value-added; quite high on political value-added and value to wider groups
Prevention, treatment, rehabilitation or improving functioning?	By planning the Urban Village quite comprehensively in advance, it was hoped to prevent many of the problems of fragmented village life
Barriers overcome	Declaration of a conservation area gave local residents the power to resist the normal economic imperatives that would drive developers to maximize the value of housing on the land and ignore all other land uses
Taken to scale?	The developer eventually decided to work closely with the community trust because the model seemed to be applicable elsewhere—and did indeed use a similar model in another part of southern England

Source: Boviard and Loefler, 2011.

Co-Design: Stockport Council's New Adult Social Care Website

Stockport Council's Adult Social Care Department co-designed, with service users, careers, partners and staff, a new *My Care, My Choice* website that guides people through the "social care maze" and has also made significant savings (further details at Governance International, Case Studies, n.d).

The council partnered with Care Services Efficiencies Delivery (CSED) and Quickheart, a specialist website design company, using a mystery shopping exercise and then ethnographic research (with a small number of randomly chosen people) to fully understand how customers wanted to see information, what language was important to them, their perception of social care as a "place of last resort" and the importance of clear and easy navigation tools on the site. It emerged that the previous website had been confusing and hard to navigate and that the service needed to reach people before they got into crisis, promoting prevention options before people came to need council-funded care. People also wanted an online charging calculator to indicate how much council care was likely to cost. Finally, staff of the council and its partner agencies needed an information hub. The emerging website was proofread for "plain speak" and tested by a number of volunteers, as well as a group of staff from all the service areas.

Since the site went live, feedback by customers, staff and partner agencies has been very positive and has led to continuous redesign and development of the site. Contacts, inquiries and observations at the contact

Table 3.4 Stockport Council: My Care, My Choice Website

Case study	Stockport Council: My Care, My Choice website
Level of co-production	High on co-design and co-assessment
Degree of outcome orientation	Quite high: focus on making available information on services which can improve users' quality of life
Aspects of public value involved	Mainly user value, with some social value and value to wider groups
Prevention, treatment, rehabilitation or improving functioning?	Strong emphasis on "treatment" through care services, but much more emphasis on prevention than in previous website
Barriers overcome	Getting different council departments and partner agencies to work together was harder than getting users to collaborate in the co-design
Taken to scale?	Website now being expanded to a wider range of services and has fed into development of similar website in LB of Kensington and Chelsea

Source: Boviard and Loefler, 2011.

center have gone down by 29 percent, freeing up resources. Although the telephone remains the main method of contact, e-mail contacts have already doubled. The number of "abandoned" and "closed" contacts have been reduced by 38 percent. The number of inquiries and observations received by the contact center that lead to a referral to social work teams has been reduced by 36 percent. Altogether, Stockport estimates that the website has saved the department about £300,000 per annum, for a cost of about £75,000.

Co- Prioritization: "You Decide!" in Tower Hamlets

The "You Decide!" project in the London Borough of Tower Hamlets began in January 2009 and ran a series of 8 events over 4 months, at which 815 residents allocated almost £2.4m of the council's budget for mainstream services—this made it rather different from most participatory budgeting (PB) exercises in the United Kingdom, which focus mainly on the ranking of new projects in neighborhoods or by specific stakeholder groups. At each event, the residents who attended were informed about the services on offer (which had to meet one of the five council priorities or a key local priority identified during the previous year), had an opportunity to deliberate about the services with other members of their community and then had the

Table 3.5   PB in Tower Hamlets

Case study	PB in Tower Hamlets
Level of co-production	High on co-prioritization, quite high on co-design
Degree of outcome orientation	Relatively low: the focus was on services and service spending
Aspects of public value involved	Main focus was on user value, with some attention to social value and value to wider groups
Prevention, treatment, rehabilitation or improving functioning?	Unclear as to how much attention voters were giving to prevention as opposed to "treatment" of problems
Barriers overcome	To reach a large number of residents, traditional techniques (such as adverts, press releases, posters and leaflets) were mixed with a networked approach involving councilors, LAP Steering Groups and Neighborhood Management teams reaching out to community groups, individuals and others and asking them to spread the word.
Taken to scale?	This approach was repeated in 2010 but did not involve a larger proportion of the council budget.

Source: Boviard and Loefler, 2011.

chance to decide which services should be purchased. Subsequently, local area partnership (LAP) steering groups—made up of residents, councilors and service providers—were involved in how the service should be operated and in monitoring its results (further details at You Decide!, Tower Hamlets (London), n.d.).

An especially interesting feature was the voting system—in the first round, all participants were asked to vote for the service they considered to be most important—the most popular was purchased and the money for that service removed from the total. Then another round took place—in each round the most voted-for service purchased, until all the money was spent. This avoided the damaging process in many recent PB exercises, whereby participants are asked what they want to *cut,* and naturally choose services that they don't know or care about, resulting in the council collecting largely uninformed information. After the events were over, all LAP steering groups vetted how service departments intended to implement the decisions of the PB process. Many of the services were changed quite considerably because of resident involvement.

Co-Financing: The Guy Fawkes
Fireworks Display in LB of Lewisham

The Blackheath fireworks display on November 5 (Guy Fawkes Day) has been a long-standing highlight in East London—about 80,000 people attended in 2009. It has traditionally been funded by Lewisham and Greenwich councils, as well as private sponsorship. In the autumn of 2010, the London Borough (LB) of Greenwich pulled out of its funding, putting the fireworks display at risk. As the LB of Lewisham could not afford to fund the shortfall, it decided to launch a public appeal for donations through both traditional and new media. It set up a PayPal account for donations, held a collection on the night and even auctioned off a VIP package on eBay—the auction ran for 10 days with a starting price of 99 pence and a winning bid of £1,000. (Further details at Governance International, Case Studies, n.d.).

The appeal attracted a lot of interest and favorable comment, especially online. Local bloggers got involved with championing the cause. The council had a significant increase in web traffic and 70 percent increase in mentions on social media channels.

In the end, £25,000 was raised toward the shortfall of £36,000. Over 350 donations were received via PayPal, amounting to £2,500, £1,000 through eBay, £4,000 through a collection on the night and the remaining £17,500 from sponsors who were attracted by the raised awareness from the campaign. Others members of the local community donated their time and skills—a local amateur took photos for the council website, and local professionals filmed the event, which can be seen on YouTube. Moreover, on the night of the event, attendance was up by 20,000.

Table 3.6   Guy Fawkes Fireworks Display in Lewisham

Case study	*Guy Fawkes fireworks display in Lewisham*
Level of co-production	High on co-financing, quite high on co-delivery
Degree of outcome orientation	Low: the focus was on continuing a popular event
Aspects of public value involved	High on user value, quite high on social value
Prevention, treatment, rehabilitation or improving functioning?	Not relevant
Barriers overcome	Legal barriers to commercial operation had to be overcome, especially in setting up PayPal and eBay accounts
Taken to scale?	Will be repeated next year, with more volunteer collectors on night, so everyone has chance to donate

Source: Boviard and Loefler, 2011.

Co-Management: KeyRing Support Networks for Vulnerable Adults

KeyRing Living Support Networks are comprised of vulnerable adults who need some support to live safely in the community and are also prepared to offer help to others. Each network enables its members to take control and responsibility for their own lives, live successfully in a place of their own and make a contribution to their local community. Since 1990, KeyRing has grown to 112 networks in around 50 local authorities across England and Wales. Initially, the organization focused on adults with learning disabilities but has now expanded its membership to other groups of people.

Typically a network comprises ten people living within walking distance of each other. Nine of these people are vulnerable adults and the tenth is a community living volunteer (CLV) who lives rent-free in the network area. The CLV provides at least 12 hours of their time each week to promote mutual support between other network members, help them build links with neighbors, community organizations and resources and provide flexible support. Network members can also draw on a structure of flexible paid support when needed. Ninety-nine percent of KeyRing members successfully sustain their own tenancy.

KeyRing members typically give and receive two hours of mutual support per person per week. The development of the network is supported through a process of local community planning, which enables KeyRing members to identify what works well in their network and their community and use it to inspire a plan of network activity. KeyRing network members are highly involved in the running of the organization, for example, through network meetings, regional and national forums, membership of

Table 3.7   KeyRing Support Networks for Vulnerable Adults

Case study	KeyRing Support Networks for vulnerable adults
Level of co-production	High on co-management and co-delivery
Degree of outcome orientation	High: focused on quality of life of network members
Aspects of public value involved	High on user value and social value
Prevention, treatment, rehabilitation or improving functioning?	High on prevention of problems and dealing with individuals underlying problems
Barriers overcome	While typically funded by local public services, KeyRing networks often find it difficult to access wider local services for their members
Taken to scale?	Growing fast through England and Wales

Source: Boviard and Loefler, 2011.

the Members' National Forum and KeyRing Board. KeyRing members are involved in all aspects of the staff and volunteer selection processes and have an equal say with managers on appointments.

In 2009, a Department of Health evaluation of three KeyRing Networks (Care Services Efficiency Delivery, 2009) concluded that KeyRing networks are effective in significantly reducing the level of paid support that members receive while enabling them to achieve good outcomes, estimating that the average saving on social care expenditure per network member was £1,491 p.a. (on a cost of around £5,000 p.a.—a savings of around 20 percent).

Co-Delivery: Peer Educators Fighting Underage Pregnancy in Lambeth

In 2002, the LB of Lambeth had one of the highest levels of teenage pregnancy in Britain. A group of young people who were members of Lambeth's youth council decided that they wanted to do something practical to address teenage pregnancy and improve sex education in schools. They were sure that they could be more effective in getting messages across to their peers than an adult could. (Further details at Governance International, Case Studies, n.d.).

In over 8 years, around 250 young people age 14 to 19 have been trained as peer educators. Most are in full-time education and around two-thirds are girls. The majority are Black African and Black Caribbean, which is broadly reflective of the composition of the borough. They get 25 to 30 hours training. Professionals contribute to the training around sexual health, substance misuse, domestic violence and lesbian, gay, bisexual and

Table 3.8   Peer Educators in Lambeth

Case study	Peer educators in Lambeth
Level of co-production	High in co-delivery
Degree of outcome orientation	Highly focused on reducing under-18 pregnancies
Aspects of public value involved	High on user value, social value and value to wider groups
Prevention, treatment, rehabilitation or improving functioning?	Highly focused on prevention of under-18 pregnancies
Barriers overcome	Allowing young people to undertake responsible activities such as giving sex education in schools has been an innovative approach
Taken to scale?	Grown significantly over eight years of operation

Source: Boviard and Loefler, 2011.

transgender issues. This means the peer educators are able to see firsthand professionals who work in the borough on these issues. Peer educators are treated as unqualified youth workers and paid accordingly (£8.31 per hour), to recognize their commitment and professionalism. Peers have subsequently been offered jobs as learning mentors and teaching assistants in schools and have worked in the youth service. Many have gone on to college or a university. Very few drop out of the training (on average only 3 out of 20) and many stay with the program for three or four years.

Over a hundred workshops are now held each year in school classrooms, at "health days" and with youth groups. The workshops are designed and delivered by the peer educators (working in pairs). Peer educators have the advantage of speaking to young people in a clear and relevant way and can credibly challenge attitudes and discuss values and beliefs. The sessions have received highly favorable feedback from young participants.

The under-age-18 conception rate in Lambeth has declined by 26 percent since 2003, a faster rate than elsewhere in London—and this program seems likely to have made a significant contribution. The program is supported by a full-time member of staff and costs around £59,000, including staffing, training materials, publicity, refreshments and payments to the peer educators.

Co-Assessment

In the United Kingdom, the Audit Commission has long co-opted tenants of social housing to work as "tenant inspection advisors" on its inspections of

Table 3.9 Co-Assessment

Case study	Co-assessment
Level of co-production	High on co-assessment
Degree of outcome orientation	Moderate: main focus is on housing services, not outcomes
Aspects of public value involved	User value
Prevention, treatment, rehabilitation or improving functioning?	Main focus is on housing service delivery rather than prevention of problems through alternative services
Barriers overcome	Tenant assessors tend to be given tasks which require the tenant's perspective, rather than tasks with a strong technical element
Taken to scale?	This approach has grown throughout the UK and is now used by many housing associations for their internal quality assurance and evaluation processes

Source: Boviard and Loefler, 2011.

social housing providers to ensure that inspection remains clearly focused on the customer's experience of housing services. (A bottom-up initiative that goes even further is the citizen inspectorate in Bobigny, France, which audits the local authority and publishes regular reports that are presented to the mayor in a public meeting (see good practice, then interviews at www. govint.org). Since 2004, the Scottish Housing Regulator has also appointed tenant assessors, volunteers who are tenants of social landlords or local authorities and who work with Regulation and Inspection staff. All tenant assessors have to sign a code of conduct and confidentiality agreement, similar to that binding professional inspection staff. They can be involved for up to three days on an inspection, carrying out tasks such as assessing samples of information that landlords provide for their tenants; attending formal meetings with tenants' groups; and taking part in onsite visits with inspectors, where they meet staff and tenants, visit properties and ask questions. An evaluation of the tenant assessors initiative found that it was seen as positive by the inspection teams, staff of inspected organizations and tenant assessors themselves (Regulation and Inspection, 2007).

CONCLUSIONS

User and community co-production appears to have been one of the best-kept secrets of public management and governance over the past few decades. It has always been important but rarely noticed, never mind discussed or systematically managed. However, it is now being "outed" as a key driver for improving publicly valued outcomes. One of the great strengths behind it is that it is not simply a "big idea" for the future but is already happening. However, this explicit recognition of the concept brings with it the challenge that the level of effort being put into co-production by users and communities must not be wasted by public agencies, as much of it currently appears to be.

Moreover, there appears to be a huge latent willingness of citizens to become more involved—but only if they feel they can play a worthwhile role. Citizens are only willing to co-produce in a relatively narrow range of activities that are genuinely important to them—but the public sector has little experience in tailoring its marketing to specific market segments. With little information on what most citizens are interested in, it is difficult to make targeted offers that are seen as relevant.

However, co-production is not always the most relevant answer to all issues in the public sector. It is strongest in producing user value, although it can also have a useful role in producing social value, environmental value and value to wider groups. It is also likely to be particularly valuable where there is a need to trigger behavior change toward prevention of future problems. However, it should not be seen as a panacea for all the problems that public agencies face.

A key issue that has not yet been properly explored is the extent to which co-production involves greater risks than professionalized service provision. Certainly, professionals are concerned that users and communities have less technical experience in coping with the risks involved in tackling public and social problems. On the other hand, there is increasing concern that public sector organizations have themselves, in the past, underestimated the risks involved in public sector provision and not properly understood how services can be quality assured more successfully through involving users and embedding them in the community.

Finally, the case studies explored in this chapter demonstrate that, while user and community co-production can achieve major improvements in outcomes and service quality and can produce major cost savings, it is not resource-free. Initiating such approaches can involve substantial set-up costs, and supporting them effectively will usually involve a flow of public sector resources. Co-production may be "value for money" but it usually cannot produce value *without* money.

ACKNOWLEDGMENTS

The authors would like to acknowledge the support of the French Presidency of the EU and of the Local Authorities Research Council Initiative for some of the research on which this chapter is based.

REFERENCES

Arnstein, S. 1971. The ladder of citizen participation. *Journal of the Royal Town Planning Institute*, 57(1): 176–182.

Barzelay, M. 2001. *The New Public Management: Improving Research and Policy Dialogue*. Berkeley, CA.: University of California Press.

Bovaird, T. 2006. Developing new relationships with the "market" in the procurement of public services. *Public Administration*, 84(1): 81–102.

Bovaird, T. 2007. Beyond engagement and participation—user and community co-production of public services, *Public Administration Review*, 67(5): 846–860.

Bovaird, T. 2009. Strategic management in public sector organisations. In: T. Bovaird, E. Löffler, eds. *Public Management and Governance*, 2nd edition. London: Routledge.

Bovaird, T. 2010. *Model Of Public Outcomes And Cost Implications: Thinkpiece For Birmingham Total Place Initiative*. Birmingham: INLOGOV.

Bovaird, T., H. Dickinson, and K. Allen. 2011. *Commissioning Across Government*. Birmingham: Third Sector Research Centre.

Brudney, J., and R. England. 1983. Towards a definition of the co-production concept. *Public Administration Review*, 43 (10): 59–65.

Department of Health. 2009. *CSED Case Study KeyRing: Living Support Networks*. London: Department of Health – Care Services Efficiency Delivery.

Etzioni, A. 1995. *The Spirit of Community*. London: Fontana Press.

Governance International, Case Studies. n.d. www.govint.org/english/main-menu/good-practice/case-studies.html. Accessed August 1, 2011.

Gunn, L. 1988. Public management: a third approach? *Public Money and Management*, 8(1–2): 5–23.

Horne, M., and T. Shirley. 2009. *Co-production in public services: A new partnership with citizens*. London: Cabinet Office.

Hood, C. 1991. A public management for all seasons? *Public Administration* 69 (1): 3–19.

Kelly, G., G. Mulgan, and S. Muers. 2002. *Creating Public Value*. London: Cabinet Office.

Kretzmann, J., and J. McKnight. 1993. *Building Communities from the Inside-Out: A Path toward Finding and Mobilizing a Community's Assets*. ACTA: Skokie, IL.

Löffler, E. 2010. *A Future Research Agenda for Co-production: Overview Paper*. London: Local Authorities Research Council Initiative.

Lovelock, C., and R. F. Young. 1979. Look to customers to increase productivity. *Harvard Business Review* 57 (May–June): 168–178.

Lyons, M. 2006. *National Prosperity, Local Choice and Civic Engagement: A New Partnership between Central and Local Government for rhe 21st Century*. London: Her Majesty's Stationary Office.

Moore, M. 1995. *Creating Public Value*. Cambridge, MA: Harvard University Press.

Moran, D. 2002. *The Real Contract*. Paper presented to Conference on Public Private Partnerships. Belfast: Chartered Institute of Public Finance and Accountancy.

National Endowment for Science Technology and the Arts. 2011. *Co-production Phase 2: Taking co-production to scale in services for patients with long term health conditions*. Strategic Partners: Call for Proposals. London: Author.

Normann, R. 1984. *Service Management*. Chichester, UK: John Wiley.

Parks, R. B., P. C. Baker, L. Kiser, R. Oakerson, E. Ostrom, V. Ostrom, S. L. Percy, M. B. Vandivort, G. P. Whitaker, and R. Wilson. 1981. Consumers as coproducers of public services: Some economic and institutional considerations. *Policy Studies Journal* 9 (4): 1001–1011.

Percy, S., 1984. Citizen participation in the co-production of urban services. *Urban Affairs Quarterly* 19 (4): 431–446.

Pollitt, C. 1990. *Managerialism and the Public Services*. Oxford, UK: Blackwell.

Porter, M. 1985. *Competitive Advantage: Creating and Sustaining Superior Performance*. New York: Free Press.

Porter, M., and M. Kramer. 2011. Creating shared value: How to reinvent capitalism and unleash a wave of innovation and growth. *Harvard Business Review* 89 (Jan–Feb): 2–17.

Putnam, R. D. 2000. *Bowling Alone: the Collapse and Revival of American Community*. New York: Simon and Schuster.

Ramirez, R. 1999. Value co-production: Intellectual origins and implications for practice and research. *Strategic Management Journal* 20 (1): 49–65.

Regulation and Inspection. 2007. *Open and Accessible?* Glasgow: Communities Scotland.

Shakespeare, T. 2000. The social relations of care. In G. Lewis, S. Gewirtz, and J. Clarke, eds., *Rethinking Social Policy*. London: Open University.

Sharp, E. 1980. Towards a new understanding of urban services and citizen participation: The co-production concept. *Midwest Review of Public Administration* 14(June): 105–118.

Warren, R., K. S. Harlow, and M. S. Rosentraub. 1982. Citizen participation in services: Methodological and policy issues in co-production research. *Southwestern Review of Management and Economics* 2 (March): 41–55.

Whitaker, G. 1980. Co-production: citizen participation in service delivery. *Public Administration Review* 40 (3): 240–246.

Wickström, S. 1996. The customer as co-producer. *European Journal of Marketing* 30 (4): 6–19.

You Decide! Tower Hamlets (London). n.d. http://www.participatorybudgeting.org.uk/case-studies/you-decide-tower-hamlets-london. Accessed August 1, 2011.

Zeleny, M. 1978. *Towards Self-Service Society*. New York: Columbia University Press.

4 Co-Production

Contested Meanings and Challenges for User Organizations

Benjamin Ewert and Adalbert Evers

INTRODUCTION

In the field of social services, co-production has become a buzzword for a set of instruments and ways of working that are meant to produce better outcomes in terms of service quality and efficiency. We understand co-production as a notion that refers to exchange relationships that include several dimensions of interaction (e.g., dialogue, practical matters and cooperation); it can relate to individual service relationships at the microlevel, as well as to the links between organizations at the mesolevel of the welfare system (Brandsen and Pestoff, 2006).

As some authors have already emphasized, as a vehicle for better, smarter and more individualized services, co-production may play a "significant role in the renewal of democratic political systems and the welfare state" (Pestoff, Osborne, and Brandsen, 2006, 593) insofar as it calls for the democratization rather than the bureaucratization of service provision relationships, whether this is achieved through the empowerment of users or better cooperative governance of service systems. However, faced with the whole set of definitions and interpretations of co-production, one might be tempted to ascribe it with a "cure-all potential" (Needham, 2008, 224). As we will argue in this chapter, it is useful to make a distinction between the various lenses through which co-production is seen, each of which classify different practices as co-production and ascribe a different nature to it. Perspectives on co-production relationships are colored by various background narratives, such as consumerism or participatory governance. And while all the different "flavors" of co-production claim to make service systems more effective and to focus more on end users, they nevertheless have a different impact and implications for new forms of "co-productive" service governance and user participation.

As we will argue, in a changed welfare environment, there is no dominant, coherent narrative for co-production. Due to various changes in welfare environments—above all, the mentalities and practices of institutions, the provision and shaping of social services, their governance in mixed welfare systems and the notions of welfare users—co-production refers to a fragmented set of activities, expectations and rationales. We will illustrate this by examining the field of health services, in general, and the German health care system in particular.

- The first part of this chapter will briefly argue that the current plurality of narratives has unfolded against a background of the waning traditional concept of preserving (health) services, in which hierarchical and paternalistic modes of service provision clearly dominate; in retrospect, one might say that something like co-production, if it ever existed at all, was in fact a synonym for "compliance" at the level of individual service provision, hierarchically ordered at the level of relationships within the public service system.
- Taking this era of "relative clarity" as a point of departure, the central second section investigates the key drivers of modernizing health care, such as shifts toward knowledge-based services, economization and marketization. Concepts of "active users" who co-produce their social services are superseding the traditional *Leitbild* of the more passive and dependent patient or welfare beneficiary. The changed environment of co-production relationships requires a new notion of the individual in the production and consumption of health and care services. In the context of the pluralism and complexity of users' relationships with social service providers (e.g., Alford, 2002), the health care user as co-producer needs to be reassessed. Given the presence of different concepts and narratives, ranging from marketization to managed care, users and systems are becoming increasingly fragmented and hybridized. Focusing on users, one can show how different role models take shape, such as the patient-consumer or the expert-patient. In each case, a different conception of "co-production" is relevant.
- The third section will focus on those dimensions of co-production that involve service-user relationships. It will change the level of argumentation by referring to the results of an empirical study of the ways user organizations in the field of health care in Germany are trying to cope with changes in practices in the system, the various types of users and concepts of reform. To what extent can they take on the role of "co-producers" who not only help patients to get what they are entitled to, but also to make the best possible choices? And to what extent does this leave room for something even more demanding— acting as *change agents*, an area where "co-production" inevitably raises questions of democratic participation?

A HERITAGE THAT CONTINUES TO CAST A SHADOW: CO-PRODUCTION AS A QUESTION OF TRUST AND COMPLIANCE

How can we characterize the co-producing relationships of the bygone golden age of the welfare state (Evers, 2008, 229–231)? Why were they so much easier to frame? Going back to the status quo ante, one can broadly state that the embeddedness of the health care co-producer was less complex. Like elsewhere in Western Europe, social citizenship in Germany until the 1980s was shaped predominantly by the political-cultural context of inclusion, redistribution and trust. For an entitled citizen (or "beneficiary"), receiving health care services was first of all a matter of legal claims; at the system level, the co-producer was conceived as a collective citizen participating through organizations that co-administered the institutions of the "*Solidargemeinschaft*" (Taylor-Gooby, 2009, 3–20), such as the system of health insurance. Within the delivery of health care services, however, the user as an autonomous social being was not really an issue. When it came to safeguarding "the active participation of those supposedly receiving the services" (Brandsen and Pestoff, 2006, 496), one could, by and large, count on the functioning of four decisive elements:

1. embededness in a prescriptive system of insurance financing and coverage
2. trust in professions
3. choice in terms of opting out for alternative services was seen as a privilege and reserved for the few better off
4. limited knowledge of health care and medical issues

At the system level as well as at the level of service provision, there was a kind of co-production as an element of interaction. However, as Alford rightly points out, "the key point is not whether there is interaction but whether the citizen's contribution is induced by the actions or behavior of the government agency" (2009, 20). With a strong impact of governments on traditional health care systems, the scope for co-production was modest, or at least tightly structured. In Germany, for example, the corporatist German system was a significant force in shaping the relationships between providers and users. For the latter, who were viewed mainly as beneficiaries, full coverage of health care services and stable insurance membership rates were more important than freedom of choice. The trust of health care users in corporate actors' care has thus far been a central resource for co-production in terms of establishing a general willingness to follow the prescriptions of experts. Most of those insured worshipped equal access and universal services and relied heavily on the recommendations of experts in their choices of doctors or institutions; general practitioners transferred their patients to local specialists or hospitals without having to consult much with their patients. Hence, the main contribution of users as co-producers was to entrust professionals with their choices by proxy.

One should remember, however, that not only in Germany but also in other welfare states in Europe there has always been a small private sector alongside the public health care system, and a minority of users that had always been used to "free choice" and different modes of "co-production" with institutions and experts. For the vast majority, however, interaction with the health system meant a kind of co-production that was embedded in dense and formalized rules and routines.

Users' limited commitment as co-producers also becomes apparent when one scrutinizes the former role models within the physician-patient relationship. As with the choice of providers, users have always played an active role in the medical treatment process. By definition, health services rely "on patients to behave in certain ways, such as resting properly and to undertake certain actions, such as taking their medicines or undergoing physical therapy" (Alford, 2009, 1). For the type of co-production that was traditionally found here, the often-used label of "compliance" would seem rather fitting. It refers to a kind of cooperation where one side—the expert—gives the directions, while the other side has to understand and comply. Even if it is well-known that many patients rejected this role—by ignoring doctors' advice or not taking prescribed medicaments, for example—that took place in an environment of unchallenged responsibilities where the only question left was how to make co-production (defined as compliance with the instructions given by the experts) work better.

What we have outlined here is the conceptual basis of an inherited, rather unitarian model of co-production, without discussing the empirical question of the degree to which this model, based on trust in the advice of experts, hierarchy and compliance, as well as trust in and support for public health protection has empirically lived up to its own goals and promises.

THE MODERNIZATION OF SOCIAL SERVICES AND ITS IMPLICATIONS FOR CO-PRODUCTION: THE EXAMPLE OF HEALTH CARE

While the involvement of users in the provision of health care services is in principle nothing new, the question remains of why and how it has become so critical in recent decades and what has led to the increase in support for a shift from a top-down regulated health system and compliance to the advice of experts to a kind of co-production that provides for a more active role for health care users.

The more general answers are well-known, and we will mention them without going into great detail. The stabilization of postwar democracies and the consolidation of welfare regimes, together with the emancipation of welfare users and individualization of welfare delivery, led to a gradual increase in users' ability to cope with public services but also their expectations with regard to decent and qualitative services. Taken together, these processes have provided fertile ground for a discourse on social services, including managerialism, consumerism and participatory governance that entailed a changed perspective on users and patients in various ways (Evers, 2009). As society and welfare environments have changed, the health care system has also been affected by new rationales.

Although we are focusing on the German case in this article, the following key drivers of modernization correspond to "global modes of restructuring health care" (Kuhlmann, 2006, 37–56). Each of them raises issues of co-production, though in sometimes different ways:

- The shift toward knowledge-based services—due to ongoing medical-technical progress and innovations, such as the personalization of treatment processes and e-health, but also due to user-oriented blueprints of health services in the light of "democratic professionalism" (Kremer and Tonkens, 2006, 131), modes of user participation have multiplied. These developments indicate that health care was integrated into the logic and rationales of modern "knowledge societies" (Stehr, 1994), which require the co-production of knowledge rather than the simple transfer of knowledge.

- The economization of health care—a reform approach that weighs cost-containment and the efficiency of public health care services the most highly. Specifically, one can speak of restrictions placed on health care in order to make tight public funds go as far as possible. Relevant policy instruments to legitimize and ration scarce goods and services concern not only the mesolevel—for example, sickness funds and doctors that are obliged to adapt their services to capped budgets—but also the overall framework in which users co-produce.

- The marketization of health care—a driver that promotes health care as a "consumer good" by fostering competition between providers and users' choice within the health care system. Unlike economization policies, which inspired the need to reduce the costs of a public sector, the principle of marketization is more about an expansion and commercialization of health care services and products, a branch that cuts across the traditional lines between the public and private sectors (see also Ewert, 2009). Being a co-producer in a marketized health care system demands consumerist behavior—that is, making the right choices among competing health care services.

Insofar as these trends are impacting on health care systems, they are first of all tending to undermine the unquestioning and one-dimensional rationale that dominated previously, as a consequence of, for example, corporatist and top-down methods of decision making and management by professional experts (the medical sciences). Market rules and market thinking, managerial and economic logics and professional forces are competing with the those of the medical professions; the previously socially protected citizen, who was treated according to the advice of medical experts, is now being asked to cooperate and invest his own money in his health, to follow medical pathways of managed care, to purchase complementary products from commercial service providers. The health care system is no longer part of the monolithic public sector but rather a cluster of public and private services with a great deal of room for organizations in between.

In such an environment, co-production on the part of health care users is being invited in very different ways: in addition to the old call for compliance, there is now the call for the "informed consent" to be negotiated with users that are seen as experts in their own right; in addition to the promise that welfare institutions will pay the bill, there is the hint that the users can and should act as consumers in health care markets and quasi markets, and in addition to models and practices in which the user simply trusts the doctor of his or her choice, there are now alternatives under which citizens feel that they have to check competing offers from managed care networks. The provision of health care is being modernized as a result of the parallelism and overlapping drivers that are activating users as co-producers. They correlate to a health care system that is simultaneously a knowledge-based service system, part of the public sector and a branch of the market. Users are addressed as and required to act as citizens, patients, consumers and co-producers, all at the same time.

Within the German health care system, these processes of modernization have merged together into specific contexts and service arrangements. While they all share a notion of the user as a "participatory" subject, economization, marketization and the challenges of a knowledge-based service system involve diverse and sometimes even contradictory co-production requirements. In order to illustrate the ambiguity of co-production as a concept of user involvement, we will look at two specific issues in more detail: the debate on new tariffs for health care insurance and the attempt to replace the traditional model of compliance in the physician-patient relationship with the concept of informed consent.

In Germany, 90 percent of those insured are enrolled in the Statutory Healthcare Insurance (SHI) system. Despite universal access to and coverage of health care services, those insured are increasingly being challenged to co-produce their insurance coverage by choosing tailor-made tariffs or packages of health care services. Specifically, the abilities of users as co-producers play a key role in making health care work as a social right. In light of the current health care reforms, SHI schemes are addressing their members more as knowledgeable, cost-sensitive and market-savvy health care consumers, rather than as entitled members.

While competition between SHI schemes was introduced in the early 1990s as a mechanism for cost-containment, the wooing of the insured through selective insurance contracts led to the reform of 2004. Untl then, the principle has been that every insured person is to receive equal health care services in the case of need. Instead, the coverage of the insured person depends increasingly on the specific terms of their enrolment with an insurance company (which are hidden away in the fine print of complex contracts). The reforms gave SHIs more leeway to negotiate service packages with health care providers and freed them from collective contracts. The result has been the economization and marketization of insurance schemes—for instance, tariffs that reward users for the nonuse of health care services within a calendar year or bind them contractually to certain health care providers or add-on insurance packages that guarantee their owners privileges, such as treatments by senior physicians or coverage for complementary and alternative medicine. In all cases, the users of health insurance have to co-arrange their health care framework as "entrepreneurs" or even "brokers," who are required to assess their own insurance needs. Furthermore, they are required to screen the market for insurance and identify suitable offers just as, in this respect, co-producing means becoming familiar with (often incommensurable) legal clauses and contract details. Co-producers who are up to these tasks can personalize their insurance coverage more appropriately, but those who are not could end up receiving substandard health care, despite their membership to an SHI scheme.

An even more awkward position could arise in modern health care systems if the process of co-production is seen at the level of individual medical treatment. Here, the creeping invasion of economization and marketization—for example, through hidden financial incentives for doctors—could disturb the equilibrium of the sensitive physician-patient relationship (see Kremer and Tonkens, 2006). Bit by bit, this could undermine mutual trust, the basis and lubricant of professional-patient interaction.

A second significant change relates to the concept of "informed consent." It is based on the assumption that patients who are given "objective" information on their diagnosis and planned treatment will then be able to make an adequate decision about whether or not to use the medical interventions they are offered. Thus, co-production in the knowledge-based framework of informed consent "presumes that 'rational' decision making can be grounded on a specific type of information provided" (Felt et al., 2009, 88). Due to the fact that this procedure does not challenge the supremacy of professional knowledge, most doctors have embraced it. The search for consensus on a routine basis, which appears to transform a patient ex ante into an informed partner, is a welcome release for professionals from the "paternalistic" responsibility of caring and protecting.

If we reconsider informed consent under the present conditions, co-production becomes much more demanding. The reasons for this are twofold: first, decisions for or against a certain medical treatment rely on very different knowledge. As well as the different layers of knowledge relating to the purely medical aspects—such as the appropriateness of a dental treatment—which will not vanish after ex ante information from the physician, nonmedical aspects are also playing an increasing role. For instance, the link between cost, quality and expected benefits, the opportunity to invest in private health care (services that are not covered by health insurance) or the comparison of the treatment offered by different physicians may play a role.

Second, the level of information is not the only issue. Patients may perceive their role as co-producers in the light of other criteria (e.g., such as how close the place of treatment is to family networks, information from informal sources), "disregarding offered formal information in their decision making and drawing on different resources instead" (ibid., 100). Consequently, the practice of informed consent between doctors and patients is becoming extended through the inclusion of other kinds of knowledge than medical information alone; the practice of consent-seeking may also be influenced by the fact that some patients doubt professional knowledge and use their own experiences, convictions and affiliations as a basis for decision making, reasons that are rarely brought up in an ex ante discussion with their doctors.

The example of informed consent underlines that co-production in health care is unfolding beyond one-dimensional mindsets (e.g., biomedical expertise) or rather isolated patterns of interaction (e.g., the patient-doctor constellation). The whole previous system of the prescribed use of health care services is being submerged by the attempts of patients to navigate through the system with maps that they are required to draw themselves. With medical professionals stepping back from their former paternalistic role of deciding on the course of treatment, patients now have more freedom but also carry more of the responsibility for mobilizing a wide range of resources for the co-production of decision-making processes in health care. Long-standing social constructs and role models for co-producers in health care must be reassessed.

THE HEALTH CARE CO-PRODUCER
IN COMPLEX ENVIRONMENTS

So far, while outlining the environment of co-production in the German health care system, we have used the terms "user," "patient" or "insured party" more or less intuitively. However, the examples previously given indicate that each of these words implies a different kind of "co-producer." The complexity of the health care environment described in the previous section is inscribed in the hybrid and kaleidoscopic nature of the co-producer. The identity of the co-producers is a patchwork, the defining characteristics of which depend on a combination of individual dispositions, patterns of health care provision, service arrangements and different health care contexts. Referring once again to the examples of health care insurance and the physician-patient relationship, we will discuss two models of the service user that reflect this intermeshing of roles and terms in co-production: the "citizen-consumer" and the "expert-patient." While the first label reflects the impact of discourses relating to rights on choice in public services, the latter concept primarily reflects the liberal attitude in reacting to the increasingly science-based nature of modern health services, modeling the doctor-patient relationship on the concept of a face-to-face discussion.

Taking the example of health care funds in Germany, co-production by citizen-consumers would ideally contribute to insurance schemes that are more efficient, effective and individualized than standardized previous versions. As a role model for co-production, the citizen-consumer (Clarke et al., 2007) pledges both the careful use of health care services by solidarity-minded citizens as well as the readiness of consumers to go for the "best buy" when it comes to private insurance coverage. However, with respect to the hybridization of the rationales of the entitled citizen and the self-responsible consumer, the question of "who commands whom" becomes central. Due to the ambiguity of service provision schemes, which come along as "opportunities" and demand knowledge from the user—or rather the mobilization of personal agency—the balancing of rationales depends on individual capabilities. In this respect, co-production means locating oneself within an area of tension, whether this is the tension between the active citizen who is able to evaluate the fine print of his insurance coverage policy independently and the passive health insurance beneficiary, or the tension between the well-informed consumer and his duped counterpart who receives poor health care without choices.

Once an individual is forced into a position between these poles, co-production inevitably alters its character. Utilitarian connotations of co-production, which reduce the term to its economic impact, can drive out its innovative and "value-creating" (Alford, 2009, 18) effect. Does Alford's praise of co-production's power to create value still apply then? Once more, one's wider view of modernity may make the difference: on the one hand, one can argue that economized welfare schemes, subjugated to market competition, are "value-destroying," since they lock co-producers into a utilitarian framework. On the other hand, if one views the modernization of health care services in a more optimistic light, value-creation in terms of co-production by citizen-consumers may trigger a process of self-assurance and self-empowerment and thus contribute to the shaping of people's social identities within complex health care service arrangements. According to this perspective, co-producers no longer serve abstract aims, such as democratic renewal, solidarity and reciprocity, but such issues are brought into play through attempts to personalize health care provision.

At the level of health care delivery, the expert-patient and the patient-consumer can be seen as equivalents to the citizen-consumer. Once again, the old terminology, such as the classic patient, is insufficient to map the current dynamics and demands within physician-patient relationships. The old protected zone of physician-patient interaction has been altered in several ways. As discussed in the previous section, doctors face incentives to purchase services privately, while patients are involved in the negotiation of treatment plans as well as in sharing emerging costs. Being "calm and patient," then, is far from the best strategy for today's patients; doctors, meanwhile, are not only medical workers but also "citizen-professionals" who help patients to translate the "concept of citizenship into the practice of welfare state services" (Kuhlmann, 2006, 16).

Classifying professionals as "facilitators" of modernity is, however, the optimistic way of viewing the processes that are unfolding. One may equally observe that physician-patient relationships suffer from the behavior of doctors who free themselves from professional role models and switch into the role of "sellers"; other physicians may be obsessed with health care managerialism, such as "managed care" or "Disease Management Programs" (DMPs), and thus almost mechanically worship a balanced budget rather than professional guidelines. Users may therefore become activated through a tense situation. They may find themselves caught in a conflictual relationship, where trusting compliance is still a precondition for benefiting as a patient—the chronically ill, for example, have to adhere to strict lifestyle rules—but where, at the same time, they are permanently co-addressed as health care consumers and cost-bearers. For patients, being addressed by professionals in either of these ways demands profound co-producing capabilities.

This means that hybrid classifications such as the expert-patient and the patient-consumer do not refer to a relaxed intermeshing of rationales but rather to a potential source of tension and conflict that health care users have to learn to cope with. Disposing of respective resources and competences then becomes critical. Who can provide information on the logics of evidence-based medicine, the budget-restraints that apply to a particular case or the quality of services offered that are not covered by SHI? This increasing demand for support and empowerment has been recognized as a new field of activity by insurance companies and user organizations (see the next section) and has led to the emergence of new educational schemes such as "patient coaching programs" or "patient universities" for future co-producers.

USERS AND USER-ORGANIZATIONS AS CO-PRODUCERS IN THE GERMAN HEALTH CARE SYSTEM

How much knowledge and competence do German health care users have? What are their intrinsic motivations, role perceptions and difficulties within co-production relationships? To answer these questions, we will draw from twenty-two expert interviews, conducted as part of an ongoing research project with consultants working in patient organizations, self-help groups and customer services in Germany. The empirical material, which serves as a basis, does not have the status of a quantitative survey on health care users' attitudes, but does indicate generalized "patterns of user behavior" as perceived by consultants.

It is obvious from the interviews that there is an emerging discrepancy between users' understanding of their own role, their actual competences and the demands on co-producers in Germany's health care system. Four different patterns of co-producing behavior and problems can be identified.

First, there are signs that cultural constraints prevent health care users from co-producing health care services in a knowing and self-confident way. Although they have the right to choose their doctor and switch health care providers freely, users are still affected by prescriptive, protective and passivating attitudes on the part of health and welfare bureaucracies. A progressively changing health care environment now requires the co-creation of specific knowledge and the acquisition of competences in order to benefit from the health care and insurance systems. This is leading to an initial loss of certainty and security for most of these *well looked after users*. With regard to the process of health care delivery, "shared decision making" or user involvement in managed care schemes remain "terra incognita" for most users.

Second, co-production in terms of choosing and purchasing insurance coverage and health care services represents a conflict for users that were socialized as entitled beneficiaries under the traditional solidarity-based SHI system, in which insurance has paid for literally every piece of adhesive tape or every journey to a health resort. Particularly *the elderly*, who are used receiving unconditional, universal health care and who have paid premiums all their lives, have a strong feeling of unease regarding cost-sharing modes. Unsurprisingly, the co-payment of dental treatments and glasses, or incentives to buy extra insurance to cover some provisions out of their own pocket conflict with their personal notion of co-production in a decent health care system.

Third, if insurance funds and physicians adopt a partly consumerist logic, the capacity of users to "shop around" in such complementary health care markets becomes critical. In this respect, co-production for personal benefit means assessing one's own requirements. According to the interviewees, *younger people, who are often more healthy and market-savvy*, or more aware citizen-consumers, do much better than average people. The latter, chiefly the elderly, require "health care trustees" to support them in the difficult process of arranging a process and package of services that will work for them.

Fourth, a significant change in co-production patterns concerns physician-patient relationships. Patients appreciate being addressed as *interlocutors* but not as *co-responsible agents with their own responsibilities*. They are still astonished if they are asked to make own complementary efforts in terms of lifestyle changes or private investment in additional arrangements and services. This means that loyalty- and trust-based partnerships—key factors for co-production—are critical. An unintended consequence is that quite often users request health care services simply because a certain form of treatment is more expensive, for fear of missing out on what is available.

In conclusion, according to what professionals from user organizations reported, German health care users are torn between different roles. On the one hand, they want to build up a trusting relationship and are ready to show compliance; at the same time, there is a growing tendency to try to become something of a self-taught expert; then again, users try to make the best buy when additional services and products are offered. Former roles, in which requests for personal agency were restricted to the task of compliance, are persistent and collide in unexpected and often unpredictable ways with the demands of modern co-production. Where the health care expectations and co-production skills of users were shaped during the traditional era of health care socialization, a relearning process will be both hard to accomplish and often frustrating. As a result, a new gap of social inequality may emerge that separates users not only with regard to their purchasing power but increasingly according to their cognitive and practical abilities.

CO-PRODUCTION BY USER ORGANIZATIONS: SIMPLE SERVICE PROVIDERS OR ALSO CHANGE AGENTS?

Within the German health care system, co-production by user organizations—mainly patient and self-help groups—has traditionally served two goals: first, the creation of a sense of community between patients that share a common fate because they suffer from a (serious) disease. This role also included providing a platform for the mutual exchange of coping strategies for members. Patient affiliation to the organization also emanated from a second goal: the promotion of (alternative) blueprints for health and health care services. In that respect, the respective organizations have also acted as change agents, whether by promoting complementary and alternative medicine, public campaigns for new and better treatment of diseases and challenges (e.g., HIV, obesity as the new plague of lower social strata, and others).

Nowadays, user organizations are in a somewhat paradoxical situation. On the one hand, collective co-production by an ever-increasing spectrum of organizations, including customer services and consumer groups, is widely seen as a necessity by all actors in the health care system. They are part of a choir that evangelizes the knowledgeable and powerful health consumer and its organizations, and advocates a strategy of opening up health care to more competition and commercial practices. Since 2004, user organizations have been consultative members (without voting rights) of the "Joint Federal Committee," the highest body of the SHI system, which has power of decision over the catalog of reimbursed health care services (Etgeton, 2009). On the other hand, alongside the many shortcomings, such as the overall lack of resources, user organizations may ask themselves whether they should become a consumer lobby and customer service, pursuing the ideal of the fully informed and competent consumer.

One currently finds that user organizations have a plurality of tasks. In analogy to mixed health care systems and multiple user identities, user organizations are also being forced to develop a hybrid profile (Brandsen, Van de Donk, and Putters , 2005; Evers and Ewert, 2010) to respond to a complex environment. Ideally, user organizations should work in a political, consultative and educative manner through political lobbying in the best interest of their members as citizens and prospective users. They should also provide meaningful advice and a variety of support services to actual consumers who are forced to make important decisions The twin demands of simultaneously being agents of change in a system that many see as being on the wrong track *and* acting as service-providers that help consumer-citizens to get along as well as possible within the system as it stands are challenging user organizations in many respects, as the following insights from the expert interviews will demonstrate.

With respect to advocacy and lobbying in a health care system driven by public and private forces, user organizations pursue strategies that depend very much on their own position in the system. Umbrella organizations, which are entitled to join the "Joint Federal Committee," rely on the power of corporate co-governance through coalition building with physicians and/or insurance and are able to influence decision-making processes in this way. In these cases, "old corporatism" generally prevails. However, the majority of user organizations, which have no direct access to SHI decision bodies, choose a different approach to lobbying. For them, collective co-production could mean launching a campaign against the price policy of pharmaceutical companies by activating members online or drawing attention to perceived health care shortcomings in the media. According to the interviewees, an opposite dynamic is also observable, characterized by user organizations that are somehow instrumentalized by government actors with the intention of strengthening political support for special reforms, such as the introduction of Disease Management Programs. In such cases of "coerced co-production" (Alford, 2009, 22), user organizations serve as channels for the dissemination of practical knowledge (e.g., to implement the reform successfully at the level of users) and for enhancing political legitimacy through cooperation. It seems that the rewards for compliant user organizations—financial support and increased public attention—are tempting.

At the mesolevel, one can find that co-production makes demands that stem from a combination of health care environments in terms of requests for cooperation and the division of labor and the prioritization of tasks between user organizations that makes them fit into system networks better. Consequently, experts are arguing in favor of "joined-up networks," by which they mean a healthy social ecology for organizations, in which political lobbying can be nourished by grassroots experiences—co-production as a softer means of co-optation. However, enhancing organizational profiles by building networks and promoting informal exchange between partners relies on scant resources: user organizations not only have to respect ideological differences, such as those relating to the impact of market mechanisms in health care; they also have to deal with the fact that they are competitors in a tough race for funds and publicity. Nevertheless, almost all the interviewees considered "being strong on all front-lines of co-production" to be an impossible task, and they therefore seek to establish unique organizational features—such as lobbying, counseling or educational services—that can differentiate them from others.

At the microlevel, user organizations have to deal with their clientele's diversity in terms of needs and competences. They have to cope with patients or citizen-consumers, but also with individuals from different social contexts and generations who require different types of support. The heterogeneity of those seeking advice requires an "organizational elasticity" in terms of both internal policy guidelines and the range of services offered. For instance, a consultant whose specialism is dentistry—a consultation-intensive field due to permanent innovation and huge differences in quality and prices—described the two poles of its organizations' clientele as follows:

> On the one hand, I have to respond to highly educated and self-conscious patient-consumers who are seeking legal advice in order to squeeze the best out of their insurance; on the other hand, there are socially deprived people and immigrants, who do not know much about the health care system, care little about dental treatment and are shocked by its cost.

Obviously, each of these target groups demands very different concepts of support or "co-production" with user organizations in mixed health and welfare systems. Experts from self-help groups reported similar experiences by identifying a growing group of smart e-users surfing for information on online forums, while, at the same time, the number of regular participants attending regular, time-consuming self-help group meetings is declining.

Coping with both ends of the clientele spectrum requires the reconciliation of two tasks: the protection of the needy, which primarily means helping them to receive basic health care provision, and the empowerment of those who are more capable. However, the interviews showed that forging such internal compromises may contradict the guiding principles of user organizations. Particularly those organizations that perceive themselves as "counterparts" or "change agents" within the established health care system are unlikely to accept a role as an extended arm of the government, taking on a co-productive role though the delivery of services that are complementary to a challenging and difficult-to-handle medical system.

To sum up, user organizations have to come up with answers to tough problems. First, they have to cope with the double role of being both a strategic partner for established health care actors and also a "change agent" and critic, reconciling its own blueprints for a better health care system with its day-to-day tasks in the current health care system. The diversity of types of users with different needs and expectations also has to be addressed. Finally, user organizations have to forge alliances with like-minded user organizations.

SUMMARY AND CONCLUSION

In this chapter, we have argued that co-production is a wide notion that can take very different meanings in competing narratives. This has been shown by looking at the field of health care services and, more specifically, the German health care system. We have looked at the interaction between organizations in personal services and the interaction of professional providers with individual users.

There is a long tradition of hierarchical management in a public system in this area, while the co-producing role of users was restricted to what is known in medical discourse as "compliance." The development of complex, knowledge-based systems, the general trend to view health care systems in terms of economic and managerial aspects and the increasing impact of marketization and commercial interests have, together with changing competences of the users, led to different ways of conceiving of co-production. For example, at the system level, one finds a simultaneous call for co-production in systems of knowledge-based managed care and incentives for greater competition between providers, who are forced to promote only their narrow self-interests. As far as the co-producing role of users in the system is concerned, former trust-based relationships are being challenged by addressing users as consumers, as well as by concepts that see them as co-decision makers. Although it is impossible to turn users into omnipotent health care co-producers and user organizations into powerhouses of multiple competences, we have pointed out that in a complex health care system, the "ability to co-produce" has taken on the status of a duty (rather than voluntary behavior).

We have argued, first, that the implications of this need for co-producing remain highly ambiguous, entailing both chances and risks. The shift toward knowledge-based services requires that capable co-producers and users must therefore be provided with the tools they need to act in this role; however, users will always remain "second-class experts" in comparison to health professionals in this respect. At its best, the economization of publicly funded health care engages patients as cost-sensitive consumers; at its worst, users could be addressed as cost-bearers who must co-produce in order to receive any service at all. The marketization of health care equates co-production through making choices on health care markets, this could mean greater freedom but also being left alone as a nonexpert to arrange one's own health care services.

Second, discussing concepts such as the citizen-consumer and the expert-patient, which combine different rationales and expectations concerning co-producing roles, we have argued that many difficulties arise due to the intermeshing of such different narratives and practices. Co-production therefore requires the skillful combination of contradictory discourses and practices, such as welfare consumerism and better governance by user involvement.

These new trends and environments are a challenge for users. If they are not to be burdened with sole responsibility for successful co-production, a supportive collective infrastructure that protects and empowers them in equal measure will need to be put in place. Based on interviews with representatives of user-organizations in the German health care system, we have shown that in reality there is a large variety of attitudes, expectations and competences among citizens and users. Some correspond more closely with the older narrative of a protective system of health care services and of professionals with rather limited expectations of users beyond compliance. Others are much more prepared and willing to take on the expectations of a modern health care system concerning their co-producing role.

As we have shown, this results in a threefold challenge for user organizations. First, they have to serve the needs of users and citizens who are basically trying to take up the challenge and make the best possible informed choices. Second, they also have to give special support and protection to the large group of those that have little chance of becoming co-producers with perfect expertise and smart consumers. However, even if user organizations do a perfect job in both of these tasks, there is the danger that they will function solely as ordinary customer services that help to make modern health care schemes more usable but have little say in their design and implementation. Third, user organizations are challenged to defend their status as potential change agents within the health care system.

At this point of the conclusion, we want to turn from a summary to some suggestions concerning the future role of user organizations in a co-productive system that entails a perspective on change toward more user centeredness and democracy.

- First, we think that this would mean questioning the widespread ideal of users being enabled to live up to the expectation of becoming perfect experts and consumers. Professionals may see expert-patients in the light of shared decision making as knowledgeable partners, willing and able to discuss diagnosis details with them face-to-face. However, patients themselves often define their expertise in terms of "how it feels" (Sennett, 2003). Consequently, they expect a different kind of co-production where their "emotional knowledge" (being a patient that is affected by a certain disease) is taken into account in the treatment process. Beyond the task of building up the skills of users in various health care contexts, user organizations could also play a key role by challenging concepts of the user and co-production that, in the name of the utopia of the perfect expert patient and smart health consumer, overlook the need for frameworks and practices that offer solid social protection and a professional ethos of a similarly protective patient support, thereby helping to re-create trust in public services and professionals.

- Second, given the broad range of tasks undertaken by user organizations, from the provision of consultancy to advocacy for neglected needs and concepts for change, the user organizations have to find ways of coping better with the dilemma of "being a jack of all trades but master of none." In this respect, it seems useful that some organizations have tried to split into different organizational units responsible for different tasks. Such a process may, in addition to the creation of units, be responsible for launching campaigns with high visibility and media impact. It may also include the marketization of organizational skills and expertise that are in great demand in the competitive health care markets, such as providing e-health portals and telephone hotlines or assisting the invention of managed care schemes. Metaphorically speaking, user organizations may co-produce like a "Swiss Army knife" by providing a toolkit to make health care services user-friendly and bring transparency into emerging health care markets but also pushing for political change in the long term.

Health care users and user organizations are forced to get used to a situation where uncertainty and ambiguity are the norm and the basis for co-production rather than the exception. As we have shown, co-production takes place in a field of tension where users and organizations are urged to cope with contradictory role expectations but similarly adopt, reinterpret and subvert given role models against a backdrop of individual identities and self-construction. Here (the generation of) mutual trust is the currency that turns co-production relationships into a success, such as by tailoring health care services to individual needs. Conversely, lack of trust can hardly be substituted by formal arrangements and procedures. If co-production is rooted in and initiated by civil society actors, promotes community-based knowledge on health and health care practices and gives co-producers sufficient entrepreneurial space, the much-praised term may be something more substantial than simply being another buzzword in the realm of welfare production.

REFERENCES

Alford, J. 2002. Defining the client in the public sector: A social-exchange perspective. *Public Management Review* 7 (2): 226–245.

Alford, J. 2009. *Engaging public sector clients: From service delivery to co-production*. London: Palgrave Macmillan.

Brandsen, T., and V. Pestoff. 2006. Co-production, the third sector and the delivery of public services: An introduction. *Public Management Review* 8 (4): 493–502.

Brandsen, T., W. Van de Donk, and K. Putters. 2005. Griffins or chameleons? Hybridity as a permanent and inevitable characteristic of the third sector. *International Journal of Public Administration* 28 (9–10): 749–766.

Clarke, J. 2007. "It's not like shopping": Citizens, consumers, and the reform of public services. In M. Bevir and F. Trentmann, eds., *Governance, Consumers and Citizens*. New York: Palgrave Macmillan, pp. 97–117.

Clarke, J., J. Newman, N. Smith, E. Vidler, and L. Westmarland. 2007. *Creating Citizen-Consumers: Changing Relationships and Changing Public Services*. London: Sage.

Etgeton, S. 2009. Patientenbeteiligung im Gemeinsamen Bundesausschuss. In W. Schroeder and R. Paquet, eds., *Gesundheitsreform 2007. Nach der Reform ist vor der Reform*. Wiesbaden: VS Verlag für Sozialwissenschaften, pp. 222–228.

Evers, A. 2008. Investiv und aktivierend oder ökonomistisch und bevormundend? Zur Auseinandersetzung mit einer neuen Generation von Sozialpolitiken. In A. Evers, R. G. Heinze, eds., *Sozialpolitik. Ökonomisierung und Entgrenzung*. Wiesbaden: VS Verlag für Sozialwissenschaften, pp. 229–252.

Evers, A. 2009. Civicness and civility: Their meanings for social services. *Voluntas, Special Issue: Civicness and the Third Sector* 20 (3): 239–259.

Evers, A., and B. Ewert. 2010. Hybride Organisationen im Bereich sozialer Dienste. Ein Konzept, sein Hintergrund und seine Implikationen. In T. Klatetzki, ed., *Soziale Dienstleistungsorganisationen*. Wiesbaden: VS Verlag für Sozialwissenschaften, pp. 103–128.

Ewert, B. 2009. Economization and marketization in the German healthcare system: How do users respond? *German Policy Studies* 5 (1): 21–44.

Felt, U., M. D., Bister, M. Strassnig, and U. Wagner. 2009. Refusing the information paradigm: Informed consent. Medical research and patient participation. *Health: An Interdisciplinary Journal for the Social Study of Health, Illness and Medicine* 13 (1): 87–106.

Gellner, W. 2006. Das Ende des klassischen Patienten? Gesundheitsreform zwischen Politik und Patienteninteresse—Eine Patiententypologie. In W. Gellner and A. Wilhelm, eds., *Vom klassischen Patienten zum Entrepreneur?* Baden-Baden: Nomos, pp. 9–17.

Kremer, M., and E. Tonkens. 2006. Clients as citizens and consumers—What are the implications for professionals? In J. W. Duyvendak, T. Knijn, and M. Kremer, eds., *Policy, People and New Professionals*. Amsterdam: Amsterdam University Press, pp. 122–136.

Kuhlmann, E. 2006. *Modernizing Health Care*. Bristol, UK: Policy Press.

Needham, C. 2008. Realising the potential of co-production: Negotiating improvements in public services. *Journal of Social Policy and Society* 7 (2): 221–231.

Pestoff, V., S. O. Osborne, and T. Brandsen. 2006. Patterns of co-production in public services: Some concluding thoughts. *Public Management Review* 8 (4): 591–596.

Sennett, R. 2003. *Respect in a World of Inequality*. New York: W. W. Norton.

Stehr, N. 1994. *Knowledge Societies*. London: Sage.

Taylor-Gooby, P. 2009. *Reframing Social Citizenship*. New York: Oxford University Press.

5 Third Sector and the Co-Construction of Canadian Public Policy

Yves Vaillancourt

INTRODUCTION

Canada does not have a unitary political system, as Sweden, France and Chile do.[1] It has a federal political system, like Germany and Brazil. This is not without implications for public policy development. In the Canadian federalist system, public policy is designed not only by one central national state, but also by thirteen provincial and territorial states. This remark is important for correctly interpreting the meaning of the expression "Canadian public policy" used in the title of this chapter. At first glance, one could conclude that it refers mainly or solely to public policy initiatives carried out by the federal state. But such an interpretation would be incorrect. Indeed, if we use the expression correctly, we should understand that Canadian public policy refers both to the public policy initiatives implemented by the federal state and to the initiatives carried out by thirteen provincial/territorial states (the Quebec state among them) and thousands of local governments across Canada.

In this chapter, we will focus on some public policy initiatives implemented by the federal government and the Quebec government. Most of the public policy initiatives examined in the chapter involve the participation of the third sector and take place in the area of social policy (our particular area of research expertise). The concept of the "third sector" will be interchangeable with that of the social and/or solidarity economy defined in an inclusive manner (Vaillancourt and Tremblay, 2002, 22; Evers and Laville, 2004). This will permit us to include nonprofit organizations (NPOs); voluntary, community-based organizations; nongovernment organizations (NGOs); consumer, worker and solidarity cooperatives; and philanthropic organizations (Vaillancourt, 2010, 58–59). Social and solidarity economy organizations and enterprises share some values on which we will focus, including the democratic participation of the users, paid or volunteer workers and other stakeholders located in the communities concerned.

More specifically, in examining the participation of the third sector in some Canadian public policies, we will take into account a distinction between two forms of participation—co-production and co-construction— and argue that the latter is more promising for fostering greater democratization of public policy and public governance. Our distinction between co-production and co-construction of public policy will be explained in the first part of our chapter.

Our chapter is divided into three parts. In the first part, we introduce our conceptual framework in which we make the distinction between co-production and co-construction. In the next part, we examine two empirical examples of third sector participation in federal public policy, the Voluntary Sector Initiative (1999–2004) and the Social Economy Initiative (2004–2006). In the third part, we look at six cases of third sector participation in Quebec government public policy. In the conclusion, we discuss the empirical results of the second and third parts within the conceptual framework presented in the first part.

DISTINGUISHING BETWEEN CO-PRODUCTION AND CO-CONSTRUCTION OF PUBLIC POLICY

At the start of this more theoretical section, we should mention that when we deal with public policy, we are looking at *state intervention* of some kind. This is true at all levels (micro, meso and macro). In this chapter, though, we look more at public policy development at the macrolevel, although the case studies we are analyzing refer to sectoral public policies, such as the role of the third sector in Quebec home care public policy. But the issue is to examine whether, in this public policy development, the state is working alone or with some other nonstate stakeholders from the private sector, the family sector or the third sector. Of course, in this chapter and this book, we are especially interested in examining scenarios of public policy initiatives in which the state is working with the third sector.

Quebec and Canadian Literature

Some of us, in our Quebec and Canadian research teams, have been working theoretically and empirically on the interfaces between the third sector and public policy in the area of human services for the last twenty years. And in the last five years (2005–2010), we have decided to deepen and apply a distinction between co-production and co-construction. Looking at the literature of the last thirty years, we have noticed that the concept of co-production, in the public policy domain, was used mainly to deal with the involvement of third sector actors in the *delivery* or *implementation* of public policy. Of course, we have found some authors, such as Pestoff (2006) and Cunill (2004), who were using the concept of co-production to say more than that (Vaillancourt, 2009a, 287–289). In other words, they were using the concept of co-production to examine the participation of the third sector in the transformation of the *institutional architecture* of public policy. But this was neither sufficient nor satisfactory, because the mainstream of the literature on co-production was captured by the focus placed on the *organizational* dimension of public policy. This means the third sector was limited to a *provider* role in the architecture of public policy, and that restricted its full innovative potentiality for public policy reforms.

Therefore, to open more conceptual space for examining the participation of the third sector in the *construction* of public policy, we decided, in interaction with other researchers from countries of the South and North, to introduce the concept of *co-construction* while maintaining the concept of co-production. "Co-construction concerns public policy when it is being designed and not merely when it is being implemented. It is deployed upstream, in other words, when public policy is being conceived. Our interest in the co-construction of public policy is tied to the idea that it can become more democratic if the state agrees not to construct it all on its own. We suggest that the democratization of such policy would gain from this, at least in some societies, at certain moments in certain specific policy areas, if the state worked to co-construct it by partnering with stakeholders from the market and civil society, not to mention from the social economy" (Vaillancourt, 2009a, 289).

But, in our theoretical work, we were not satisfied merely with introducing the concept of co-construction. We were also concerned with the need to advance some elements of reflection about different forms of co-construction and about the conditions to be brought together to foster the realization of more democratic co-construction of public policy involving the participation of the third sector. In that context, we conducted some historical and empirical research to unveil different "configurations" of third sector (or social economy) participation in co-production and co-construction of public policy. This led us to explain that the conditions for *democratic co-construction* are more demanding than those permitting *corporatist co-construction* or *neoliberal co-construction* of public policy (ibid., 291–295). For the third sector and other civil society stakeholders involved in it, democratic co-construction of public policy means something more than effective lobbying to convince the political decision makers to integrate their proposals in policies and programs. It means entering into a deliberative process with a variety of other stakeholders, rooted either in representative democracy or in participatory democracy, working together to construct public policy decisions aimed at the general interest (Lévesque, 2007; Vaillancourt, 2009a, 2010).

It may be helpful here to say a word about the circulation of this distinction between co-production and co-construction within social research circles in Quebec, Canada, and other countries and on other continents.

In Quebec and Canada, in the last three years, our theoretical and empirical work on the contribution of the third sector to the co-production and co-construction of public policy has been discussed and used in different research in partnership networks specializing in the themes of social and solidarity economy, public policy, social policy, local development and community economic development. Cases in point include such research units as CRISES (*Centre de recherche sur les innovations sociales*); CURA (Community-University Research Alliance) on the Social Economy; CURA on Social Innovation and Community Development; LAREPPS (Research Laboratory on Social Practice and Policy); CIRIEC-Canada; *Chantier de l'économie sociale*; GESQ (*Groupe d'économie solidaire du Québec*); the Canadian Social Economy HUB of the University of Victoria and its Public Policy Facilitating Committee; the various Social Economy Regional Nodes in six regions of Canada; and the Canadian CEDNET (Community Economic Development Network). Consequently, a significant number of social research publications have started to give a central place to the concept of co-construction (Proulx, Bourque, and Savard, 2007; Lévesque, 2007; Jetté, 2008; Vaillancourt and Jetté, 2009; Vaillancourt and Jetté, 2011; Bourque, 2009; Klein et al., 2010, 98; Amyot, Downing, and Tremblay, 2010; Elson and Rogers, 2010; Tremblay, 2010).

European and International Literature

Paradoxically, the Quebec and Canadian contributions to the significant distinction between co-production and co-construction could not be understood without paying attention to the social, political and intellectual connection with some international networks that have produced some innovative literature on the contribution of the social and solidarity economy to the democratization of public policy. Among these international networks mobilizing researchers and practitioners are the following:

- *The international CIRIEC based in Liège.* We are particularly noting here of the theoretical contributions of Enjolras (2008) and Lévesque and Thiry (2008). Enjolras is interested in the relationships between regimes of governance and the formation of public policy (2008, 12). For him, the success of public policy depends not solely on the ability of public stakeholders but also on the ability of the state to enter into a form of governance involving the mobilization and co-operation of a variety of players, whether they are program beneficiaries, stakeholders from civil society or the world of business (ibid., 17). Enjolras distinguishes between two regimes of governance, one he terms competitive or quasi market, the other partnership-oriented (ibid., 18–21). Then he emphasizes the contribution of the social and solidarity economy to partnership-oriented governance. For their part, Lévesque and Thiry use the distinction made by Enjolras between the two modes of governance to apply it to the transformations in health and social service policies in various countries (2008, 236–241). In so doing, they highlight the fact that partnership-oriented governance fosters the democratic co-construction of policy and services by differentiating between co-construction and co-production (ibid., 251, note 11). We note in passing that the concept of partnership-oriented mode of governance developed by Enjolras, Lévesque and Thiry relates closely to the concept of co-governance introduced by Pestoff in chapter 2 of this volume.

- In France, the dynamic *Réseau des territoires pour l'économie solidaire* (RTES) established in 2002 promotes the co-construction of public policy at the local and regional levels. This network is headed by Christiane Bouchart, a Lille city councilor, and works in partnership with the solidarity economy research trend led by Jean-Louis Laville. In the publications of the RTES and Laville, the theme of the contribution of the solidarity economy to the democratic co-construction of public policy occasionally arises. This is the case in some chapters of a book presenting a dialogue between French and Brazilian stakeholders and researchers, who see the participation of players from civil society as "fundamental" in the development, implementation and evaluation of public policy (Laville et al., 2005, 223, 98).

- RIPESS (*Réseau intercontinental de promotion de l'économie sociale et solidaire*) has given priority to the theme of co-construction of public policy in its last two international meetings, in Dakar in November 2005, and in Luxembourg in April 2009. At the Dakar Conference, the theme was strongly articulated by some West African leaders, such as Salam Fall (Favreau and Salam Fall, 2007). At the Luxembourg conference, a workshop on the co-construction of public policy lasted four days and was attended by seventy-five people.

Latin American and Caribbean Literature

The RIPESS regional network in Latin America and the Caribbean, RIPESS-LAC, is very dynamic and is interested in the theme of co-construction of public policy with a major contribution from Peruvian and Brazilian intellectuals and practitioners. The same is true of another, complementary Latin American network, RILESS (Network of Latin American Researchers on the Social and Solidarity Economy). This network, coordinated by José Luis Coraggio, Luiz Gaiger, Paul Singer and Jean-Louis Laville, publishes *La Otra Economía* and organizes regional conferences. The third RILESS international meeting took place in Buenos Aires in December 2010, and the co-construction perspective was debated there.

In Latin America and the Caribbean, a significant number of researchers from different disciplines are de facto working theoretically and empirically on the participation of the third sector in the democratization of public policy. Very often, they develop research practices at the micro- and mesolevels more than at the macrolevel. This is the case in some research teams and projects led by Dagnino, Olvera and Panfichi (2006) on "democratic construction in Latin America," in which we are exposed to a variety and wealth of case studies dealing with Mexican, Brazilian and Peruvian experiences. In addition to that, the empirical chapters of this book are introduced by a substantial, coherent, innovative theoretical chapter in which the essence of co-construction is present, although that term as such is never actually used. Indeed, Dagnino, Olvera and Panfichi occasionally use the similar concept of "co-gobierno" and "co-management" (ibid., 40, 54–58), giving it a meaning very close to that of our concept of co-construction. They refer to the participation of "new political subjects" (social movements, civil society organizations, and social and solidarity economy actors) not only in the "management of the state," but also in the fabrication of "political decisions," as is the case in the practice of "participatory budgets" in many Brazilian municipalities (ibid., 58–59). We can even suggest with these authors that the idea of citizens' participation in the co-construction of public policy is implicitly present in the Brazilian Constitution of 1988 (ibid., 84), as it is in the Ecuadorian Constitution of 2008.

At the end of this theoretical part of our chapter, we would like to underline a research conviction: In the current international context—the end of the first decade of the twenty-first century—what is going on in Latin America makes it a rich laboratory for research on social and political innovation. Indeed, the social transformations taking place in many countries of Latin America led by progressive governments of different kinds (Brazil, Venezuela, Bolivia, Ecuador, El Salvador, Nicaragua, Uruguay) and in other countries now led by neoliberal governments (Peru, Colombia, Mexico) offer stimulating reference points for conducting research on third sector participation in the co-production and co-construction of more democratic public policies.

In a country such as Ecuador, for example, where the government of Rafael Correa has, since 2007, been pursuing the "citizens' revolution," some research writings produced by civil society and government researchers offer much food for thought on co-production and co-construction. For instance, section 85 of Ecuador's new Constitution of 2008 contains a statement that de facto addresses the issue of co-construction: "In the formulation, execution, evaluation and control of public policies and services, the Constitution guarantees the participation of individuals, communities, villages and nations." The same thing occurs in some government papers promoting the concept of "participatory planning": "*participatory planning* which is constructed through active participation by and deliberation with civil society. Traditionally, national planning experiences have been a process controlled by a small number of specialists and civil servants. In an effort to overcome the planning vision of the 1970s, centered on state action, the National Government has committed to implementing a broad process of participatory planning aimed at development." (Secretaría Nacional de Planificación y Desarollo, 2009, 62–63). In some Ecuadorian government departments, such as the Department of Economic Policy Co-Ordination, we have even found that the concept of co-construction was used with the meaning developed in this chapter: "Without doubt, there is still a long way to go before the actual *co-construction* of public policy, in order to avoid for the socio-economic stakeholders the alienating separation between the design and the application of public policy" (Ministerio de Coordinación de la Política Económica del Ecuador, 2009, 4). So, now let us examine the Canadian and Quebec reality, using the conceptual tools presented in this part.

TWO FEDERAL STATE PUBLIC POLICIES TO EMPOWER THE THIRD SECTOR

In this part, we will examine the record of the Canadian federal state with regard to the participation of the third sector in the co-construction of public policy over the past fifteen years (1995–2010). During that period, the federal government took two policy initiatives to provide acknowledgement and institutional support to the third sector. We are referring to the Voluntary Sector Initiative and the Social Economy Initiative.

Voluntary Sector Initiative (1999–2004)

The Voluntary Sector Initiative (VSI) was developed by Jean Chrétien's Liberal government. Chrétien was Prime Minister in a majority government from 1993 to December 2003, when he stepped down, to be replaced by Paul Martin, who had been his finance minister for ten years.

The VSI was announced in the 1999 Throne Speech and launched in June 2000 as a five-year initiative (2000–2004) with a budget of $94.6 million. This budget was used to run the National Survey of Nonprofit and Voluntary Organizations (NSNVO). From 1999 to 2004, the VSI led numerous meetings, launched the establishment of various working groups, built an accord "much like the British Compact to govern future relations between the two sectors" (Brock, 2010) and fostered the drafting of numerous papers enabling government leaders and senior officials as well as leaders of voluntary, community-based organizations (VCBOs) to work together to identify priorities, objectives and means of action. The VSI was evidence of a degree of recognition of the voluntary and community sector by the federal government. This initiative received far more exposure and commentary in English Canada than in Quebec (Vaillancourt and Thériault, 2009, 336–337; Brock, 2010).

The VSI ended dramatically with the departure of Jean Chrétien and the arrival of Paul Martin as Prime Minister of Canada in December 2003, although both politicians belonged to the same political party, the Liberal Party of Canada (LPC). For Thériault (2010), one flaw of the VSI lay in the fact that it followed a "top down approach" and was unable to pay attention to the importance of provincial governments' role with regard to state-third sector relationships. For Brock (2010), "the VSI did have an impact on future relations between the state and sector and changed the perception of the sector in different ways."

Social Economy Initiative (2004–2006)

The Social Economy Initiative (SEI) was developed by the Paul Martin government (2003–2006). Martin was Prime Minister for only twenty-six months. During that time, he headed two Liberal governments: a majority government from December 2003 to October 2005, and a minority government from October 2005 to the elections of January 26, 2006, which led to the advent of a new minority government headed by Stephen Harper of the Conservative Party of Canada (CPC). In reality, on coming to power in late 2003, Martin already had his plan for the SEI in mind. In the preceding months, with his political team and senior bureaucrats, he had been involved in deliberations with some leading figures in the social economy movement in Quebec and some of their allies in the community economic movement in the rest of Canada. In other words, the idea of a social economy plan and public policy had, to some extent, been *co-constructed*. We will qualify this co-construction later in this chapter. For the moment, let us sum up the characteristics of the SEI.

The SEI was a $132-million five-year plan announced in the 2004 to 2005 budget speech to support the social economy as a whole. This sum was primarily earmarked for improving "the access of social enterprises to programs and services for small and medium-sized enterprises" in the various major regions of Canada. Within the overall envelope, an amount of $15 million over five years was to pass through the Social Sciences and Humanities Research Council of Canada (SSHRC) to support partnership-oriented research on the social economy in Canada as a whole (Vaillancourt and Thériault, 2009, 339). But, with the change of government in January 2006, the new SEI policy created by the Martin government did not survive the advent of the Harper government. Within the five-year, $132-million budget, the major components were not spent. The research component was maintained. Funds targeted to development of trusts to provide "patient capital" to permit the development of new social economy projects in all regions of Canada were not made available, except in the Quebec region, where the "Chantier de l'économie sociale Trust" was saved at the last minute (Vaillancourt, 2010, 72). In the meantime, the rest of these financial instruments were not made available, to the disappointment of many social economy and community economic development practitioners (Guy and Heneberry, 2010).

Paradoxically, the two federal policy initiatives examined in this section were adopted by governments of the same political party, the LPC. In addition, *objectively*, they had substantial points in common. Indeed, both policy initiatives referred to the third sector and the social economy, defined broadly. On the one hand, the VSI dealt mainly with voluntary, community-based organizations, or nonmarket components of the social economy. On the other hand, the SEI dealt mainly with cooperatives and social economy enterprises, or with market components of the social economy. But *subjectively*, at that time, for most people inside and outside the respective federal governments, even for third sector and social economy activists and intellectuals, the two policy initiatives were seen as totally distinct and even contradictory. Even within the Liberal party, those in favor of the Chrétien plan were not the same as those in favor of the Martin plan. Not surprisingly, the capacity of each plan to survive a change of government was weakened. In other words, both plans were not well co-constructed within the LPC and the other four political parties in the Canadian Parliament, nor did they have adequate support from civil society and the third sector.

SIX QUEBEC STATE PUBLIC POLICIES TO EMPOWER THE THIRD SECTOR

In this part, focusing on the last fifteen years (1995–2010), we will examine the record of the Quebec provincial state with regard to the participation of the third sector in the co-production and co-construction of public policy. To do so, we will look at the public policy initiatives of the Quebec state in six concrete areas (recognition of community-based organizations, recognition of the social economy, child care, home care, social housing and the fight against poverty). To set the political scene, let us recall that over those fifteen years, two political parties were in power:

- The Parti Québécois (PQ) from 1994 to 2003, with three different premiers, Jacques Parizeau (1994–1995), Lucien Bouchard (1996–2000) and Bernard Landry (2000–2003)
- The Quebec Liberal Party from 2003 to 2010, with Jean Charest as premier, heading three different governments

In addition, it is important for us to point out that we have written extensively in the last twenty years on most of the cases we have selected, and that our objective in this part is to update and synthesize the results of our past writings, looking at how they relate to the concepts of co-production and co-construction of public policy.

Policy to Recognize Autonomous Community Organizations

Voluntary, community-based organizations (VCBOs) had been almost forgotten in the 1960s and 1970s, at a time of rapid development of the welfare state in Quebec. Since the 1980s, and especially in the 1990s, VCBOs were rediscovered and recognized increasingly as indispensable by the state and civil society. This was particularly the case in the area of health and social services, but also to varying degrees in twenty-five areas of human life and services, such as family violence. There are now some 5,000 VCBOs representing 29,000 full-time jobs interfacing with the Quebec state. In the last thirty-five years, many of these organizations, often organized and federated on a province-wide, sectoral or regional basis, have been struggling to obtain more recognition from the Quebec state, as well as financial support and respect of their identity and autonomy. They have been struggling and negotiating with a view to establish a *partnership* relationship with the state. They have been demanding institutional arrangements to minimize financial and political instability. Over the years, a first step was accomplished with the Côté reform in the early 1990s for VCBOs in health and social services; a second step was taken in 1995, when the Parizeau government agreed to start organizing a secretariat for "autonomous community organizations"; finally, a third step was realized in the early 2000s, under the Bouchard government, with the creation of the *Secrétariat à l'action communautaire autonome* (SACA, later changed to SACAIS) and the adoption of a public policy for all VCBOs with a contractual and financial relationship with the Quebec state (Vaillancourt, 2009b, 162–163; Jetté, 2008; Secrétariat à l'action communautaire autonome, n.d.).

This means that some institutional arrangements have been achieved. These arrangements acknowledge three main principles, among others: first, that the state provides funding support for VCBOs not only for what they do as service co-producers, but also for what they are; second, state funding distinguishes between "core funding" and "project funding"; third, VCBOs can be awarded three years of funding arrangements in exchange for an evaluation conducted with a co-constructed policy. Of course, with this public policy, the autonomy of the VCBOs remains fragile, and their relationship with the state is not fully symmetrical. In spite of these shortcomings, VCBOs interfacing with the Quebec state have managed historically to be not only co-producers in the sense of co-providers, but also "co-builders" of the policy in which they are a major stakeholder. Therefore, in the subtitle of his excellent book dedicated to VCBOs that have a relationship with the Quebec state, Jetté (2008) highlights a real issue when referring to "three decades of co-construction of public policy in health and social services."

Policy to Recognize the Social Economy

After the YES side was narrowly defeated in the October 1995 referendum on Quebec sovereignty, a new PQ government led by Lucien Bouchard took power in 1996. Targeting the problem of Quebec's public deficit, Bouchard quickly launched the proposal to organize a socioeconomic summit. After preliminary discussions with some civil society leaders, it was decided to organize a broader summit than the classical tripartite events with representatives of government, business organizations and trade union organizations. The idea was to mobilize representatives of civil society and third sector organizations as well, that is, community, women's, cooperative, church and education organizations.

In fact, two socioeconomic summits took place, a preliminary one in early 1996, and a larger-scale, better prepared one in the fall of 1996 called "the Summit on Economy and Employment." At the first summit, the decision was made to achieve a "zero deficit" within four years. In addition, the Bouchard government, influenced by pressure from social movement leaders, agreed to include issues of socioeconomic reforms in the summit agenda, such as job creation, fiscal reform, the fight against poverty, family policy, local development and the social economy.

Between the two summits, a working group on the social economy was created. Led by Nancy Neamtan, a well-known community economic development leader, this working group arrived at the October summit with a forty-page report containing a broad, inclusive definition of social economy (SE) and concrete proposals for launching twenty specific social economy projects (in day care, home care, environment, social housing etc.). Many of these SE projects were seen as bringing new services and new jobs complementary to those already existing in the public sector. The proposals prepared by the SE working committee were presented, discussed for hours and transformed into public policy decisions during the three-day socioeconomic summit (Vaillancourt and Jetté, 2009, chapter 2).

To understand the productivity of the democratic deliberation with representatives of the Quebec government and a variety of stakeholders in the labor market and civil society, we have to take into account the various debates, struggles and deliberations accomplished through socioeconomic and sociocultural events and mobilization activities developed in the preceding years. Among these, the "Bread and Roses" women's march was rather significant. With such a background in mind, in some of our research on the 1996 summits and recognition of SE, we argued that the 1996 public policy decisions related to social economy were *democratically co-constructed* during the preceding years (Lévesque, 2007; Vaillancourt and Jetté, 2009; Vaillancourt, 2010).

Consequently, because they had been democratically constructed, the public policy decisions made at the October 1996 summit to recognize and empower SE initiatives were, in subsequent years, to have various structural and institutional implications. In other words, the thrust of these public policy decisions was even able to survive several changes of government after 1996. This does not mean each government was capable of delivering the same quality of support to SE in the years following the 1996 summits. We will return to this point in our Conclusion.

Early Childhood Day Care Services Policy

Since the early 1970s, the social economy has played an essential role in early childhood day care services. In its 1997 family policy—prepared at the 1996 summit—the Quebec government confirmed its preference for nonprofit day care over commercial day care (Vaillancourt and Tremblay, 2002, 37–42; Vaillancourt, 2009b, 263–264). The history of day care since the 1970s and of the early childhood policy since the mid-1990s testifies to the capacity of third sector stakeholders to co-construct and co-produce, with other stakeholders from the state, the market and civil society, a new public policy now seen as highly innovative in the rest of North America. This new policy is a symbol of a new sharing of responsibilities among the state, the third sector and the private sector. This includes the following features:

- The planning, regulation and evaluation of the policy are under the responsibility of the state. But, in some key aspects, they have been co-constructed with the contribution of the third sector (among other stakeholders) (Briand, Bellemare, and Gravel, 2006).
- Funding is mixed, but principally public, with the state covering 80 percent of costs and parents paying 20 percent of costs ($7 a day for each child receiving day care services).
- Child care centers (*centres de la petite enfance*, or CPEs) are the main providers or co-producers of services. In 2008, there were 980 CPEs or nonprofit day care agencies (297 with more than one "facility"), accounting for 38 percent of the places. There were also 683 for-profit day care agencies, providing 18 percent of the places. Finally, there were 165 "coordinating bureaus" managing the provision of 44 percent of the places (Government of Quebec, 2009).
- Management of services is mainly in the hands of the CPEs, with strong voluntary participation from parents. At least two-thirds of board members have to be parents using the services of the CPEs (Giguère and Desrosiers, 2010).
- One third of the CPEs' primarily female labor force is unionized and, over the years, trade union practices have been innovative and capable of respecting social economy values, such as parents' participation in their management. The union presence has contributed to improving not only employees' wages and working conditions, but also service standards (Gravel, Bellemare, and Briand, 2007).

From 1997 to 2010, the number of early childhood day care centers places increased from 55,000 to 210,000, and the number of employees also rose significantly. In this area of collective services and public policy, we find a "partnership governance regime" more than a "competition governance model," to borrow the distinction suggested by Enjolras (2008) and

Lévesque and Thiry (2008). In such partnership governance, one of the key conditions is the strong participation of the third sector in terms of co-production and co-construction. But it is necessary to add that under the Charest governments (2003–2010), this public policy did survive, but the partnership and co-construction dimensions were often downsized.

Home Care Policy

Home care is another area of social policy in which we find participation from the third sector and on which we have been working and writing regularly over the last twenty years. (Vaillancourt and Tremblay, 2002, 42–50; Vaillancourt, 2009b, 265–266). In our recent writings (Vaillancourt and Jetté, 2009; Jetté and Vaillancourt, 2011), we have severely criticized both the Quebec home care policy taken as a whole and the specific policy with regard to the shortcomings of the state support for participation by the third sector in some segments of home care policy. Our analysis shows that in this area of human services policy, the third sector co-produces a great deal, but does not co-construct sufficiently.

Briefly, let us recall that in Quebec home care policy, two third-sector niches have historically received state support. The first, starting in the late 1970s, involved some voluntary, community-based organizations (VCBOs) delivering community home care services (meals on wheels and similar). The second niche relates to the new policy co-constructed at the 1996 summit and launched in 1997 to develop a network of one hundred social economy enterprises to deliver domestic services (house cleaning and similar). In Quebec province, these two niches receive financial support from the state, which represents 10 percent of the public home care budget. But in fact, regional and local public sector institutions (regional health and social services agencies and local centers) remain the principal providers of home care services while purchasing an undisclosed portion of them from private sector providers.

Let us now talk briefly and in somewhat simplified terms about the niche occupied by SE enterprises:

- In 1997, the Quebec government created a state organization, PEFSAD (financial exemption program for domestic help services) to deal administratively with "recognized" SE enterprises following the rules of the game as established by government decree.
- Of the 102 SE enterprises recognized in 2010, 54 are nonprofit organizations and 48 are cooperatives.
- The funding of SE enterprises is mixed. About half comes from fees paid by users (mainly elderly people, but also disabled people and regular households).
- In 2009, the network created 6,000 jobs (mainly for women), delivering 5.5 million hours of service to 80,000 people.

- Because of the shortcomings of the institutional arrangements as they evolved from 1996 to 2010, SE values are suffering, mainly because of the poor working conditions of a female labor force.

In sum, in this area of public policy, the co-construction aspect was present at the beginning in 1996, but almost disappeared in the following years. This means SE enterprises in that sector play an important provider role without being permitted to influence the evolution of the public policy they are living with. In other words, the SE sector in that policy area, so far, is having difficulty pulling itself out of a "competition governance regime" and entering more of a "partnership regime" with the Quebec state.

Social Housing Policy

Social housing is another particular area of public policy in which the third sector has been both a major and a creative participant in the last fifteen years. In spite of its limitations, Quebec social housing policy has effectively allowed third sector actors, often in conjunction with their allies in the social movements and the public sector, to be involved in a co-production and co-construction process (Vaillancourt and Tremblay, 2002, 50–55; Vaillancourt, 2009b, 264). Yet another of the social policy initiatives energized at the 1996 summit was the new housing program, *AccèsLogis*, which was co-constructed on the basis of experiments conducted in the preceding years.

Social housing is a concrete example we have often used with an in-depth analysis to illustrate our definitions of co-production and co-construction of public policy (Vaillancourt, 2009a, 295–302; Bouchard and Hudon, 2008). So we will limit ourselves here to referring briefly to some key elements of that policy. The *AccèsLogis* program, launched in 1997 in a difficult budget context of "zero deficit," allowed the Quebec state, under different governments, to enable the development of more than 25,000 new social housing units belonging to the third sector and also to address the economic and social needs of vulnerable individuals and families. This means 25,000 new housing units owned and managed by cooperatives and nonprofit organizations, many of them using the innovative community support formula. As we have explained elsewhere, the ability of the *AccèsLogis* program to survive and its success, recognized not only in Quebec but also in the rest of Canada, is tied to the mobilization and coalition of a great variety of individual and collective social and political actors interested in housing issues and capable of co-constructing together in the general interest.

Quebec Legislation to Combat Poverty and Social Exclusion

The *Act to combat poverty and social exclusion*, known as Bill 112 (Government of Quebec, 2002) was unanimously adopted by Quebec's National Assembly on December 13, 2002. As Aubry says, this was "an exceptional accomplishment" (2010) not only because of its content, but also because of the process that developed before and after the adoption of the legislation.

The seven-year *process* leading to the emergence and drafting of Bill 112 was a masterpiece of dialogue between participatory democracy and representative democracy. On the one hand, this progressive piece of legislation received the unanimous support of all Members of the National Assembly from all three political parties in late 2002. On the other hand, this umbrella act was the result of broad mobilization and democratic debate that involved the participation of a variety of individuals and civil society organizations between 1995 and 2002. Briefly, aspects of this mobilization included: the "Bread and Roses" march of 1995; the idea of "zero poverty" proposed by community and women's organizations at the 1996 socioeconomic summit; the organization by CAPMO (*Carrefour de pastorale en monde ouvrier de Québec*) of a one-month "street parliament" held in 1997 near the Quebec Parliament building; the creation in 1998 of a collective for legislation on the elimination of poverty, with ten founding organizations; the circulation of a petition in favor of legislation on the elimination of poverty, which received 215,316 signatures in November 2000; the hundreds of discussion meetings during a campaign to discuss the Bill in different regions of the province; and so on (Ninacs, 2003).

With regard to the *content* of Bill 112: (1) it contains a preamble that, among four principles, states one underlying principle that "persons living in poverty and social exclusion are the first to act to improve their situation" (Aubry, 2010, 7); (2) it offers a broad definition of poverty as "the condition of a human being who is deprived of the resources, means, choices and power necessary to acquire and maintain economic self-sufficiency or to facilitate integration and participation in society" (Government of Quebec, 2002); (3) it proposes among five strategic goals one to "encourage persons and families living in poverty to participate in community life and social development" and another "to develop and reinforce the sense of solidarity throughout Quebec so that society as a whole may participate in the fight against poverty and social exclusion;" and (4) it requires the government to establish a five-year "action plan" to combat poverty and social exclusion and make an annual "report on the activities carried out" (Aubry, 2010, 8).

In sum, Bill 112 was a "major political innovation" (Noël, 2003). It represents another Quebec public policy initiative that was *democratically co-constructed* in a very original, impressive way with a major contribution from many community-based organizations from the third sector and a great variety of stakeholders and social actors. This factor allowed the legislation "to acquire greater institutional strength and durability than if it had been the work of a single political party and had not been strongly rooted in civil society" (ibid., 2). This helps explain why this policy, four months after its adoption in April 2003, was capable of surviving, in spite of the advent of a neoliberal government under Jean Charest. This new government was obliged to respect the parameters of the legislation in 2003 and thereafter, because of the importance of the co-construction dimension. So the Charest government, despite leaning somewhat to the right, adopted a first five-year action plan (2005–2009) in 2004 and a second one in June 2010. But it is fair to say that the first plan was fleshed out and was well received, while the second was less attractive and was severely criticized by various community-based organizations involved in the fight against poverty and social exclusion.

CONCLUSION

In this chapter, we looked at the participation of the third sector in the development of public policy in Canada. To that end, we drew attention to the fact that third sector participation in public policy development can take two forms: *co-production*, when third sector organizations participate in the application of public policy; and *co-construction*, when third sector organizations also participate in the design of public policy. After introducing this distinction and showing its basis not only in Quebec and Canadian literature, but also in European and Latin American writings, we pointed out that Canada's political system was not unitary, but *federal*, meaning that Canadian public policy emanates not only from the federal state, but also from thirteen other provincial and territorial states, the Quebec state among them. In this vein, based on the findings of prior research, we drew attention to cases of public policy from the federal state and the Quebec state in which third sector participation is found in the form of co-production or co-construction. We did this in the second part of the chapter, examining two cases of federal public policies, as well as in the third part, looking at six cases of Quebec provincial public policy. It now remains for us to synthesize some points that emerge from the various public policy cases we have examined, bearing in mind our distinction between co-production and co-construction of public policy.

1. *Co-production exists more often than co-construction.* Third sector participation in the co-production or implementation of public policy is a phenomenon we encounter more frequently than third sector participation in the co-construction of such policy. That is what emerges from the six cases of Quebec public policy reviewed. Even in the case of home support policy, where we emphasized that participation of the third sector in co-construction of the policy was lacking, the third sector nevertheless appears to be an essential co-producer of services, with input from 100 social economy enterprises in the provision of home help services to 80,000 households, particularly to households comprising frail elderly people. In the other public policy cases where we mentioned that there was more co-construction, in particular in

cases of social policy, such as day care centers and social housing, the social economy stakeholders comprising day care centers, cooperatives and housing NPOs play an indisputable role as service providers. In any case, this observation comes as no surprise to us, because in the history of social policy, in both southern and northern societies, there are numerous examples of third sector participation in the co-production or application of public policy, stretching over several decades. They are more numerous than examples of third sector participation in the co-construction of public policy, anyway. In fact, in Canada as elsewhere, it often happens that the third sector takes on considerable responsibility in the application of policies that were constructed by others without its participation.

2. *The short life span of the two federal public policies examined.* In fact, the two federal public policies studied in the second part of this chapter were rather short-lived. Indeed, neither policy survived a change of government. On the one hand, the VSI policy launched by the government of Jean Chrétien in 1999 was relegated to the back burner when Paul Martin took over as prime minister of Canada in December 2003. But these two heads of government both belonged to the Liberal Party of Canada. Similarly, the policy developed by Paul Martin to support the social economy when he came to power in December 2003 did not survive—at least as far as most of its components are concerned—the Liberal defeat and the advent of a new, Conservative government headed by Stephen Harper following the January 2006 elections.

3. *The Quebec public policies examined show greater resilience.* Unlike the federal policies studied, in the case of the six Quebec policies examined, the policies are still in effect in 2010. But four of these policies appeared at the 1996 socioeconomic summit (those concerning the social economy, social housing, day care centers and domestic help social economy enterprises), while the other two appeared in the early 2000s (those concerning community organizations and the fight against poverty). Thus, in the six cases we examined, we observe that the public policies adopted were able to survive not only one but several changes of government. Indeed, these policies were all adopted under a Parti Québécois government (under Bouchard or Landry) and have remained in effect under Charest's three provincial Liberal governments.

4. *The democratic ingredient in co-construction varies from one public policy to another.* Why do the Quebec public policies examined show greater durability than the federal policies? To our mind, the answer to this question lies in the fact that the co-construction, which accompanied the genesis of the Quebec policies studied here, was more inclusive and democratic than that accompanying the emergence of the federal public policies studied. Inclusive, democratic co-construction is distinguished in our view from corporatist co-construction and

lobbying. In these last examples, one or more organizations from the third sector and civil society can very well have a decisive impact in the development of a new government initiative or policy. But in those cases, the social actors involved in co-construction leave aside the participation of other stakeholders from civil society and political society. This means that the base of support for a policy co-constructed by too small a number of stakeholders remains more narrow and fragile in co-construction built on democratic deliberation involving a large variety of stakeholders. That is why the policy of recognition of the social economy co-constructed by Paul Martin's federal government in 2004 proved less long-lasting than that developed by the Quebec government of Lucien Bouchard in 1996. The difference between the 1996 Quebec policy and the 2004 federal policy is that the former was based on a broad coalition of social actors who had had the opportunity to deliberate democratically together, whereas the latter was the outcome of more rapid, narrow, secret negotiation between Paul Martin and a small number of socioeconomic stakeholders. A similar explanation holds true for the astonishing institutional stability of the Quebec public policies that emerged in the mid-1990s concerning social housing, day care centers and community organizations. In those three cases, there was a successful confluence of the contributions of participatory democracy and representative democracy. There was also a mobilization of a great variety of stakeholders concerned, over a longer period of time, reflecting the short- and long-term preparations of the public policies studied. Finally, among the examples chosen, one of the most impressive in terms of the institutional solidity of a democratically constructed public policy is without doubt that of Bill 112—the *Act to combat poverty and social exclusion*. That legislation, adopted in December 2002, had received the unanimous support of all political parties represented in Quebec's National Assembly, following long-term preparations in civil society over a six-year period, which had involved a whole range of struggles, debates and consultations between social and political leaders. That explains why this legislation, despite a change of government four months after its adoption, has lasted so long. Indeed, insofar as this policy had been democratically co-constructed, the Charest government felt bound by it and obliged to apply it, even if it was not always excessively enthusiastic in doing so.

Conditions for Democratic Co-Construction

For us, the democratic co-construction of public policy in which the third sector is a key participant requires something other than efficient lobbying and something more than corporatist co-construction. Unlike a lobbying operation and corporate co-construction, the democratic co-construction of a public policy involves the mobilization and participation of a broad variety of individual and collective stakeholders from civil society, the labor market and political society.

Bearing in mind the lessons learned from the concrete cases examined in our chapter, we can summarize the conditions for democratic co-construction as follows:

- *Co-construction of public policy concerning the third sector begins within the third sector itself.* This means that the various components and trends of the third sector must consult successfully together before working with other stakeholders from civil and political society. It is this lack of internal co-operation among various segments of the third sector that explains the fragility of the Chrétien government's VSI policy in 1999 and of the Martin government's 2004 policy to support the social economy. While both these policies concerned the third sector, they did not involve the same segments. On the one hand, Chrétien's VSI policy focused more on the nonmarket components of the third sector, that is, voluntary and community organizations that do not sell the goods and services produced. On the other hand, Martin's policy on support for the social economy was aimed more at social economy enterprises that have commercial activities, selling their goods or charging for their services. As a result, the third sector stakeholders who were happy with Chrétien's policy were not the same as those who were happy with Martin's. Consequently, the two policies concerned the third sector but did not have the support of the entire third sector, and this made each policy more fragile.

- *Democratic co-construction of public policy concerning the third sector involves public (not secret) deliberation in which not only third sector stakeholders participate, but also other stakeholders from civil society and the labor market,* notably stakeholders from the public sector, private sector and social movements (not forgetting the labor union and women's movements). It was precisely because that condition was taken into account that the Quebec policies concerning social housing and day care centers may be considered to fall under democratic co-construction. It is also because of the absence of participation in Quebec's home care policy by the third sector and the public sector in the past few years that this policy does not appear to have stayed democratically co-constructed, even though it was when it was conceived at the 1996 Summit (Vaillancourt and Jetté, 2009).

- *The democratic co-construction of public policy concerning the third sector requires participation in the deliberation by stakeholders from political society,* meaning not only elected officials in authority in government, but also opposition members and representatives of the public administration. We have observed that this condition clearly made the difference in the case of the policy concerning the fight against poverty and exclusion adopted in Quebec in 2002. We have also seen that it was lacking on the adoption of the two federal policies examined in the relevant section.

• *Democratic co-construction requires intermediate locations and institutions where leaders from both civil and political society can meet in conditions conducive to deliberation and consensus building.* Finally, we would add that among these leaders, the involvement of consensus facilitators capable of moving beyond both political partisanship and the corporatism of interest groups is a prime condition for success.

NOTES

1. David Llewellyn translated this chapter from French.

REFERENCES

Amyot, S., R. Downing, and C. Tremblay. 2010. *Public Policy for the Social Economy: Building a People-Centred Economy in Canada.* Victoria, Canada: Canadian Social Economy Hub, The Canadian Community Economic Development Network and the University of Victoria.

Aubry, F., in collaboration with C. Plamondon. 2010. *The Québec Act to Combat Poverty and Social Exclusion: How Does It Tackle the Situation of People with Disabilities?* Study conducted for the Community-University Research Alliance, "Disabling Poverty and Enabling Citizenship," Winnipeg: Council of Canadians with Disabilities.

Bouchard, M. J., and M. Hudon. 2008. L'histoire d'une innovation sociale. In M. J. Bouchard, ed., *Se Loger Autrement au Québec.* Montreal: Éditions Saint-Martin, pp. 15–53.

Bourque, D. 2008. *Concertation et Partenariat. Entre Levier et Piège du Développement des Communautés.* Quebec City: Presses de l'Université du Québec.

Briand, L., G. Bellemare, and A. R. Gravel. 2006. Contraintes, opportunités et menaces de l'institutionnalisation: le cas des centres de la petite enfance. In P.-A. Lapointe, and G. Bellemare, eds. *Innovations sociales dans le travail et l'emploi, Recherches empiriques et perspectives théoriques*, Quebec City: Presses de l'Université Laval, pp. 185–207.

Brock, K. L. 2010. *Charting Government-Third Sector Relations for Effectiveness: Canada, England, and the United States*, Paper prepared for presentation at ANSER/ARES 2010, Concordia University, Montreal, June 2–4, 2010.

Cunill Grau, N. 2004. La democratización de la administración pública. Los mitos a vencer. In Bresser Pereira et al., eds., *Política y Gestión Pública.* Buenos Aires: Fondo de Cultura Económica, CLAD.

Dagnino, E., A. J. Olvera, and A. Panfichi, eds. 2006. *La Disputa por la Construcción Democrática en América Latina.* México City: CIESAS, Universidad Veracruzana and Fondo de Cultura Económica.

Elson, P., and D. Rogers. 2010. *Voices of Community: The Representation of Nonprofit Organizations and Social Enterprises in Ontario and Quebec.* Toronto: Social Economy Centre, University of Toronto.

Enjolras, B., ed. 2008. Introduction. In B. Enjolras, ed., *Gouvernance et Intérêt Général dans les Services Sociaux et de Santé*. Brussels: P.I.E. Peter Lang, pp. 11–22.

Evers, A., and J.-L. Laville, eds. 2004. *The Third Sector in Europe*. Cheltenham, UK: Edward Elgar.

Favreau, L., and A. Salam Fall, eds., 2007. *L'Afrique qui se refait. Initiatives Socioéconomiques des Communautés et Développement en Afrique Noire*. Quebec City: Presses de l'Université du Québec.

Giguère, C., and H. Desrosiers. 2010. *Les Milieux de Garde de la Naissance à 8 Ans: Utilisation et Effets sur le Développement des Enfants*. Quebec City: Institut de la Statistique.

Government of Quebec. 2002. *RSQ, c, L-7: An Act to combat poverty and social exclusion*. Quebec City: Quebec Official Publisher.

Government of Quebec. 2009. *Situation des Centres de la Petite Enfance, des Garderies et de la Garde en Milieu Familial au Québec en 2008*. Quebec City: Government of Quebec.

Gravel, A.-R., G. Bellemare, and L. Briand. 2007. *Les Centres de la Petite Enfance: Un Mode de Gestion Féministe en Évolution*. Quebec City: Presses de l'Université du Québec.

Guy, D., and J. Heneberry. 2010. Building bridges with government: The social economy in practice. In J. J. McMurtry, ed., *Living Economics. Canadian Perspectives on the Social Economy, Co-operatives, and Community Economic Development*. Toronto: Emond Montgomery, pp. 217–267.

Jetté, C. 2008. *Les Organismes Communautaires et la Transformation de l'État-providence. Trois Décennies de Coconstruction des Politiques Publiques dans le Domaine de la Santé et des Services Sociaux*. Quebec City: Presses de l'Université du Québec.

Jetté, C. and Y. Vaillancourt. 2011. Social economy and homecare services in Quebec : Co-production or co-construction ? *Voluntas*, 22 (1) : 48-69.

Klein, J.-L., J.-M. Fontan, D. Harrisson, and B. Lévesque. 2010. L'innovation sociale dans le contexte du modèle québécois. *The Philanthropist* 23 (3): 93–104.

Laville, J.-L., J.-P. Magnen, F. De França, C. Genauto, and A. Medeiros., eds 2005. *Action Publique et Économie Solidaire. Une Perspective Internationale*. Paris: Éditions Érès.

Lévesque, B. 2007. *Un Siècle et Demi d'Économie Sociale au Québec: Plusieurs Configurations en Présence (1850–2007)*. Montreal: Joint publication CRISES/ÉNAP/ARUC-ÉS.

Lévesque, B., and B. Thiry. 2008. Conclusions. Concurrence et partenariat, deux vecteurs de la reconfiguration des nouveaux régimes de la gouvernance des services sociaux et de santé. In B. Enjolras, ed., *Gouvernance et intérêt général dans les services sociaux et de santé*. Brussels: P.I.E. Peter Lang, pp. 227–261.

Ministerio de Coordinación de la Política Económica del Ecuador. 2009. *Agenda de la Revolución Económica*. Draft 7. Quito: MCPE.

Ninacs, W., with the collaboration of A.-M. Béliveau, and F. Gareau. 2003. *The Collective for a Poverty-Free Quebec: A Case Study*. Ottawa: Caledon Institute of Social Policy.

Noël, A. 2003. Une loi contre la pauvreté : La nouvelle approche québécoise de lutte contre la pauvreté et l'exclusion sociale. *Lien social et politiques* 48 (Fall): 103–114.

Pestoff, V. 2006. Citizens as co-producers of welfare services: Preschool services in eight European countries. *Public Management Review* 8 (4): 503–520.

Proulx, J., D. Bourque, and S. Savard. 2007. The government-third sector interface in Québec. *Voluntas* 18 (3): 293–307.

Réseau des territoires pour l'économie solidaire. n.d. http://www.rtes.fr/. Retrieved August 1, 2011.

Secretaría Nacional de Planificación y Desarollo. 2009. *Consolidación del Estado Nacional para alcanzar el Buen Vivir. Memoria Bienal 2007–2009*. Quito: SENPLADES.

Secrétariat à l'action communautaire autonome. n.d. www.mess.gouv.qc.ca/sacais Retrieved August 1, 2011.

Thériault, L. 2010. *Les Collaborations de Recherche sur l'Économie Sociale au Canada Anglais: Quelques Réflexions Critiques*. PowerPoint presentation prepared for the "23ᵉ Entretiens Jacques-Cartier," IEP de Grenoble, November 22–23, 2010.

Tremblay, C. 2009. *Advancing the Social Economy for Socio-Economic Development: International Perspectives*, Public Policy Papers No. 1, Victoria: Canadian Social Economy Hub at the University of Victoria.

Vaillancourt, Y. 2009a. Social Economy in the co-construction of public policy. *Annals of Public and Cooperative Economies* 80 (2): 275–313.

Vaillancourt, Y. 2009b. Vers un État stratège partenaire de la société civile. In L. Côté, B. Lévesque, and G. Morneau, eds., *État Stratège et Participation Citoyenne*. Quebec City: Presses de l'Université du Québec, pp. 235–274.

Vaillancourt, Y. 2010. The social economy in Quebec and Canada: Configurations past and present. In J. J. McMurtry, ed., *Living Economics: Canadian Perspectives on the Social Economy, Co-operatives, and Community Economic Development*. Toronto: Emond Montgomery, pp. 57–104.

Vaillancourt, Y., and L. Thériault. 2009. Social economy, social policy and federalism in Canada. In A. Gagnon, ed., *Contemporary Canadian Federalism. Foundations, Traditions, Institutions*, Toronto, University of Toronto Press, pp. 330–357.

Vaillancourt, Y., and L. Tremblay, eds. 2002. *Social Economy, Health and Welfare in Four Canadian Provinces*. Halifax: Fernwood.

6 From Co-Production to Co-Governance

John M. Ackerman

INTRODUCTION

While the forty years after World War II were characterized by a faith in state intervention and the following twenty five years were marked by the acceptance of the market model, the new wave of development thinking is grounded in a solid commitment to civic engagement and government transparency.[1] We should welcome this paradigm shift as an opportunity to rethink accepted categories and as a chance to give a dynamic boost to studies of development. Nevertheless, as with all new concepts and intellectual fads, we need to carefully analyze and evaluate the many meanings and practices embedded in this new current of thought.

Specifically, strategies based in the local co-production of public goods and services and basic government transparency are normally not enough to set off the positive feedback loops necessary for making government action accountable at the highest levels (Ackerman and Sandoval, 2006). To achieve a true democratization of state power (O'Donnell, 1999) it is important to scale-up such initiatives and open the inner chambers of the state to direct citizen participation (Ackerman, 2004, 2005).

Even the poorest citizens are exceptionally willing and able to actively work with government in constructive ways once they perceive that their participation can make a difference. In addition, effective societal participation is by no means limited to the provision of basic services. It is a grave mistake to think that the poor are incapable of mobilizing themselves in the pursuit of larger social goals.

New public management (NPM) policies, such as managed competition and performance contracts, involve citizens but simultaneously keep them far away from the core activities of the state. Although NPM does have a participative or "social control" current within it (Bresser and Cunill, 1999; Peters, 2001), this is usually marginalized in favor of marketization strategies. Marketization itself allows citizens to let their opinions be known through "exit" options, but it prohibits their active participation in government. Indeed, studies show that such policies may even directly undermine community organization and social capital in the developing world (Cunill, 2000; Wallis and Dollery, 2001).

The "voices of the poor" (Narayan and Petesch, 2000) usually find their way back in, but they are often left speaking into a void. Governments and international development agencies have moved "participatory development" up their discursive agendas, but actual practice has lagged far behind. Participation is usually seen to be important only insofar as it reduces government costs and responsibilities. It suddenly appears to be "practical" and attractive when governments can offload service delivery to NGOs and community groups or convince local residents to donate volunteer labor or materials. The direct involvement of citizens and societal groups in the core functions of government continues to be extremely rare.

In the end, one's definition of accountability will depend on one's vision of the role of the state. Insofar as one conceptualizes the state as fundamentally an obstacle to development, as a predator that must be controlled in its unceasing desire to take over the market and the private sector, one will tend to grasp onto a more external, ex-post, legal, hierarchical vision of government accountability. Insofar as one imagines the state as a possible facilitator of development, as a central actor in the provision of public goods and the stimulation of investment and citizen participation, one will lean toward a more ex-ante, performance-based, proactive, horizontal concept of accountability.

This chapter encourages the latter strategy. Such initiatives are usually more difficult to implement, but they are well worth the effort. By transgressing the boundaries between state and society, institutional reformers can unleash invaluable pro-accountability processes that are almost impossible to tap into through less ambitious strategies. Through an exploration of case studies from a wide variety of contexts (Brazil, Mexico, United States, India) and policy areas (poverty reduction, infrastructure provision, school reform, electoral administration, police reform), this chapter shows that state reformers should move beyond strategies based on "exit" and even "voice" (Hirschman, 1970; Paul, 1992) to establish spaces of full "co-governance" with society. Instead of sending sections of the state off to society, it is often more fruitful to invite society into the inner chambers of the state.

The first section below gives an overview of the literature on accountability and society. It begins by defining accountability and discussing the various ways it can be enforced. It then focuses on a wave of works on society's pro-accountability role by authors such as Avritzer, Cunill, Evans, Fox, Goetz, Jenkins, Isunza, Paul, Peruzzotti, and Smulovitz. Finally, it defines and proposes the concept of "co-governance for accountability."

The following section includes various case studies of successful examples of "co-governance for accountability." The emphasis is on successful cases because, as Tendler has pointed out, "the mainstream donor community's advice about public-sector reform arises from a literature that looked mainly at *poor* performance. . . . This means that countries and the experts that advise them have few models of good government" (1997, 2; emphasis in original). Development professionals are acutely aware of the ways that governments fail. There is a need for the sustained study of successful government innovations to inspire and direct positive action.

The cases are organized according to the level at which state actors have opened themselves up to and encouraged the participation of civil society in the structuring of accountability arrangements. The section begins with the case of participatory budgeting (PB) in Porto Alegre and moves on to the case of Mexico's Federal Electoral Institute. It then turns to the case studies of police and school reform in Chicago and decentralization and rural development in Mexico. It ends by discussing a pair of examples of "social auditing" from India. Finally, the chapter concludes with a summary of the principal lessons for those interested in strengthening government accountability through the full involvement of society.

ACCOUNTABILITY AND SOCIETY

Good government does not emerge spontaneously or naturally out of the good hearts of individual bureaucrats and politicians. It is the result of a tough and often conflict-ridden process of institutional design. The principle element that assures good government is the accountability of public officials. This involves both answerability, or "the obligation of public officials to inform about and to explain what they are doing" (Schedler, 1999a, 14) and enforcement, or "the capacity of accounting agencies to impose sanctions on power holders who have violated their public duties" (Schedler, 1999a, 14). Although some individual officials may never need institutional structures to assure their commitment to the public good, most do need it at least some of the time. The only way to guarantee good government is by institutionalizing powerful accountability mechanisms that hold every public official responsible for his or her actions as a public servant.

The celebration of free and fair elections is one of the most powerful pro-accountability mechanisms in existence. Through periodic elections, political leaders who work for the common good are supposed to be reelected, and leaders who use public office for particularistic ends are supposed to be removed from office. Nevertheless, there are both structural and contextual problems with elections in the developing world.

There are at least three different structural problems with elections as accountability mechanisms. First, elections only hold elected officials accountable. The vast majority of public officials are appointed bureaucrats who are not directly accountable to the public through the electoral process. Second, because elections only occur once every few years and force an incredible diversity of opinions and evaluations together into a single ballot, it is virtually impossible for elections to give clear *accountability signals* to individual office holders (Przeworski, Stokes, and Manin, 1999). Third, even if the accountability signal were somehow clearly discernible, the fact that most politicians are elected by only a small portion of the population often forces politicians to favor patronage, "pork" or corruption over initiatives that would bring long-term benefit to the public as a whole (Varshney, 1999).

The situation appears even worse when we take into account the empirical context. Democratic institutions are extremely weak in the contemporary world. The effectiveness of elections as mechanisms of sanction and control are weakened by the distance between political and civil society, the clientelistic nature of many political parties, the excess private funding for candidates, and the lack of public information about the general workings of government and even less information about the specific behavior of individual office holders.

As a result, "vertical accountability" mechanisms, like elections, that require government officials to appeal "downward" to the people at large have been complemented by "horizontal accountability" mechanisms that require public officials and agencies to report "sideways" to other officials and agencies within the state itself. O'Donnell has defined horizontal accountability in the following manner.

> The existence of state agencies that are legally enabled and empowered, and factually willing and able, to take actions that span from routine oversight to criminal sanctions or impeachment in relation to actions or omissions by other agents or agencies of the state that may be qualified as unlawful. (1999, 38)

Examples of horizontal accountability mechanisms include institutions such as human rights *ombudsman*, corruption control agencies, legislative investigative commissions and administrative courts.

There has been a phenomenal growth of such institutions throughout the world in recent years.[2] Unfortunately, as with elections, these many new agencies of horizontal accountability are plagued by both structural and contextual problems. Structural difficulties include the impossibility of monitoring the almost infinite number of government actions (and inactions), as well as the political isolation that results from these agencies' statutory or constitutional independence (Maor, forthcoming). Contextual difficulties include the lack of adequate funding, reduced enforcement capacity, the absence of second-order accountability (i.e., holding accounting agencies accountable) and the overall weakness of the rule of law needed to enforce agency sanctions.

Fortunately, there is a third way to hold government accountable. In addition to elections and horizontal accountability agencies, societal actors can directly oblige government actors to answer for their actions and sanction them for wrongdoing. Paul's 1992 article in *World Development* on "Accountability in Public Services: Exit, Voice and Control" was one of the first to put forth such an agenda.

The traditional public accountability mechanisms such as expenditure audits and legislative reviews seem unequal to the task of ensuring accountability for public services at the micro level. . . . Public service accountability will be sustained only when the "hierarchical control" (HC) over service providers is reinforced by the public's willingness and ability to exit [i.e., marketization] or to use voice [i.e., direct participation]. (1047–1048)

Paul here simultaneously articulates the accountability function of marketization strategies and, even more important, makes the crucial argument that direct societal participation is often even more effective than strategies based on "exit."

The 1996 symposium on "Development Strategies across the Public-Private Divide," also published in *World Development*, then expanded and filled out an initial discussion of society's pro-accountability role. This series of articles argued that "state-society synergy" (Evans, 1996a, 1996b) is one of the best ways to strengthen government accountability. In sum,

the image of the good bureaucrat—carefully insulated from constituents—has its usefulness, but openness to the role of the "co-producer" . . . may be the best way to increase effectiveness and ultimately the best way to preserve the integrity of increasingly besieged public institutions. (Evans, 1996a, 1131)

For instance, in her contribution to the symposium Ostrom documented how the involvement of citizens in the planning and implementation of water and sanitation projects greatly improved their effectiveness and reduced corruption in urban Brazil (Ostrom, 1996). Lam's contribution showed how community participation in irrigation programs in Taiwan has made service delivery much more efficient and effective (Lam, 1996). This is also consistent with Tendler's path-breaking work in *Good Government in the Tropics* (1997), which demonstrated the salutary effects of the co-production of services by street-level bureaucrats and societal actors.

This literature performed a great service insofar as it pushed academics and development professionals to take societal participation seriously. No longer was society viewed as a "bother," a "contaminant" or as the source of bureaucratic "capture." States and societies could be strengthened simultaneously. Nevertheless, this first wave of writings was also limited in scope insofar as it tended to emphasize depoliticized forms of participation, circumscribed societal action to specific local services and to the implementation phase of government projects, and left out the important discussion of the legal institutionalization of participative mechanisms.

In recent years, two different currents of research have arisen that expand on this earlier literature. First, authors such as Smulovitz, Peruzzotti, Cunill and Waisbord have argued that more political forms of societal participation, such as mass mobilization, media exposés and the use of the courts, are also effective ways for society to improve government account-ability. Smulovitz and Peruzzotti distinguish this form of accountability from the electoral and the horizontal forms by calling it "societal account-ability." They define this as

> a nonelectoral, yet vertical mechanism of control that rests on the actions of a multiple array of citizens' associations and movements and on the media, actions that aim at exposing governmental wrongdoing, bringing new issues into the public agenda, or activating the operation of horizon-tal agencies. (Peruzzotti and Smulovitz, 2000a, 150; 2002, 32)

For example, in their analysis of the social response to two extra-judicial killings in Argentina, the authors have documented how the combination of mobilization, legal action and media exposure can effectively guaran-tee that the judicial system operates impartially, even when the perpetra-tors are well connected or even part of the government apparatus itself (Peruzzotti and Smulovitz, 2000a, 2000b, 2002). Waisbord has comple-mented this analysis by focusing on the role of investigative journalists and media scandals in obliging public servants and politicians to be more accountable (2000).

Cunill (1997, 2000) follows this same line of research but focuses more on the action of citizens in general than on that of organized civil society. For her, the most important society driven pro-accountability mechanisms are legal reforms, such as popular referendum laws, administrative proce-dure acts that require public consultations, "amparo" laws, and freedom of information acts (Cunill, 2000, 25–39). Because laws open up the state to the action of the common citizen, they create space for the active enforce-ment of accountability by the public.

This literature is a welcome addition to the accountability debate because it obliges us to look beyond "well behaved" local participation in specific government projects to a more openly political and even confrontational engagement with the government apparatus as a whole. Nevertheless, these writings still envision and defend an arm's length relationship between state and society. As Cunill has written, "co-management is irreconcilable with control. The efficacy of [social control] is directly dependent on the independence and the autonomy that societal actors maintain with respect to state actors" (Cunill, 2000, 9, my translation).

The second alternative current of research is more "transgressive" inso-far as it explicitly violates the separation between state and society. For instance, Isunza has recently written about "transversal accountability," in which societal actors participate directly in the leadership and operation of state pro-accountability agencies (Isunza, 2003). This parallels Goetz and Jenkins description of the "The New Accountability Agenda" (Goetz and Jenkins, 2002b), which emphasizes "hybrid" or "diagonal" forms of accountability (Goetz and Jenkins, 2001) in which "vertical" actors carry out intra-state "horizontal" accountability functions.

In a similar spirit, Avritzer has put forth the idea of "participatory publics," which occur when societal participatory practices are taken up by and embedded within the state (Avritzer, 2002). Fung and Wright have also followed this line of research in arguing for "empowered participatory governance," which expands the sphere of democratic participation beyond formal electoral politics to involve society at large in deliberation over the design and operation of fundamental government services, such as schooling, policing, environmental protection and urban infrastructure (Fung and Wright, 2001). In addition, Fox has argued for an "interactive approach" to state-society relations that envisions the improvement of accountability through the participation of society in the core functions of government (2000).

This group of authors goes beyond the circumscribed participation implicit in the "co-production" literature as well as the arm's length action of the "societal accountability" literature to posit a full "co-governance for accountability" that confuses the boundary between state and society. In addition to co-producing specific services and pressuring government from the outside, societal actors can also participate directly in the core functions of government itself. This form of civil society participation is special because, as Goetz and Jenkins have written, it "represents a shift towards augmenting the limited effectiveness of civil society's watchdog function by breaking the state's monopoly over the responsibility for official executive oversight" (Goetz and Jenkins, 2001, 365). This chapter looks both to bring together these various texts into a coherent literature and to demonstrate the salience of this budding "transgressive" school of thought by offering some examples of how it works in practice.

CASE STUDIES

Participatory Budgeting in Porto Alegre, Brazil

The Porto Alegre city government represents one of the most effective schemes of state-society collaboration for accountability in the developing world. Since 1989, when the Worker's Party (PT) first won the city government, Porto Alegre has placed spending decisions for over 10 percent of its annual budget in the hands of the people. Every year, more than 14,000 citizens in this city of 1.3 million participate in neighborhood meetings as well as 16 regional and 5 thematic assemblies to set priorities for government investment in infrastructure and basic social services. Each assembly then elects two councilors to serve on a citywide Council of Participatory Budgeting (COP), the organ responsible for putting together the final citywide budget plan. At each level of the process (neighborhood, district, citywide), decisions are made through intense negotiation and the use of sophisticated weighted voting systems designed to assure a fair distribution of resources. At the end of the process, the proposed budget is then submitted to the local legislature for final approval and promulgation. During the following year, the regional and thematic assemblies, councilors and neighborhood groups evaluate the previous year's negotiation process and monitor the implementation process of the previous year's budget.

The participatory budgeting (PB) process is an excellent example of "co-governance for accountability." Normal citizens are involved directly in the planning and supervision of public spending, activities normally under the exclusive purview of public officials. This arrangement is clearly a step beyond both the "co-production" and the "societal accountability" models of civil society participation. Instead of trying to influence policy from the outside or only at the local community level, the citizens of Porto Alegre are invited inside the governmental apparatus itself.

This arrangement has had an important impact on accountability. First, it has drastically reduced the possibilities and incentives for corrupt behavior on behalf of bureaucrats. Each neighborhood and region is informed as to the exact amount of funds that will be invested in which products and services in its area and, even more important, because the citizens themselves participate in designing the budget, they feel that they have a personal *stake* in making sure the government complies with it (Navarro, 1998, 70–71).

Second, the budgeting process reduces the political use of public funds by opening up alternative channels for the participation of civil society. The crucial element is the entirely open and public nature of the budget assemblies. Any adult can attend, speak and vote in the assemblies (Avritzer, 2000, 18). Moreover, it is easy to form a new group and thereby gain access to special organizational representation in the popular votes. This leads to easy "exit" options for members of clientelistic groups where "voice" is not an effective form of protest.

Third, PB limits the capture of state institutions by wealthy interests. Popular participation itself does this by replacing the power of money with the power of voice. In addition, the special design of Porto Alegre's system reinforces this tendency even further. The algorithm used for determining budget priorities intentionally tilts investments toward poorer neighborhoods. Due to this built-in pro-poor bias, the same need presented by two neighborhoods is much more likely to be implemented in the poorer one than the wealthier one (Baiocchi, 2001, 48). Marquetti (2003) has recently empirically demonstrated the significant redistributive impact of the PB.

The origins of this successful pro-accountability arrangement can be found in society. First, the *idea* of instituting a participatory budget had its origins within civil society. It was the Union of Residents' Associations of Porto Alegre (UAMPA) that first advocated the introduction of such a mechanism in the city in 1986 (Avritzer, 2002, 145). Second, Avritzer documents how the expression "participatory budget" did not exist in the PT's electoral platform for city government in 1988. The design of today's PB arrangement only arose after a period of intense negotiation and participation between the new government and civil society groups (Avritzer, 2000, 9). Third, the particular institutional form developed by the Porto Alegre government was largely modeled on already existing practices of deliberation and negotiation in civil society groups (Navarro, 2002).

The Porto Alegre experience offers many lessons for pro-accountability state reformers. First, poor, uneducated people can and do effectively participate in the core activities of governance. Abers (1998) documents that while in 1991, 29 percent of Porto Alegre's residents earned three times the minimum wage or less, 45 percent of the budget participants fit this profile. The underprivileged not only actively participate, but they even participate *more*, relative to their size in the population, than better-off groups.

Second, governments can only get back as much as they put into efforts to activate civil society participation for accountability. In Porto Alegre, citizens are taken out of their usual role as only "advisors" or information providers to government projects and thrust directly into the decision-making process itself. In addition, the government actively encourages the participation of unorganized citizens through the use of government employed community organizers (Abers, 1998, 514). As has been shown to be the case in other cities that have tried participatory budgets, without such full involvement by the government, "participation" schemes can easily end up only strengthening previously existing clientelistic networks and unbalanced intracommunity power relations (Goldfrank, 2002; Nylen, 2002).[3]

Third, governments need to take civil society into account in the design of the participative mechanisms themselves. The PB did not spontaneously arise out of the minds of enlightened bureaucrats. It originated in civil society, was pushed forward by social actors and was ultimately modeled on previously existing practices in civil society by a new government that itself consisted mostly of individuals who had made their careers as community and social activists. Participatory mechanisms usually hold the mark of their birth.

Fourth, according to Fung and Wright (2001), the Porto Alegre experience is an excellent example of how a healthy balance can be struck between "devolution" and "centralized supervision and coordination." Although devolution and decentralization are important because they bring government closer to the people, if carried out blindly, they tend to reinforce inequalities both within the newly "autonomous" local units as well as between them. Decentralization is only productive if the center remains responsible for the supervision and coordination of activities in the local units.

Mexico's Federal Electoral Institute

Mexico's Federal Electoral Institute (IFE) stands out as another example of successful "co-governance for accountability."[4] The IFE's principal activities include organizing federal elections, distributing public funds to the political parties, monitoring the use of both public and private funds by the parties, checking for media bias in the coverage of political campaigns, putting together and cleaning up the official electoral roll and running public education campaigns (IFE, 2000a). The IFE actively involves societal actors at five different levels.

First, the IFE is run by an independent, nine member "citizen-run"[5] General Council that serves as both a special horizontal accountability agency for electoral affairs and as the IFE's principal directive body (Schedler, 1999b). Second, the meetings of the General Council are public. The minutes and decisions are widely publicized, reported on by the media, and are available via the Internet. Third, one representative from each registered political party sits on the General Council. These party representatives can fully participate in the discussions of the General Council and have access to all of the same information as the councilors but do not have the power to vote on initiatives or decisions. Fourth, the IFE commissions that are responsible for organizing and supervising the federal elections at the state level are also "citizen-run" insofar as they are appointed by the General Council without any formal interference from local or state governments (Isunza, 2003).

Fifth, during its most important moment of "service delivery," the organization of the federal elections, the IFE recruits a huge army of citizen volunteers. For instance, during the months leading up to the 2000 elections, the IFE trained over 800,000 volunteer citizens to run 113,423 polling sites (Woldenberg, 2001). All of the participants received two training courses that were designed and implemented by the IFE. In addition, the IFE trained both national and international observers in the basics of electoral law (Pozas, 1996). Finally, each political party is permitted to send one representative to each voting booth on election day. In total, more than one million citizens were mobilized in 2000 to assure the realization of free and fair elections.

Overall, the IFE has been remarkably successful. The lack of significant post-electoral protests and mobilizations in the year 2000 was unprecedented for a presidential election in Mexico. In addition, the fact that there has not been a new electoral reform since 1996 is a testament both to the great breakthrough of this reform and to the legitimacy that the institution continues to enjoy up through the present. Other than the 1933 to 1942 and 1963 to 1970 periods, the seven years from 1996 to 2003 marks the longest period the Mexican political system has gone without an electoral reform since the promulgation of the Mexican constitution of 1917 (Molinar, 1996). Finally, the IFE's recent historic $100 million fine of the Party of the Institutional Revolution (PRI) and its aggressive investigation of the irregular financing of the campaign of sitting president Vicente Fox demonstrates its ability to stand up to even the most powerful interests.

The stimulant for the 1996 reform was the widespread social unrest and demands for democracy that arose out of the economic meltdown of 1994 and 1995, as well as the Zapatista uprising. In addition, one of the most important influences on this electoral reform was the activism of non-profit electoral watchdog groups. The leading group during this period was *Alianza Cívica*. For the 1994 elections, this group mobilized over 12,000 national electoral observers and 400 international observers, carried out its own parallel "quick count" of the electoral results, published a report on bias in media coverage of the campaigns, as well as a guide for electoral observers and a final evaluation of the election as a whole (Olvera, 2003). This organized civic activity motivated the 1996 reform and many of the activities that the IFE carries out today (e.g., the "quick counts," the training of electoral observers and the analysis of the media) are based in practices that *Alianza Cívica* first initiated (Olvera, 2003).

In addition, the successful 1996 reform was the first electoral reform negotiated, designed and implemented by all of the important actors in political society. The 1990 reform that first created the IFE had been pushed through by the ruling Party of the Institutional Revolution (PRI) with the support of only a part of the rightist opposition party, the Party of National Action (PAN). The 1994 reform gave the IFE an increased level of autonomy and was passed by the PRI and the PAN along with a small fraction of the leftist opposition, the Party of the Democratic Revolution (PRD). Finally, the 1996 reform was negotiated, designed and passed by all three of the main parties from left, right and center (Prud'homme, 1996).

This case study offers a number of important lessons for state reformers. First, it confirms the willingness and capacity of poor people to participate in the core activities of governance. Second, the rule of equal and opposite reaction applies here once again. Normal citizens will only participate at such massive levels if the policies being implemented are seen to respond to demands that have originated in civil society, are designed with the participation of a broad range of actors and actively incorporate citizens into the process of implementation itself.

Third, none of the achievements of the IFE would have been possible without a significant amount of resources dedicated to the reform and operation of the IFE itself. Societal participation is best stimulated when it is perceived as a complement rather than as a replacement for government action. Without a core group of 2,500 civil servants, significant salaries for the General Council and a large operating budget (US$480 million in the year 2000) (Instituto Federal Electoral, 2000b), the IFE would not have been able to successfully carry out its tasks nor stimulate the popular legitimacy it needed to involve the active participation of civil society.

Fourth, the case of the IFE forces us to question the commonly accepted idea that neutrality arises exclusively out of the absence of partisanship.

Although some of the IFE's effectiveness does indeed arise out of the professionalization and nonpartisanship of its staff, a great deal of its legitimacy
also arises out of the saturation of partisanship or the radical plurality of
those who participate in the decision-making processes of the IFE. The
General Council is made up of nine citizen councilors, but also surrounded
by a whirlwind of party representatives and media "intrusions." Each voting booth is staffed by trained members of civil society, but also intensively
watched by representatives from each political party. One of the principal reasons why the electoral reform of 1996 was more effective than the
reforms of 1990 and 1994 is because a greater diversity of political positions were taken into account at the negotiating table in 1996 than during
the other two reforms.

Police and School Reform in Chicago

Like many cities in the developing world, Chicago has a "tradition of
machine politics, insular administrative bureaucracies installed in reaction
to political manipulations, a vibrant tradition of neighborhood activism
[and] extreme socioeconomic inequality" (Fung, 2001, 73). Research by
Fung shows how the Chicago city government has improved the performance of its schools and police forces by actively incorporating the participation of civil society. As in Porto Alegre and with Mexico's IFE, the
Chicago government has gone far beyond methods of consultation, co-
production and protest to open itself up to full "co-governance" with the
citizenry at large.

This is particularly true in the case of school reform. In 1988, the city assembly passed the Chicago School Reform Act, which created a "local school council" (LSC)[6] for each of the Chicago Public School's (CPS) 530 elementary and
high schools. The LSC's principal tasks are hiring and firing school principals,
approving school budgets, developing long-term strategic planning documents
called School Improvement Plans (SIP) and dispersing all Chapter 1 funds[7]
(Fung, 2001, 77). These reforms have made the Chicago school system one of
the most open to participation in the entire United States.

Chicago's police reform also involved a significant increase in citizen
participation. The 1995 reform of the Chicago Police Department (CPD)
organized police officers into 279 "beat teams" that are required to hold
open "community meetings" each month in which police officers and citizens work together to identify problems and plan solutions (Skogan and
Hartnett, 1997; Fung, 1999). Here the mode of participation is more akin
to "societal accountability." Citizens are not given any direct legal power
over the operations of the police. They simply provide information and
pressure the officers to attend to specific problems. Nevertheless, the close
citizen oversight of police activities does serve as a powerful accountability mechanism because citizens' complaints can trigger existing internal
mechanisms of supervision and control (Walker, 2001).

There is evidence that both school and police services have greatly improved as a result of the reforms. Between 1994 and 1998, the murder rate declined 24 percent, robbery fell 31 percent and sexual assault fell 21 percent in Chicago, results that are comparable to radically different "zero-tolerance" strategies, such as those imposed by Rudolph Giuliani in New York (Skogan and Hartnett, 1997; Fung, 1999). In addition, school performance as measured by a specially developed "metric of school productivity" shows that between 1987 and 1997 "while students entering the system have become increasingly disadvantaged and less well prepared, the majority of schools have become more effective in educating them" (Fung, 2001, 99).

The origins of the two reforms are quite distinct. School reform arose out of conflict between state and society and was driven by social protest.

> In the Chicago schools, reform resulted from a pitched battle that pitted a diverse social movement composed of parent organizations, "good government" civic groups, educational reform activists, and a coalition of business groups against traditional school insiders such as the Chicago Teacher's Union and the Board of Education. (Fung, 2001, 77)

In contrast, police reform arose out of consensus between government and civil society and was principally directed by reformers within the state. "Absent the street heat and legislative pressure that drove school reform, [the reform] discussions at the intersection of professional, political and civic interests led quietly to the formulation of a participatory variant of community policing . . ." (Fung, 2001, 78). Nevertheless, neither of these reforms were the independent creation of "far sighted" bureaucrats. Both state and society actors were crucial in the development of each participation mechanism, and the more active civil society was involved in the development of the reform proposals, the more complete the opening up of the state to society was achieved.

These institutions are excellent examples of what Fung calls "accountable autonomy." For both cases,

> the role of central power shifts fundamentally from that of directing local units (in the previous hierarchical system) to that of supporting local units in their own problem-solving endeavors and holding them accountable to the norms of deliberation and achievement of demanding but feasible public outcomes. (Fung, 2001, 87)

For example, while local school councils in Chicago are responsible for drawing up budgets and sanctioning principals, they are also simultaneously monitored and evaluated by central agencies. This adds an interesting new twist to our theoretical discussion of accountability because local participative bodies are accountable to centralized bureaucratic agencies.

Instead of civil society holding government accountable, it is now government that is holding civil society accountable.

These Chicago cases reinforce the previously mentioned lessons. First, the most active participants in Chicago are once again the poor and uneducated. In addition, Fung documents that minority dominant areas tend to have higher participation rates than White dominant areas. (Fung, 1999). Second, the success of these Chicago cases also depended on the government opening the process beyond already organized civil society organizations and employing community organizers to stimulate participation and facilitate community decision making.

Third, civil society participation in the design phase of participatory structures proved to be crucial here as well. Neither of the Chicago reforms arose purely out of the minds of social planners, and their relative success depended on the ability of the government to involve social actors from the very beginning. Fourth, as with Porto Alegre and the IFE, the supply side of the equation is crucial. Without a capable and well-financed state apparatus that can actually respond to popular demands and participation, such accountability mechanisms would create more disenchantment than hope.

Finally, these cases push us further toward the conclusion that the supposed either/or choice between centralization and decentralization is a false dichotomy that needs to be reanalyzed. Although devolving power is important, there is an equal need to strengthen the center, at least in its coordinating and monitoring capacities.

Nevertheless, the accountability mechanisms in Chicago are clearly not as open and participatory as those in place in Porto Alegre or the IFE. On the one hand, the local school councils are elected bodies that do not bring a clear popular mandate arising out of popular assemblies, such as the COP in Porto Alegre. On the other hand, the police "community meetings" do not have any direct legal authority over police behavior as does the IFE's General Council. Indeed, this may be why the level of citizen participation in Chicago is also much lower than it is in Porto Alegre and with the IFE. An average of only 20 to 25 people participate in each beat meeting per month, and there are only an average of 1.5 candidates in the elections for each open spot in the school councils (Fung, 1999).

Decentralization and Rural Development in Mexico

Decentralization on its own is just as likely to strengthen corrupt local networks as it is to promote participation and accountability. Pro-accountability arrangements cannot be expected to arise spontaneously from devolution, but need to be intentionally structured. This is the central lesson of Fox's research on the use of World Bank funds for municipal development projects in rural Mexico.

The Mexican Municipal Funds Program has been almost entirely financed by two large loans received from the World Bank, one for US$350 million for the period from 1991 to 1994 and a second for US$500 million for the period from 1995 to 1999. This money was targeted for use in basic infra-structural improvements for the poorest communities in the rural areas of the poorest states. The program was implemented through municipal governments. Autonomous "solidarity committees" were to be organized in each community to supervise government spending, decide which projects would be funded and contribute the necessary labor power.

Unfortunately, because the solidarity committees did not have any legal standing or formal authority over the Municipal Funds program itself, the actual level of participation and the effective autonomy of the committees from the municipal, state and federal government depended entirely on the whims of local bureaucrats. Many committees were therefore entirely ignored or allowed to participate only in the implementation phase of the projects.

Nevertheless, this participatory mechanism was actually relatively successful in the state of Oaxaca. In this state, the community assemblies made the project selection decisions in 63 percent of the cases (Fox and Aranda, 1996, 37). Fox and Aranda argue that one of the principal reasons for this high level of participation is that Oaxaca is an area that is endowed with a very high level of "horizontal social capital"[8] due to a long and rich indigenous tradition of community collaboration and self-governance. Equally important, the government of the State of Oaxaca was flexible and open to working with these traditions. Instead of imposing a new organizational structure on society, a healthy mixing between state and social forms was permitted (Fox, 1994). Indeed, in Oaxaca, this tolerance of autonomous social forms goes back much further than the Municipal Funds program. The state's municipal structure itself, with 570 different municipalities based in local organizational forms, demonstrates the government's long-standing commitment to accommodate legal forms to traditional practices.

The communities that had higher levels of participation had more effective development projects. When the community was directly involved, it tended to monitor the use of funds more closely and to pick projects that were more useful for the population as a whole. In contrast, when the selection process was manipulated from the outside, investment tended to be shifted toward highly visible although not always useful projects (Fox and Aranda, 1996, 37).

A few years into the program the government intervened in order to increase community participation and make the distribution of resources fairer. The formulas used for poverty measurement and funds distribution were improved and, even more important, made public. Also, the amount of funds that could be spent in the municipal capital was limited to 25 percent, thus requiring municipalities to channel funds to the most needy, isolated areas. Finally, the required amount of community contributions was made variable depending on the impact on poverty the selected project would have. High impact projects required less community contribution than low impact projects, thus encouraging investment in true "public goods" (Fox and Aranda, 1996, 12; Fox, 2002, 104–105).

These changes stimulated community participation and strengthened social capital. This occurred because the reforms made communities aware of their right to a precise amount of funds, which was actively involved the poorest areas, and empowered those actors who looked beyond their particular interests and toward the development of the community as a whole. Here institutional reform had a direct impact on trust, fairness and participation (Fox, 2002).

Nevertheless, the origins of this particular scheme of state-society synergy for accountability was entirely "top-down." Instead of arising out of intense negotiations between social actors and government reformers, the participation scheme was thought up and designed by the federal government in consultation with World Bank staff. This may go a long way in explaining why community participation has not been more dynamic in the Municipal Funds program, and why the case of Oaxaca is more of an exception than the rule. Indeed, the "top-down" nature of the entire National Solidarity Program (PRONASOL), of which the Municipal Funds program was only a part, has led many scholars to disqualify it entirely as an attempt at social manipulation intended to help the former ruling party, the PRI, and the powerful interests it defends remain in control (Dresser, 1994, 144; Soederberg, 2001, 104).

Such evaluations of the program as a whole are solidly supported by the extreme level of pro-government propaganda that accompanied almost every step of the solidarity program. Moreover, the distribution of solidarity funds corresponded much more closely to political criteria than to need-based criteria (see Cornelius, Craig, and Fox, 1994). Nevertheless, these well-documented facts should not lead us to ignore exceptional cases, such as those of the more participative communities of Oaxaca that support the prospect of successful co-governance for accountability, even under difficult conditions.

There are various lessons to be learned from this case study. First, as we have already seen, the direct involvement of social actors and practices from the design stage greatly contributes to the success of accountability mechanisms that depend on active participation from civil society. Second, this case also confirms the importance of the formal, legal empowerment of participatory bodies. Without a clear institutionalized location in the decision-making process, these bodies are left open to the winds of manipulation and are quickly bypassed by unwilling or authoritarian public officials.

Third, government transparency and institutional design have an important impact on community participation. Co-governance for accountability stands a much better chance at success when government actors respect social actors enough to fully inform about the details development programs and design participatory institutions so as to assure the active involvement of the most marginal actors. Finally, this case also demonstrates the value of what Norman Long has called "interface analysis." This type of analysis pushes us to "focus upon intervention practices as shaped by the interactions among the various participants, rather than simply on intervention models, by which is meant the ideal-typical constructions that planners, implementers or their clients have about the process" (Long, 1999, 4).[9] The best way to evaluate experiences of societal participation is to delve into how state-society relations work themselves out on the ground in specific contexts.

Grassroots Anticorruption Initiatives in India

One area of government that seems to be particularly resistant to societal participation is the auditing of government expenditure. This task is usually thought to be far too technically sophisticated and politically delicate for the average citizen. Freedom-of-information acts have recently started to sprout up around the world, and citizens are encouraged to use public information to pressure corporations or governments from the outside to comply with their duties or to decide their votes (e.g., Fung and O'Rourke, 2000). But it is difficult to find examples in which normal citizens are as directly involved in the activity of auditing government expenditure as they are, for example, in the activity of budget design in Porto Alegre.

Nevertheless, as Goetz and Jenkins have cogently argued, the cases of the *Mazdoor Kisan Shakti Sangathan* (MKSS) movement in Rajasthan, India, and the *Rationing Kruti Samiti* (RKS), or Action Committee for Rationing, movement in Mumbai, India, show that when reformist bureaucrats are faced with an active pro-accountability movement in civil society, it is possible to make important inroads into the area of social auditing. The central accountability problem that both of these organizations face is the widespread corruption in the provision of government services to the poor. Wages for public works projects are frequently skimmed off by public managers and the materials used in these projects are often artificially overpriced and of bad quality so as to allow the maximum room for kickbacks. In addition, the nation's Public Distribution System (PDS), which is in charge of channeling basic food items and other fundamental household goods, such as kerosene, to the poorest households, is rife with corruption. One of the principal problems here is the selling of these goods by owners of "ration shops" for personal profit (Goetz and Jenkins, 2002a).

Most communities in India already have local "participatory" institutions that are supposedly responsible for monitoring the performance of government programs. Nevertheless, these "Vigilance Committees" and "Village Assemblies" are often captured by actors who are implicated in the process of corruption itself. For instance, they are frequently chaired by the representative of the municipal ward and their members are appointed in a top-down fashion. In addition, many government ration shops are owned or controlled by the very same politicians who are on the committees that are supposed to supervise them (Goetz and Jenkins, 2001, 371).

As a result of the failure of these state-run participatory mechanisms, movements such as MKSS and RKS have found it necessary to create their own autonomous society-driven mechanisms for auditing public projects. The MKSS has developed a methodology through which they independently investigate government spending practices and then expose and compare this information to reality through public hearings (*jan sun wai*) (Goetz and Jenkins, 2002b, 41–42). In the hearings, obvious discrepancies and missing accounts are presented and the public is given the opportunity to check their own personal experience as public employees or suppliers with the accounts. Public officials often attend, and many cases exist in which this process has worked to directly shame them into returning large amounts of "misdirected" funds.

Goetz and Jenkins present the case of the RKS in Mumbai as another example of what they call "diagonal accountability," or the participation of "vertical" actors in "horizontal" enforcement activities. Because the official "Vigilance Committees" are ineffective, the RKS has developed its own parallel system of informal vigilance committees. For each ration shop, five local women who are clients of the shop monitor and evaluate the quality and prices of the goods being sold. This activity has been facilitated by the RKS citywide campaign to oblige shop owners to publicly display prices as well as samples of the goods on sale. The reports of the informal committees are then put together and presented both to the user community and to the central coordinating bureaucracy of the PDS in the city (Goetz and Jenkins, 2002a).

This process was particularly successful during the period immediately following the 1992 riots in Mumbai, after which the city government was very interested in being perceived as being responsive to the poor. In addition, during this period, an important reform-minded bureaucrat held the job of Regional Controller of Rationing. Nevertheless, once this reformist left his post, the process became much less effective. The authors therefore claim that the RKS's experience with "diagonal accountability" has been only a "limited success story" (Goetz and Jenkins, 2001). As we saw with the case of the MKSS, society-driven pro-accountability initiatives that confront the state and demand inclusion in the basic activities of government can be highly effective. Nevertheless, the RKS experience also shows us that ultimately the success of these movements often also depends on constructing alliances with progressive government officials as well.

From this pair of cases, we can learn various lessons. First, they give us a fascinating alternative to "participative" mechanisms, such as the "Bangalore Scorecard," which are limited to simply surveying and reporting on the opinion of the public concerning the performance of government services. As Goetz and Jenkins argue, such initiatives are grounded in a fundamentally naive view of politics and bureaucratic inefficiency because they assume that bureaucrats are simply ignorant of the problems with government (Jenkins and Goetz, 1999). Bureaucrats need to be made directly accountable to the citizenry, and the best way to do this is to allow citizens to get involved in the activity of auditing from the inside and to confront bureaucrats face-to-face with their complicity in bad performance or corruption.

Second, co-governance for accountability does not need to begin with reformist or progressive governments. Success can also arise out of the action of independent organizations and social movements that press their demands on the state and push their way into the auditing of government programs. Third, it seems that at some point in the process, these movements do need allies within the government. Without state support or at least tolerance, such movements will most likely be repressed or rendered ineffective by state action. Finally, both of these cases confirm that sensitive and complex activities, such as public auditing, are not beyond the capacity of poor, illiterate citizens.

LESSONS FOR INSTITUTIONAL REFORMERS

This chapter has argued that the active involvement of civil society and the strengthening of the state apparatus are not mutually exclusive or even contradictory initiatives. This is the central idea of "co-governance" as a concept. If institutions are properly designed, a virtuous cycle that reinforces both state and society is possible. This is particularly important to emphasize today given the thrust of much of the NPM literature that proposes the devolution of state responsibilities to social actors via the market.

In addition, this chapter questions those strands of the "old" public management literature that emphasize the insulation of bureaucracy from societal actors. As Kaufman has recently argued,

> The implication of accountability reform is different, however, when it refers to the establishment of popular assemblies and other forms of direct grassroots participation in administrative decisions. Although some forms of inclusion, such as partnerships with non-governmental organizations (NGOs) may enhance capacity, others, such as popular assemblies, may be a step backward in terms of the efficiency, effectiveness, and even the accountability of state organizations. (2003, 284)

The previous case studies challenge this sort of circumscription of societal participation to "well behaved" or "enlightened" actors, such as NGOs, and argues for the full inclusion of the citizenry as a whole in the core activities of government.

The first step for government reformers looking to construct co-governance for accountability should be to trust and actively involve societal actors from the very beginning of the process. Reformers should not wait for civil society to start trusting government, nor should they wait to involve society until after the government has already designed a new participatory mechanism "from above." As the case studies show, the earlier societal actors are involved in the design process, the more effective participatory measures tend to be. The best "entry points" are therefore those issues and locations where there are previously existing social demands and practices surrounding a specific accountability issue.

In addition, when designing participatory mechanisms, government reformers should be aware that transparency is not enough. Governments cannot expect information provision to single handedly generate the positive feedback loops between state and society outlined in the case studies. Governments should directly stimulate the participation of society. Otherwise, the only actors who will put to use the new information are journalists, academics, nonprofit organizations and already-existing community organizations. Although these groups are indeed crucial in maintaining accountability, the cases show that there is a qualitative forward leap when the population at large and the poor in particular are directly involved in enforcing accountability.

Once initiated, the best way to assure the sustainability of a participatory framework is through its full institutionalization. As we saw in the case of the Municipal Funds program, the formalization of even limited "top-down" participatory schemes allowed for the development of much fuller participation. The case of the RKS in Mumbai, India, provides us with important negative examples of this same point. Here, the absence of a clear legal framework left participation up to the whims of individual bureaucrats, leading to the eventual overturning of participatory schemes once there was a change of heart on the part of government. The difference between the two Chicago cases also reveals the importance of formalizing participatory procedures. One of the major reasons why the school reform has been more effective than the police reform is because the former institutionalized the involvement of civil society in the formal legal structure much more clearly and explicitly than the latter.

There are three different levels at which participatory mechanisms can be institutionalized. First, participatory mechanisms can be built into the strategic plans of existing government agencies. Second, new agencies can be created whose goal is to assure societal participation in government activities. Third, participatory mechanisms can be inscribed in law.

Although the first level of institutionalization is more or less widespread in the developing world and the second level is relatively common, the third level is extremely rare.[10] Why this is the case is more or less evident. Law making under democratic conditions involves the messy process of legislative bargaining and a full role for political parties. State reformers and multilateral agencies tend to shy away from such arenas, especially when they are dominated by opposing parties or factions. Therefore, reformers usually settle for executive procedures, special agencies or innovative individual bureaucrats to carry out their participative strategies.

This is a mistake. As the case studies show, if dealt with in a creative fashion, partisanship can be just as effective as isolation in the search for effective accountability mechanisms. It is necessary to involve political parties and the legislature to fully institutionalize participative mechanisms through the law.

In general, professionalism and independence are necessary but by no means sufficient to assure the long-term survival of accountability. Effective pro-accountability structures need to be legitimated by society both at their founding moment and during their everyday operations. This requires the multiplication, not the reduction, of "external eyes" (Smulo-vitz, 2003) and the diversification, not unification, of political and ideological perspectives.

Finally, these case studies also show us that decentralization alone does not automatically lead to an increase in societal participation or an improvement of government accountability. Although devolution and decentralization are important because they bring government closer to the people, if carried out blindly, they tend to reinforce inequalities both within the newly "autonomous" local units as well as between them. Decentralization is only productive if the center remains responsible for the supervision and coordination of activities in the local units.

If carefully applied, co-governance can be much more rewarding than alternatives such as marketization, bureaucratic insulation, "co-production" or "societal accountability." Co-governance for accountability is usually more difficult to implement, but it is well worth the effort. By transgressing the boundaries between state and society, institutional reformers can unleash invaluable pro-accountability processes that are almost impossible to tap into through less ambitious strategies.

NOTES

1. This chapter is based on previous work published as Ackerman, J. M. 2004. Co-governance for accountability: Beyond "exit" and "voice." *World Development*, 32(30): 447–463.
2. In Latin America, Belize, Brazil, Columbia, Costa Rica, Chile, Peru and Mexico have all recently created or revived such institutions. This trend is also present in Asia, Africa, Australia and Eastern Europe. Some recent examples include the new *Ombudsmen* in Poland (founded in 1987), the Philippines (founded 1989) and South Korea (founded in 1994), the National Counter Corruption Commission in Thailand (founded in 1998), the Independent Commission Against Corruption in New South Wales, Australia (founded in 1988), the Public Protector in South Africa (founded in 1994), and the Inspector-General of Government in Uganda (founded in 1996) (Schedler, Diamond, and Plattner, 1999; Pope, 2000). Over eighty countries currently have a national *Ombudsman* (Bennett, 1997).

3. Navarro (2003) has recently argued that such intense involvement of the government is one of the principal problems with the PB scheme. This is because it violates the "autonomy" of civil society and opens up the process to manipulation by party and governmental interests. Following the "societal accountability" line of thinking, Navarro therefore advocates for what he calls the full "institutionalization" of the PB process by allowing societal actors to decide on the allocation of public funds without any interference from the government (Navarro, 2003, 124–125). Needless to say, from the point of view of the present article, the full interpenetration of state and society present in the Porto Alegre PB process is one of its most important strengths, not one of its weaknesses.

4. I am not the first to draw a parallel between Porto Alegre's PB and Mexico's IFE. In his text on *Democracy and the Public Space in Latin America*, Avritzer claims that these experiences are two of the best examples of the institutionalization of what he calls "participatory publics" (2002, 135–164) or the embedding of societal practices within the state. My approach differs from Avritzer's insofar as I give equal credit to government and party "entrepreneurs," while he tilts the balance toward the role of societal actors.

5. The councilors are elected by two-thirds of the legislature for non-renewable seven-year terms and are chosen among the most well-known scholars and leaders of civil society.

6. LSCs are formed by six parents, two community representatives, two teachers, the school's principal and an additional nonvoting student for high schools.

7. Special state funds allocated to schools on the basis of economic disadvantage of their student body.

8. Fox understands "horizontal social capital" to be the existence of social practices of mutual trust and cooperation within a given community (Fox, 2002, 113).

9. I would like to thank Ernesto Isunza for bringing this extremely valuable text to my attention.

10. There are some exceptions, including the above Porto Alegre and IFE cases, as well as Bolivia's Law of Popular Participation (Cunill, 2000; Oxhorn, 2001), Mexico City's Law of Citizen Participation (Mellado, 2001) and Brazil's 1995 administrative reform that formalizes social control through the legal category of "Social Organizations" (Barreto, 1998; Nassuno, 1998; Bresser, 1999). Nevertheless, these exceptions only prove the rule that participatory mechanisms are usually vastly underinstitutionalized and depend too much on the ingenuity and good will of individual bureaucrats.

REFERENCES

Abers, R., 1998. From clientelism to cooperation: Local government, participatory policy, and civic organizing in Porto Alegre, Brazil. *Politics & Society* 26 (4): 511–538.

Ackerman, J. M. 2004. Co-governance for accountability: Beyond "exit" and "voice." *World Development* 32 (3): 447–463.

Ackerman, J. M. 2005. *Social Accountability for the Public Sector: A Conceptual Discussion*. Washington DC: World Bank.

Ackerman, J. M., and I. M. Sandoval. 2006. The global explosion of Freedom of Information laws. *Administrative Law Review* 58 (1): 85–130.

Avritzer, L. 2000. *Civil Society, Public Space and Local Power: A Study of the Participatory Budget in Belo Horizonte and Porto Alegre*. http://www.chs.ubc.ca/participatory/docs/avritzer.pdf. Retrieved August 1, 2011.

Avritzer, L. 2002. *Democracy and the Public Space in Latin America*. Princeton, NJ: Princeton University Press.

Baiocchi, G. 2001. Participation, activism and politics: The Porto Alegre experiment and deliberative democratic theory. *Politics & Society* 29 (1): 43–72.

Barreto, M. I. 1998. Las organizaciones sociales en la reforma del estado. In L. C. Bresser, N. Cunill, eds. *Lo Público No Estatal en la Reforma del Estado*. Buenos Aires: Paidós, pp. 115–156.

Bennett, C. 1997. Understanding ripple effects: The cross-national adoption of policy instruments for bureaucratic accountability. *Governance* 10 (3): 213–233.

Bresser, L. C. 1999. Managerial public administration: Strategy and structure for a new state. In L. C. Bresser and P. Spink, eds. *Reforming the State: Managerial Public Administration in Latin America*. Boulder: Lynne Rienner, pp. 1–14.

Bresser, L. C., and N. Cunill. 1999. Entre el estado y el mercado: lo público no estatal. In L. C. Bresser and N. Cunill, eds. *Lo Público No Estatal en la Reforma del Estado*. Buenos Aires: Paidós, pp. 25–58.

Bresser, L. C., and P. Spink, eds. 1999. *Reforming the State: Managerial Public Administration in Latin America*. Boulder: Lynne Rienner.

Cornelius, W., A. Craig, and J. Fox, eds. 1994. *Transforming State-Society Relations in Mexico: The National Solidarity Strategy*. La Jolla: Center for U.S.-Mexican Studies.

Cunill, N. 1997. *Repensando lo Público a Través de la Sociedad: Nuevas Formas de Gestión Pública y Representación Social*. Caracas: Nueva Sociedad.

Cunill, N. 2000. Responsabilización por el Control Social. *United Nations Online Network in Public Administration and Finance (UNPAN)*. http://unpan1.un.org/intradoc/groups/public/documents/clad/unpan000183.pdf.

Dresser, D. 1994. Bringing the poor back in: national solidarity as a strategy of regime legitimation. In W. Cornelius, A. Craig, J. Fox, J., eds. *Transforming State-Society Relations in Mexico: The National Solidarity Strategy*. La Jolla: Center for U.S.-Mexican Studies, pp. 143–166.

Evans, P. 1995. *Embedded Autonomy*. Berkeley: University of California Press.

Evans, P. 1996a. Government action, social capital and development: reviewing the evidence on synergy. *World Development* 24 (6): 1119–1132.

Evans, P. 1996b. Introduction: Development strategies across the public-private divide. *World Development* 24 (6): 1033–1037.

Fox, J. 1994. The difficult transition from clientelism to citizenship: lessons from Mexico. *World Politics* 46 (2): 151–184.

Fox, J. 2000. *Civil Society and Political Accountability: Propositions for Discussion*. Presented at the conference "Institutions, Accountability and Democratic Governance in Latin America," The Helen Kellog Institute for International Studies, Notre Dame University, May 8, 2000.

Fox, J. 2002. La relación recíproca entre la participación ciudadana y la rendición de Cuentas. *Política y Gobierno* 9 (1): 95–133.

Fox, J., and J. Aranda. 1996. *Decentralization and Rural Development in Mexico: Community Participation in Oaxaca's Municipal Funds*. La Jolla: Center for U.S.-Mexican Studies.

Fung, A. 1999. *Street Level Democracy: Pragmatic Popular Sovereignty in Chicago Schools and Policing*. Paper presented at the American Political Science Association Annual Meeting, Atlanta, September 2–5, 1999.

Fung, A. 2001. Accountable autonomy: toward empowered deliberation in Chicago schools and policing. *Politics & Society* 29 (1): 73–103.

Fung, A., and D. O'Rourke. 2000. Reinventing environmental regulation from the grassroots up: Explaining and expanding the success of the toxics release inventory. *Environmental Management* 25 (2): 115–127.

Fung, A., and E. Wright. 2001. Deepening democracy: innovations in empowered participatory governance. *Politics & Society* 29 (1): 5–41.

Goetz, A. M., and R. Jenkins. 2001. Hybrid forms of accountability: citizen engagement in Institutions of public-sector oversight in India. *Public Management Review* 3 (3): 363–383.

Goetz, A. M., and R. Jenkins. 2002a. *Civil Society Engagement and India's Public Distribution System: Lessons from the Rationing Kruti Samiti in Mumbai.* Paper presented at "Making Services Work for Poor People," World Development Report Workshop (WDR) 2003/04, Oxford, November 4–5, 2002.

Goetz, A. M., and R. Jenkins. 2002b. *Voice, Accountability and Human Development: The Emergence of a New Agenda.* Background paper for Human Development Report 2002. New York: United Nations Development Programme.

Goldfrank, B. 2002. The fragile flower of local democracy: A case study of decentralization / participation in Montevideo. *Politics & Society* 30 (1): 51–83.

Grindle, M. 1996. *Challenging the State: Crisis and Innovation in Latin America and Africa.* New York: Cambridge University Press.

Hirschman, A. 1970. *Exit, Voice, and Loyalty: Responses to Decline in Firms, Organizations, and States.* Cambridge, MA: Harvard University Press.

Instituto Federal Electoral. 2000a. *The Mexican Electoral Regime and the Federal Elections of the Year 2000.* Mexico City: Author.

Instituto Federal Electoral. 2000b. *Proceso Electoral Federal 2000: Datos y Numeralia Más Importantes,* Mexico City: Author.

Isunza, E. 2003. *Construcción de la Democracia y Rendición de Cuentas: Una Mirada Regional de Nuevas Interfaces Socio-Estatales en el Contexto de la Transición Política Mexicana.* Presented at the meeting of the Latin American Studies Association, Dallas, March 27–29, 2003.

Jenkins, R., and A. M. Goetz. 1999. Accounts and accountability: Theoretical implications of the right-to-information movement in India. *Third World Quarterly* 20 (3): 603–622.

Kaufman, R. 2003. The comparative politics of administrative reform: some implications for theory and policy. In B. Schneider and B. Heredia, eds., *Reinventing Leviathan: The Politics of Administrative Reform in Developing Countries.* Miami: North-South Center Press.

Lam, W. F. 1996. Institutional design of public agencies and co-production: a study of irrigation associations in Taiwan. *World Development* 24 (6): 1039–1054.

Long, N. 1999. *The Multiple Optic of Interface Analysis.* Background Paper on Interface Analysis. Paris: United Nations Educational, Scientific and Cultural Organization.

Manzetti, L. Forthcoming. Political manipulations and market reform fiascoes. *World Politics.*

Maor, M. Forthcoming. Feeling the heat? Anti-corruption agencies in comparative perspective. *Governance.*

Marquetti, A. 2003. Participação e redistribuição: o Orçamento Participativo em Porto Alegre. In L. Avritzer, and Z. Navarro, eds., *A Inovação Democrática no Brasil: O Orçamento Participativo.* São Paulo: Cortez Editora, pp. 129–156.

Mellado, R. 2001. *Participación Ciudadana Institucionalizada y Gobernabilidad en la Ciudad de México.* Mexico City: Plaza y Valdés.

Molinar, J. (1996). Renegotiating the rules of the game: The state and political parties. In M. Serrano, and V. Bulmer-Thomas, eds., *Rebuilding the State: Mexico After Salinas.* London: Institute of Latin American Studies, University of London, pp. 24–40.

Narayan, D., and P. Petesch, eds. 2002. *Voices of the Poor: From Many Lands.* New York: Oxford University Press.

Nassuno, M. 1998. El control social en las organizaciones sociales en el Brasil. In L. C. Bresser and N. Cunill, eds., *Lo Público No Estatal en la Reforma del Estado*. Buenos Aires: Paidós, pp. 333–360.

Navarro, Z. 1998. Participation, democratizing practices and the formation of a modern polity—the case of "participatory budgeting" in Porto Alegre, Brazil (1989–1998). *Development* 41 (3): 68–71.

Navarro, Z. 2002. *Decentralization, Participation and Social Control of Public Resources: "Participatory Budgeting" in Porto Alegre (Brazil)*. Presented at the workshop on "Citizen Participation in the Context of Fiscal Decentralization: Best Practices in Municipal Administration," Inter-American Development Bank and Asian Development Bank, September 2–6, 2002, Tokyo and Kobe, Japan.

Navarro, Z. 2003. O'Orçamento Participativo' de Porto Alegre (1989–2002): um conciso comentárico crítico. In L. Avritzer, and Z. Navarro, eds., *A Inovação Democrática no Brasil: O Orçamento Participativo*. São Paulo: Cortez Editora, pp. 89–128.

Nylen, W. 2002. Testing the empowerment thesis: the participatory budget in Belo Horizonte and Betim, Brazil. *Comparative Politics* 34 (2): 127–145.

O'Donnell, G. 1999. Horizontal accountability in new democracies. In A. Schedler, L. Diamond, M. F. Plattner, eds. *The Self-Restraining State: Power and Accountability in New Democracies*. Boulder: Lynne Rienner, pp. 29–52.

Olvera, A. 2003. Movimientos sociales prodemocráticos, democratización y esfera pública en México: el caso de Alianza Cívica. In A. Olvera, ed., *Sociedad Civil, Esfera Pública y Democratización en América Latina: México*. Mexico City: Fondo de Cultura Económica, pp. 351–409.

Ostrom, E. 1996. Crossing the great divide: Co-production, synergy, and development. *World Development* 24 (6): 1073–1088.

Oxhorn, P. 2001. *La Construcción del Estado por la Sociedad Civil: La Ley de Participación Popular de Bolivia y el Desafío de la Democracia Local*. Documentos de Trabajo del INDES. Washington: Inter-American Development Bank.

Paul, S. 1992. Accountability in public services: exit, voice and control. *World Development* 20 (7): 1047–1060.

Peruzzotti, E., and C. Smulovitz. 2000a. Societal accountability in Latin America. *Journal of Democracy* 11 (4): 147–158.

Peruzzotti, E., and C. Smulovitz. 2000b. *Societal and Horizontal Controls: Two Cases about a Fruitful Relationship*. Presented at the conference "Institutions, Accountability and Democratic Governance in Latin America," The Helen Kellog Institute for International Studies, Notre Dame University, May 8, 2000.

Peruzzotti, E., and C. Smulovitz. 2002. Accountability social: la otra cara del control. In E. Peruzzotti, and C. Smulovitz, eds., *Controlando la Política: Ciudadanos y Medios en las Nuevas Democracias Latinoamericanas*. Buenos Aires: Editorial Temas.

Peters, G. 2001. *The Future of Governing*. 2nd ed. Lawrence: University Press of Kansas.

Pope, J. 2000. *Confronting Corruption: The Elements of a National Integrity System*. Berlin: Transparency International.

Pozas, R. 1996. La observación electoral: una modalidad de la militancia ciudadana. *Revista Mexicana de Sociología* 59 (2): 23–40.

Prud'homme, J. F. 1996. La negociación de las reglas del juego: tres reformas electorales (1988–1994). *Política y Gobierno* 3 (1): 93–126.

Przeworski, A., S. Stokes, and B. Manin, eds. 1999. *Democracy, Accountability and Representation*. New York: Cambridge University Press.

Rose-Ackerman, S. 1999. *Corruption and Government: Causes, Consequences and Reform.* New York: Cambridge University Press.

Schedler, A. 1999a. Conceptualizing accountability. In A. Schedler, A., L. Diamond, M. F. Plattner, eds., *The Self-Restraining State: Power and Accountability in New Democracies.* Boulder: Lynne Rienner, pp. 13–28.

Schedler, A. 1999b. Las comisiones y la pirámide: notas sobre la conflictiva recentralización del Poder en el IFE. *Política y Gobierno* 6 (1): 187–222.

Schedler, A., L. Diamond, and M. F. Plattner, eds. 1999. *The Self-Restraning State: Power and Accountability in New Democracies.* Boulder: Lynne Rienner.

Skogan W., and S. Hartnett. 1997. *Community Policing: Chicago Style.* New York: Oxford University Press.

Smulovitz, C. 2003. How can the rule of law rule? Cost imposition through decentralized mechanisms. In J. M. Maravall, and A. Przeworski, eds. *Democracy and the Rule of Law.* Cambridge, UK: Cambridge University Press.

Soederberg, S. 2001. From neoliberalism to social liberalism: Situating the National Solidarity Program within Mexico's passive revolutions. *Latin American Perspectives* 28 (3): 104–123.

Tendler, J. 1997. *Good Government in the Tropics.* Baltimore, MD: Johns Hopkins University Press.

United Nations Development Programme. 2002. *Human Development Report 2002: Deepening Democracy in a Fragmented World.* Oxford, UK: Oxford University Press.

Varshney, A. 1999. *Democracy and Poverty.* Presented at the conference on the 2000 World Development Report, Caste Donnington, England, August 15–16, 1999.

Vellinga, M., ed. 1998. *The Changing Role of the State in Latin America.* Boulder: Westview Press.

Waisbord, S. 2000. *Watchdog Journalism in South America: News, Accountability and Democracy.* New York: Columbia University Press.

Walker, S. 2001. *Police Accountability: The Role of Citizen Oversight.* Belmont: Wadsworth / Thompson Learning.

Wallis, J., and B. Dollery. 2001. Government failure, social capital and the appropriateness of the New Zealand model for public sector reform in developing countries. *World Development* 29 (2): 245–263.

Woldenberg, J. 2001. Lessons from Mexico. *Journal of Democracy* 12 (2): 151–156.

World Bank. 1997. *World Development Report 1997: The State in a Changing World.* Oxford, UK: Oxford University Press.

World Bank. 2003. *World Development Report 2004: Making Services Work for Poor People.* Oxford, UK: Oxford University Press.

Part II

How Does Co-Production Work?

7 Co-Production from a Normative Perspective

Edgar S. Cahn and Christine Gray

The systematic engagement of the citizenry as co-producers, at least in the United States, arguably dates back to Jane Addams's work in founding the Hull House in the early twentieth century. The emergence of co-production as a framework for understanding and analyzing the role of citizen engagement stems directly, in the United States, from the civil rights movement in the 1950s and 1960s, the sit-in movement, and the implementation of "maximum feasible participation" as the major idea underpinning President Lyndon Baines Johnson's war on poverty. Both the funding and the impetus for many of the instances of co-production stem from efforts to address the entrenched racial divides in America. This was especially true of efforts mounted through public services to address and rectify the historically rooted inequality and the disenfranchisement on political and economic fronts of African Americans.

For many, the term co-production stems from the work of Elinor Ostrom, most specifically her studies of urban services in 1975, which examined urban reform and the role of co-production within the framework of public administration. Ostrom defined co-production broadly as "the process through which inputs used to produce a good or service are contributed by individuals who are not 'in' the same organization." Her real focus, however, was more specific. Ostrom's work focused on the roles that citizens could play in producing goods and services provided by the government. In a comment that echoes the spirit of "maximum feasible participation," she asserted that "co-production implies that citizens can play an active role in producing public goods and services of consequence to them." "The term 'client' is a passive term" she observed: "Clients are acted upon" (Ostrom, 1990; Ostrom, 1999, 347). Citizenship implied a far more active role.

Ostrom's groundbreaking analysis of co-production's utility focused on the question of co-production's efficiency in the production of needed public services and outputs. She analyzed co-production in terms of whether citizens' and officials' inputs are strictly substitutable, or whether the inputs from citizens are complementary to those already being provided by public officials. The least interesting case is where the inputs of the one can be substituted for the inputs of the other. In this case, the most efficient form of production is easy to determine as a matter of price. The combination of inputs (paid officials versus citizens) that will yield maximum output for the least cost is simply computed by comparing the wage rate of officials with the opportunity costs of the citizens. The more meaningful occurrence of co-production explored by Ostrom occurred when inputs from citizens are complementary—that is, when citizens bring something to the table that public officials either cannot or choose not to provide. In this case, the achievement of co-production goes beyond mere efficiency to produce outcomes that are qualitatively or quantitatively better. However, Ostrom (1999, 102) cautions that designing the institutional arrangements that induce successful co-productive strategies "[are] far more daunting than demonstrating their theoretical existence"—and she notes that "[i]t is notoriously difficult to specify a clear production technology for education, health, and police service."[1]

Wholly independently of Ostrom's work, one such technology, Time-Banking, emerged in the 1980s and continues to develop. By coincidence, the founders of TimeBanking utilized the same term, co-production (Cahn, 2004), to describe the principles underpinning TimeBanking's ability to generate efforts to address social problems by systematic utilization of client or citizen labor to complement, enhance or transform public services. Those who were associated with TimeBanking sought to distill those factors that would lead TimeBanking to be used most effectively to achieve social justice through citizen engagement. Unlike Ostrom, the "original position" of their analysis was a normative framework linked explicitly to the agendas of the civil rights movement and to the subsequent efforts by President Lyndon Johnson's war on poverty to rectify the economic implications of inequality (Cahn, 1994, 2000). For them, the concept of co-production was the result of an empirical inquiry into what had worked best to achieve the equivalent of maximum feasible participation. Ostrom's articles focused on how best to understand the dynamics of citizen engagement from an economic perspective. They, on the other hand, were seeking to understand how best to achieve engagement for specific ends.

As the TimeBanking movement undertook to formalize the status of labor inputs by clients, citizens and community, Co-Production™, as a specific social technology was so central to its distinctive mission that TimeBanks USA, the organization that developed this technology, applied for and actually secured a trademark for the term, Co-Production™ for two purposes: (1) to vest that labor with economic and programmatic significance worthy of quasi-brand name recognition and (2) to redefine TimeBank members as contributors and as civic assets rather than as objects of largesse.

This chapter submits that the understanding of co-production is usefully expanded by examining how TimeBanking defined the elements of co-production and by appreciating the extent to which those elements emerged as progeny of the civil rights movement and the statutory mandate "maximum feasible participation" in the war on poverty (Economic Opportunity Act, 1964, 516; Cahn and Cahn, 1969; Boyle, Slay, and Stephens, 2010). To be sure, both Ostrom and the TimeBank movement refer to the engagement of citizens by the government as co-producers of public goods. The difference lies in the rationale, the methodology and the purpose of TimeBanking's efforts to transform citizens from consumers of public goods and services into co-producers of those goods and services (Cahn, 2006, 10–19). When TimeBanking is utilized to implement co-production, we see the transformation of the client that Ostrom envisioned in her contrasting the agency of "citizens" as against the passivity of "clients."[2] But we see something else. We see co-production involving a reflexivity that leads to transformation at a different level. The system itself undergoes change. Producer and product, process and outcome are transformed.

This chapter cautions that attempts to analyze co-production purely in terms of efficiency can be a trap. As an economic concept, "efficiency" suggests a context-free, value-free measure of improvement. But efficiency improvements are in fact always relative to *something* to which value is attached. Ostrom's analysis is empirical, not normative. However, normative values creep into Ostrom's work through the back door with terms such as "citizens" and "clients" that implicitly at least contribute to the idea that superior "efficiency" of co-production only emerges when efficiency incorporates normative criteria like equity and justice. That is why TimeBanking generated a definition of co-production that injected core normative principles drawn from the civil rights movement and the war on poverty (Cahn, 2004, 32).

We argue that an appreciation of the relationship of co-production to the war on poverty and "maximum feasible participation" is more than a historical inquiry. It is a source of experience that can help us appreciate the critical role that certain core values play when they function as operating principles in efforts to generate co-production. It can draw attention to the implications that go beyond mere efficiency. Understood from a historical context, it becomes apparent that co-production is not only a method of production; it is both a means and an end, method and purpose, process and outcome. When citizens help to produce the public goods and services that are, in the words of Elinor Ostrom (1999, 86), "of consequence to them" that activity has the potential to be transformational.

A HISTORICAL PERSPECTIVE ON MAXIMUM FEASIBLE PARTICIPATION

The war on poverty came on the heels of—and was partly an offspring of—the civil rights movement, so that mandate was as much a normative mandate as an economic one calling for civic, economic, social and political enfranchisement (Davies, 1996, 103). The Thirteenth Amendment to the US Constitution had established in 1865 that people of African descent were no longer chattel. But a virtual apartheid still reigned in the United States, more evidently and overtly in the South, but also in the segregated neighborhoods of the North. Among populations of color and in some rural areas of the country, poverty and deprivation—including severe malnourishment—were still not uncommon (Lui et al., 2006, 11). In a post-World War II world, where the United States was becoming increasingly dominant, such levels of poverty had become intolerable in the nation that was not only the richest on earth, but that laid claim to being a model for free societies everywhere. A century after slavery had been brought to a close, and as the civil rights era crested in the 1960s, the war on poverty was initiated to usher in an era in which cheap labor could no longer be extracted from human beings based on ethnic identity or unfortunate circumstance. It is no coincidence that the identical period, the 1960s to 1970s, was also when the women's movement attained a new scale in addressing the status of women and de facto inequalities in both the family and the workplace (Freidan, 1963).

When Congress passed the Economic Opportunity Act of 1964, programs funded by the legislation were required to incorporate "maximum feasible participation" of the poor (Economic Opportunity Act, 1964, 516). Although the term "co-production" was not then in use, "maximum feasible participation" was to be implemented in a way that would be readily recognizable to anyone versed in co-production as mandating partnerships between government officials and citizens in multiple modalities: governance, management and actual service delivery (Economic Opportunity Act, 1964, 516). From an historical perspective, "maximum feasible participation" was a battle cry that grew out of the civil rights movement that was buttressed by the experience of minority groups with a national program called urban renewal. Through the 1950s, in city after city, the bulldozer was the primary vehicle of renewal (Anderson, 1964; Avila and Rose, 2009; Baldwin, 1965). Leveling entire communities, officials declared, was necessary in order to bring economic and social well-being to blighted and disadvantaged neighborhoods. The neighborhoods designated for urban renewal were inner-city neighborhoods occupied by African Americans. Federal law had guaranteed what would now be viewed as classic co-production: that the residents would be engaged in the planning, would approve of the plan and would be guaranteed a return to homes that replaced those being demolished (Economic Opportunity Act, 1964, 516). The reality was altogether different. In fact, vibrant, organic communities were destroyed, often replaced by highways that encouraged and facilitated White flight and an expedited commute to and from White suburbs. In the African American community, urban renewal was referred to as Negro removal (*The Negro and the American Promise*, 1963).[3]

Maximum feasible participation, therefore, was call for citizen mobilization as much as it concerned citizen engagement. It grew out of a sense of outrage and injustice spurred by a different kind of war that had left the poor as civilian casualties of a campaign waged allegedly on their behalf and for their benefit. An article, "The War on Poverty: A Civilian Perspective," which was widely disseminated by the Office of Economic Opportunity (OEO) (Cahn and Cahn, 1964) put this framing front and center. Speaking to a promise that the "war on poverty" would not be merely a spectator sport for residents, as professionals fought for and against their interests, it is credited with supplying the blueprint for the establishment of the National Legal Service program. That program provided lawyers as advocates who could not be silenced when they represented the poor (Stossel, 2004, 433). Whereas Legal Aid had existed for well over half a century, the new legal services program sought to utilize legal representation as a strategy to empower the poor in their efforts to reach for economic opportunity. It was expressly justified as a strategy of enfranchisement needed to hold officials to their word, to secure entitlements guaranteed by law, to enforce laws such as housing codes and consumer protection and to challenge patterns and practices that perpetuated past racial discrimination (Cahn and Cahn, 1964, 1334–1336).

Many of the programs in the United States subsequently studied and cited in the literature on co-production had originated, been supported or grew out of programs funded as part of war on poverty and related initiatives. Perhaps the best known of those was the preschool Head Start program (Head Start Act, 2007). Because 50 percent of those living in poverty were children, Head Start was launched with an express requirement to engage the parents as essential "co-producers" of preschool child development (Head Start Act, 2007, §§ 9833, 9836(c)(9)(J), 9836(c)(9)(v)(VI), 9836(g)). Community based health clinics funded by the war on poverty incorporated the same participatory philosophy in delivering health care to communities (Schorr, 1988, 130–134). Governing boards of OEO-funded programs were required to be recruited from the community to represent the poor (Gillette, 2010, 79, 82). And OEO programs expressly employed substantial numbers of residents from the community (Gillette, 2010, 79, 82).

During those years, paraprofessional programs opened multiple pathways for citizens as consumers and clients to become citizens as co-producers by unbundling tasks previously regarded as the exclusive preserve of professionals. In 1965, one year after the war on poverty was launched, Congress passed the Elementary and Secondary Education Act (1965), which required schools to involve parents in their child's education and in the activities of the school. The act defined parental involvement as the participation of parents in regular, two-way communication involving student academic learning and other school activities (Elementary and Secondary Education Act, 1965). That effort stimulated extensive experimentation in peer tutoring and the use of peer systems where student achievement was promoted by students teaching other students (Gartner and Reissman, 1993). Multiple community-policing programs were funded to enlist the residents in curtailing crime and reducing delinquency (U.S. Department of Justice, 2011b). The Community Action Program was designated a centerpiece of the entire war on poverty, designed to mobilize the entire community in a collective effort to expand opportunity that would reduce poverty (Stossel, 2004, 363–367; Gillette, 2010, 13, 65–88).[4]

In the context of the civil rights movement, OEO programs provided the first major opportunity for people of color to assume leadership and management responsibilities for substantial human service programs. Many civic leaders and elected officials of color in the later part of the twentieth century served a kind of apprenticeship provided by positions funded as part of the war on poverty (Gillette, 2010, 213, 371).[5]

Both the cost and the political backlash from the Vietnam War brought an end to Johnson's presidency, and with it, an end to the war on poverty. The Nixon administration did not shut down the underlying idea, however. The Weed and Seed program of the Department of Justice funded many community-based initiatives (U.S. Department of Justice, 2011a), and under other auspices, many community-based experiments that had been started through the war on poverty took on a life of their own.[6]

Many of the programs that Ostrom and others analyzed grew out of initiatives begun as part of the war on poverty and later the Model Cities program (Peterson, 2009). Consistently, resident participation and citizen participation went beyond consultation or representation on governing or advisory boards. Maximum feasible participation aimed at active, dynamic engagement in the delivery of services by people drawn from the communities the programs were designed to benefit. Co-production then partakes of the normative energy of the civil rights movement and the broader concerns over poverty, subordination and discrimination that it helped fuel.

TIMEBANKING AND CO-PRODUCTION

The next part of this chapter deals with TimeBanking and the examples and forms of co-production that it has generated. TimeBanking is a lineal descendant of "maximum feasible participation" and the struggle of the civil rights movement for equal citizenship and enfranchisement. That history and those origins have added some distinctive elements to co-production and to its implementation utilizing the TimeBanking technology.

Perhaps the most unprecedented element that TimeBanking brought to co-production was its use of a medium of exchange that explicitly rejected market price as the sole measure of economic value (Cahn, 2004, 5–7; Cahn, 2006, 1–2). With TimeBanking, all hours of labor, regardless of the type of labor or the qualifications of the laborer, were rewarded at the rate of one unit for one hour, and were thus regarded as equal (Cahn, 2004, 6). Different names for the currency have emerged: Time Dollars, service credits, hour credits, community credits. But all take exception to market price. One hour equals one unit of the medium of exchange that all TimeBanks apply, regardless of nomenclature.

The reasons for this rejection of market price were simple but profound, and they bring together empirical, theoretical and normative concerns. We tend as a society to view the design of our economic system as given—as a fact of nature, not a social institution that has been developed over the course of history as the result of many individual decisions, and subject, therefore, to being changed at will. Within that institution, market price is a given. As such, it operates through the interplay of supply and demand to determine price—hence, in a very specific way, value. If a capacity is scarce relative to demand, the cost, in money terms, goes up. Within that market frame, it is valued more highly. If the capacity is abundant, it is viewed as less valuable in terms of price, and the cost goes down. The logical extension of this approach is that if a capacity is universal, it has close to zero market value. Thus, when we choose market price as our chief indicator of value, we inadvertently devalue every capacity that we share as humans and that defines us as human beings. But these may be the very capacities that enabled our species to survive and develop. Taking this into account led the founder of TimeBanking to make the rejection of market price a central feature, choosing instead to place an hour-for-hour value on all service transactions. In this way, the human capacities that the market easily overlooks become, in the TimeBanking economy, valued equally: an hour of care giving is no less and no more valuable than an hour of accounting, an hour of medical treatment, or an hour of music-making or gardening.

As a social technology aimed at generating co-production, TimeBanking supplied another transaction-fostering element: databases of skills, talents and passions aimed at linking supply and demand by documenting unutilized capacity, unmet need, availability and reliability. If co-production means enlisting citizen labor, then knowledge of where that labor can be found and who might need it is essential.

As mentioned earlier, TimeBanking was originally inspired by the war on poverty's aim of achieving maximum feasible participation, thereby mobilizing citizens to be involved themselves in building a more just society. When TimeBanking began, the only means for achieving that goal were two: the egalitarian nature of the currency with its eschewal of price, and the development of databases that listed the capacities of community members. As Ostrom observed, however, generating co-production is far easier in the abstract and theoretically than it is in "real life." The pioneers of TimeBanking struggled to find their footing; many TimeBanks never grew beyond twenty to thirty individuals and then collapsed, having exhausted those who set them up. Some, however, thrived. In examining which ones succeeded and which failed, it became clear that fundamental core values were at play in the successful TimeBanks that were not at play in the failures. These core values were empirically derived, but, because the original starting point of TimeBanking had been a normative one, the core principles function both as principles *and* as values. For those who are used to a strict division between normative and empirical or analytical thinking, this merging of empirical and normative categories can be profoundly disquieting. Nevertheless, from our experience, we have no trouble in asserting that TimeBanking's core principles and values operate on both fronts simultaneously. Over time, it has been repeatedly confirmed that they are "best practices" in a double sense: as guides to "what works" operationally, and as pointers to normative ideals. Thus, TimeBanking and Co-Production as a trademarked concept call for fidelity to those core principles/values, which can be summarized briefly as follows:

- *An Asset Perspective*: Every human being has capacity to help in ways that will meet needs in others.
- *Honoring Real Work:* Work that the market does not value—caring, mentoring, civic participation, cultural celebration, social justice campaigns, environmental preservation—done by people regardless of whether they are in the labor force or not, is still real work that needs to be recorded, valued and rewarded.[7]
- *Reciprocity:* One-way helping transactions disempower and devalue those who receive services relative to those from whom they receive help. Giving back through generalized reciprocity empowers the recipients of services. Pay-it-forward needs to be intrinsic to receiving help.
- *Community:* No man is an island. We are social beings. We are interdependent. The confidentiality imposed by professional services can perpetuate isolation and vulnerability. Collective events and projects can empower.
- *Respect:* Those with power and wealth need to be held accountable by those in community who may be silent and who feel powerless. We need to create ways to amplify their voices and create effective feedback loops (Cahn, 2004, 87–99, 111–131, 144–154, 169–179; Cahn, 2006, 10–19).

Because of its roots in the civil rights movement and the war on poverty, the TimeBanking approach to co-production has been designed to address the absence of each of those core principles/values. The principles/values in turn have functioned as a normative mandate calling for co-production as a remedial strategy. Thus, the asset perspective was formulated as an imperative: no more throw-away people (Cahn, 2004, 87–99; Cahn, 2006, 10–11). The need to honor work that the market did not value was reformulated as a pointed exhortation: no more labor exacted from the subordination of women, discrimination against ethnic minorities or exploitation of immigrants and children (Cahn, 2004, 111–131; Cahn, 2006, 12–13).

Reciprocity as a principle of mutuality became a directive: do not exact dependency as the price of receiving help (Cahn, 2004, 144–154; Cahn, 2006, 14–15). Community, as a principle of interdependence, became a pointed indictment: Do not permit rules involving confidentiality or privilege to leave people isolated and vulnerable (Cahn, 2004, 169–179; Cahn, 2006, 16–17). Respect meant: amplify voices that tell you truths you may not want to hear (Cahn, 2006, 18–19).

As noted earlier, each of these values stems directly from the struggles of the civil rights movement and the war against poverty to enlist both government and the citizenry in a joint effort to create a more just and equitable society. We see them, too, engendering the kinds of complementary inputs that Ostrom's first articles on co-production depicted. Moreover, to the extent that co-production has emerged more broadly as a framework designed to achieve a more equitable and just society, the efforts of Time-Bank programs, drawing on that history, provide examples and, hopefully, some useful principles that can be employed in different contexts to create new social enterprises.

TimeBank programs take two basic forms: Community of Place and Community of Mission. The first is a neighbor-to-neighbor network of mutual assistance (Time Dollar Institute, 2003, 19–24). The second is a special purpose TimeBank where participants earn time credits doing specific, predetermined tasks to achieve a mission-defined outcome (Time Dollar Institute, 2003, 39–62).

Community of Place TimeBanks

Time credits can be earned doing an unlimited variety of tasks; there are TimeBanks with a list of over 800 services offered by members to members (Simon, 2010, 30–31; Dane County TimeBank, 2011). A public purpose is served and government dollars are saved when TimeBanking is used to rebuild community. The public purpose takes many forms: reduction of crime, provision of care and supervision to children whose parents are working, environmental clean-up and restoration, mentoring and tutoring for children having difficulty at school, employment opportunities for people needing to build a work record because they are new to the world of work or because past conduct or a condition presents a barrier to employment, care for the elderly or for people discharged from a hospital. Because this operates as a neighborhood exchange system, this is not a "public" service in the formal sense. That protects it from "free riders," a problem encountered by other co-production efforts. In this sense, it is not the public sector that is being expanded or public services being performed.

These efforts in effect rebuild what Neva Goodwin has called the "Core Economy" of household, neighborhood, community, civil society (Goodwin et al., 2009, 383–385; Cahn, 2004, 203–205). That economy may not be the "public economy" normally referred to in co-production literature.

Relationships and friendships and trust are not just by-products; they may be the central products of this form of co-production. The public sector is less burdened the more that critical needs are adequately addressed by the core economy.

The question then arises: is creating a community of place with Time-Banking co-production? In TimeBanking, we would say "Yes." Indeed, we take the position that no public outcome can be fully realized without there being a double-layered partnership, one occurring on an individual, person-to-person level, the other occurring at the level of community. On the person-to-person microlevel, individuals are enlisted as co-producers; on the community level, co-production takes the form of a partnership between the community more broadly and those who operate from within the monetary economy.

Special Purpose: Community of Mission TimeBanks

This second form of TimeBanking is much more programmatic. Time-Banking has repeatedly generated co-production in contexts where traditional governmental and philanthropic interventions have been ineffectual or where outcomes reflect racial disparities that are entrenched and resist efforts at change. This is the form of co-production that utilizes TimeBanking specifically as a catalyst for system change. Part of the change stems from the transformation that comes when people designated as useless discover, step-by-step, hour-by-hour, that they can make a difference—and, in fact, they can achieve the very outcomes that professionals and agencies and programs had been unable to produce. Some examples illustrate that aspect of co-production.

In Chicago, Albany and St. Louis disadvantaged youth have earned Time Dollars tutoring younger students. They have cashed the Time Dollars in for recycled computers and in TimeBank stores located in some schools—but the real breakthroughs have been in test scores, attendance, morale and violence reduction (Royer, 2000; City School District of Albany, 2005; U.S. Department of Commerce, 1999, 1–2).

In Washington DC, a Time Dollar Youth Court handles over 65 percent of nonviolent juvenile crime. Recidivism has gone down by more than 50 percent. But perhaps the most significant accomplishment was captured by one former offender serving as a juror when she told an official Juvenile Justice Board: "I learned my acts had consequences" (Time Dollar Youth Court, 2008, 9–10).

In Oakland California, the Department of Public Health facing violence between long time Black residents and newly arrived Hispanic neighbors realized after shootings that it needed to confront the latest form of lead poisoning: bullets. A previously all-Black church became the home of the TimeBank program with both a Hispanic and African American matchmaker. A rigorous evaluation designed to measure changes in the "collective efficacy" of that community found a significant decrease in violence coupled with an increase in trust and sense of control. Jointly, African Americans and Hispanics were reclaiming habitat—and in doing so, they were welcoming back people returning from prison who would otherwise have been treated as social lepers. Instead, they were enlisted in the Time-Bank as homecomers and co-workers. (Caplan et al., 2008).

In New York City, local newspapers have been describing the Time-Bank groups set up by the Visiting Nurse Service as mini-United Nations gatherings, where exchanges are continually bridging traditional divides of nationality, language, ethnicity, gender, age and class (Visiting Nurse Service of New York, 2009).

In Rhode Island, an organization led by families whose children have been diagnosed with serious emotional disturbance now utilizes Time-Banking to provide support to other families throughout the state for children who may be bipolar, autistic or schizophrenic, but who with mutual support are able to function, learn, develop and contribute. The Rhode Island Department of Children, Youth and Families now contracts with this family centered organization to assist in the redesign of the entire state system for children at risk of institutionalization (Parent Support Network of Rhode Island, 2011).

In Phillippi, West Virginia, euphemistically designated a "distressed county," seniors in wheelchairs describe ways they earn Time Dollars. One on oxygen says: "I stuff envelops to get my grass mowed." Another points to a young man, a veteran from Iraq, who says he still can't be around large groups of people. She says: "He's asked me to help him with his job. He trains seeing-eye dogs. And he needs me because those dogs have to learn to be around people in wheel chairs." Everyone is needed; everyone is valued.[8]

There is a tendency in the world of policy makers, human service professionals and others to characterize all those who do unpaid work as "volunteers." So long as they are relegated to that status, we will see extensive contribution but we will not see the kind of synergy that co-production, tracing its roots to "maximum feasible participation," seeks to generate. TimeBanking provides both a tracking system and a network management technology that can exclude free riders while simultaneously creating a reward system that can reduce the burn-out and attrition that afflicts many efforts to secure voluntary citizen engagement efforts.

There is at least one other distinctive element of co-production that Time-Banking has been used to generate: the feedback loop needed as a corrective for any system. In this country, government initiatives typically lack an effective feedback loop. Those served by government initiatives are often the disenfranchised, lacking a voice or political clout. They may be silenced by being blamed for their own misfortunes. Or they may need help because they are casualties of dysfunctional public programs. TimeBanking has been used to create a different form of co-production: feedback loops that let those in charge know when they are failing and whom they have left out.

Thus, for instance, youth who served on the Youth Court expressed a desire to deal with more than individual problems. They were organized as a Youth Grand Jury to conduct an inquest into how the Sistrict government was dealing with drugs and youth. After six months of hearings held alternative weekends, they indicted the mayor and the drug rehabilitation agency for ignoring youth, for having no programs for youth except two that were ineffectual, for spending over $37 million on programs for people other than youth, and for failure to implement any of the truly effective programs that the youth had learned were operating in other jurisdictions (D.C. Youth Grand Jury, 2000, 6–16). As a result, the mayor put in $2 million in his budget for community-based programs for substance abuse and youth (Cahn, 2002, 1).

THE SPREAD OF CO-PRODUCTION
THROUGH TIMEBANKING

Use of co-production of the TimeBank variety stemming from the war on poverty is now spreading to other countries. At present, Great Britain is the place where this is occurring most. For instance, the volunteer movement in the United Kingdom is now embracing TimeBanking; Adoption of TimeBanking by volunteer Time Centers in Scotland is widespread (Volunteer Development Scotland, 2011). Similar developments are emerging in Wales and England. (TimeBanking Wales, 2011; TimeBanking UK, 2011). The growth of TimeBanking in Great Britain has been spurred by major awards: Castlemilk, an impoverished community of relocated families in Scotland won the Queens Award for Volunteering (Queen's Award for Voluntary Service, 2008). Clapham Park TimeBank addressing major mental health problems in a low-income community in London won the Residents Involvement award from Metropolitan Housing Group (Metropolitan Housing Group, 2010, 19). The Rushey Green TimeBanks operating out of a medical center where patients are referred to the TimeBank won the Sustainable City Award from the City of London. A major housing developer operating vast housing complexes includes TimeBanking as part of its core infrastructure for tenants.

We contend that when TimeBanking is utilized as a vehicle for co-production, the normative principles implicit in co-production become explicit. Unless those values are made explicit, co-production can be misunderstood and misused as a euphemism for cheap labor by citizens. Precisely because co-production entails system change that advances social justice, enthusiasm can easily lead to overstatement. First, we must note that the achievements have come only after a long time and great effort. Persuading public officials of the value of co-production (with or without TimeBanking) has been uphill work for two decades. Only now are officials in the United States beginning to embrace the idea. In Great Britain, there has been much greater willingness to embrace co-production; leading figures at NESTA, the New Economics Foundation, Improvement and Development Agency, and the Office of Public Management have all written pieces endorsing co-production as a catalyst to transform service programs. (Boyle, Slay, and Stephens, 2010; Improvement and Development Agency, 2010; Cummins and Miller, 2007).

Moreover, as Ostrom noted at the outset, an embrace of the concept of co-production does not necessarily translate into practice. Elevating clients and communities previously defined as "problems" to the status of co-producers requires significant system change; but as is well known, systems operate to entrench behaviors, expectations and incentives—entire cultures. They do so in a world that is organized around the dynamics of money and price, so that "needs"—for nothing other, say, than genuine caring and love—become synonymous with "services." And organizations that supply services earn their money by paying staff to manage caseloads. Status comes from one's role in parsing out limited supply of time and resources.

Funders do not pay service providers to generate co-production—at least not yet. On the other side of the ledger, building the infrastructure of a TimeBank has costs. They, like any other operation, require staff, computer capacity, phones, brochures and space. Evaluating their performance and impacts also takes effort and (however ironically) money. Those costs have to be justified. Slowly, however, over time the successes of TimeBanking and its ability to generate multiplier effects are becoming more broadly known. TimeBanking is moving from its pioneer stage, when only the early adopters stepped forward. More organizations and systems are becoming willing to make the initial investment and take the gamble that co-production will produce unique outcomes at a time when money is scarce and competition is brutal.

Thus, we end this chapter by taking a leap. From our vantage point, nothing short of retrofitting obsolete service systems will enable highly professional agencies to tap the vast renewable energy of community. We believe that the evidence to date suggests that TimeBanking, taken to scale and implemented with integrity, will be the carrier for an expanded vision of co-production. In an era of fiscal austerity, a re-engaged citizenry may represent the only option for agencies that are already overburdened and in crisis. Anchoring co-production in the core operating principles/values that were developed through TimeBanking can, we think, help to prevent co-production from being perverted into a vehicle for exploiting citizens. We are at an epoch-making juncture when principled-based co-production can become a catalyst for creating both a more equitable global community and a more sustainable planet.

CONCLUSION

This chapter has sought to highlight how, in the United States, the notion of "maximum feasible participation" on the one hand and TimeBanking on the other, lay the groundwork for an expansive vision of co-production that is premised on normative principles stressing the value and capacity of all individuals to become valued and engaged citizen contributors, helping to generate a sense of community and common good. TimeBanking, as a medium exchange created to value and reward such contributions, was designed as a new social technology to achieve the kind of social well-being that the war on poverty in the United States sought to offer. Since then, we have learned that government cannot "go it alone,"

The TimeBank movement developed its own version of co-production as a catalytic vehicle that takes "maximum feasible participation" to a new level. Co-production can supply a framework that has the potential to realize the vision laid out by leaders, such as Mahatma Gandhi and Martin Luther King, of a world where all can dwell in dignity and realize their full potential as contributors. That vision is inherently connected with a notion of justice: justice within our own species, justice to other species and justice between current and future generations. Co-production must yield more than efficient service delivery; it must also enlist the human spirit on an evolutionary journey.

NOTES

1. Ostrom describes the conditions that would heighten the probability that co-production would be "an improvement over regular government production or citizen production alone." "First, the technologies in use must generate a complementary production possibility frontier rather than merely a substitutive one . . . Second, legal options must be available to both parties [meaning that potentially productive options are not restricted or off limits]. Third, participants need to be able to build a credible commitment to one another so that if one side increases output, the other will continue at the same or higher levels. Fourth, incentives help to encourage inputs from both officials and citizens" (Ostrom, 199, 105–106).
2. Ostrom writes: "We developed the term coproduction to describe the potential relationship that could exist between the 'regular' producer and 'clients' who want to be transformed by the service into safer, better educated or healthier persons" (Ostrom, 1999, 99–100).
3. James Baldwin famously states that urban renewal is "Negro removal."
4. See also Cahn and Cahn, 1969, 14–23 for illustrations of war on poverty programs using the poor as a resource.
5. For example, the Reginald Herber-Smith program was an apprenticeship program that trained many Black lawyers.
6. For example, the Head Start Program, Job Corps, VISTA and the Legal Services Program.
7. A five-year-old, complete with pigtails, earned Time Dollars for dance lessons when she went up to a former gang member (after a truce had been negotiated) and explained: "We have trash cans here and we use them." He had just thrown a candy wrapper on the ground and her TimeBank job was to keep the grounds cleaned up.
8. The author attended a meeting at the Phillippi TimeBank in January 2009, and this is his firsthand account.

REFERENCES

Anderson, M. 1964. *The Federal Bulldozer: A Critical Analysis of Urban Renewal 1949–1962*. Cambridge, MA: MIT Press.

Avila, E., and M. H. Rose. 2009. Race, culture, politics and urban renewal: An introduction. *Journal of Urban History* 35 (3): 335–347.

Baldwin, J. 1965. The American Dream and the American Negro. *New York Times*, March 7. http://www.nytimes.com/books/98/03/29/specials/baldwin-dream.html. Accessed January 6, 2011.

Boyle, D., J. Slay, and K. Stephens. 2010. *Public Services Inside Out: Putting Co-Production into Practice*. London: New Economics Foundation, Improvement and Development Agency.

Cahn, E. S. 1994. Reinventing poverty law. *Yale Law Journal*, 103(8): 2133–2155.

Cahn, E. S. 2000. Co-producing justice: The new imperative. *UDC/DCSL Law Review*, 5, 105–123.

Cahn, E. S. 2002. *Report of Time Dollar Youth Court Accomplishments 2001–2002*. Unpublished report. Washington DC: Time Dollar Youth Court.

Cahn, E. S. 2004. *No More Throw-Away People: The Co-Production Imperative*. Washington DC: Essential Books.

Cahn, E. S. 2006. *Priceless Money*. Washington DC: TimeBanks USA.

Cahn, E. S., and J. C. Cahn. 1964. The war on poverty: A civilian perspective. *Yale Law Review* 73 (8): 1317–1352.

Cahn, E. S., and J. C. Cahn. 1969. Maximum feasible participation: A general overview. In E. S. Cahn, and B. A. Passett, eds., *Citizen Participation: A Case Book in Democracy*. Trenton: New Jersey Community Action Training Institute.

Caplan, J., L. Maker, S. Walton, and M. Luluquisen. 2008. *Sobrante Park Time Bank, 2006–2008 Documentation and Evaluation*. Unpublished report, Oakland, CA.

City School District of Albany. 2005. *"Time-Dollar Store" Program Provides Incentives to volunteer*. www.albanyschools.org/district/communications/District%20News/2009–10/Hackett%20Time%20Dollar%20store.htm. Accessed January 6, 2011.

Cummins, J., and C. Miller. 2007. *Co-Production, Social Capital, and Service Effectiveness*, London: Office for Public Management.

Dane County TimeBank. 2011. *Services Commonly Available*. http://www.danecountytimebank.org/. Accessed January 6, 2011.

Davies, G. 1996. *From Opportunity to Entitlement: The Transformation and Decline of Great Society*. Lawrence: University Press of Kansas.

D.C. Youth Grand Jury. 2000. Youth speaking truth to power: An investigation and indictment. *The Final Report of the D.C. Youth Grand Jury*. Washington DC: Youth Grand Jury.

Economic Opportunity Act of 1964, 78 Stat. 508 (repealed 1981).

Elementary and Secondary Education Act. 1965 (6318), Washington.

Freidan, B. 1963. *The Feminine Mystique*. New York: W. W. Norton.

Gartner, A., and F. Reissman. 1993. *Peer-Tutoring: Toward a New Model*. Washington DC: ERIC Clearinghouse on Teaching and Teacher Education.

Gillette, M. L. 2010. *Launching the War on Poverty: An Oral History*. New York: Oxford University Press.

Goodwin, N., J. A. Nelson, F. Ackerman, and T. Weisskopf. 2009. *Microeconomics in Context*. Armonk, NY: M. E. Sharpe.

Head Start Act. 2007. (9801 et seq.).

Improvement and Development Agency. 2010. *A Glass Half-Full: How an Asset Approach Can Improve Community Health and Well-Being*. London: Improvement and Development Agency.

Lui, M., B. Robles, B. Leondar-Wright, R. Brewer, and R. Adamson, 2006. *The Color of Wealth*. New York: New York Press.

Metropolitan Housing Group. 2010. *Clapham Park Homes Annual Report to Residents 2009–10.* www.mhp_online.co.uk/documents/CPH-TSA_131010. pdf. Accessed January 15, 2011.

The Negro and the American Promise. 1963. Online video. WGBH. http://www. pbs.org/wgbh/amex/mlk/sfeature/sf_video.html. Accessed January 12, 2011].

Ostrom, E. 1990. *Governing the Commons: The Evolution of Institutions for Collective Action*. Cambridge, UK: Cambridge University Press.

Ostrom, E. 1999. Crossing the great divide: Co-production, synergy, and development. In M. McGinnis, ed. *Polycentric Governance and Development: Readings from the Workshop in Political Theory and Policy Analysis*. Ann Arbor: Michigan University Press.

Parent Support Network of Rhode Island. 2011. *Vision and Mission*. www.psnri. org/html%20docs/overview/visionmission.html. Accessed January 16, 2011.

Peterson, P. E. 2009. Nobel Prize winner Elinor Ostrom and her theory of co-production. *Education Next*. http://educationnext.org/nobel-prize-winner-elinor-ostrom-and-her-theory-of-co-production. Accessed January 12, 2011.

Queen's Award for Voluntary Service 2008. *2008 Winner Case Studies*. www. direct.gov.uk/prsd_consum_dg/groups/dg_digitalassets/@dg/@en/documents/digitalasset/dg_181024.pdf. Accessed January 12, 2011.

Royer, J. 2000. Toys for have-nots: bridging the great tech divide. *Chicago Reader Newspaper*, December 22.

Schorr, E. B. 1988. *Within Our Reach: Breaking the Cycle of Disadvantage*. New York: Doubleday.

Simon, M. 2010. *Your Money or Your Life: Time for Both,* Whitechapel, UK: Freedom Favours.

Stossel, S. 2004. *Sarge: The Life and Times of Sargent Shriver*. Washington DC: Smithsonian Books.

TimeBanking UK. 2011. www.timebanking.org/. Accessed January 15, 2011.

TimeBanking Wales. 2011. http://www.timebankingwales.org.uk. Accessed January 15, 2011.

Time Dollar Institute. 2003. *The Time Dollar How-To-Manual: A Comprehensive Gide to Creating and Running Your Time Dollar Exchange*. Washington DC: Time Dollar Institute.

Time Dollar Youth Court. 2008. *A Five Year Look at Participation in the Time Dollar Youth Diversion Program: Progress Report 2004–2008*. Washington DC: Time Dollar Youth Court.

U.S. Constitution. 1865. (amend. XIII, § 1).

U.S. Department of Commerce, National Telecommunications and Information Administration. 1999. *Evaluation of the Telecommunications and Information Infrastructure Assistance Program,* Washington DC: U.S. Department of Commerce.

U.S. Department of Justice. 2011a. *Community Capacity Development Office*. www.ojp.gov/ccdo/ws/welcome.html. Accessed January 12, 2011.

U. S. Department of Justice. 2011b. *Community Oriented Policing Services*. www. cops.usdoj.gov/Default.asp?Item=36. Accessed January 12, 2011.

Visiting Nurse Service of New York. 2009. *Impact of the TimeBank of Its Membership: Research Study Results*. New York: Visiting Nurse Service of New York.

Volunteer Development Scotland. 2011. *TimeBanking Scotland*. www.vds.org. uk/Volunteers/VolunteerNow/TimeBankingScotland/tabid/156/Default.aspx. Accessed January 15, 2011.

8 Co-Production and Network Structures in Public Education

David O. Porter

EMERGENCE OF THE CONCEPT OF CO-PRODUCTION

The notion of co-production emerged at particular time and place—during the 1970s in the United States. Americans were struggling to cope with a vast increase in public sector activities that resulted from a myriad of events and initiatives during the 1960s. The continuing arms race of the cold war, the civil rights movement, urban violence, the Great Society and the Vietnam War converged to produce an unprecedented scope and scale of government activity at all levels—federal, state and local. Not surprisingly, in pluralist America there were competing notions about the institutional arrangements for governments as they grappled with diverse demands for administrative effectiveness, citizen participation and democratic accountability.

These discussions were driven by both ideological and technical considerations. Large government bureaucracies were perceived by many as insensitive and ineffective. Some of the alternatives to direct provision by large government agencies were sought from the discipline of political economy, especially in the case of services that involved citizens directly when they were created. Vouchers (or voucher-like instruments) for education, housing allowances, food stamps and health insurance for senior citizens emerged as alternatives to direct provision by government. These proposals and/or legislation were sometimes associated with pro-market biases. Most obviously, education vouchers were vigorously advocated by Milton Friedman (1962). But political economy approaches were not uniformly, or perhaps even predominately, associated with antigovernment and/or pro-market advocacy. Many analysts were motivated to improve effectiveness by involving citizens/clients more directly in the creation of government services, as a technical consideration. The concept of co-production emerged in the middle of these ideological and technical debates.

That many public services are co-produced was in general discussion in 1970s. Many investigators realized that the model of the traditional economic transaction did not apply to what Garn, Springer and Flax at the Urban Institute called "jointly produced output."

[T]he person being served (the client or customer) is inevitably part of the production process, if there is to be any production whatsoever. Therefore, the resources, motivations, and skills brought to bear by the client or consumer are much more intimately connected with the level of achieved output than in the case of goods production. The output is always a jointly produced output. (1976, 14–15)

For Garn and his colleagues, this was a production function in which inputs such as "resources, motivations, and skills" provided by a client or consumer are combined with inputs provided by a producer to jointly produce a good or service. But it was Elinor and Vincent Ostrom and their colleagues at the Workshop in Political Theory and Policy Analysis at Indiana University who gave joint production sustained attention: "the productive role of consumers as co-producers of the services they receive has been a continuing interest for us" (Parks et al., 1981, 382). They coined the word *co-production* and sharply distinguished it from traditional production functions.

Skepticism about the ineffectiveness and unresponsiveness of centralized public bureaucracies were enduring concerns for Vincent and Elinor Ostrom, co-founders of the workshop. In *Intellectual Crisis in American Public Administration* (1989, first published 1972), Vincent Ostrom introduced mainstream public administration scholars to political economy. He argued in part that any advantages from economies of scale or opportunities for specializations that derived from consolidated bureaucratic agencies were often offset by scale inefficiencies and unresponsiveness to citizen preferences. It was in this atmosphere of skepticism about the advocacy of consolidated metropolitan governments and school districts that the Ostroms introduced their notion of co-production:

> Users of many public services are themselves essential co-producers. Teachers cannot produce education without the co-productive efforts of students; police cannot produce public order without the co-productive efforts of citizens. Public servants help to accomplish these tasks. They rarely produce the results themselves. Units of government of varying size are necessary to take account of the diverse situations and patterns of community preferences that may exist in different and overlapping communities that make joint use of various public goods and services. (Ostrom, 1989, 148)

Several scholars at the workshop collaborated with the Ostroms over the years to define and develop the concept. An article by a team of workshop scholars summarized their notions about co-production:

> [I]ndividual consumers or groups of consumers, acting outside of their regular production roles, may contribute to the production of some goods and services they consume. In such cases they act as consumer producers.

> In many instances, consumer production is an essential complement to the efforts of regular producers; without the productive activities of consumers nothing of value will result. This appears to be characteristic of much public service production. (Parks et al., 1981, 381)

The relationships between producer and consumer in a co-production function differ significantly from the relationships assumed between producer and consumer in a traditional economic transaction. In a traditional economic transaction, producer and consumer have discreet roles and discreet self-interests. A producer's role is to create a good and offer it for sale. A consumer's role is to express his or her preference by offering money equal to their preference for a specific quantity and quality. A co-production function includes inputs—"resources, motivations and skills" (Garn et al., 1976)—from the consumer as well as the producer. The "regular producer" and "consumer producer" jointly contribute inputs in the creation of output (Parks, et al., 1981).

This overlap of the consumer role with the production role leads to a number of difficulties in using traditional economic analysis in situations of co-production. For instance, Rosentraub and Sharp (1981) note that during a co-production process consumers often change their perception and preferences, or alter the characteristics of the service:

> [I]f, in the process of contributing to service production, citizens change their conception of what the service should be and direct their contributions toward the production of a service of a different character, assessment of [economic] efficiency becomes more complicated. From the perspective of the public school teacher, youth who teach "subversive" ideas to other youth may be subtracting from rather than adding to, service delivery; from the perspective of the "consumers" themselves, there may be more education not less. In traditional economics, this problem is not considered; the efficient level of production of a good depends in part upon the different valuations of that good by different potential consumers but, in such analysis, the nature of the good is stable. In considering productions [sic] of human services, the efficiency problem is complicated by the fact that in contributing to the production of a service, consumers can fundamentally alter its character. (Rosentraub and Sharp, 1981, 516)

Folbre identified a similar problem for the "idealized competitive markets of conventional economic theory" because the "process of exchange itself may modify the exchangers—altering product quality in unanticipated ways" (2008, 1769). Producer and consumer may develop emotional "attachments":

> Unlike many other services, successful care work . . . requires collaboration between worker and consumer. Doctors often must cajole

patients to take medication or change their life-styles; teachers must persuade students to study. Child care and elder care workers require a high level of personal cooperation from their wards. Care services have idiosyncratic and emotionally sticky aspects that affect both their cost and their quality—people's preferences and feelings can be modified by the very process of exchange. They form attachments. (ibid., 1770)

Elinor Ostrom added a significant dimension to the notion of co-production in 1996, when she used it to bridge the "Great Divide" between "Market and State," thereby integrating institutional arrangements from both markets and bureaucracies. She went beyond the notion of a co-production function and added normative content—co-production as an alternative institutional rule:

> I think the great divide between Market and the State or between Government and Civil society is a conceptual trap arising from overly rigid disciplinary walls surrounding the study of human institutions . . . I proceed on the assumption that contrived walls separating analysis of potentially synergistic phenomena into separate parts miss the potential for synergy. By developing more fully the theory of co-production and its relevance to the study of synergy and development, I hope to change the views of social scientists to the hypothetical "Great Divide." . . . By co-production, I mean the process through which inputs used to produce a good or service are contributed by individuals who are not "in" the same organization. The "regular" producer of education, health, or infrastructure services is most frequently a government agency. Whether the regular producer is the only producer of these goods and services depends on both the nature of the good or service itself and the incentives that encourage the active participation of others. All public goods and services are potentially produced by the regular producer and by those who are frequently referred to as the client. The term "client" is a passive term. Clients are acted upon. Co-production implies that citizens can play an active role in producing public goods and services of consequence to them. (Ostrom, 1996, 85–86)

The Ostroms and workshop scholars, then, have used the notion of co-production in two related but distinct ways. Earlier research drew heavily on political economics and an analysis of the relationship between the producer and consumer. The co-production function for a good or service combined inputs from both a "regular producer" and a "consumer producer" (Park et al., 1981). In later research Elinor Ostrom (1997) also considers co-production an alternative institutional rule that may or may not be used to create a service.

The differences between these two uses of the concept are not trivial. In the first, co-production is associated with a specific good or service where inputs from both producer and consumer are combined. Examples are given, for example, education services (Ostrom, 1989; Parks et al., 1981; Whitaker, 1980), in which if co-production is omitted the service will not be created. Inputs from the consumer producer are required to create a public service in the first usage; but in the second usage, inputs from consumers may be contingently added to enhance qualities and quantities of a public service.

The second usage is more normative. Co-production adds qualities to a service even if the service could be created without inputs from the consumer producer. Co-production becomes an alternative institutional rule through which decentralized institutions may contribute to the creation of a public service. If combined with complimentary institutional rules that permit, facilitate or encourage inputs from consumer producers, a co-produced service is changed because different or additional inputs are included in the co-production function. Institutional rules may include, for instance, procedures for more citizen participation and/or democratic decision processes.

Both uses of the concept of co-production are necessary for a full analysis of co-production in education. The co-production function for education services requires inputs from the teacher (traditional producer) and student (traditional consumer), at what I call the student/teacher nexus. There will be no learning without active, willing participation by the student. There are also a relatively large number of contingent inputs from parents, student peers, community organizations and public media that may impact the quality and quantity of education services. Education services of differing quality and quantity result as the co-productive activities of students, parents and districts vary. If these inputs are few or omitted, education services may still be created but will have very different qualities and quantities. Further, there are strong norms that students, parents, student peers and others should contribute positively to co-production. These norms and the resulting practices may be considered as some of the institutional rules bearing on the co-production function for education services.

But before moving to a detailed analysis of the concept of co-production as applied to education services, it may be useful to provide a somewhat selective summary of the more general literature on the concept:

- Co-production refers to a co-production function in which both the producer and consumer provide inputs as a good or service is created (Ostrom, 1989; Parks et al, 1981; Garn et al., 1976).
- The process of co-production involves consumers[1] in positive, voluntary and active interactions with the producer (Brudney and England, 1983).
- Resources provided by consumers may be substitutes, complementary or required by the co-productive technology (Ostrom, 1997).
- In most cases, resource inputs provided by consumers are not included in the regular budgetary process and are therefore undervalued, ignored or in other ways not taken into consideration by "regular producers" (Gross, 1964; Porter, 1973).

- Co-production may occur at one or more steps of the productive process. Processes such as policy formation, planning, managing, coordinating and evaluation may be co-produced (Ostrom, 1996; Pestoff, Osborne, and Brandsen, 2006).
- Consumers are often transformed during the co-productive process in ways that either enhances the qualities and quantities of the service or as a part of the service itself (Whitaker, 1980).
- Co-produced services are inherently more variable than those produced without co-production. The most fundamental reasons for variability are great differences between and among the consumer producers and variability in their relationships with regular producers (Porter, 2007, 2009). Some citizens/clients/students are advantaged (or disadvantaged) in their access to regular producers (Rosentraub and Sharp, 1981). Some citizens/clients/students are more skilled as co-producers of services (ibid.).
- And, because co-production involves mutual adjustments between consumers and producers, coordination and administration must include a strong decentralized, localized component. Uniformity in the quantity and quality of the service across jurisdictions is highly unlikely (Porter, 1976; Rosentraub and Sharp, 1981)

CO-PRODUCTION OF EDUCATION SERVICES

The co-production function for education is a very particular type of co-production. Inputs are required from students. Without active, willing and voluntary participation by students, there is no learning. Workshop scholar Gordon Whitaker emphasized that in education the "primary objective" is "the transformation of the student and that the student must be involved" (Whitaker, 1980, 240):

> In "delivering" services the agent helps the person being served to make the desired sorts of changes. Whether it is learning new ideas or new skills, acquiring healthier habits, or changing one's outlook on family or society, only the individual served can accomplish the change. He or she is a vital "co-producer" of any personal transformation that occurs. The agent can supply encouragement, suggest options, illustrate techniques, and provide guidance and advice, but the agent alone cannot bring about the change. Rather than an agent presenting a "finished product" to the citizen, agent and citizen together produce the desired transformation.

Rosentraub and Sharp reinforced the idea that when consumer inputs are required, the "role of the professional agent" is as a "helping agent":

[Whitaker's] definition is obviously linked to a particular understanding of human services—one that emphasizes that human services involve a transformation in the recipient of the service. While Whitaker does not ultimately restrict the co-production concept to this type of service, he stresses the special importance of the concept in this situation. This approach to co-production has two important implications—the *necessity* for client involvement if any service is to be achieved and the role of the professional as a helping agent. As Whitaker states: "The agent can supply encouragement, suggest options, illustrate techniques, and provide guidance and advice, but the agent alone cannot bring about the change (in the client.)" Note also that his approach to co-production emphasizes a micro-view of the process, i.e., it stresses the direct, personal interaction between a service delivery agent and a client. (1981, 509; emphasis in original)

The requirement for student involvement at the student/teacher nexus is particularly stringent in the creation of education services. In the absence of voluntary, active co-production by a student, the prescribed learning for a course will not take place.

Many potential co-production inputs to education services are discretionary, contributed at points away from the student/teacher nexus. Coleman (1966), Cremin (1998), Kozol (1991) and Rothstein (2004)—to name but a few of a long list of researchers—have documented contributions to student learning from parents, peers, community and religious organizations and public media. Also, on the teacher side of the student/teacher nexus, peer teachers, principals, student advisors and other professionals make contributions to learning processes. These contributions are contingent, that is, they may or may not occur. If regularly and skillfully contributed, these inputs enhance the qualities and quantities of education services. Expectations about the qualities and quantities of education services usually assume that inputs from outside the student/teacher nexus are effectively contributed.

To summarize, the co-production function for education services includes two broad types of co-production. A first type of required co-production occurs at the student/teacher nexus. If students are not voluntarily and actively involved, the intended learning will not occur. The teacher must also be involved, if for no other reason than to certify that the learning for the prescribed course of study was achieved. Much of the prescribed learning, however, may take place in spite of teacher contributions. A second type of contingent co-production occurs on either side of the student/teacher nexus. Inputs from parents, student peers, more or less effective teachers, community organizations and public media contribute to the co-production of education service. These contributions are contingent and vary in intensity and quality.

CO-PRODUCTION AT THE STUDENT/TEACHER NEXUS

A brief vignette of the beginning of a very ordinary day at school unambiguously illustrates, first, required co-production at student/teacher nexus and, second, opportunities for enhancing co-production by family and school peers.

Vignette

Tom, age ten, is roused by his parents an hour and a half before he must walk out the door to meet his school bus. He dresses in clothes purchased and kept clean by his parents. A parent makes sure Tom eats a sufficient breakfast. As he heads out the door, a parent checks to see he has all of his books, school supplies and lunch or lunch money. Tom is greeted at school by his home room teacher. Instruction begins by reading aloud a chapter in social studies. The teacher and students listen to each other, offering corrections and help as needed. Next the teacher moves to a lesson in mathematics, introducing a new concept on the blackboard. Students are asked to complete a workbook exercise that includes a couple of story problems requiring reading comprehension and reasoning. The teacher and student peers help Tom figure out how to begin the calculations. Tom is initially stumped on the story problems. He takes longer than most students learning to read carefully and then figuring out the problem to be solved. He gives up and begins to talk with other children a couple of times. Tom and another child do not return their full attention to the workbook exercise and do not master solving the problems. The teacher observes that Tom and his friend are not attentive to their math lesson and makes a note for the after school teacher aide to complete this assignment with Tom and his friend.

Getting Tom out of bed, fed and off to school is overseen by parents. The teacher observed and reacted to Tom's learning. When he faltered, the teacher assisted him. When that assistance was not sufficient, the teacher arranged for an additional resource, a teacher aide. Thus, a "self-organizing" process of co-producing education services was coordinated jointly by Tom, his teacher and his parents. To be successful, Tom must have sufficient motivation for learning prescribed lessons, give attention during class sessions, attempt to understand new materials and complete assignments. His teacher must take actions to help each child in the learning process, observe learning-related behaviors of each child in class and mobilize resources from outside the classroom that may enhance learning.

More generally, the teacher, Tom and his parents are reciprocally interdependent and exercise discretion in the course of their mutual adjustments as they co-produce education services. Boundaries between the classroom, the families, the school, the school district and their task environments are open, with continuous adjustments to meet constraints and contingencies at the student/ teacher nexus (Parks et al., 1981; Thompson, 1967; Whitaker, 1980).

As a summary, I want to reinforce three aspects of co-production implicit in the vignette. First, co-production is not optional when it comes to education services. "Students can supply much of their own education in the absence of teacher inputs, but teachers can supply little education without inputs from students" (Parks et al., 1981, 384). Second, as the Ostroms and their colleagues recognized, there is an inherent asymmetry in co-productive contributions by student and teacher. If a student is absent, inattentive, actively resistant, intellectually unable or unprepared, there will be no learning and no education services. Whitaker makes the point that teacher and student must willingly participate in mutual adjustment to be successful in the co-production of a public service such as education:

> In an exchange of this type [mutual adjustment], both the citizen and the agent share responsibility for deciding what action to take. The citizen co-producer is not a "client" in the sense that he or she is not a supplicant seeking the favor of the agent. (Whitaker, 1980, 244)

Finally, significant inputs are provided from outside the classroom by parents, peers, community organizations and others. Few of the costs for these resources are included in the school's budget.

EMPIRICAL FINDINGS SUPPORT CO-PRODUCTION

A large number of studies have found that education services are created through a co-production function. These findings are among the few generalizations in social science that have withstood repeated challenges and replication from a number of perspectives and methodologies. Efforts associated with U.S. President Lyndon B. Johnson's war on poverty were the catalyst for the first spate of these studies, most notably a major, multiyear study lead by James S. Coleman (Coleman et al., 1966). Title I of the Elementary-Secondary Education Act of 1965 annually earmarked millions of dollars for school districts to use on compensatory programs for low-income and minority students. Coleman, however, found little or inconsistent evidence that the extra inputs to school districts narrowed the achievement gap between low income/minority students and their middle class peers. He found instead that inputs from parents, student peers and community environment (i.e., co-production) explained at least as much of the variation in student achievement as inputs related to schools and teachers. These findings have been amplified and verified in numerous subsequent studies.

> [S]cholarly efforts over four decades have consistently confirmed Coleman's core finding; no analyst has been able to attribute less than two-thirds of the variation in achievement among schools to the family characteristics of their students. (Rothstein, 2004, 13–14)

A couple of recent Colman-inspired research projects give relevant details on inputs by "consumer producers" to the co-production processes. Melhuish and colleagues (2008) studied the impact of preschools on later academic performance. They found three variables associated with a student's home life that impacted later learning more than the effectiveness of a preschool or primary school. Mother's education, home learning environment and family socioeconomic status were all shown to have substantial influence on later student achievement:

> HLE [home living environment] effects were substantial and occurred across the whole population. The HLE had low correlations with parents' socioeconomic status or education . . . and showed independent effects slightly less than mother's education but greater than father's education and family income. This indicates that what parents do is as important as who parents are. (Melhuish et al., 2008, 1162)

Lahaie (2008) studied the impact of parental inputs on achievement by students from immigrant families. Lahaie developed a relatively comprehensive, three-part variable on parental involvement. The first part, Cognitive Learning at Home, included literacy activities such as reading a book to child, telling stories to child; activities with academic content, such as building projects, teaching about nature, creating art, singing songs, playing games; other activities without academic content, such as sports and doing chores. The second part, Cognitive Learning Outside the Home, tracked the types of care arrangements in the years before kindergarten-parental care, center-based care, Head Start, other forms of care. The third part, Parental Involvement at School, was a dichotomous measure on whether the parent met with teacher at least once during the school year (ibid., 688–689). She also included as covariates the usual list of child and family characteristics—birth weight, current weight and height, age, gender, race/ethnicity, family structure, family size, city/rural, region of country, educational attainment of each parent, work status for both mother and father, mother's age at first birth, household income, family use of welfare assistance (ibid., 689).

She found that for immigrant children, "[t]he joint impact of all in-home cognitive learning activities is significant for both math scores and English proficiency" (ibid., 695). Lahaie also found that for children from both immigrant and non-immigrant families, "[a]ll cognitive learning activities in home still have a joint impact that is significant. . . . Parental involvement appears beneficial for all children and especially for the children of immigrants whose parents speak another language" (ibid., 702).

The Coleman report (1966) sparked a decades-long policy dispute about the efficacy of increased expenditures in public schools that, in its own way, demonstrate how widely the idea that education services are co-production is accepted. Conservative analysts reasoned that because inputs from outside the schools had a bigger impact on learning than inputs from the schools, there was less justification for increased public expenditure on schools. Hanushek conducted a number of very careful economic analyses where he and his collaborators found that student outcomes on standardized tests were not be correlated with changes in such school inputs as lower student/faculty ratios, higher teacher compensation or enhanced professional qualifications for teachers (Hanushek 1996, 2007; Rivkin, Hanushek, and Kain, 2005). In the end, Hanushek ends up heavily discounting inputs from the schools and teachers—the "regular producers." Inputs from non-school sources make such substantial contributions to student achievement on standardized tests that he is reluctant to recommend increases in school budgets:

> The existing research suggests inefficiency in the provision of schooling. It does not indicate that school do[es] not matter. Nor does it indicate that money and resources never impact achievement. The accumulated research surrounding estimation of education production functions simply says there currently is no clear, systematic relationship between [school-provided] resources and student outcomes. (Hanushek, 2007, 6)

A group of researchers at Columbia Teachers College, while they strongly agreed that education services are co-produced, nonetheless rejected Hanushek's conclusion that putting more money into school districts probably would not lead to improved student outcomes. Rothstein, formerly an education affairs journalist with the *New York Times*, summarized their position in *Class and Schools: Using Social, Economic, and Educational Reform to Close the Black-White Achievement Gap* (2004). Schools, he argued, make a difference in learning, but they cannot by themselves make up for the differences in skills and motivation that children bring to the classroom:

> Think of Coleman's finding in this way: all students learn in school, but schools have demonstrated limited ability to affect differences in the rate at which children from different social classes progress. Children from higher social classes come to school with more skills and are more prepared to learn than children from lower classes. All children learn in school, but those from lower classes, on average, do not learn so much faster that they can close the achievement gap. (Rothstein, 2004, 15)

To close the achievement gap between middle class and underperforming poor and minority students, the Columbia researchers recommended concurrent increases in expenditures in schools, public health, housing subsidies, child care and adult education. Rothstein summarized their case for co-productive inputs from outside the "regular producer," that is, the school, as follows:

These differences [in achievement] appear not only in how families can support children from current income, but also in how families support children from other economic resources like savings for college, home equity, or access to stable rental housing; in their varied childrearing philosophies, conversational styles, literacy practices, role modeling, and parental social networks; in children's health that impacts learning, with differences in vision, hearing, dental care, lead poisoning, asthma, immunizations, birth weight and maternal smoking and alcohol use; in the ethnically and racially patterned cultural expectations about the payoff to education; and in the athletic and other enriching experiences that children enjoy in the after school hours and in the summer. Each of these contributes only a tiny bit to the learning gap between lower-class and middle-class children, but combined, the effects could be huge, and it is hard to see how even the greatest schools could overcome them. (ibid., 61)

The contributions of such inputs as stable housing, literacy practices and role modeling take place, for the most part, outside of the student/teacher nexus. They enhance the qualities of the mutual adjustments at the student/ teacher nexus, and because all too often there are too few of these enhancements, achievement gaps persist between students coming from homes and communities where "school learning" skills are emphasized and those coming from homes where they are not.

IMPORTANT INSIGHTS IN FOUR POLICY AREAS

What are the payoffs from a careful analysis of co-production? In this section, I consider policies in four areas in which an analysis of co-production provides special insights.

Skills to Co-Produce

The co-production function in education requires that students, parents and teachers work together. But is it reasonable to assume that all students, parents and teachers will be equally skilled co-producers? Both Hanushek and Rothstein give ample evidence that the co-productive skills of students, teachers and families vary greatly. Some teachers are better at co-producing than others (Hanushek, 2007; Ripley, 2010; Wingert, 2010); some students and their families are more skilled at co-producing than others (Rosentraub and Sharp, 1981; Rothstein, 2004). Rosentraub and Sharp (1981) are almost singular among researchers on co-production in recognizing: (1) that some parents and students are more skilled in co-producing education services, (2) that these variations in skills are systematically associated with the education and income levels of parents and (3) that students and families with better co-productive skills often receive a disproportionate share of education services:

> Implicitly, co-production appears to raise equity issues. Wealthier, better-educated, or non-minority citizens may be more willing or able to engage in co-production activities. To the extent that co-production raises the quality of services received, it may exacerbate gaps between the advantaged and disadvantaged classes. (Rosentraub and Sharp, 1981, 517)

Aside from Rosentraub and Sharp, attention on variations in co-productive skills has focused almost exclusively on teachers. In the Coleman report, education researchers learned that there was more variation in student achievement scores within a school than between schools and/or districts, and that these variations were associated with variations in co-productive skills among teachers (Hanushek, 2007; Rothstein, 2004). There is strong evidence, in fact, that the most important school-provided inputs are stimulating and skillful teachers (Rivkin, Hanushek, and Kain, 2005). To be certified, a professional teacher must complete a number of specialized pedagogical courses, but evidence that these courses actually contribute to making outstanding teachers is thin. How to train or even identify excellent teachers remains something of a mystery (Ripley, 2010).

There has been far less systematic attention given to improving student and parental skills in co-production. Students are routinely advised by their teachers to improve study habits, but that advice is almost always ad hoc with little or no systematic follow-up. Faculty and staff in most public schools annually engage in ritualized efforts to involve parents in the learning of their children. Given the well-documented importance of parent, peer and community inputs to the co-production of education services, these efforts are surprisingly superficial and inadequate. Few staff or faculty are specifically assigned to improve the skills of parents, or to specifically train teachers to evaluate and improve the co-productive skills of parents and community organizations.

Motivation to Co-Produce

How to sustain, day in and day out, the motivations of students, parents and teachers is a central concern in the co-production of education. Without active participation students cannot learn. Parents cannot be commanded by school officials to contribute essential enhancing inputs. An unmotivated or alienated teacher is less likely to capture the interests of students and parents. Students, parents and teachers must be motivated to voluntarily participate.

Younger students famously spend more time thinking about recess than arithmetic and language arts. American high schools have long rationalized expensive extracurricular activities as vehicles for keeping students motivated. Requirements for passing grades as a prerequisite for participation in sports or popular music programs have kept many distracted adolescents focused sufficiently on their academic subjects to graduate. Motivating parents who are untrained in core academic skills to become actively involved in co-producing takes more than well-intentioned exhortations. Finding ways to motivate and reward teachers is currently receiving a great deal of attention (e.g., see Ripley). Policy makers seem to agree that motivated (and skilled) teachers are at least as important as a teacher's knowledge of his or her subject. In all three cases—student, parent and teacher—an understanding of the co-production function in education suggests that systematic long-term efforts be made to sustain and augment their motivations to participate in co-production.

There has been considerable indirect attention given in the co-production literatures to the issue of motivating consumers to perform their co-production roles. Brudney and England (1983) recognized that co-production must be voluntary. Implicitly, it follows that for a citizen to voluntarily participate in co-production he or she will have to be motivated by self-interest, civic obligation or belonging to a co-producing social group. For Whitaker (1980), the transformative nature of co-production is an essential characteristic of co-production in a service such as education. To be transformed, he implies, a student must be motivated. Alford (2002) is among the few investigators to specifically study why citizens voluntarily participate in co-production:

> Material rewards and sanctions are ineffective in eliciting the requisite client contribution for all but the simplest of [co-production] tasks. Instead, clients are motivated by the more complex nonmaterial incentives that co-production scholars have identified as influencing other kinds of co-producers such as volunteers or citizens: intrinsic rewards, sociality, and expressive values. (Alford, 2002, 51)

In the management literatures more generally, studies of motivation are almost exclusively restricted to problems of motivating employees, that is, producers (Miner, 2002). Except in specific industries, such as health care, little attention has been given to motivating consumers to co-produce. Even so, many of these studies are relevant to co-production in education.

Budgets for Co-Produced Inputs

A co-production function is defined as combining inputs from both the "regular producer" and the "regular consumer" to create a good or service. Conventional accounting and budgeting practices focus almost exclusively on inputs provided by regular producers. Few conventions or concepts attempt to account for inputs from "consumer producers." This is a crippling omission in education services. As we demonstrated, half or more of the inputs come from or through the regular consumer, that is, from students, parents, local community institutions and public media.

Even following the most advanced practices, school budgets are limited to a set of accounts listing official revenues and expenditures in monetary units. How much revenue is allocated from local government? How much money is allocated to pay teachers? And so forth. Such budgets are well suited to monitor whether public monies are spent as allocated and are not stolen. But if used to evaluate effectiveness in co-producing education services, they unavoidably provide an incomplete, distorted analysis. Calculations in any reliable scheme of cost accounting must include all inputs into the co-production processes. In a school budget, there is not even a simple listing of the essential inputs from students, parents and community institutions.

Gross conceived a budgetary process that included resources mobilized from all sources, only some of which are available for purchase (1964, 699–702). In education, many of the most important of these resources are intangible, indirect and not exchanged through sale and purchase. For instance, one of the more important resource suppliers is a student's mother. More specifically, the mother's education is the strongest predictor of student achievement (Melhuish et al., 2008). She supplies this resource through years of conversations, encouragement, physical nutrition and protection. When a mother's inputs are in short supply or not available, it has been very difficult to find adequate or effective substitutes (Rothstein, 2004). Without more systematic accounts of all inputs to co-production, teachers and other school leaders can only guess at what resources may need augmentation.

It will be a long learning process as schools, policy makers and researchers struggle to assemble accounts for the inputs from "consumer producers" in education. It must be attempted, I strongly suggest, if schools are ever to come to grips with what is *perceived* to be chronic ineffectiveness and a lack of accountability in education systems. Basic questions on how to organize, coordinate and administer the co-production of education will not be effectively confronted until this is done. Industrial firms went through a similar struggle in the early twentieth century as they adapted strategies and organization structures (Chandler, 1962).

Polycentric Network Structures

With education services, there is a fundamental constraint in that no education services can be co-produced without willing, active participation by a student at the student/teacher nexus. In addition, there are many inputs from the immediate task environment. Students are impacted by contributions from parents, peers, community and many others. Enhancements by teachers may be affected by the particular skills and personality of the teacher, interactions with colleagues and general working conditions. All of these inputs are contingent and may or may not be available or contributed effectively. In current assessments of schools, however, it is assumed that the fundamental constraint of willing, active student participation is satisfied and assumed that enhancing inputs from parents and teachers are made in sufficient quantity and quality. Neither of these assumptions would be as readily made after even a cursory analysis of the co-production function for education. It is unrealistic to assume that all students will be willing, active participants; that all parents are equally effective in playing their roles in co-producing education services; and that all peer and community inputs will be efficacious.

The institutional arrangements through which these reciprocal interdependencies have been coordinated are polycentric network structures. The student/teacher nexus spans the boundary of the focal organization, that is, the school district; crucial enhancing (or contributing) inputs are unambiguously contributed from participants located in the task environment. Therefore, a more comprehensive conception of the purposive unit of action must be taken into account because of the network structures inherent in a co-produced service. Adjustments to the design of the focal organization need to take account of the polycentric network structures in which it is embedded and to mobilize and coordinate important inputs that come from outside the boundaries of the focal organization.

The polycentric network structures for education services have numerous and dispersed nodes of co-production and decision making. Many of these nodes are self-organizing (Ostrom, 1999). The primary polycentric node should organize around the student/teacher nexus (see especially Thompson, 1967, 61–64). Discretionary actions by student and teacher continually mediate through mutual adjustments the reciprocal interdependence inherent in the co-production function. These adjustments are dependent on the motivations and skills of students and teachers. In other words, the learning prescribed in an education curriculum will not occur unless student and teacher voluntarily and actively co-produce.

There are a number of polycentric nodes clustered adjacent to the student/teacher nexus. Their inputs enhance the co-productive activities of the student/teacher nexus. Learning is enhanced if parents are skilled and motivated to co-produce; enhanced if parents get their children to school each day, provide proper food, insist homework is finished, provide proper health care; enhanced if parents are good role models; and enhanced if students and families share enriching experiences. Learning is enhanced if teachers learn from their peers how to be effective in motivating and engaging students; enhanced if school facilities are adequate; and enhanced if the school district is effective in engaging and training parents in co-production. But these enhancements cannot succeed without at least minimal success at the nexus. And these enhancements are all contingent. Learning can take place without them, although it is clearly enhanced if they do take place.

The literatures on networks have largely overlooked co-production as the basis for organizing networks. Studies that dealt with aspects of education services, for instance, did not deal with co-production at the student/ teacher nexus. Meier and O'Toole (2003) studied networking among school district superintendents; Pestoff in Chapter 2 of this volume analyzed co-productive contributions by parent-teacher associations (PTAs). While superintendents and PTAs indisputably make important contributions to the performance of school districts and schools, their networking and co-production activities are several steps removed from the network structures and co-production so central to the core activity of an education system.

It is routinely asserted that managing network structures is fraught with complexity (e.g., Ospina and Sax-Carranza, 2010). I am not convinced. When a co-production function is understood by participants in the network structure, they self-organize and coordinate their activities around their shared commitment to and understanding of the co-production function. There is relatively little central direction, few allocations of resources through market transactions. Yet, as the vignette about Tom's school day illustrated, instrumentally effective actions are self-coordinated.

Understandings of the working of the co-production function for education are not, to be sure, uniform. This core technology is instrumentally uncertain. Nor is there consensus on which of several possible educational outcomes should get priority. But even with these uncertainties and ambiguities, Tom's parents knew they should help him get up each morning in time to arrive at school on time. Tom knew he should pay attention and try to master the day's lessons. The teacher monitored and responded to Tom's progress each day. In the aggregate—day to day, for ten, twenty or a hundred students—these mutually adjusted, coordinated activities may be considered to be so numerous as to be beyond the grasp of any single participant or administrator. And so they are. But a self-organizing, self-monitoring division of labor is coordinated via a shared understanding of the co-production function. Participants may be stumped or overwhelmed from time to time, but few would characterize their day-to-day experiences co-producing education services as inherently more complex or difficult than many other problems in their lives (Hjern and Porter, 1981).

A final task in this section is to integrate the concept of polycentricity and the co-production function for education. I rely on the classic essay by Vincent Ostrom for my discussion of polycentricity (Ostrom, 1999). Ostrom argued that a continuing polycentric system would satisfy four conditions (ibid., 59–60): first, the provision and co-production of the service must be too diverse and scattered to be comprehended by a central administrator. The co-production of education services easily satisfies this condition. Second, participants spontaneously self-organize:

> Spontaneity implies that patterns of organization within a polycentric system will be self-generating or self-organizing in the sense that

individuals will have incentives to create or institute appropriate patters of ordered relationships. (ibid., 59)

Polycentric network structures in education services self-organize around a shared understanding of the division of labor inherent in the co-production function. And, it should added, self-organizing around a production function is not unique to education services. A central element of the industrial revolution was a division of labor around the steps in a production function, thus allowing more specialization and more effective use of machinery. An automobile, for example, is created by a network of more and less specialized workers coordinating their activities through the logic of the production functions for assembling cars. Thompson argued that the central activities of organizations should be arranged to satisfy the requirements of the core technology. And, almost by default, private sector firms self-organize around their core technology (Thompson, 1967). Public sector organizations, on the other hand, have often used other criteria as organizing principles—democracy, ethics, responsiveness and universal access.

Third, conditions of entry and exit must be publically understood. In the case of education services, participants know conditions of entry and exit through general rules and expectations set by the state, learning certifications formulated by education professionals, administrative rules and conventions made by school districts and the organizing logic of the co-production function. Motives to enter, continue or exit are grounded, in large part, by self-interest and the personal desires to learn.

Fourth, some of the participants within the polycentric network structures must enforce the rules and norms of the system:

> If individuals or units operating in a polycentric order have incentives to take actions to enforce general rules of conduct, then polycentricity will become an increasingly viable form of organization. (Ostrom, 1999, 60)

Teachers, disciple-based professions, school districts and states enforce conduct by promulgating rules regarding eligibility to participate, certifying mastery of courses of study, and granting diplomas and degrees. Enforcement is finely calibrated to the performance of individual students in each examination, course, specialization and diploma. Students and parents also have strong incentives to enforce compliance. The value of certifications and diplomas will be degraded if rules are inconsistently enforced.

There must be many detailed case studies of local education institutions in which there are descriptions of sustaining polycentric network structures. One of the next steps in this research project will be to survey those case studies. In the meantime, I offer as an example of a polycentric network structure a case study written by Elinor Ostrom (1997). The case, dealing with a waste water project in an urban area in Brazil, demonstrates how government authorities may facilitate the co-production of a public service.

> A key point of this [waste water system] is the activation of local citizens to participate from the very start in the planning of their own condominial systems. To accomplish this goal, project teams first set up a series of neighborhood meetings where a general overview of the process, opportunities, and costs of a condominial system is presented. Then, meetings are held in each block, where detailed discussions center on the choices that residents will have to make, their implications in regard to cost, and in regard to the maintenance of the system. Block meetings are called off if half of the households on a block are not in attendance to ensure that there is wide availability of relevant information and good discussion among those living on a block. All of this effort to involve citizens is directed, however, toward facilitating their making real decisions in a process of negotiation among neighbors and with project personnel. Residents decide on the layout of the systems they want, which affects the cost of the system and the charges that they will pay. Arriving at these decisions can take considerable time if some neighbors want the less expensive (but more intrusive) front yard or sidewalk options. Much of the costs of determining and achieving rights-of-way agreements are borne by residents themselves. (ibid., 88–89)

AN ADMINISTRATIVE MODEL FOR EDUCATION?

The project of which this chapter is a part aims at guiding the practice of education administration. Its theory is framed around the common sense notion that administrative arrangements and practices should take into account the co-production function for education. The challenge posed to education administrators and policy makers is to design focal organizations that take account of the polycentric network structures in which education services are embedded.

The primary network structure is the student/teacher nexus. Students must be (1) present and (2) voluntarily and actively participate in the learning process. No learning, in school at least, will take place if those two constraints are not satisfied. Teachers must first coordinate among a number of crucial contingencies in the classroom. Students respond individually to a classroom environment. What is stimulating and motivating to one student may be boring or off-putting to another.

The teacher must also take account of contingencies in the task environment of the school and students. How supportive are parents of student learning? Does the school provide adequate physical facilities? Are there enough textbooks? Is the school a safe and socially supportive environment where students want to be? It falls to the teacher to coordinate these contingencies and facilitate compensatory measures if needed. The colleagues and peers of classroom teachers may be mobilized to help solve specific classroom problems. These actions often include the mobilization of resources from within the school, such as tutoring and counseling. Just as often, nonbudgeted resources are mobilized from parents, student peers and the community.

On the student side, a widely variable range of potential resources may be contributed from the network structures that include parents, student peers and community organizations. That is the point of the Coleman report (1966) and its follow-up studies. Researchers at Teachers College were right to emphasize the contributions of parents, extended family, community and public media (Rothstein, 2004).

What does all this mean for education policy and administration? A more comprehensive response will be given in subsequent research and writing. I anticipate that discussion by offering an initial four points.

First, there is no administrative model or gimmick that will be the next silver bullet that solves all the ills of an education system. The co-production of education services is dependent on the voluntary, active participation of each student. Circumstances affecting student motivation, skills and expectations vary widely within families, schools and regions. The student/teacher nexus is embedded in not one but multiple clusters of interwoven polycentric network structures. Students themselves and classroom teachers are the primary mediators of those networks. If they are not effective as mediators, it is less likely other potential resources and inputs from these network structures will be effectively coordinated. Understanding student specific circumstances within the network structures of education services comes close to exceeding the limits of bounded rationality at the level of single classrooms. For whole schools, or whole school districts, the limits of bounded rationality are exceeded many times over. An effective education system must, therefore, build from the bottom up.

Second, whatever administrative arrangements are adopted, they must share a focus on empowering, motivating and supporting classroom teachers. Not surprisingly, effective teachers are the single most important resource provided by schools (Rivkin, Hanushek, and Kain, 2005). But the selection and training of people who will become effective teachers is very uneven (Ripley, 2010). Folks satisfying the requirements for full credentialing are no more likely to be effective in facilitating student achievement than folks who have not. Further, our analysis of the co-production function suggests the more effective teachers will also have skills in community organizing and improving the co-producing skills of student and parents.

Third, principals and superintendents need to learn to inventory, evaluate and more effectively utilize the nonbudgeted resource inputs available to students from family, peers and the community. Inventories of specific family and community resources around a school and district need to be regularly updated. Where deficiencies are found, principals and superintendents need to be able to facilitate efforts to nurture network structures that may improve, augment or compensate. Classroom teachers need support and professional guidance as they develop procedures and techniques to more systematically build the co-productive skills of parents and students. Principals and superintendents should facilitate seminars and workshops on these subjects in schools and districts. These are new skills and missions for education administrators, the centrality of which is highlighted by analysis of the co-production function.

Fourth, education services are unavoidably co-produced through network structures. Teachers, education administrators and policy makers therefore need to expand their understandings and skills in facilitating and coordinating the resource inputs contributed through network structures. Default skills learned from administering the hierarchies of schools districts will be counterproductive in these network structures. Command and control will need to be replaced by persuasion, convincing, guiding and facilitating. Most participants in the polycentric network structures of education are not subject to their bureaucratic authority. Polycentric means, after all, many independent centers of decision making.

Principals and superintendents may look to the burgeoning literatures in public administration for insights into coordinating and managing network structures. Case studies, theory building and empirical research have been accumulating on the implementation of a variety of programs through networks (Hanf, Hjern, and Porter, 1978; Hjern and Porter,1981; Provan and Milward, 1995; O'Toole, 1997), network structures (Hall and O'Toole, 1997); Hjern and Porter, 1981; Keast et al., 2004; Porter, 1990) and managing network structures (Keast et al., 2004; McGuire, 2002; Meier and O'Toole, 2003; Milward and Provan, 2006; Provan and Milward, 2001; Ospina and Sax-Carranza, 2010). This chapter is indebted to these inquiries for many concepts and insights on purposive networks.

The four previous points are derived from a common sense analysis of the intensive co-produced technology of education services. Teachers and education administrators intuitively understand this technology. They do not need to be told students must to be present and motivated, or that effective and loving parental contributions are more important than what teachers can do. This exercise simply looks carefully at constraints and contingencies embedded within the co-production function and asks what implications for coordinating and administering are posed by interdependencies within that core technology. Classroom teachers and firstline administrators, as they carefully think through the co-production function, are probably the folks to continue the list of things to do to improve education outcomes.

NOTES

1. The word consumer is often not descriptive of the citizen, client, student or patient involved as a co-producer of a particular service. When writing in general about co-production I use consumer as shorthand to cover where

a citizen, client, student or patient may be the co-producer. When writing about a specific service I use the word that best describes the role of the consumer in co-producing the service. The same is true for the producer. When writing in general I use producer, when writing about a specific co-produced service I use the word best describing the agency or organization.

REFERENCES

Alford, J. 2002. Why do public-sector clients coproduce? Toward a contingency theory. *Administration & Society* 34 (1): 32–56.

Brudney, J. L., and R. E. England. 1983. Toward a definition of the co-production concept. *Public Administration Review* 43 (1): 59–65.

Chandler, A .C., Jr. 1962. *Strategy and Structure: Chapters in the History of the American Industrial Enterprise*. Boston: MIT Press.

Colman, J. S., et al., 1966. *Equality of Educational Opportunity*. Washington DC: Government Printing Office.

Cremin, L. A. 1998. *American Education: The Metropolitan Experience 1876–1980*. New York: Harper and Row.

Folbre, N. 2008. When a commodity is not exactly a commodity. *Science* 319 (March): 1769–1770.

Friedman, M. 1962. The role of government in education. In M. Friedman, ed. *Capitalism and Freedom*. Chicago: University of Chicago Press.

Garn, H., M. Flax, M. Springer, and J. Taylor. 1976. *Models for Indicator Development: A Framework for Policy Analysis*. Urban Institute Paper 1206–17. Washington DC: Urban Institute.

Gross, B. M. 1964. *The Managing of Organizations Vol. II*. New York: The Free Press.

Hall, T. E., and L. O'Toole, Jr. 1997. Shaping formal networks through the regulatory process. *Administration & Society* 36 (2): 186–242.

Hanf, K., B. Hjern, and D. O. Porter. 1978. Local networks of manpower training in the Federal Republic of Germany and Sweden. In K. Hanf, and F. W. Scharpf, eds., *Interorganizational Policy Making*. London: Sage.

Hanushek, E. A. 1996. School resources and school performance. In G. Burtless, ed., *Does Money Matter?* Washington DC: Brookings Institution.

Hanushek, E. A. 2007. Education production functions. In S. N. Durlauf, and L. E. Blume, eds., *The New Palgrave Encyclopedia of Economics*. Basingstoke, UK: Palgrave Macmillan.

Hjern, B., and D. O. Porter. 1981. Implementation structures: a new unit of analysis. *Organization Studies* 2 (3): 211–227.

Keast, R., M. P. Mandell, K. Brown, and G. Woolcock. 2004. Network structures: Working differently and changing expectations. *Public Administration Review*, 64(3): 363–371.

Kozol, J. 1991. *Savage Inequalities: Children in America's Schools*. New York: Crown.

Lahaie, C. 2008. School readiness of children of immigrants: Does parental involvement play a role? *Social Science Quarterly* 89 (3): 684–705.

McGuire, M. 2002. Managing networks: Propositions on what managers do and why they do it. *Public Administration Review* 63 (6): 689–699.

Meier, K. J., and L. J. O'Toole, Jr. 2003. Public management and educational performance: The impact of managerial networking. *Public Administration Review* 63 (6): 559–609.

Melhuish, E. C., et al. 2008. Preschool influences on mathematics achievement. *Science* 321 (August): 1161–1162.

Milward, H. B., and K. G. Provan. 2006. *A Manager's Guide to Choosing and Using Networks*. Arlington, VA: IBM Endowments for the Business of Government.

Miner, J.B. 2002. *Organizational Behavior: Foundations, Theories, and Analyses*. Oxford, UK: Oxford University Press.

Ospina, S. M., and A. Sax-Carranza. 2010. Paradox and collaboration in network management. *Administration and Society* 42 (4): 404–440.

Ostrom, E. 1996. Crossing the great divide: Co-production, synergy, and development. *World Development* 24 (6): 1073–1088.

Ostrom, V. 1999. Polycentricity Part I and II. In Michael D. McGinnes, ed. *Polycentricity and Local Public Economics*. University of Michigan Press.

Ostrom, V. 1989. *The Intellectual Crisis in American Public Administration*. 2nd ed. Tuscaloosa: University of Alabama Press.

O'Toole, L. J., Jr. 1997. Implementing public innovations in network settings. *Administration & Society* 29 (1): 115–138.

Parks, R., P. C. Baker, L. Kiser, R. Oakerson, E. Ostrom, V. Ostrom, S. L. Percy, M. B. Vandivort, G. P. Whitaker, and R. Wilson. 1981. Consumers as co-producers of public services: some economic and institutional considerations, *Policy Studies Journal* 9 (7): 1001–1011.

Pestoff, V., S. P. Osborne, and T. Brandsen. 2006. Patterns of co-production in public services. *Public Management Review* 8 (4): 591–595.

Porter, D. O. 1976. Federalism, revenue sharing and local government. In C. O. Jones and R. D. Thomas, eds., *Public Policy-making in a Federal System*. London: Sage.

Porter, D. O. 1990. Structural pose as an approach for implementing complex programs. In M. P. Mandell and R. Gage, eds., *Strategy for Managing Intergovernmental Policies and Networks*. New York: Praeger.

Porter, D. O. 2007. Structuring institutions for a radical new strategy in public education. In W. Taylor, J. Lewis, and M. Massoud, eds., *Economic Development, Environment, Energy and Ethics in a Global Economy*. Dean Frear, Proceedings of the Congress of Political Economists International (COPE), 18th Annual Meeting, July 14–21, 2007, Berlin, Germany.

Porter, D. O. 2009. *Co-production's Specific Challenges to Education Administration*. Paper presented at the annual conference of the European Group for Public Administration, Third Sector Study Group; Malta. September 2–5, 2009.

Porter, D.O., with D. C. Warner, T. W. Porter. 1973. *The Politics of Budgeting Federal Aid: Resource Mobilization by Local School Districts*. London: Sage Professional Paper in Administrative and Policy Studies 03–003.

Provan, K .G., and H. B. Milward. 1995. A preliminary theory of network effectiveness: A comparative study of four mental health systems. *Administrative Science Quarterly* 40 (1): 1–33.

Provan, K. G., and H. B. Milward. 2001. Do networks really work? A framework for evaluating public-sector organizational networks. *Public Administration Review* 61 (4): 414–423.

Ripley, A. 2010. What makes a great teacher? *The Atlantic Online*, January/February 2010. http://www.theatlantic.com e/doc/print/201001/good-teaching. Accessed January 6, 2011.

Rivkin, S. G., E. A. Hanushek, and J. F. Kain. 2005. Teachers, schools, and academic achievement. *Econometrica* 73 (2): 417–458.

Rosentraub, M. S., and E. B. Sharp. 1981. Consumers and producers of social services: Co-production and the level of social services. *Southern Review of Public Administration* 4 (March): 502–539.

Rothstein, R. 2004. *Class and Schools: Using Social Economic, and Educational Reform to Close the Black-White Achievement Gap.* Washington: Economic Policy Institute and Teachers College, Columbia University.

Thompson, J. D. 1967. *Organizations in Action.* New York: McGraw-Hill.

Whitaker, G. P. 1980. Co-production: citizen participation in service delivery. *Public Administration* I 40 (3): 240–246.

Wingert, P. 2010. Blackboard jungle, *Newsweek*, March 15, 2010, p. 22.

9 The Conditions for Successful Co-Production in Housing
A Case Study of German Housing Cooperatives

Taco Brandsen and Jan-Kees Helderman

INTRODUCTION

The erosion and decline of social cohesion in contemporary society is a recurring theme in social science. It is difficult to say how far this deterioration is really taking place, how far new types of social bonding are developing and what kind of social bonding is actually desirable. But the fact that new forms of social cohesion are being called for is, in itself, possibly a sign that old ties are no longer functioning as they should. In recent years, it has often been argued that self-organization and active citizenship need to be encouraged. This also applies to the field of housing. Few would deny that it would be desirable for more citizens to become more actively involved in their living environment. That much is clear. What is less obvious is what, specifically, can be done to encourage this involvement. Could housing providers act to strengthen social cohesion from their current position? More specifically still, could residents become more actively involved in management and decision making, not only as individual customers, but also as a community? This is a question that is increasingly being raised in a sector where discussion has traditionally centered on the socioeconomic consequences of the choice between the two dominant tenures in housing: private home ownership and the (social) rental sector.

Co-production has thus become an important focus for discussion in the housing sector, one that is usually referred to as participation and self-organization. The field of housing has a particularly important place within public service provision because the quality of housing and the immediate living environment have a strong influence on personal quality of life and are often an expression of the lifestyle of the individual. Many of today's private social landlords have been born out of initiatives undertaken by citizens and communities who wanted to create an alternative to the existing supply on the housing market.

The capacity of citizens for self-organization in social housing has actually decreased over time. In recent decades, housing professionals have made many attempts to stimulate this capacity, but these have run into institutional barriers. Bureaucratization, mergers and up-scaling have meant that existing suppliers of housing have become estranged from the communities that they were once active in or, in the case of private non-profit organizations, that they were once linked to. When these suppliers are positioned somewhere between the state, the market and civil society, they have tended to move toward either the state or the market: civil society seems to be a weak point. The question is whether they can strengthen this link with civil society.

In order to answer this question, we have searched for other forms of organization in the field of housing, which might be better placed to mobilize the civic potential of their residents. We have carried out research among small-scale cooperatives in Germany, which in terms of their social dynamics come close to what we would understand as co-production. These coopera-tives are so widespread that they cannot—unlike similar initiatives in most other countries—simply be dismissed as a marginal phenomenon. They thus constitute a "critical case" that could shed light on the circumstances under which co-production could be made to work in the field of housing.

We will work on the basis that the housing market is not a blank canvass. It would be unrealistic to assume that co-production could be used mean-ingfully on any scale without the involvement of existing housing suppliers. Housing is a capital good that requires significant financial investment and a considerable degree of professionalism, and this means that the likelihood of "bottom up" initiatives is limited. Even in the private housing sector, the scope for projects undertaken by individuals is limited. Co-production in this area thus requires cooperation between citizens, but also between citi-zens and institutions that see such initiatives as an opportunity.

First, we will set out our theoretical foundation and methodological choices. We will then focus on the specific functions of housing as a capital good, a consumer good and a form of social investment. We will subse-quently discuss what we encountered in the German housing cooperatives. This will lead us to the formulation of some conditions that need to be met in order for successful co-production in this area to be able to occur. We will also address the specific question of the role for housing suppliers in encouraging co-production.

INDIVIDUAL MOTIVATION AND COLLECTIVE ACTION

To analyze co-production properly, we first need a clear picture of the moti-vations of the citizens involved. Co-production in the field of housing must begin with communities of individuals with a shared goal. How does this shared goal come about, and how does it stand the test of time? This will be the starting point of our analysis, and we use the work of Elinor Ostrom as a basis on which to work.

However, we can in fact begin our exploration with a quotation from former British Prime Minister, Margaret Thatcher: "There is no such thing as society. There are only individual men and women" (Thatcher, 1987).

From this perspective on society, the individual assumes the most important place, and what is more, it is assumed that an individual acts solely and exclusively out of self-interest. Any collective interest that people may share is, from this perspective, simply the sum of their individual interests. Under Thatcher's individualistic approach, it is difficult to understand and explain collective action. In reality, we can observe that people are certainly capable of organizing themselves in such a way that they can accomplish goals that would remain unattainable if they all acted as individuals. We also know that people often act out of mixed motivations. In other words, we want to achieve something good for ourselves and for other people, and as long as we are confident that other people want the same and will behave accordingly, we are prepared to contribute to communal arrangements. In fact, collective arrangements that are based either on self-interest or on altruism exclusively are, in practice, the least sustainable (Le Grand, 2003).

In this chapter, we will work on the basis that a contradiction between individual and collective interests is one possible scenario, but not the only possibility. It is of course possible that the interests of the individual and collective interest may not coincide—for example, when collective investment detracts from the quality of life of some residents and they oppose this investment. However, it is also possible for the interests of the individual and the collective interest to coincide, for example, when an individual invests in communal property and by doing so enhances his own quality of life. The question then becomes—how can housing be organized in such a way that these two types of interest are made to coincide?

We know from research already conducted that people need rules and structures for this. The question is, which rules and structures will bring about an alignment of individual interests with collective interests? This has always been an important issue in social science, and it remains an extremely complicated question for today's policy makers. The solution has traditionally been to establish small-scale, voluntary arrangements, which have been seen as the antidote to large-scale, professionalized institutions. Even Margaret Thatcher, for example, saw the potential for individuals to organize themselves, particularly within the family (households) and in small communities. Within social science, too, where the dilemma of collective action is essential, an exception is often made for small social groups. The sociologist Mary Douglas put it this way:

> Small-scale societies are different. Many who are well apprised of the difficulty of explaining collective action within the theory of rational choice are content to make exceptions. Smallness of scale gives scope to interpersonal effects. . . . Consequently, there seems to be no theoretical problem about altruism when the social organization is very small. (1986, 2)

As mentioned, we do not wish here to work on the basis of a contradistinction between small-scale collectives and professionalized institutions.

However, we could use small-scale forms of organization as a source of inspiration for the realization of social cohesion on a larger scale. For this, we will need to have a good understanding of the social dynamics of these communities: what is it precisely that makes a small group or organization less susceptible to the problems associated with collective action?

HOW SUSTAINABLE COLLECTIVE ACTION CAN BE ACHIEVED

The American political scientist Elinor Ostrom set out to discover the conditions under which individual interests and community interests can be aligned. More specifically, she researched the large variation in the ways in which common-pool resources become institutionalized and are managed (Ostrom, 1990). Common-pool resources are associated with specific collective action problems that relate to the fact that the good involved is, by definition, semi-collective. As shared resources or supplies, common-pool resources are significant to all those entitled to use them, but individual members may end up using so much of the resource that other members (or potential future members—and thus future generations too) may be left without enough. These common-pool resources are characterized by the fact that individual allocation and distribution decisions have an effect on the sustainable management of the supplies, and vice versa.

The two most common ways of managing common-pool resources with individual usage rights are either the wholesale nationalization of the resource (so that individual usage rights are effectively eliminated), or alternatively, its wholesale privatization (so that the good is no longer a common-pool resource). Both options are simple enough to bring about, but for various reasons neither of these options represents the most effective course of action. The question that Ostrom sought to answer was under which institutional and social conditions common-pool resources can really be created and managed on the basis of co-production.

Both a dwelling and the housing stock can be conceived of as a common-pool resource (Helderman, 2007). More specifically, they can be seen as a form of insurance against future investment risks in the field of housing. A dwelling, for example, can serve as collateral for new investment and at a collective level, the entire housing stock and the capital that is tied up in it can serve as a similar source of funding for future investments (Kemeny, 1995). If there is effective management and a certain level of scale is achieved, a stock of housing can even serve as a "revolving fund"—a form of funding that finances itself entirely. But when too many homes or too much capital are taken out of the collectively managed housing stock, the stock becomes exhausted and a collective tragedy may ensue. In a deregulated housing market, an individual home owner may use the excess value of his home to purchase unrelated consumer items, for example, and that excess value will no longer then be available for housing purposes. This will also lead to inflation. When the housing stock is owned communally, the municipal council or national government may decide to sell off rented housing at below its market value, but in the long term this will also mean that the housing stock will become exhausted. The "Right to Buy" program implemented under Thatcher in the United Kingdom in the 1980s had just this effect. Creating and managing a stock of housing therefore requires collective action and more complex forms of institutionalized ownership. It is a classic example of a co-production issue.

Ostrom's research focused specifically on the question of under what institutional conditions common-pool resources can be managed in a sustainable way. Her research concerned communal water resources, but what she discovered about the conditions that lead to successfully managed communal water resources can easily be transferred to the management of housing stock. On the basis of empirical research, she reached the following design principles for the successful management of common-pool resources (Ostrom, 1990, 90).

- The boundaries of the common-pool resource itself and the group of users must be clearly defined.
- Rules concerning use and provisions (such as the division of living space or investment) must be adapted to local circumstances.
- Using collective choice mechanisms, the actors involved in the collective housing stock must be given the opportunity to participate in decision making in some way—whether directly or through representation.
- Monitoring must be carried out in a way that is transparent and accountable to the actors involved.
- Sanctions for violations of the rules must be graduated according to the seriousness of the violation.
- Social infrastructure must be put in place for the resolution of any conflicts that arise between the actors involved.
- The right of the community to organize itself must not be undermined by external authorities.
- When the common-pool resource is part of a larger system (such as the social housing stock), activities involving the removal of resources from the system, provision, monitoring and other relevant forms of management, must be organized as close as possible to local level.

The specific way in which systems of social housing are instituted differs from country to country, and the specific origin and development of each national system can only be explained through historical institutional research (Helderman, 2007).

There are private home owners in all countries, and the use they make of their own dwellings, including for economic purposes, is subject to varying degrees of regulation. All countries also make provisions for the section of the population that has no access to home ownership. In most cases this is for economic reasons—after all, home ownership requires income security and a considerable amount of capital. Most of the housing that is provided for those who do not or cannot own their own dwellings is rented. In Anglo-Saxon countries, the social housing stock has long been managed by municipal housing authorities, although in the United Kingdom that role is increasingly being taken over by not-for-profit housing associations. In the Netherlands, meanwhile, private not-for-profit housing associations have long played an important role in managing the social housing stock. Only in a few countries—the Scandinavian countries and Germany—have housing cooperatives been able to find a long-term niche for themselves between the two dominant forms of ownership—home ownership and the rental sector.

The case of the Scandinavian countries is remarkable because the cooperative form of ownership has many of the same characteristics as private home ownership (Grosse, 2007). It is possible to buy and sell one's membership of a housing cooperative in the same way as one would buy or sell a private home. In Germany, where the research for this chapter was carried out, housing cooperatives have more in common with the rented sector. Of the three forms of ownership previously described, the cooperative sector resembles most closely what is referred to, for the purposes of this book, as co-production. This still leaves us, however, with the empirical question, what exactly is being co-produced between the public sector and the private citizen inhabitants of the housing cooperatives? That is, whether these housing cooperatives also promote public housing goals or whether they are more exclusively oriented toward satisfying the housing needs and demands of their (potential) members?

METHODOLOGICAL CONSIDERATIONS

The German housing cooperatives were chosen for two reasons. To begin with, research had already indicated that a number of the *Wohnungsgenossenschaften* had succeeded in getting their residents to play a more active role in and around their immediate living environment and that lively communities had formed around these organizations. That made them an interesting case study through which to look at co-production. The second reason was that the cooperative housing sector houses a very broad cross-section of the population that includes both recently established and much older organizations. This enabled us to form a varied picture of the various phenomena in the sector and the development of co-production.

In Germany, housing cooperatives account for around 10 percent of the housing market. As such, Germany is one of Europe's frontrunners when it comes to cooperative housing (Harloe, 1995). In many other countries, cooperatives in the field of housing are a marginal phenomenon, and separate statistics are not even recorded for them. While in many countries, real property prices began to rise steeply from the start of the 1990s, the German housing market has been characterized by relatively stable price levels. This is illustrative of the fact that in the German housing market, housing bears a closer resemblance to a consumer good than in Anglo-Saxon markets, where its function as a capital good is more dominant (Muellbauer, 1994; Helderman, 2007). This has been confirmed by research into household perceptions (Elsinga et al., 2007). In Germany, owning one's own home is perceived principally as a form of investment in one's future security. Any rise in the value of housing is assessed in terms of its effect on security, rather than in terms of property. Tenants and home owners also share a very similar perception of the economic value of their home in Germany (Tegeder and Helbrecht, 2007). In Anglo-Saxon countries, on the other hand, property markets are unstable and subject to large price fluctuations, and tenants and home owners have a quite different perception of their own homes. In fact, this observation reveals the first important characteristic that can enable co-production in housing in the form of housing cooperatives. The way in which the housing market is institutionalized and the economic dynamic associated with it is a significant factor. Housing cooperatives are better able to flourish in a stable housing market where the economic purpose of housing is perceived principally in terms of its practical use.

When collecting data, we were able to limit ourselves to qualitative data. Some years ago, large-scale quantitative research was carried out into the *Wohnungsgenossenschaften*, which meant that some basic data concerning the scale and institutional form(s) of this type of organization in the German housing market were already available (Expertenkommission Wohnungsgenossenschaften, 2004). This enabled us to concentrate our efforts on intensive research at the organizational level. Some basic questions about structures and procedures were answered using documentation analysis. In addition to that, we carried out intensive case study research. This was based on interviews with the board members, residents and municipal officials in and around seven mainly smaller organizations. The *Wohnungsgenossenschaften* we worked with were located in the cities of Berlin, Hamburg and Munich, which enabled us to research the role of the cooperatives in various types of local property markets.

The research was financed by Futura, a network of housing corporations in the Netherlands. The research objectives were arrived at in consultation, but the authors of this chapter determined the research methods themselves. Of course, given the scale of the research, it can only be seen as exploratory in nature. Nevertheless, it does go some way to revealing the factors that are behind successful co-production. Some of these factors are specific to the field of housing and, for that reason, it is now necessary to take a closer look at this specific field.

THE FUNCTIONS OF HOUSING

The previous section explained the conditions under which co-production can occur in general terms. We will now focus specifically on the field of housing. After all, the conditions necessary for co-production are closely linked to the functions of the product or service in question and with the specific consequences of co-production at the sectoral level (Pestoff et al., 2006). We will now analyze the field of housing on the basis of its three functions: its capital function, its consumer function and its social investment function (Brandsen and Helderman, 2004, 2010). Each of these functions can have an impact at various levels: at the level of the individual resident, or at higher, collective levels such as that of the community that the resident belongs to, or of the city as a whole.

Clearly, housing is constructed to last for the very long term, and this means that the supply of housing available consists predominantly of the existing housing stock. High production costs mean that only a very limited number of dwellings are added to that stock—on average just a few percent each year. As a result, the demand for housing often changes much more quickly than the supply. This can lead to significant shortages or surpluses, and this type of imbalance can last for long periods of time. In fact, the supply of housing does not reflect current demand, but rather the demand of decades ago. Changing tastes and requirements are therefore only reflected in the existing housing stock to a limited extent.

The nature of housing as a good that is supplied almost exclusively from an existing stock means that the rewards and expenses involved will vary from place to place and over time. Although housing requires some level of maintenance over time, most of the finance is needed "up-front" to make the purchase itself. Loans are often used to raise this finance, sometimes in the form of a personal loan (a mortgage) or sometimes on a larger scale through the capital market. These costs are paid back in installments while the dwelling is being used. In some cases, a proportion of this finance can be provided by the state, whether this is through direct subsidies (object subsidies) or by funding individual users or owners (through housing benefits or tax rebates). When large-scale ownership is involved, more finance options become available. Because there are many individual dwellings, it is possible to bring anticipated income forward, postpone expenditure or (in the case of collective ownership) channel money from one dwelling to another. For example, the income from certain dwellings (income from sales or in the form of rent) can be used to finance investment (in whole or in part) elsewhere. Low rents can be compensated by higher rents at later time, or certain groups of tenants can be subsidized by other tenants. The larger and the more varied the number of dwellings in the hands of one owner, the more possibilities there are to juggle their finances in such a way.

The considerable investment required and the fact that this is often extended over the long term means that housing has a function as a *capital good*. Here, the important factor is the extent to which the market value of the dwelling is passed on. This comes down to the fact that it is possible not only to live in a house, but also to live from it. Where the dwelling is the property of an individual home owner, the resident shares directly in the increase (or decrease) in its value. Viewed in these terms, living in a house is a form of investment.

When a property is owned collectively, the range of possibilities is greater. If the sum paid by the individual for using the property is independent of any changes in the value of the property, capital profits can also be used to maintain the collective property and make new investments. At the collective level, the capital function can thus be translated into an arrangement that provides maximum security of tenure. Traditional German housing cooperatives, for example, expressly emphasis this type of security, which is passed on to the residents at an individual level.

Second, housing has a *consumer function*, which in market terms we can call a consumption function. In basic terms, the consumer function of housing stems from the simple fact that a resident also needs a roof over his head. However, housing can also fulfill several consumer functions simultaneously. The diversification of the services provided by social housing providers in countries such as the United Kingdom and the Netherlands in recent decades has meant that living arrangements are increasingly enabling residents to lead a variety of individual lifestyles (Brandsen, Cardoso Ribeiro, and Farnell, 2006). For example, partnerships between health institutions have significantly widened the options available to the elderly. Housing is becoming a means through which to offer a variety of services that can enhance residents' quality of life. Residents can also organize themselves and pursue their collective interests—independently of or in addition to the services provided by professionals. When residents live together in a shared residential environment, they can also help and support each other in various aspects of their lives. Parents can babysit for each other's children, and people with handicaps can give each other a helping hand. Individual interests are thus served by the community, enhancing the consumer function of housing.

Finally, housing has a social investment function. Housing provides the opportunity to realize social ideals, such as empowerment. The housing market has always been closely associated with socioeconomic status and social mobility. Ecological sustainability is also becoming ever more prominent nowadays as an ideal to be put into practice. All this means that housing suppliers can take on a social enterprise role. Landlords may, for example, choose to focus on individual social advancement or invest to enhance the environmental sustainability of their housing.

It is impossible to define the conditions necessary for co-production without referring to the different functions of housing previously outlined. After all, the success of co-production can be defined in different ways. The definition of success is most often framed in terms of the consumer function of housing, but the effect of co-production on the other functions of housing must also be taken into consideration, otherwise we will only see one side of the story, in which only the advantages of this form will be emphasized. As we will see in the following sections, co-production in housing has both advantages and disadvantages, and both should be taken into account.

SMALL GERMAN HOUSING COOPERATIVES: ET IN ARCADIA EGO?

This section shows how co-production is present in the organizations we studied and the circumstances that lay behind this. The cooperatives that we researched often had something of the utopian idyll about them. On some occasions that was clear as soon as we arrived. The first cooperative that we visited had traditional red brick courtyards with benches, flowers and balconies looking out. There were a couple of children's bicycles lying on the ground. Elsewhere, we visited colorfully painted rows of family houses, each with a long strip of garden out back, tended attentively by the residents. As we walked past, many of the residents were out clipping their hedges. In another location, we visited an area of architecturally surprising modern housing with an abundance of wide open green spaces and attractive communal areas. Of course, not all the buildings owned by the cooperatives were as striking as these, but many organizations prioritized architectural quality, and this was also a source of pride. Many of them view the design and maintenance of the buildings they own simply as part of their social responsibility.

There is a relatively low turnover among tenants. Germany is characterized by a relatively high proportion of vacant housing, particularly in Eastern Germany, but this is significantly lower among housing cooperatives than in other types of housing providers. In the majority of residents of newer cooperatives, the residents are still those who originally established them. The mix of residents in the traditional *Genossenschaften* is fairly varied, but they are particularly popular among certain groups. These are mainly households who can help each other directly—the elderly, families with children and the handicapped. Additionally, some managers pointed out growing interest among single people over the age of forty, particularly women. In fact, many of the managers were themselves middle-aged women—a group that has traditionally played a significant role in voluntary work. The cooperatives are particularly attractive to one and two-person households with a certain lifestyle—often these are people who could actually live independently but who have much to gain from life in an integrated community. But where cooperatives have already been established for a long time, the preference of the residents for living in a certain neighborhood can also be decisive.

Managers pride themselves in their active residents. This usually involves some kind of self-help. Particularly in smaller communities, mention was made of mutual assistance, such as doing shopping for one another or babysitting for each other's children. In addition, during our interviews with many traditional housing cooperatives, they referred to a wide range of organized activities—the elderly go on coach trips together, as far as the Arctic Circle; games and treasure hunts are organized for children; and those who love walking go off to the woods together. Every cooperative has a yearly winter street party with mulled wine, and countless cups of tea and coffee are enjoyed together.

Yet the larger *Genossenschaften* experienced familiar problems. All these activities tended to depend on a core of mainly older residents. Many of the members acted just like tenants of regular social housing, doing nothing more than paying their monthly rent. Some cooperatives had begun experimenting with other forms of participation, such as funds to be spent by residents for which residents could submit their own ideas. But here, too, falling levels of participation were a cause of concern. Nevertheless, the long average tenure of residents and the small-scale of the organizations (achieved by, for example, transferring the democratic decision-making structure to the level of individual housing complexes) contribute to a relatively high level of involvement. What is more, most small cooperatives seem to be able to involve their members even more intensively—members typically participate in management and forms of direct democracy, which are anchored in their organizational structure.

BORN OUT OF SOCIAL MOVEMENTS

There is a significant amount of variation among German housing cooperatives. The clearest difference is between the older *Genossenschaften* and those that have been instituted more recently. Many of the older cooperatives were founded in the second half of the nineteenth century and vary greatly in size, from a few thousand residents to tens of thousands of dwellings, although they are smaller on average than the municipal housing organizations. The newer cooperatives are significantly smaller, with sometimes only a few hundred dwellings.

The older cooperatives have a history similar to that of housing corporations in the Netherlands. During the Industrial Revolution, there was a massive movement of workers to the urban centers, where they could not all be housed. Families were squeezed together into tiny dwellings where living conditions were often squalid. This was at its most severe in Berlin, where they joked: "There's a basement flat above us that's going to be vacant soon." Benevolent groups of idealists, often with connections to the workers movement, founded new colonies around the edges of town where they sought to promote community spirit and mutual assistance, and provide housing with more light and air. Even today, many of the cooperatives still have close political links to the Social Democratic Party of Germany (SPD). Later, many of the *Genossenschaften* helped in the postwar reconstruction of the cities that had been bombed. They were given state grants to build social housing. But these grants came with strings attached: if a dwelling was built with the aid of object subsidies, the municipality was then entitled to house whoever it wanted there—and these were not always neighbors of the sort that the existing residents would look favorably on.

The newer *Genossenschaften* have their origins in more recent social movements. For example, in cities such as Hamburg, collective forms of housing were a means of tackling the issue of squats in the city. Following German reunification, there was a new wave of *Genossenschaften*, supported by favorable local subsidy schemes and spurred on by worries about housing being sold off to private property speculators (the "cherry-pickers"). During the 1990s in Dresden, for example, the municipality sold 47,000 dwellings from its stock of social housing to foreign investment companies. Particularly in the eastern part of the new Germany, residents took matters into their own hands and bought up existing housing estates or plots of land. This type of initiative and the associated financial risks were linked to a desire for security of tenure and self-determination, and for a home that would never have to be sold again and where the only risks residents had to take were risks they chose to take themselves. A number of new initiatives had links with the ecological movement and, in these, sustainable buildings were given a high priority.

The internal structure of the cooperatives is partly laid down by law. In smaller organization, the highest administrative organ is the general meeting of members. In larger *Genossenschaften*, members are represented indirectly. Management duties are carried out by two or three members—in smaller cooperatives they may work on a partly voluntary basis. The management has a supervisory board that is consulted regularly and whose members have the power to dismiss the management if necessary. The administrative structure consists mainly of technical staff and caretakers. This democratic structure is fixed and replicated on a smaller scale within individual housing complexes.

As so often in Germany, history has left its mark very clearly on the *Genossenschaften*, which have been shaped by social transformations. The older cooperatives were a response to rapid urbanization during the Industrial Revolution of the nineteenth century. The more recently formed cooperatives were formed during the turbulent period that followed German reunification and the globalization of capital markets at the end of the twentieth century. Few new *Genossenschaften* are being formed today because both public and private forms of funding are less freely available. But it is possible that the demographic turning point that is due to take place around the middle of the twenty-first century may result in a new wave of *Genossenschaften* for two reasons. First, in a shrinking housing market, the *Genossenschaften* will face lesser competition from for-profit investors in the land market, the capital market and the housing market. Second, the *Genossenschaften* seem to be particularly well suited to combine the provision of housing services with the provision of care services for the elderly. Hence, with an aging population, the potential demand for sheltered housing in cooperatives may rise.

FINANCIAL BACKGROUND

In the field of housing, unlike in many other forms of service provision, it is possible to function for long periods without the financial support of government or other financial backing. Capital invested in housing generates its own income through rents or the proceeds of sales. A very large investment is required "up-front," however, and support from external financiers is nearly always necessary for this.

The *Genossenschaften* vary in the degree to which they have received financial support, but only a few have managed without any form of subsidy at all (when implicit subsidies are included). After all, they cater for a stratum of the population, which is not the lowest in economic terms (or they would not be able have any capital to contribute) but not particularly rich either (or they would probably choose to own their own home). There is also very little room for maneuver: the cooperatives promise their residents absolute security and any sale of the properties is virtually out of the question. The scope for rent increases is also limited, both in legal terms and by the financial position of the tenants. The legal support measures from which the cooperatives used to benefit were abolished during the first decade of this century. Direct subsidies do still exist, and come mainly from the regional (*Länder*) or municipal levels of government. But even so, the cooperatives are forced to keep an eye on every penny. Larger cooperatives are often financially stable, but for the smaller ones it is often a constant struggle for survival. In a few cases known to us, established cooperatives have lent their support to new cooperatives during the start-up phase by providing advice, but there is no question of any financial support between cooperatives. Not only are there limited resources available to share, but cooperatives tend to focus on their own community and their own immediate environment; this is both their strength and their weakness.

The main way in which cooperatives receive external financial support is through favorable terms of credit. The largest risks are during the set-up phase. Many new initiatives have had to be abandoned during this phase. Groups of residents who wanted to set up cooperatives have had to rely almost entirely on state banks or banks motivated by other ideals than purely profit alone. Regular banks have remained reluctant to help and have only really shown interest once the risky phase is over. A few years ago, bank managers invited a housing cooperative customer to visit them and politely explained that the cooperative was no longer an attractive customer for the bank, with only a few millions in credit (a further ironic twist in this story: on the day of our interview with this cooperative in 2009, the very same bank was about to collapse due to taking on subprime mortgage debts from the United States).

In the past, some cities have also supported alternative forms of housing directly, albeit sometimes on a temporary basis. For example, the municipality of Berlin extended grants for set-up and renovation costs, which were later scrapped when the city ran into financial problems. However, this did provide a window of opportunity that enabled a number of cooperatives to become established. These kinds of arrangements existed throughout Germany, although they have by no means always been successful. Hamburg is an interesting case: the city government began to encourage housing communities there in the 1980s. A proportion of land in the city—which is in short supply and thus expensive—is set aside for collective housing and a subsidized foundation supports residents who want to prepare applications and get established. It is interesting to note that the traditional cooperatives also began by setting up housing communities because it was one of the few ways of being able to acquire land.

In short, cooperatives have to get established in a difficult and sometimes fickle environment, where the support they require cannot always be found. Those cooperatives that survive are only able to achieve some degree of stability over time. So it seems that even this form of self-organization requires a push to get it started. But just how strong does that push need to be? As we shall discover, the answer to that question involves finance, but has social aspects too.

At first glance, decision-making structures play an important role in this. Cooperatives that have been set up more recently usually incorporate some form of direct democracy or associational democracy through which members can be involved in decisions on strategy and management. Older, larger cooperatives are usually run on the basis of indirect representation. Their identity is influenced to a significant extent by their democratic structure. Even in the traditional cooperatives, members have the power to dismiss those that run them. However, the cooperatives we researched did not differ radically from the housing corporations of the Netherlands. The decision-making procedures were reminiscent of the original housing associations, and many of the initiatives at the level of individual housing complexes have equivalent forms in the Netherlands.

More important than the formal structure are the informal ties between residents. A number of cooperatives succeed in aligning their residents' interests as individuals and the interests of the community as a whole. The most important factor in this is how residents' involvement is built up over time. The smaller, newer cooperatives are without exception based on communities that were already in the process of being formed before the housing cooperative itself was established. Sometimes these communities are strengthened further by some form of participation in the physical construction process itself. To a certain extent, social bonds also have an important role to play in the more traditional cooperatives. They often have a loyal core of resident families who, over the generations, have long made up part of the community as a result of allocation mechanisms. In both cases, the housing communities are based on established social or family ties, or both.

Communities cannot be created, but they can evolve and thereafter can be maintained. As our description has shown, housing cooperatives in Germany are characterized by a combination of closed membership and community interests. The original community is carefully protected by laying down clear boundaries for what can be changed—both in terms of the residents and financial and economic conditions. Members of the smaller cooperatives in particular have a clear interest in preserving their own communities—and the survival of the community depends on closed membership.

CONTROLLING THE BOUNDARIES OF THE COMMUNITY

We do not wish to give a distorted picture of the German *Genossenschaften*: not all of them excel in building an active sense of community. Even in the housing cooperatives of Germany, only a limited number of organizations have residents who are highly active. But why do some organizations manage it, while others do not?

It is true that residents stay in their homes longer, that there are close relations between managers and residents, and that there was a relatively large amount of contact between residents. Certainly in the smaller organizations, residents are closely involved in management. This means of management is also essential to smaller organizations as a means of cost reduction—they are kept running through voluntary work and low turnover.

The German cooperatives exhibit all the classic hallmarks of strong communities: membership is—to some degree—closed, they are kept deliberately small in scale and there is a clear community interest. Herein lies both the strength and the weakness of housing cooperatives. This is a model from which there is much to learn, but also one that comes with a price tag attached.

To start with, it should be emphasized that the communities have not come into existence through the cooperatives, but rather the cooperatives have been built around existing groups. New organizations were set up by groups of enterprising individuals, who then went on to enlist more residents. These groups put a great emphasis on relations between residents before the first brick was laid. In one of the cases we researched, the future residents of the cooperative were obliged to help finish off the buildings in the final phase of construction so that they would get to know each other properly. The cooperative is thus an instrument rather than an end in itself. More important still, perhaps, the cooperative is the instrument of a specific group that has its own goals.

What also plays an important role here is that cooperatives have remained relatively small in scale. There are a few large cooperatives with over 10,000 homes, but two-thirds of all cooperatives own less than 20 percent of the total stock of cooperative housing, with the average cooperative extending to a total of 1,200 homes. The *Wohnungsgenossenschaften* generally have a strategy of limited expansion, and sometimes limit themselves simply to renovation and maintenance. This means that the number of homes that become vacant is consistently low.

This leads us logically to the question of how accessible the cooperatives in fact are. On this point, the cooperatives we researched provided some very contradictory evidence. They invest a great deal in the transparency of their housing distribution methods. Allocation decisions are usually published and explained. Sometimes residents receive a personal letter to explain why they have not been allocated a specific dwelling. In principle, anyone is free to apply for housing. The sum required—between €500 and €1,000—is by no means excessive. Some cooperatives offer a savings variant, which involves acting as a kind of bank for members as a means of raising extra capital from them. There are no limits on income.

On paper, then, the cooperatives could hardly seem more welcoming. But in practice, the situation is rather more complex. As mentioned, in reality, very few homes actually become vacant. In addition, those that do become vacant are generally taken rather quickly. In principle, anyone who is prepared to accept the obligatory share purchase can apply for the dwelling. In reality, though, many family homes stay in the hands of the same families. It is common practice for children who are born within the cooperative to be registered as members immediately and to receive shares as gifts from their parents or godparents. Thirty years later, they will have been registered for long enough to be entitled to a family home. This intergenerational transfer of homes means that cooperatives often retain an intergenerational core of residents who are closely involved. All of this is perfectly within the rules of registration, but the length of registration is so long that outsiders hardly ever get the chance to move into the most sought after family houses. The only way into some *Genossenschaften* is by being born into them or by first occupying a single-person's home. Those who want to move up to a larger home are then put on a very long internal waiting list.

CONFLICT-AVOIDING BEHAVIOR

The low turnover in tenants of housing cooperatives is linked to the priority that they accord to ownership rights. This means there are seldom grounds for any conflict. Increases in property values hardly exert any influence at all in the cooperatives that we studied. Each member is obliged to invest a certain amount in shares in the cooperative—a relatively low sum for traditional cooperatives, but substantially more in new cooperatives. In return, they receive an annual dividend, usually a fixed percentage of between 2 percent and 4 percent. As a financing mechanism, this is similar to a deposit savings account with a bank (since the credit crisis, we perhaps ought to clarify this further: the type of bank account where you are guaranteed your original deposit back). The difference is that members of German housing cooperatives seldom leave and thus seldom have their original deposit returned. In the event of a member leaving, he or she will only be given their deposit back. It is a sober system that minimizes conflicts concerning financial distribution and makes profit-seeking strategies impossible.

In this way, the principle of security of tenure is translated onto every level. This security is very much a key principle for cooperatives, and it also leads to a scrupulous investment policy. Any expansion of cooperatives is usually limited—sometimes a small housing complex will be added. A conscious effort is made to strike a balance between economies of scale and retaining the small-scale of the cooperative. This means that hardly any cross-subsidization takes place—in principle, each housing complex needs to be financially self-sufficient. This also contributes to the conciliatory nature of relationships within the cooperatives—existing organizations can gain from economies of scale through expansion, but do not need to invest to do this. The model is limited in ambition, but very clear. Residents know where they stand.

Finally, the internal structure of cooperatives, particularly smaller ones, ensures that residents are well-informed about any developments. Communication plays an essential role in organizations of all sizes—they organize meetings, hold open days, write letters and employ wardens. This does not mean that managers and members are of equal rank, however. The difference in the levels of knowledge between the two groups is enormous even under this form of housing ownership, and it cannot be denied that some managers act paternalistically. But the bottom line is that residents are secure in their homes and ultimately they have the power to dismiss managers. This too gives residents a feeling being able to decide their own destiny.

A LIMITED FOCUS

Even the most dynamic of the *Genossenschaften* have a view that is restricted only to their own neighborhood—they are very active within their own "territory" but no further. There is also criticism on the part of local authorities. "Our experience is that there is little willingness to feel responsible. If there was coordination between them, that would be different, but often they don't even know what their immediate neighbor is doing." The cooperatives look inward, first of all, and have neither the financial capacity nor the personnel to take on a broader role. Certainly, the cooperatives are islands of stability with a favorable influence on their immediate environment. Their residents are relatively closely involved in managing their housing complexes and the streets around them. They attract volunteers, are attentive and reliable, and maintain their properties well—the perfect neighbors, one might say. But when it comes to broader concerns such as urban renewal, it is the project developers and the municipal housing authorities that call the shots, not the *Genossenschaft*. Although the *Genossenschaften* have their local federations, it should be emphasized that these federative organizations and the individual cooperatives are more oriented toward satisfying the housing needs and demands of their members than toward contributing to local and regional housing issues.

CONCLUSION: THE CONDITIONS REQUIRED FOR CO-PRODUCTION

Home ownership and renting are the two dominant tenures in the housing sector. It is only in a few countries that housing cooperatives have been able to find a niche between these two forms of ownership. Our research has focused on the German *Genossenschaften*, and we have asked ourselves the question of under what conditions this form of co-production in housing has been able to succeed there. It is important to point out, first of all, that external conditions play an important role. The specific structure of the housing market and the economic dynamic associated with it are important factors. Cooperatives can thrive in a housing market where competition from other forms of ownership is not too strong. The cooperatives also need institutional space. In the Netherlands, where housing corporations have long enjoyed a dominant position within the rental sector, the institutional space for cooperatives is limited. In countries where home ownership is dominant in the housing sector and is often used as a means of making personal profits, there is also only limited institutional space for cooperatives.

The housing market in Germany is relatively stable, and this has allowed the cooperatives to develop. But what internal requirements did the cooperatives meet? In fact, almost all of them resembled the "small-scale societies" that Douglas referred to. Interpersonal contact was important and was emphasized consistently by our respondents. A certain degree of altruism probably also plays a role, but much more important in this type of small-scale community, the shared interests of the cooperative are also clearly understood as forming part of the individual's own self-interest.

The eight conditions that Ostrom identified for the successful management of common-pool resources can easily be recognized in the *Genossenschaften* that we researched. That is: the boundaries of the cooperatives are well defined, as well as the eligibility criteria that potential members must satisfy; rules concerning the use of the provision, including the withdrawal of housing services and decisions concerning new investments, are by definition adapted to local circumstances; furthermore, the cooperatives have simple collective choice mechanisms and decision rules, often based on direct democracy; monitoring of the management board is directly accessible by the members of the *Genossenschaften* and the general meeting usually also serves as an effective social infrastructure for the resolution of potential conflicts; and last but not least, they are explicitly based on the right of communities to organize themselves.

We have also shown that the *Genossenschaften*—once they have got off the ground—are capable of surviving in the long term. Managing their existing housing stock sustainably is seen as being more important than making risky investments to attract potential new members or groups. The *Genossenschaften* seldom dispose of the financial means to initiate risky new investments, and their internal decision-making structures have an intrinsically conservative effect. To conclude, there are both economic and social aspects associated with co-production in German housing cooperatives.

The Price of Co-Production

On the basis of our research, we have sought to portray a realistic picture of co-production in the organizations under discussion. This type of small-scale housing providers has many positive effects on their environment, but it is also important to explore their limitations.

There is significant variation among the German cooperatives, but it is possible to discern some general characteristics. On the one hand, there are the more recently established communities that have an independent legal status, are more inclined to take larger risks and have little capacity for investment, but that excel in terms of self-organization and openness. On the other hand, there are the more traditional cooperatives, in which there is a greater distance between managers and members, which sometimes means that they bear a suspiciously close resemblance to larger-scale providers of social housing in countries such as the Netherlands or Sweden. Some of these traditional cooperatives have also been able to replicate the original basis of their community through a core of highly active residents whose involvement spans many generations. In almost all cases, the cooperatives have chosen to pursue a cautious investment policy. They focus almost exclusively on the physical upkeep of the housing and on promoting social involvement among residents—they ignore considerations such as service provision, freedom of choice and profit making. As a model, this is by no means attractive for everyone and many feel it to be distinctly restrictive. But for many others, the cooperatives are the ideal form of housing organization, even though their influence remains strictly confined to their own neighborhoods.

As we have already mentioned, in a number of cases, the German housing cooperatives have demonstrated that they are extremely good at mobilizing their residents for collective action. In this, co-production in housing takes on a concrete form. But at the same time, there are limitations and short-comings. The cooperatives make limited use of their capital. As indicated, the cooperatives emphasize security of tenure above all else, which means that they avoid making any risky investments. There is very limited cross-subsidization, or none at all: each housing complex is expected to provide for itself. The emphasis on security of tenure also means that the sale of properties is often virtually impossible. That means that there is a high level of stability and conflicts between members are rare, but it is not the most productive strategy when it comes to activating the capital that has been invested in the housing stock. A second disadvantage of cooperatives is the limited reach of their community. In fact, they often do not look any further than the next street corner. There is no denying that within these boundaries, the German *Genossenschaften* can be home to very pleasant communities with a high degree of social involvement, many volunteers and a positive influence on their immediate environment. Nevertheless, these cooperatives do remain friendlier versions of the "gated community," in which the "in-group" assumes a central position.

In terms of the functions of housing, the user function and the social investment function are enhanced within smaller-scale organizations, but not within those on a larger scale. When it comes to the capital function of housing, by contrast, the larger organizations make much more effective use of the capital invested. In other words, co-production in housing comes with a price tag attached. Of course it would be wonderful if all the functions of housing could be fulfilled equally well on any scale level. The ideal housing organization would be one that invested broadly across the whole city, where residents shared in the return on capital investments and at the same time were happy to work tending the communal gardens with a cheery whistle. However, the conditions that optimize performance for fulfilling one function are not compatible with the optimization of performance in terms of other functions. If one wishes to enable residents to share in the rise in the value of their property, this is almost impossible to reconcile with maintaining the closed communities that are needed to preserve social stability. Scandinavian owners' cooperatives, in which shares are tradable at market prices, have a completely different social dynamic and bear only a superficial resemblance to the German tenant cooperatives. In other words, where individual residents interpret capital function of housing as an investment, this can prevent the user function of housing from developing into a community.

The question is: at what scale are collective interests served the best? The difference between social landlords in the Netherlands and the United Kingdom and the smaller-scale German housing cooperatives is illustrative here. Dutch and British social landlords often have an active role in the city, which means that they have a wider field of view than their own properties alone. They are important partners for municipalities and, in that sense, they are able to act as a more effective force in the wider process of urban renewal. This concern for the interests of the wider community is embedded at the organizational level. However, larger-scale housing providers—as we mentioned at the start of this chapter—are not characterized by a close relationship with communities of residents. Residents are viewed first and foremost as individual tenants. The German cooperatives that we investigated are, to some extent, a mirror image of this. They have a much more limited field of view, but within that narrow field they are able to mobilize residents more effectively. In other words, they invest mainly at the community level and much less at the level of the city or even city district. This means that smaller-scale housing providers replicate, to some extent, the disadvantages of private home ownership when it come to inter- or cross-communitarian solidarity.

IN SEARCH OF ALTERNATIVE FORMS OF ORGANIZATION

To conclude, there seems to be a trade-off between the internal communitarian orientation of the German cooperatives and the external societal orientation of Dutch and British social landlords. This brings us to the question whether it is possible to combine the advantages of different types of organization within a single model? As we have mentioned, the conditions required for fulfilling the different functions of housing at various scales levels are often contradictory. Enhancing the function of housing as a capital good demands larger-scale organization, but this seems to be incompatible with co-production, which requires smaller-scale communities. It would be ideal if these two functions could be combined in some way so that there is a more optimal balance between *social efficiency* and *social equity* (efficiency and equity across different communities), while at the same time also benefitting from the more responsive intra-communitarian quality of the cooperatives toward the needs and demands of their residents or tenants. It goes without saying that the social investment function of housing would also need to be incorporated at different levels (individual, community and city).

One way of combining the different functions of housing may be to decouple the different levels within one organization from one another. It would be unrealistic to expect a community to form around a total housing stock of, for example, 5,000 dwellings. Equally unrealistic would be to expect an organization with a stock of 100 dwellings to play a role in the development of the city as a whole. However, a provider with 5,000 dwellings could accommodate an organization for a housing community of 100 dwellings. In Hamburg, for example, some large cooperatives have allowed smaller housing communities a place within their housing stock when those communities are housed within one building or within a clearly demarcated area. At a lower scale level, it may be possible for existing housing providers to provide the conditions necessary for communities to form and co-production to occur.

Existing housing suppliers would continue to have a dual role in that respect. On the one hand, they will have to seek to colonize "bottom-up" initiatives. After all, the sense of community that we encountered in the German housing cooperatives depends to a considerable degree on the residents' capacity for self-organization and a hands-off approach on the part of existing organizations. This system works when the smaller communities really do bear some of the risks themselves, too. This is an argument for the established housing providers to keep their distance. At the same time, it is unrealistic to assume that "bottom-up" initiatives will simply manage to find their own way into a rigid framework of relationships within the housing market without the support of existing providers. Such initiatives need external support, certainly in the start-up phase at the very least. In that sense, it would seem that established housing providers, particularly social landlords with a municipal or private sector background, may be the best place to encourage such new initiatives. This will involve striking a difficult balance between giving them a helping hand and taking a hands-off approach where necessary.

If such an approach were to prove successful, existing housing providers could function as a roof over the heads of initiatives at lower levels. New forms of organization within and around the existing housing providers could lead to a proliferation of new opportunities for co-production, while at the same time allowing for more variation within their portfolio. Perhaps this process could enable these organizations to realize the potential they have to bring about social innovation without having to relinquish their traditional position, which over the years they have worked so hard to attain.

REFERENCES

Brandsen, T., T. Cardoso Ribeiro, and R. Farnell. 2006. *Housing Association Diversification in Europe*. Coventry, UK: Rex Group.

Brandsen, T., and J.-K. Helderman. 2004. Volkshuisvesting. In H. Dijstelbloem, P. Meurs, and E. K. Schrijvers, eds., *Maatschappelijke dienstverlening. Een onderzoek naar vijf sectoren*. Amsterdam: Amsterdam University Press, pp. 65–131.

Brandsen, T., and J.-K. Helderman. 2010. *Coöperatieve Verenigingen in Duitsland*. Tilburg, The Netherlands: Futura Wonen.

Douglas, M. 1986. *How Institutions Think*. Syracuse, NY: Syracuse University Press.

Elsinga, M., P. De Decker, N, Teller, and J. Toussaint, eds. 2007. *Home Ownership beyond Asset and Security*. Amsterdam: IOS Press.

Expertenkommission Wohnungsgenossenschaften. 2004. *Wohnungsgenossenschaften: Potenziale und Perspektiven*. Berlin: Bundesministerium für Verkehr, Bau- und Wohnungswesen.

Grosse, I. 2007. *Political Parties and Welfare Associations*. Doctoral thesis at the Department of Sociology, Umeå University, Sweden.

Harloe, M. 1995. *The People's Home: Social Rented Housing in Europe and America*. Oxford, UK: Blackwell.

Helderman, J.-K. 2007. *Bringing The Market Back In? Institutional Complementarity and Hierarchy in Dutch Housing and Health Care.* Dissertation at the Department of Public Administration, Erasmus University Rotterdam.

Kemeny, J. 1995. *From Public Housing to the Social Market: Rental Policy Strategies in Comparative Perspective.* London: Routledge.

Le Grand, J. 2003. *Motivation, Agency and Public Policy: Of Knights and Knaves, Pawns and Queens.* Oxford, UK: Oxford University Press.

Muellbauer, J. 1994. Anglo-German differences in housing market fluctuations, the role of institutions and macroeconomic policy. *Economic Modelling* 11 (2): 238–249.

Ostrom, E. 1990. *Governing the Commons: The Evolution of Institutions for Collective Action.* Cambridge, UK: Cambridge University Press.

Ostrom, E. 2005. *Understanding Institutional Diversity.* Princeton, NJ: Princeton University Press.

Pestoff, V., S. P. Osborne, and T. Brandsen. 2006. Patterns of co-production in public services: Some concluding thoughts. *Public Management Review* 8 (4): 591–595.

Tegeder, G., and U. Helbrecht. 2007. Germany: Home ownership, a Janus-faced advantage in time of welfare restructuring. In M. Elsinga, P. De Decker, N. Teller, and J. Toussaint, eds., *Home Ownership beyond Asset and Security.* Amsterdam: IOS Press.

Thatcher, M. 1987. "Aids, education and the year 2000". Interview by Douglas Keay with Prime Minister Margaret Thatcher in Woman's Own, October 31, 1987: 8-10.

10 Co-Production in an Information Age

Albert Meijer

TECHNOLOGICAL PROMISE

> In Ramsey County, Minn., you don't have to be a cop to fight crime. In fact, you don't even have to leave your desk. All you have to do is join the county's virtual neighborhood watch network and you'll be able to lookout for suspicious activity from your computer. (Nichols, 2010)

New practices of co-production are being facilitated by the new media. The Ramsey County example is telling: citizens are asked to help the police by monitoring online safety cameras. Thirty cameras have been put up at criminal hot spots, or areas with frequent vehicle break-ins, thefts and assaults. The wireless technology allows law enforcement officers to watch what is going on but the police have a limited number of "eyeballs." To extend their number of "eyeballs," they have created a website (www.ramseycountysheriffwebcop.com) that enables users to gain access to fourteen of the county's surveillance cameras set up in various public areas. If users spot any suspicious activity, they can report this to the local authorities. The authorities can then watch the cameras more closely and dispatch police to the location if this is needed. The citizens help the authorities to focus their attention. Sheriff Bob Fletcher says in an introduction video on the site: "We want you to help us look for suspicious activity" (Nichols, 2010).

Technology holds a similar promise for public service support: On the finance discussion forum, a citizen posts the following question: "I drive 50 miles one way to work, Can I take my fuel cost off on my taxes?" He receives several answers that all stress that commuting cannot be deducted. "If you are self-employed or you are going to see clients, you can deduct the mileage, and not your fuel costs. If this is just your commute every day, then no, you cannot deduct anything" (Financial Crisis, 2009).

The finance discussion forum enables citizens to obtain public service support from other citizens. Instead of calling the Internal Revenue Service (IRS), they can pose their questions on the forum and they receive various answers. One could argue that this type of activity takes some of the burden of the shoulders of the IRS because citizens are now doing part of the work themselves. Specific questions may still need to be asked to the IRS, but other questions are taken care of by citizens. Public service support is no longer the sole responsibility of government: it is co-produced by government and citizens. This new form of public service support is facilitated by web technology.

In essence, co-production is about creating new connections between government and citizens. Fruitful connections can contribute to solving societal problems, such as crime and theft, by improving public service delivery (see Chapter 1). Although co-production has been explored since the 1970s, we are witnessing a new wave of attention for this form of citizen participation. The new media are an important facilitator for new forms of co-production because the costs of connecting to citizens have been reduced drastically and the new technologies create opportunities to interact 24–7. In short, new media hold the promise of strengthening co-production in an information age.

Will the new media deliver their promise? It is too early to evaluate the effects of technology on co-production between government and citizens. Various forms of experimenting are taking place. New practices are being developed and redeveloped. Enthusiasts inside and outside government are developing ideas to enable citizens to connect in new and meaningful ways to government agencies. These experiments are taking place in policy areas such as social welfare and health care but also in policing and service delivery. On the basis of these experiments, we can provide a preliminary assessment of the value of technology for co-production between government and citizens.

A pure instrumental assessment of new media, however, would provide too narrow a focus. Research into the impact of new media in the public sector has constantly shown that new media do not only have an instrumental but also an institutional effect (Kling and Dunlop, 1991; Snellen and Van de Donk, 1998). Values embedded in the media have an effect on the practices that are carried out through these media. This has been formulated most notably by McLuhan (1964) in his famous phrase "The medium is the message." The safety cameras in Ramsey County may not only strengthen police effectiveness: it may also fundamentally alter the relations between police and citizens. We need to explore these changes as well.

This chapter is based on theories about new media in social practices and hence adds another dimension to the multidisciplinary analysis of co-production. In line with the ambition of this book to show how co-production actually works in practice, it is based on two empirical research projects. The first project is an analysis of the value of websites for co-production in public service delivery (Bekkers and Meijer, 2010). The second project was an analysis of the use of mobile phone technology in the co-production of safety between police and citizens (Bekkers and Meijer, 2010). The empirical research consisted of a combination of qualitative methods. The main part of the research of co-production in public service delivery consisted of an analysis of 150 posts on the forum.werk.nl. Additionally, an interview and a limited survey were carried out. The analysis of co-production of safety consisted of an interview, a media analysis and a secondary analysis of two evaluation studies. The empirical findings from these projects are used to enhance our understanding of the role of technology in co-production. What will be the character of co-production in an information age?

This chapter consists of a theoretical and empirical analysis of the relation between new media and co-production. The theoretical part starts with a brief discussion of co-production in general and then proceeds with a more focused discussion of the theoretical role of new media in co-production. The empirical part presents the results of the studies into the co-production in the domains of public service delivery and safety. The chapter ends with a discussion of the instrumental value and cultural aspects of co-production in an information age.

CO-PRODUCTION

Research into co-production of public services has a long history, and strong conceptual papers about co-production of public services were published in the 1970s, 1980s and 1990s (Ostrom, 1978; Whitaker, 1980; Parks et al., 1981; Normann, 1984; Ostrom, 1996; Alford, 1998, for overviews see: Bovaird, 2007; Pestoff, 2006). The idea of co-production of public services can be positioned within the wider debate in the scientific and practitioner communities on public services (Bovaird, 2007). The starting point was the traditional, government-centric model of public services that was based on the assumption that civil servants should emphasize the legality and equity of public services. Traditional bureaucrats were not interested in customer satisfaction or citizen input in production services. Bureaucratic procedures were central to public service delivery and correct service delivery was measured by adherence to (legal) procedures. Ostrom reinforces: "For some time, most social scientists have conceptualized public agencies producing human services (police, education, welfare) as the primary producers of these services. This conception relegates the citizen to a passive role" (1978, 102).

This model of public service production was challenged by "new public management" (Pollitt, 1990; Hood, 1991; Osborne and Gaebler, 1993; Barzelay, 2001). New public management emphasized the importance of customer satisfaction, and the basic idea was that civil servants should not only strive to follow formal procedures but they should make an effort to serve customers. The private sector was presented as a guiding ideal for making citizens more satisfied with services in the public sector. Osborne and Gaebler (1993) emphasized that an "entrepreneurial spirit" should transform the public sector. A range of publications challenged this idea of public service delivery, and many authors emphasized that public service delivery was fundamentally different from service delivery in the private sector (Pollitt and Bouckaert, 2000). An alternative approach is the so-called "new public services" (Denhardt and Denhardt, 2007). This approach highlights the fact that public services are different from private services. Reacting to Osborne and Gaebler's claim that public services should focus on steering and not on rowing, Denhardt and Denhardt emphasize that public services are about serving and not steering.

Whereas both the new public management and new public services focus on the role of governments and civil servants, a different strand of critique on new public management focuses on the role of citizens in the production of public services. The argument here is that in new public management, citizens are generally regarded as consumers, whereas citizens should be regarded as co-producers of public services (Bovaird, 2007). This strand of thinking focuses our attention on an older alternative for a government-centric perspective on public services. The term co-production was originally coined by Ostrom (1978). In the 1990s, Ostrom emphasized that "the great divide between the Market and the State or between Government and Civil Society is a conceptual trap arising from overly rigid disciplinary walls surrounding the study of human institutions" (1996, 85–86). She sees co-production as a core component of most forms of public service delivery.

Renewed attention for co-production of public service delivery has been triggered by technological developments. The success of Internet communities such as Wikipedia and Linux have led to a new wave of attention for the idea of co-production (often referred to a co-creation). The proponents of co-production in the public sector refer to these developments and they suggest that the Internet creates new opportunities for rearranging relations between government and citizens (Eggers, 2005; Tapscott and Williams, 2006). Ideas about co-production have been revitalized by the new Internet technologies.

NEW MEDIA

How can new media facilitate co-production? Beautiful scenarios of co-production in an information age have been developed by creative thinkers. A great example of these scenarios is Leadbeater and Cottam's (2007) argument to organize public services in the form of a "user generated state": "A public sector that just treats people as consumers—even well-treated ones—will miss this dimension of participation that is at the heart of the most successful organizational models emerging from the interactive, two-way Internet." They argue that new forms of co-production are the key to revitalizing the public sector.

The potential of these new models has been highlighted, but they are only slowly diffusing into the public sector. The idea of a "user generated state" not only conflicts with bureaucratic standards but also hardly fits within the dominant discourse on technology. The dominant discourse on contributions of information and communication technologies to public services has been heavily dominated by new public management and pays little attention to the idea of co-production (Bekkers and Homburg, 2007). Improvements have been sought in improving service to individual customers by enabling 24–7 access, integrating services and connecting services to the experience of users. The basic model underlying these improvements is a relation between a public service provider and an individual consumer. The perspective of co-production opens up the arena to other actors who could possibly play a role in the provision of public services. From this perspective, involvement of citizens, intermediaries and stakeholders strengthens the provision of public services. This idea fits recent shifts in thinking about Internet technology: from the Internet as an information medium to the Internet as a platform for communication and interaction.

The dominant, consumerist ideas about technology in government are being challenged by a coalition of advocates of co-production and social media enthusiasts. Ideas of co-production as developed in the administrative sciences match well with ideas about co-production as they have been developed in the Internet community and by technology gurus (Raymond, 1998; Tapscott and Williams, 2006). Leadbeater and Cottam (2007) state:

> Traditional professional public services will be more effective the more they are designed to help and motivate users to generate their own content and solutions. [. . .] That is why promoting participation should be at the heart of a new agenda for public services. Not participation in formal meeting or governance but participation in service design and delivery.

Wikipedia and Linux are inspiring examples that lead the way toward new models of service production in which services are not only produced for consumers but also by consumers (cf., Toffler, 1980).

The idea of co-production on the Internet has received new attention with the thrust of what has been labeled "Web 2.0" (O'Reilly, 2005). Frissen and colleagues (2008, 62) indicate that web 2.0 consists of new platforms for interactions with extensive input from users, integration of knowledge and user participation in the production of web services. One of the core assumptions of web 2.0 is that users generate content. Content is no longer produced and provided by the public service provider but rather being created (i.e., co-produced) in networks and communities. Content is made available to all members of the community and generally stored in an accessible format to create an online interaction platform and repository for the virtual community.

In IT-circles, the instrumental perspective on new media and co-production is dominant: the basic idea is that objectives can be attained more efficiently with new technologies. Media theorists such as McLuhan (1964), Postman (1986) and Winner (1977) emphasize that media should not only be analyzed as instruments to obtain certain objectives because the use of media also influences these objectives. McLuhan emphasizes that "the media is the message," Postman stresses that "to a man with a hammer everything looks like a nail" and Winner talks about "reverse adaptation" to indicate that the means shape objectives. Applying their views to the use of new media for co-production in the public sector, we need to analyze not only goal attainment and side effects. A reflective perspective on the emerging new practices is needed to understand the meaning of these new media for shaping relations between citizens and government.

To enhance our understanding of the instrumental value of new media for co-production and to reflect on the changing meaning of it, we investigated emerging practices of co-production in two different domains of government activity: public service support and safety. New practices are described and analyzed in terms of their value for government and citizens. We will present a reflection of changing meanings in the conclusions.

NEW MEDIA AND THE CO-PRODUCTION OF PUBLIC SERVICES

The first empirical domain in our analysis of new media and co-production is public service support. Public service support is meant to help clients in the process of public service provision. Most government agencies have call centers and a website to provide their clients with the information they need. One can also think of co-production as a form of providing this information. In 2002, the Dutch Agency for Unemployment Benefits started a forum—forum.werk.nl—to enable citizens to ask each other questions and to discuss various issues related to jobs and unemployment. The central idea behind this forum was that public service provision could be improved by enabling citizens to exchange experiences and answer each others' questions. The forum was set up in an open, easy and accessible manner to enable all users to participate, and the agency communicated the existence of the forum to potential users. In their interactions, citizens were assisted by the agency because fourteen employees at the Center for Work and Income spend part of their time moderating discussions at form. werk.nl. Moderators provide valuable answers to the questions that are not answered by other users. An example is the following quote:

> If you gain some money from incidental selling of things on e-Bay, that is not a problem. It is wise to contact the agency if you start gaining a profit of 50 Euro or more a month on average. Your contact person will—in contact with you—determine to what extent this counts as additional income and whether this influences your unemployment benefit.

These answers are based on the previously mentioned forum with questions and answers. If a client would call the contact center of the Dutch Unemployment Benefit Agency, he would get the same answer. Moderators also organize and connect discussions in the forum. If users show behavior that does not comply with the rules, moderators intervene.

Do the efforts of the agency trigger participation from citizens? Our analysis indicates that there is a small group of active participants and a large group of "lurkers." With nearly 1,000 members of the forum, the forum has a substantive group of users, albeit that this is only a small fraction of the total number of clients of the Center for Work and Income (165,000 in December 2008). The number of active participants is small: 91 members have posted 10 to 50 messages, 47 members have posted more than 50 messages and 2 frequent posters have posted nearly half of all messages. The number of users is not known, but a calculation on the basis of the average total number of visits for certain discussion indicates that the forum attracts thousands of visitors per week. This indicates that the number of people that use the information—lurkers in Internet terms—is much higher than the number of people that post information on the forum.

What is the content of citizens' contributions? In the first place, many users post questions about their personal situations. An example: "Does anybody know what I can tell an employer to convince him that he should hire an employee for 32 hours a week?"

Second, the forum is used to discuss various issues that are related to jobs and benefits. An example is the following poll, which got 5 votes, 32 comments and was visited 14,666 times: "I find it a good idea to create a blacklist or web register or something like that to list employers who exhibit improper behavior in job application procedures."

Third, the forum is used to share personal experiences. Descriptions of experiences do not result in questions to other users but rather in a call for attention and understanding. Mostly users want to share negative experiences but sometimes they also want to share positive experiences.

Critics such as Keen (2007) have emphasized that there are risks in the provision of information by "amateurs": this information may not be as adequate as the information provided by professionals. The forum.werk.nl does not seem to run this risk because moderators from the government agency can monitor the quality of the answers. The presence of the moderators may have a preemptive effect: in our empirical research, we found no evidence for a lack of quality in the information provided by other users.

What is the value of this form of co-production to the government agency? First, the forum provides an additional channel of interaction with citizens. Moderators provide answers to questions of citizens when these questions cannot be answered by other citizens. Second, the forum provides the agency with additional signals about customer satisfaction. Discussions about overactive marketers, problems with digital systems and improper job ads form triggers for the agency to improve its public services. Third, and probably most interesting, the forum supplies an additional function to the existing forms of service provision in the sense that citizens can provide each other with information that the agency cannot. Citizens exchange specific experiences, and they can tell each other how they have dealt with specific situations. Emotional support is also an important additional function that citizens can provide to each other, whereas the agency cannot do this.

Does the forum provide additional value to citizens? Strong quantitative evidence is not available, but the interview with respondents at the government agency and the content analysis provide indications of the value of the forum. Our analysis indeed seems to show that citizens obtain valuable answers to their questions. The second value of the forum could be that the forum enables citizens to exchange experiences with companions. The qualitative analysis shows that many of the postings contain stories about negative experiences of citizens when applying for a job. Reactions are generally understanding and supportive. We note that these discussions may result in a negative atmosphere concerning the issue of finding a job. The third potential value of the forum is support in finding a job. Neither the interview nor the content analysis provide evidence that the forum helps citizens to find a job.

NEW MEDIA AND THE CO-PRODUCTION OF SAFETY

The second empirical domain in our analysis of new media and co-production is safety. The police need citizens to assist them in their intervening police work, for example, to provide information about the direction in which a criminal has run away. The traditional approach to engaging citizens is to ask bystanders for information. Important limitations of this approach are that only a limited number of bystanders can be reached and that the intervening police officer has to spend his time on gathering information from citizens instead of intervening in a situation by pursuing the criminal.

The Dutch police developed a new system for engaging citizens in intervening police work called Burgernet (Citizens Net). The system was tested on a small scale in 2004 in the city of Nieuwegein and on a larger scale in 2008 in nine Dutch cities. Over the next years, Citizens Net will be implemented in every police department in the Netherlands. The basic idea behind the system is that the police contact citizens over the telephone when they need direct information from them. They can contact them in the so called "golden hour," the time directly after something has been reported.

How does Citizens Net work? Citizens sign up for the system and provide information about their home or work address. The police can contact this network of citizens at this real time: directly after a crime or missing person has been reported, the police can contact citizens to ask for information. Citizens are contacted on the basis of their geographical characteristics. If, for example, a thief has been seen running away in a certain direction, citizens in that area are contacted. The emergency center of the police can start a so-called Citizens Net action, which means that a voice or text message is send to all participants to tell them who or what the police are looking for. The following message is an example: *"Stolen in Maarssen* (a Dutch city): *red Volkswagen Golf Cabriolet. License Plate Number: TN-DG-23. If you see this vehicle, please call 112"* (Police Nieuwegein, 2010).

The participants receive a new message when the Citizens Net action is terminated. They can also obtain additional information about this action on the Citizens Net website. The website presents information about the results of the action. This may mean that the police are still looking for a suspect, or it can also mean that a lost child has been found. The website shows the number of citizens that have been contacted and the number that has actually been reached. The website does not contain any interactive element: interaction between police and citizens only takes place over the telephone.

The police have three broad objectives for Citizens Net. The first objective is to strengthen the subjective safety, citizens' perception of safety in their own environment. The basic idea is that citizens will feel safer when they can do something about safety. The second objective is to strengthen objective safety. Tracking suspected or missing people faster will enhance the effectiveness of intervening police work. A third objective is to strengthen trust in government and the police. If citizens are engaged in police work, they can be expected to develop a more positive perception of the police.

Citizens' interest in this form of co-production is high, with an average of 4.6 percent of the citizens in the nine cities signing up for participation in Citizens Net. The evaluation of Citizens Net in the nine cities shows that only 24 percent of the participants are less than 36 years old. Most of the participants, 62 percent, are male. This lack of representativeness may not be a problem when it comes to findings lost people, but it may both reflect and affect trust of immigrants and young people in the police and lead to skewed perceptions of safety.

Why do citizens engage in Citizens Net? A citizen's duty and wanting to contribute to the safety of the neighborhood are the strongest motives for engaging in Citizens Net (Van der Vijver et al., 2009, 49). The expected effects in terms of apprehension of criminals and a safer neighborhood along with the idea of a better hold on the safety in the neighborhood score somewhat lower. The latter two can be seen as motives based on group interest. Television broadcasts about Citizens Net reveal another motive that was not measured in the evaluative study by Van der Vijver and colleagues: excitement. In a television program about Citizens Net, a citizen reveals that he found it exciting to receive a phone call from the police and to look out of the window to spot the suspect. De Wit (2006, 47) also found that a substantial minority of interviewed participants mentioned excitement as a reason for participating in Citizens Net.

Does this form of co-production contribute to police's effectiveness? The hard contribution of Citizens Net to intervening police work is substantial: 9 percent of all the cases that were qualified as fit for a Citizens Net action were solved on the basis of information from this action. This number seems limited in terms of the total number of actions, but it amounts to more than 50 percent of the successful police actions. This indicates that Citizens Net is not a miracle product with which all crimes can be solved, but it certainly forms an important addition to the existing means.

How does Citizens Net affect subjective safety? Do citizens feel safer? The evaluation study indicates that Citizens Net has no effect on citizens feeling of safety in their own neighborhood. Van der Vijver and colleagues (2009, 51) argue that these feelings are based on their own perceptions of the neighborhood and are not affected by Citizens Net. At the level of the city, Citizens Net does have a positive effect on subject safety. Van der Vijver and colleagues (2009, 51) indicate that these feelings are not based on direct perceptions but on mediated perceptions. These mediated perceptions are influenced by the creation of Citizens Net and the information they receive about how the police work and what the results of these actions are.

TECHNOLOGY MATTERS!

Instrumental Value

What have we learned from these cases about the instrumental value of new media for co-production? The forum.werk.nl can clearly be identified as forms of co-production. Value is generated through joint efforts of moderators from the Center for Work and Income and citizens who post questions and experiences and react to each other's postings. This form of co-production is limited to the co-production of public service support. The production of public service delivery, the provision of the benefits, is still carried out by the agency. It is interesting to see that this form of co-production on the Internet is facilitated by proven technology. There is no need for cutting-edge technology to facilitate new forms of interactions between the agency and its clients.

The empirical findings indicate that the forum.werk.nl supplies an addition to the government-centric form of public service provision in three ways:

- *The forum provides an additional channel for public service support.* The forum provides an additional channel for obtaining formal information about jobs and unemployment and disability benefits. This information is provided by other citizens and moderators. The forum creates a new channel for providing formal information to citizens.
- *The forum provides access to citizens' experiences.* The forum also gives citizens access to the experiences of companions. Formal channels of the Center for Work and Income and the Disability Agency cannot provide citizens with this information. Offline channels

provide the same information, but the forums open up the exchange of experiences to a much larger group of citizens.

- *The forum provides a social and emotional function.* The forum provides citizens with a channel for sharing experiences. Government-centric service provision has a businesslike character and creates few opportunities for delving into social and emotional issues related to being unemployed. The forum gives citizens the opportunity to set up a mutual support structure.

The value and role of the digital forum should not be exaggerated. Less than a percent of the clients of the Center for Work and Income is a member of the forum, and less than one-tenth of a percent of the clients actively participates in the discussions. Even though thousands of people visit the forum and obtain information from it, the forum.werk.nl still plays a limited role compared to other channels of public service provision, such as the telephone and face-to-face meetings.

Citizens Net can also be regarded as a form of co-production because information from the police is combined with information from citizens to strengthen intervening police work. The police direct this form of co-production: they have all the information from citizens and feed little information back. The website is used to present information about Citizens Net, but it contains little information about the input from citizens. The police deliberately choose to use technology only to facilitate citizen-police interactions and not citizen-citizen interactions. This is an understandable choice in view of the risks of reprisals to individuals, but it also means that citizens do not have the opportunity to contact each other to start new initiatives for improving the safety of the neighborhood. In the end, the police want to stay in control.

The empirical analysis shows that this form of co-production is an important addition to existing instruments in the following ways:

- *Citizens Net enhances police effectiveness.* Citizen engagement has provided a substantial addition to the existing opportunities for engaging citizens in intervening police work. Citizens Net is not a miracle product, but it certainly forms an important addition to the instruments: it amounts to more than 50 percent of the successful police actions.
- *Citizens Net strengthens subjective feelings of safety.* Although Citizens Net has no effect on citizens' feeling of safety in their own neighborhood, it does have a positive effect on subjective safety at the city level. This perception is influenced by the creation of Citizens Net and the information citizens receive about the police work and what the results of these actions are.

The advantages of this type of citizen engagement are substantial. The combination of information technology at the side of the police (database with information about participants, geographical layer for choosing relevant participants, system for managing Citizens Net actions, Internet site with further information) and (cell) phones at the side of citizens form a perfect couple. This type of technology use does not demand access to technology for citizens or knowledge about complicated systems. Nearly everyone has a telephone and knows how to use it. Technology does not form a barrier to participation.

Although positive effects for police effectiveness and legitimacy were identified, the study also provided information about (potential) risks. These risks build on the normative debate in the literature about the "dystopian dangers of unreflexive communitarism" (Hughes and Rowe, 2007, 318). Negative side effects concern infringements on the privacy of citizens and the risk of practices of vigilantism. Both risks relate to the idea that the benefits of co-production will not equally be divided among citizens. In the practices of co-production in investigative police work, suspects face a deterioration of their position because of the infringements on their privacy. These infringements follow the general trend of prioritizing safety over privacy (Rubenfeld, 2008).

Overall, the findings indicate that technology facilitates new forms of co-production. The forum.werk.nl facilitates new connections between citizens and the public service provider, and Citizens Net facilitates new connections between citizens and the police. Creating the same connections without new media would hardly be possible in view of the numbers of participants and their geographical dispersion. The new media help to create new connections. These connections help to strengthen the effectiveness and efficiency of public service delivery and safety policies. Although these contributions are limited—one should not expect the miracles from co-production through social media that gurus talk about—they present promising venues for improving the work of government.

Co-Production as a Social and Emotional Encounter

What is the meaning of new media for co-production? The empirical research into the co-production of public service provision highlights a first pattern: a shift from a rational to a more social encounter. Services are not provided to an individualized "homo economicus" but to a "homo sociologicus," who is a member of a community of citizens. Public service provision is positioned within networks of citizens who interact with the government agency, an independent intermediary and each other. What does the Internet do with these interactions? The creation of a forum to facilitate these interactions leads to interesting couplings between domains that are traditionally separated:

- *Mixing of information sources*. In a traditional system, citizens can obtain information from either government or their peers. In the new system, the distinction between these two is fading away. Citizens ask a question, and they can get an answer from either the moderator or a fellow citizen.

- *Mixing of functions.* In a traditional system, citizens obtain factual information mostly from government agencies and emotional support from their peers. The forum challenges this distinction by creating a virtual space in which both factual information and emotional support is provided.

The value of the forum is that the community of citizens is created. The postings on the forum show that there is the idea of a shared identity based on the fact that they are in the same situation, which is similar to what has been found for patient groups (Madara, 1997). This shared identity, however, can only result in a community when citizens have a communication platform to exchange information and experiences. This community is a partial and not a holistic community in the sense that most members only contact other members on issues related to jobs and benefits. The community consists of networked individuals as indicated by Castells (2001) and Wellman and Haythornthwaite (2000): individuals create new connections, but these do not take the form of traditional communities.

The community of citizens in forum.werk.nl is similar to the many patient groups on the Internet and can be classified as "communities of interest" (Van Bockxmeer, Frissen and Van Staden, 2001). These groups also provide both factual and personal information, as well as informative and emotional functions. Traditional perspectives on co-production emphasize factual and informative functions. Relations between government and citizens are the central focus in many analysis of offline co-production, whereas here we see a shift to citizen-citizen connections and community building. The analysis of the forum.werk.nl clearly shows that public service delivery also entails personal information and emotional functions. Co-production should not only be conceptualized as a rational process but also as a series of social and emotional interactions.

Co-Production as Real-Life Gaming

What can we learn from a reflection on new practices of co-production in the police? Important for a reflective perspective on co-production in the public sector was the identification of entertainment and excitement as motives for citizens. Intervening police work turns into a real-life game in which everybody can participate. Get a text message, look out of your window and catch the thief. An interesting feature of this new form of co-production is that it seems to be integrated in the life of citizens. Citizens can receive a text message from the police any time of day and wherever they are. The distinction between serious participation and real-life games is thinner than it is in offline co-production. While television may reduce everything to a form of entertainment (Postman, 1986), the new media arguably transform all content into a game. Interviews with drivers of tanks in war zones have indicated that these drivers feel that they are in computer game. In the co-production of safety, stakes are not as high, but the impact of new media may be identical.

One can think of several reasons why people play games. A first reason to play games is to kill time and have something to do. Participation in Citizens Net is specifically high among senior citizens. One could assume that these citizens need something to do, and Citizens Net provides them with a useful alternative. A second reason to play games is to have an intellectual challenge. One can play a puzzle, do a sudoku or get involved in Citizens Net. This type of puzzle may be relevant to more investigative police tasks. A third reason to play games is to compete with others and attain a higher social status. The motives for participating in the Citizens' Net seem to indicate that people want to obtain social value, and we could even propose that they want more value than others by presenting relevant information to the police.

The idea that the new media transform co-production into a game has important implications. The police may even have to compete with other "games" to get the attention of citizens. Will they play Dungeons and Dragons or watch the police cameras in Ramsey County? Developing meaningful relations in our "attention economy" (Davenport and Beck, 2001) may be a matter of developing the right games. Issues of privacy and protection of the rights of suspects may become less important in the new forms of online entertainment. Previously, religious duties seemed to have formed the model for citizen participation as secular institutions replaced preexisting religious institutions (Tocqueville, 2000). Visiting police neighborhood meetings was not considered to be "fun," but it appealed to a sense of civic duty, just like going to church (Verba and Nie, 1972). Now these contacts with the police are based on the idea of gaming. Dungeons and Dragons may be the new model for co-production.

CO-PRODUCTION IN AN INFORMATION AGE

What have we learned from these emerging practices about co-production in an information age? The key lesson is that technology matters in both an instrumental and an institutional sense. Technology facilitates new practices of co-production: new media lower the costs of large scale and dispersed interactions and therefore enable practices of co-production that could hardly be created offline. The new media also transform these practices into more social and more playful interactions: co-production in an information age seems to be less serious than offline co-production. An important question here is what these changes mean for government. Is government capable of developing social and playful interactions? And is this a task for government? Or are citizens capable of developing these forms of interactions themselves?

Let us first consider co-production in public service support. Why should governments not leave it to citizens to organize their information provision about public services? The Center for Work and Income has chosen to set up this forum because there was not yet a similar forum available. The forum is fairly active and seems to meet unmet needs (Madara, 1997, 21). An important benefit for the agency was that this also means that they can monitor the discussions and that they can react to rumors and incorrect information. On the other hand, one can question whether government agencies should penetrate the personal sphere of citizens (cf. Habermas, 1984) to improve the provision of public services. Should government agencies be involved in the exchange of personal experiences of citizens? And should government be the one that provides these facilities? The finance discussion forum in the introduction presents an interesting alternative: citizens answer each others' questions without government involvement. One could argue that government should only develop this type of co-production when citizens have not developed a similar platform by themselves.

The considerations may be different when it comes to the domain of safety. Citizens are developing their own communities in the form of neighborhood watches. These communities have much value but do not enable the exchange of information between citizens and the police. This exchange is crucial because citizens and police both hold part of the information and need each other to produce safety. For privacy reasons, the police cannot put their information out in the open, and citizens will also be reluctant to share certain information with anybody else other than the police. These constraints on the exchange of information call for the design of effective forms of co-production. Citizens Net shows that playful interactions can be designed, and these forms of play can contribute to public safety.

In the information age, governments need to reassess the need, opportunities and forms of co-production. Social media enable the construction of new connections between government and citizens, and these connections could hardly be created offline. The value of these connections depends on the policy domain, institutional situation and existence of citizen communities. The challenge for governments is to design forms of co-production that appeal to citizens' motives. The Internet as a virtual space for social support and serious gaming challenges traditional bureaucratic orientations of governments.

REFERENCES

Alford, J. 1998. A public management road less travelled: Clients as co-producers of public services. *Australian Journal of Public Administration* 57 (4): 128–137.

Barzelay, M. 2001. *The New Public Management.* Berkeley: University of California Press.

Bekkers, V., and V. Homburg. 2007. The myths of e-government: Looking beyond the assumptions of a new and better government. *The Information Society* 23 (5): 373–382.

Bekkers, V., and A. Meijer. 2010. *Cocreatie in de Publieke Sector. Een Verkennend Onderzoek naar Nieuwe, Digitale Verbindingen tussen Overheid en Burger.* Den Haag: Boom Juridische Uitgevers.

Bovaird, T. 2007. Beyond engagement and participation: User and community co-production of services. *Public Administration Review* 67 (5): 846–860.

Castells, M. 2001. The *Internet Galaxy. Reflections on the Internet, Business and Society.* Oxford, UK: Oxford University Press.

Davenport, T. H., amd J. C. Beck. 2001. *The Attention Economy: Understanding the New Currency of Business.* Cambridge, MA: Harvard Business School Press.

Denhardt, J. V., and R. B. Denhardt. 2007. *The New Public Service: Serving, Not Steering.* Armonk, NY: ME Sharp.

De Wit, E. 2006. *Burgernet: Een Trendsetter? Over Burgers en Responsibilisering.* Unpublished Master Thesis, Rotterdam, Erasmus University Rotterdam.

Eggers, W. D. 2005. *Government 2.0: Using Technology to Improve Education, Cut Red Tape, Reduce Gridlock and Enhance Democracy.* Plymouth, UK: Rowman and Littlefield.

Financial Crisis. 2009. Financial Forum>Taxes thread. http://www.financialcrisis2009.org/forum/Taxes/I-drive-50-miles-one-way-to-work-Can-I-take-my-fuel-cost-off-on-my-taxes-291931.htm. Retrieved August 2, 2011.

Frissen, V., et al. 2008. *Naar een 'User Generated State'? De Impact van Nieuwe Media voor Overheid en Openbaar Bestuur.* The Hague: Report for the Dutch Department for the Interior.

Habermas, J. 1984. *The Theory of Communicative Action.* Cambridge, UK: Polity.

Hood, C. 1991. A public management for all seasons? *Public Administration* 69 (1): 3–19.

Hughes, G., and M. Rowe. 2007. Neighbourhood policing and community safety: Researching the instabilities of the local governance of crime disorder and security in contemporary UK. *Criminology and Criminal Justice* 7 (4): 317–46.

Keen, A. 2007. *The Cult of the Amateur. How Today's Internet is Killing Our Culture.* New York: Doubleday.

Kling, R., and C. Dunlop, eds. 1991. *Computerization and Controversy: Value Conflicts and Social Choices.* San Diego: Academic Press.

Leadbeater, C., and H. Cottam. 2007. *The User Generated State: Public Services 2.0* http://www.charlesleadbeater.net/archive/public-services-20.aspx.

Madara, E. J. 1997. The mutual-aid self-help online revolution. *Social Policy* 27 (3): 20–26.

McLuhan, M. 1964. *Understanding Media: The Extensions of Man.* New York: McGraw-Hill.

Nichols, R. 2010. Neighborhood Watch Goes Digital in Ramsey County, Minn. *Government Technology.* http://www.govtech.com/public-safety/Ramsey-County-Minn-Neighborhood-eWatch.html. Accessed November 22, 2010.

Normann, R. 1984. *Service Management.* Chichester, UK: John Wiley.

O'Reilly, T. 2005. *What is Web 2.0? Design Patterns and Business Models for the Next Generation of Software.* www.oreillynet.com/lpt/a/6228. Accessed December 1, 2010).

Osborne, D., and T. Gaebler. 1993. *Reinventing Government.* New York: Penguin Books.

Ostrom, E. 1978. Citizen participation and policing: What do we know? *Nonprofit and Voluntary Sector Quarterly* 7 (1–2): 102–108.

Ostrom, E. 1996. Crossing the great divide: co-production, synergy and development. *World Development* 24 (6): 1073–1087.

Parks, R. B., P. C. Baker, L. Kiser, R. Oakerson, E. Ostrom, V. Ostrom, S. L. Percy, M. B. Vandivort, G. P. Whitaker, and R. Wilson. 1981. Consumers as co-producers of public services: Some economic and institutional considerations. *Policy Studies Journal* 9 (7): 1001–1011.

Pestoff, V. 2006. Citizens and co-production of welfare services: Childcare in eight European countries. *Public Management Review* 8 (4): 503–519.

Pollitt, C. 1990. *Managerialism and the Public Services*. Oxford, UK: Blackwell.

Pollitt, C., and G. Bouckaert. 2000. *Public Management Reform*. Oxford, UK: Oxford University Press.

Postman, N. 1986. *Amusing Ourselves to Death*. New York: Penguin Books.

Raymond, E. S. 1998. The Cathedral and the Bazaar. *First Monday* 3 (3). firstmonday.org.

Rubenfeld, J. 2008. The end of privacy. *Stanford Law Review* 61 (1): 101–162.

Snellen, I.Th.M., and W. Van de Donk. 1998. *Public Administration in an Information Age. A Handbook*. Amsterdam: IOS Press.

Tapscott, D., and A. Williams. 2006. *Wikinomics: How Mass Collaboration Changes Everything*. New York: Portfolio.

Tocqueville, A. de. 2000. *Democracy in America*. Chicago: University of Chicago Press.

Toffler, A. 1980. *The Third Wave: Democratization in the Late Twentieth Century*. New York: Bantam Books.

Van Bockxmeer, H., V. Frissen, and M. Van Staden. 2001. *Nieuwe media en gemeenschappen*. Delft: TNO Strategie, Technologie en Beleid.

Van der Vijver, K., et al. 2009. *Burgernet in de Praktijk. De Evaluatie van de Pilot van Burgernet*. Dordrecht: Stichting Maatschappij, Veiligheid en Politie.

Verba, S., Nie, N.H. 1972. *Participation in America: Political Democracy and Social Equality*. New York: Harper and Row.

Wellman, B. A., and C. Haythornthwaite, eds. 2000. *The Internet in Everyday Life*. Oxford, UK: Blackwell.

Whitaker, G. 1980. Co-production: citizen participation in service delivery. *Public Administration Review* 40 (3): 240–246.

Winner, L. 1977. *Autonomous Technology: Technics-out-of-Control as a Theme in Political Thought*. Cambridge, MA: MIT Press.

Part III

How Does
Co-Management Work?

11 Co-Management to Solve Homelessness

Wicked Solutions for Wicked Problems

Kerry Brown, Robyn Keast,
Jennifer Waterhouse, Glen Murphy
and Myrna Mandell

INTRODUCTION

While governments are heavily engaged in developing social policy responses to address intractable, complex, "wicked" issues, such as poverty, homelessness, drug addiction and crime, resolving these issues in the long-term through government action has been problematic. Homelessness is a critical area to develop new approaches for securing better outcomes for members of society, as housing is considered a basic right for citizens (Human Rights and Equal Opportunity Commission, 2008) and homelessness is a problem that has outweighed the resources and policy intent dedicated to it by traditional "emergency" service delivery approaches (Culhane and Metraux, 2008; Gladwell, 2006). Not only is homelessness a social issue that affects many individuals, including young people, those with mental illness, drug and alcohol problems or a history of family violence, recent research that identified those who are without shelter has expanded to include new categories, such as family homelessness brought on by rental shortage and financial stress.

This widening of the domain of homelessness has severely strained the ability of governments and the community sector to deal effectively with people who are homeless, let alone find ways of assisting those at risk of being homeless. The use of vehicles for joint action and partnership between government and the community sector, such as co-management, has been offered as a way of harnessing the productive capability and innovative capacity of both these sectors to resolve these complex problems. However, it is suggested that while there is a well-advanced agenda with the intent for collaboration and partnership working, the frameworks and models for undertaking this joint action are not well understood and have not been fully developed or evaluated (Keast and Brown, 2006).

In their role as a service provider, community organizations have always relied on other organizations, to some extent, in terms of funding their programs. This is especially true in terms of their relationships with government

212 Brown, Keast, Waterhouse, Murphy and Mandell

agencies and/or foundations. In addition, they have often worked together with each other in order to better serve their clients. More recently, in terms of their relationships with government, they have become involved in a more active role, one in which they work alongside government agencies and other stakeholders in new forms of collaborations. In this role they actively work with government and other individuals, groups and organizations to make decisions, not only regarding service delivery, but more important to develop innovative solutions for changing the existing systems that currently deliver services (Keast and Waterhouse, 2006).

These new forms of relationships are becoming more prevalent. They represent alternative ways of harnessing the capacities of various partners, bringing about strategic renewal and innovative responses and maximizing resources. However, they also represent a challenge to those engaged in them. In Australia, this idea has been taken up and reflected in an experiment in co-management geared to meet these challenges. It is applied to the problem of homelessness. Here, the concept is of a "hub" of government agencies and community organizations working together to produce a new coordinated way of providing easy and early access to clients of a variety of services. As a result of this unique application of co-management, the hub model has led to a number of social innovations. The purpose of the service hubs is to provide homeless people, or those at risk of homelessness, with coordinated and therefore easy access to a wide range of housing and support services. The underlying conceptualization for the hub model of service provision centers on the understanding that "joined up" services are inherently more accessible to clients, as well as being more effective and efficient (Department of Communities, 2006). Moreover, there was an expectation that the hubs would become a service location where specialist knowledge and intervention skills would amass, creating a collective service space. It is evaluated to determine whether this approach can be considered a more effective method of co-management, leading to social innovations, and what the requirements for developing, improving and extending this model might involve.

For Mulgan (2006), social innovation involves innovative action and approaches motivated by an objective of addressing a social need diffused through organizations with a primary purpose of supporting social requirements. Innovation in the context of this chapter is the ability to establish a new underlying paradigm for the operation of the service system surrounding the issue of homelessness.

This chapter examines this model and its impact on co-management. In this chapter, the use of the term co-management refers both to the changing role of community groups in delivering government services as well as to the involvement of the government in the production and programmatic intent of services. The chapter uses the approach of Osborne and McLaughlin (2004), which regards co-management as part of a suite of integration and connection frameworks whereby the government and third or community sector work together. For Osborne and McLaughlin (2004), co-management is specifically focused on arrangements in which community sector organizations develop and administer services in conjunction with government. This type of activity then puts government and community sector organizations in the delivery arena of social programs as part of a co-management framework rather than at the co-governance level for the planning of services and service delivery systems or developing responses whereby citizens co-produce their own service solutions (Osborne and McLaughlin, 2004; Brandsen and Pestoff, 2006).

The chapter concludes that third sector organizations may be better positioned through their on-the-ground presence, their ability to undertake "innovation on the run" and their already-established linkages necessary to bring together the elements of the services system to foster innovation. Thus, these community organizations bring to the service delivery system a more flexible and adaptive response in areas of extreme social disadvantage that is more difficult to cultivate for their public or commercial counterparts working alone. However, the capacity of a financially constrained and, in some areas of geographical remoteness, skills-deficient community sector to deliver a complex policy and services, such as the homelessness policy and program agenda, may be put at risk. Further, while linkages are evident in many areas of service delivery, the ability of new entrants to enter and play an integral part in the service delivery framework may take time for adjustment by long-standing community organizations operating in the homelessness space.

HOMELESSNESS AS A WICKED ISSUE AND INTEGRATION AS A WICKED SOLUTION

In an evaluation of homelessness in the District of Columbia, Burt, Pearson and Montgomery (2005) conclude that the most effective strategies to prevent homelessness rely on a mix of community and institutional initiatives comprising a range of programs and policies, such as supportive services coupled with permanent housing, the establishment of Housing Courts and their effective use of mediation, access to cash assistance for rent or mortgage arrears, and finally, the use of shelter only as a fast transition to housing. Burt (2009) outlines developments in response to homelessness in California as focusing on providing integrated approaches to provide more permanent housing options.

The focus on co-management through integrated responses and service delivery to resolve homelessness is a common policy and practice prescription across many Western nations. However, the ways in which integration is achieved differ according to the mix of public, private and third sector parties involved in service delivery, and the systems change, integration vehicles and ability to create new approaches to chronic homelessness rather than through simply providing supported accommodation. The hub model of community sector organizations working across organizational boundaries used in Queensland, Australia, is an example of an integrated approach to developing a response to homelessness. Sereacki's (2007) research also adopted a case study approach to examine Canadian innovations for improving social housing that also mirrored and supported a hub model in that it provides examples of cases where collaborative alliances were used to reduce costs and increase the pool of resources.

Case studies of a suite of policies and programs in Queensland, Australia, are used to illustrate the multiplex issues in developing a system of co-management, through the use of joined up or integrated responses to resolving homelessness. At a national level, there is recognition that the issue of homelessness has strained the limits of a service system that cannot rely on traditional single agency or organizational responses to achieve sustained housing for people:

> The current response is not working. Mainstream services like schools, health services, and employment programs often fail to help people who are homeless or who are at risk of homelessness. Services don't always work together and people are forced to go from one service to another to try and get help. (Australian Government, 2008)

New responses to homelessness across the globe have focused on proposing joint action between stakeholders, including between all levels of government, from federal through to state and local spheres and across health, welfare and law enforcement functional departments together with the community sector (Australian Government, 2008; for U.S. examples, see Burt and Hall, 2008; Burt, 2009; and for Canada, see Pierre, 2007; Sereacki, 2007; and for Scotland see, Anderson and Tulloch, 2000). This chapter analyses an attempt to move away from traditional bureaucratic structures of welfare departments operating through single functional "silos" to a new horizontal "hub-based" model of service delivery operating in one jurisdiction in Australia that seeks to integrate actors across many different service areas and organizations. The hub model and the various innovative approaches of co-management emergent through integration and working together is argued to create, as stated by one of the case study respondents, "compelling new social relationships between previous separate individuals or groups that matter greatly to the people involved."

As the case studies indicate, where the institutional integration arrangements have deliberately and genuinely involved the community sector, stronger and more sustained commitment and effort has evolved. Based on the hub model, these integration mechanisms establish a range of "place" and "space" based initiatives that have improved access to services and provide links between various stages and locations on the homelessness pathway.

We argue that resolving homelessness needs a "wicked solution" that goes beyond simply providing emergency shelter. Community organizations and government working to develop and establish innovative ways of giving people the skills and capacity to move along the pathway from homelessness to sustained tenancy is a key strategy to begin addressing homelessness. In examining this approach, this chapter offers the results of a policy initiative to respond more effectively to the problem of homelessness. The methodology draws on the evidence of a suite of case studies to demonstrate and assess a new role the third sector can play in the provision of services to people who do not have sustained access to housing.

CASE STUDY METHOD

Similar to other studies investigating homelessness, a case study methodology is adopted in this research. A case study is ideal to map the situational context of policy and programmatic responses in specific locales (Yin, 2003). The method is flexible in that policy documents, interviews and focus groups with key informants can be added to the mix of techniques, and this approach was adopted in this study. It focuses on one jurisdiction in Australia as a case study of a particular type of co-management strategy and is examined to develop an understanding of the complex array of issues that need to be considered when resolving a wicked issue, such as homelessness. The case study sets out the overarching policy and reform agenda and investigates several embedded case studies of a government department working together with community sector program responses to this policy agenda.

Case study evaluation examined the impact of the strategy and levels of integration and service coordination and innovation across three selected sites: Townsville, Gold Coast and Brisbane. Distributed across the state of Queensland, these sites offered different social, economic and geographic contexts for understanding the impact of policy that sought to bring the service delivery stakeholders into a new paradigm and relationship for addressing homelessness. Specifically, the case studies provide an in-depth qualitative view of the selected service initiatives and their outcomes, highlight examples of innovative practice and identify the level of interconnection within the service system, as well as factors that have impacted on the achievement of these outcomes.

In June 2005, the Queensland Government committed $235.52 million (Australian dollars) to the *Responding to Homelessness Strategy* (the strategy). This whole-of-government approach sought to extend existing services and develop new and innovative models. Specifically, the aim of the strategy was to "create an integrated homelessness service system and to reduce, over time, the number of people who are completely without shelter by enhancing existing, and implementing new initiatives, responding to homelessness and public intoxication" (Queensland Government, 2005). In practice, the strategy comprises a suite of some thirty-two initiatives based within a number of government departments developed and offered in conjunction with community agencies organized under six themes: providing more accommodation and support options, connecting people with services, responding to homelessness and public space issues, meeting the health needs of homeless people, meeting the needs of homeless people in the legal system and helping residential services stay open.

Initiatives have been implemented across the state, but predominantly the five key locations of Brisbane, Gold Coast, Townsville, Cairns and Mt Isa were targeted for specific attention. Funding of $56.45 million (Australian dollars) was allocated to the Department of Communities. The following key initiatives fall within the remit of the department: Service Hubs for Homeless People (Service Hubs), Roma House Crisis Accommodation, Homeless Persons Information Queensland (HPIQ), Public Intoxication and Homelessness Early Intervention Services.

FINDINGS: THE IMPACT OF THE HUB MODEL ON CO-MANAGEMENT

As part of its change agenda the strategy was looking for new and innovative ways to enhance and link up services and systems. As Figure 11.1 displays, these innovation types occur at the client service, process and strategic/systems levels of operation. Examples of key innovations based on the Hub model at the different levels are outlined next.

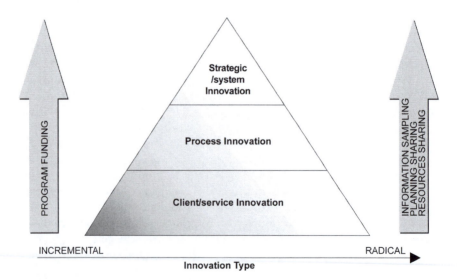

Figure 11.1   Integration innovation spaces.

Strategic Level of Co-Management

The strategy seeks to restructure the entire system of services to resolve homelessness. The inclusion of departments previously not directly engaged in addressing homelessness helped to garner a more holistic government approach. The introduction of initiatives such as the Homelessness Diversion Courts have impacted at the structural level by addressing public order homelessness as a social not legal issue and the referral of offenders to support services. This innovation is considered to be an important advance on dealing with homelessness issues.

Program Level of Co-Management

The findings distilled a number of innovations as a result of the use of the hub model that coalesced at the program level of operation. Three different hub operating models were evident. All were successful in their service role and context. This outcome highlights the benefits of a range of model options to accommodate locational variance.

Co-location established a new way of operating, bringing services together to share common resources and avoid duplication. Virtual network models provide for access to an expanded, more loosely connected service set whereby an administrative core acts as both a direct service provider and a "throughway" to other services and support. A linear-mobile model is evident on the Gold Coast, where the geographic requirements necessitate a chain of service linkage. This approach is facilitated by network membership hosting mobile crews.

Client Service Level of Co-Management

The activity programs have been operating on a small-scale, but with far-reaching consequences for those who are homeless. Two quite different programs have delivered positive outcomes of encouraging well-being and employment. The employment program at the Drop-In Centre and the art program run by a community organization offer new ways of engaging those who are homeless. The framing of a zero-alcohol policy for participation within an Occupational Health and Safety requirement has eased the burden of a "policing" approach to alcohol and has also had positive results for those participating in the activities. Mobile service options, such as outreach, and mobile services clustered around a client have shifted the service model from an agency to a place-based model, which is more client-centric. Tapping into the existing mobile phone connectivity of clients has enabled service providers to better stay in contact with clients and remind them of forthcoming appointments and use these as vehicles to contact other, more disconnected clients. The availability of free calls, including mobile phone calls to a community organization, allows clients safe and more immediate access to information and services. It also acts as a connector between clients and service agencies where previously there was a need for agencies to use resources to identify client whereabouts.

Of particular note, the hub model of co-management has led to a number of solutions to early intervention cases in each of the three case locations.

EARLY INTERVENTION PROGRAMS

Brisbane

There are examples, such as facilitating interagency coordination through memoranda of understanding, joint strategic planning, information sessions, joint funding submissions and regular partnership meetings in particular neighborhoods and localities where more people are at risk of homelessness; using brokerage funding to assist clients to establish themselves in new accommodation; working closely with "first-to-know" agencies, which alert the early intervention service to people at risk of becoming homeless; and outreach work in particular neighborhoods and localities where more people are at risk of homelessness or are already homeless.

This innovation culture was transferred to the suburbs of Brisbane. Over five broad locations, early intervention services were linked through a conceptual framework group. The purpose of this group was for workers and line managers across the services to engage and develop some common understanding of early intervention and how it might be operationalized in the field. A representative from the Department of Communities and Dr. Phil Crane of the Queensland University of Technology were part of the group.

The intentions of the initiative were to actively inform about early intervention and to establish some agreed guidelines that, in turn, could be used to inform government policy and expectations. A grant was also sought to work on issues of public advocacy, mental health and disability issues that can lead to homelessness. All of this activity led to wider discussion and wider recognition of the issues, as well as a more targeted approach to service provision. The cumulative benefit of this creative response to the definitional deficit was the building of new and the strengthening of existing networks. As a result of this work, it was stated by one case study respondent that: "the whole early intervention network across Brisbane has been raised on what we did."

The hub model has reframed early intervention through inclusive participation of all parties and has provided Brisbane with a project that advanced both the nongovernment and government sectors' understanding of early intervention issues and meanings. At a more on-site level, Brisbane early intervention innovations that were identified include outreach teams to identify needs and direct clients to services, use of brokerage expenditure tied to case management plans thus providing accountability processes and use of external community resources.

More closely linking brokerage with a case plan allowed for additional innovations, such as help with transport and moving assistance. For all three sites in this case study, transport was a commonly identified problem. All of these innovations are addressing how to become resource rich and enhance understanding in the community of the benefits of early intervention processes and help. In addition, the service hubs, in their various operational models, have provided a coalescing point for clients and service support that was previously dispersed and lacked a client-centric approach. In the Brisbane context, the presence of alternative hub models serves different client needs and, as such, is thought to be complementary.

Gold Coast

Service innovations that were identified included new approaches for young people, particularly in using a strengths-based approach to help empower clients to resolve their difficulties and provide more lasting results, to continue to provide follow-up and monitoring clients' tenancies for varying periods of time, and outreach work in particular neighborhoods and localities where more people are at risk of homelessness or are already homeless.

The most prominent innovation in co-management apparent in the Gold Coast area is the level of experimentation on new ways of working together. In the words of the Department of Communities' Stocktake Report (2008), the lesson is one of:

> Recognizing that while outcomes are hard to capture and measure, the culture of the SAAP [Supported Accommodation Assistance Program] network [and] the new version of it called the Gold Coast Homelessness Network, are critical and important to the success of the R2H [Responding To Homelessness] initiative—[the] network puts . . . real focus on clients rather than empire building, [provides a] good sense of succession planning with network collaboration, . . . enhanced funding . . . [and] has allowed a new model with an outreach function which is very effective.

The network approach to practice, planning and resourcing underpins much of the creativity of the service approach occurring within this area. Most important, the Gold Coast hub model, which actively engages with the nongovernment sector to develop local responses, presents as a way forward for sustained focus and committed action. Creating opportunities for advancement in solutions to homelessness through this model indicates a profound connection with the community and with the services collaborating in delivery of these services.

TOWNSVILLE

In Townsville, the hub model was not fully established. Instead, breaking into an existing service system required that the Red Cross adopt an innovative approach based on steady engagement, building relationships and through the strategic use of brokerage funds to bridge service gaps. The unique approaches adopted by Red Cross include: facilitating interagency coordination (a new experience in Townsville Red Cross), using brokerage funding to assist clients to establish themselves in new accommodation, including clients with higher support needs and using a strengths-based approach to help empower clients to resolve their difficulties and provide more lasting results.

OVERALL INNOVATION IN CO-MANAGEMENT

The hub model approach to co-management is based on the commitment to improving service to their clients, even in the face of doing something that is new, not always clearly defined and in need of development and redesign. Innovations identified by the early intervention services as enhancing support for clients cover three arenas: (1) early identification, (2) service promotion and interagency coordination and (3) improved operating methods and tools. The case study interviews have found the following details regarding these three arenas of innovation that have been found to be successful. They are:

- early identification of clients—people at risk of homelessness
- working closely with "first-to-know" agencies, which alert the early intervention service to people at risk of becoming homeless
- outreach work and having this occur in particular neighborhoods and localities where more people are at risk of homelessness or are already homeless
- service promotion and interagency coordination
- regular promotion of the early intervention service
- operationalising integration through memoranda of understanding, joint strategic planning, information sessions, joint funding submissions and regular partnership meetings
- community education sessions with rental property managers, the Real Estate Institute of Queensland forum and real estate agencies on homelessness risks in the community
- operating methods and tools
- developing a package containing general information for all early intervention service clients
- using brokerage funding to assist clients to establish themselves in new accommodation, including clients with higher support needs
- using a strengths-based approach to help empower clients to resolve their difficulties and provide more lasting results
- continuing to provide follow-up and monitoring clients' tenancies for varying period of time, especially the tenancies of clients with higher needs

Other specific innovations in the three sites include:

- a homelessness early intervention conceptual framework working group (Brisbane)
- renewed efforts to engage local doctors and dentists in accepting early intervention patients (Gold Coast)
- projects and forums increasing a culture of inquiry, learning and collaboration among early intervention
- Rent It to Keep It program on sustaining tenancies that teach the basics of how to rent a house (Townsville)
- cross-cultural promotional materials where appropriate (Brisbane)
- developing links with local governments and politicians (Brisbane)
- budgeting and sharing costs of staff training and workshops and group workshops with clients (Gold Coast)

Incremental innovation is the main outcome of co-management generated by the hub model that is highlighted. Due to the intractable nature of the complex problems addressed by the community sector, novel ways of dealing with short-term issues have been developed. "Innovation-on-the-run" is the norm for services that have been stretched beyond capacity and still are required to find shelter and draw on scarce resources to not only house clients but bring together the requisite services (health, medical, counseling, budgeting and welfare) for their complex needs.

DISCUSSION: THE IMPACT OF THE HUB MODEL OF CO-MANAGEMENT

Despite the variance in models and approach, each of the three hub models implemented has made significant contributions to improving homelessness service delivery in their geographic areas. The two Brisbane-based hubs have a more noticeable presence and contribute strongly to service integration as well as systems integration. The aim of the strategy in terms of developing wholesale innovation in services, processes and systems and the impact of this nexus on integration may have been too ambitious. This result is made evident in the lack of recognition of the community and government sector workers in articulating their work in an innovation context. Nevertheless, the findings of this study indicate that innovation in co-management can be identified.

Changing the Role of Community Organizations

It should be noted that the bulk of the innovation activity is occurring at the client service level. It is likely this outcome is a product of both the immediate need for creative service responses and the funding models that have allowed flexibility and space at the service delivery rather than the strategic level. It is possible this result reflects the funding intent that focused on incremental rather than large-scale systems change. This result concurs with the findings of Walker and colleagues' (2002) study of housing innovation in the United Kingdom, which found that most innovation was evolutionary rather than revolutionary for the sector and also supports the view of Osborne and Brown (2005) that innovation occurs at various layers within a service system.

The community sector was much less involved at the process level of innovation. Where such initiatives were identified, they appeared to be a result of longer term effort and higher level planning, often accompanied by a program champion.

Less evident across all case studies were innovations at the strategic/systems level. In the Gold Coast case study, there was horizontal and vertical strategic links forged, over time, which deliberatively incorporated new actors into the strategic decision-making and planning processes. This cross-fertilization of personnel and expertise was innovative and also contributed to strategic innovation, the outcome of which is meshed knowledge and action being directed to the Gold Coast region. This sustained level of interaction was not a common feature of the other cases. Creating such an innovation space at the strategic level requires significantly more funding, joint planning and pooled resources. Furthermore, it is highly dependent on an ongoing commitment from all parties to bring the objectives to fruition. System innovation is derived from individuals who can see "the big picture," know the steps to achieve this and have the capacity to mobilize people to collective action. It is argued that together these elements create an innovation space to develop new processes and systems.

The formation of the hub has enhanced services because it acts as a ring of support, and the outreach part of the concept provides initial outreach, makes assessments, and coordinates what is needed, which builds a more complete picture and a defined situation so that others can respond in a much better and effective way. The connections are essential.

There are excellent foundations for a hub success story on the Gold Coast. The Gold Coast homelessness network was built on collaboration, and the addition of the hubs can do a lot of the work and make the job of the other services a lot easier because the whole network has agreed to link together and meet monthly, and meet in the one place at the one time, and be out in the community in multiple places at the same time.

There is a pre-strategy existing ethos of working together, and there is a cultural valuing of what each person and service can add, and all are welcomed to the group. There is a vision of shared resources and doing the best for the consumers at the center. It is essential that there is, in creating a linear hub, an overall Gold Coast set of values and shared commitment to similar goals. The network of the service groups and their values are critical. That impacted how the hub in the Gold Coast was developed. A lot of people were involved in the development of the model. If there had not been a network and the values of working relationships in place, the hub would be a totally different concept. Everyone also then saw the hub as an improvement based on everyone's ideas of what was needed, what would happen and how it should work.

Involvement of the Community in the Delivery of Services

New service models have added depth to the array of services and support previously available to clients. In doing so, the new services shift the intervention focus from predominately a crisis orientation and have offered additional resources and support to better meet the complex and multiple needs of homeless people. Working with clients in their own locations offers an important additional service dimension, especially to more vulnerable clients and those less willing to go to formal sites.

Findings indicate the hub teams are widening the options available to clients. The hub teams are also enhancing awareness of services and reaching more of the people experiencing homelessness, which is adding to the number of people requesting services. The system could be acknowledged, and is said by service providers, to be working too well! Of serious concern to such an innovative co-management model as this one, therefore, is the increase in clients and client access to a system in which there are resource limitations. The system introduced by the strategy, however, requires further examination of the resourced infrastructure that underpins the capacity to do the support work.

Other agencies commented on the inherent benefits that co-location through a hub model offers in terms of stronger relationship building and overcoming agency "turf" issues. Informants theorized that these strengthened relationships could be used as a catalyst to enhance integration, which could then be leveraged particularly for the more difficult or intractable client issues. On the other hand, concern was expressed that in such a tightly coupled arrangement, clients may be reluctant to raise service complaints and that confidentiality and privacy rights may be compromised.

The Role of Government

While the community sector has developed innovations in a range of areas, it is suggested that government has a role in helping develop the capability and capacity to undertake these tasks. Moreover, government investment in developing in-house capacity and a commitment to innovate in the area of co-management is an important aspect of co-management. While innovative individuals operating at the grassroots level are found to be vital for the services system to operate and adapt, innovation capacity remaining only at this level puts in jeopardy the ability to achieve process and systems change through innovation.

CONCLUSION

In conclusion, integration and new services provided a strong foundation to an overall improvement to the homelessness service system. The new hub service models have added depth to the array of services and support previously available to clients. These new service models, which cross an array of areas, including housing and support, early intervention, service and referral hubs, health outreach teams and court diversion, relieve some of the pressure experienced by existing services with limited intervention options. In doing so, the new services shift the intervention focus from predominantly a crisis orientation and have offered existing supported accommodation services the additional resources and support to better meet the needs of homeless people with complex and multiple needs.

Innovative strategies and practices were found to occur primarily at the service system and client level of operation of community organizations by drawing on the knowledge, expertise and networks of service providers to creatively navigate the service system. Future research should consider whether additional support and resourcing is required to advance beyond improvisation or "innovation-on-the-run" to a more deliberate and considered approach to innovation.

From the insights generated from the case studies, coupled with the extant literature, it becomes apparent that for such innovative services in co-management to occur, the array of programs, processes and systems to be developed and embedded takes time, commitment and targeted and adequate funding. Success of innovative endeavors relies not just on developing integration mechanisms and structures between stakeholders, but on building relational capital between the parties—in essence, the development of "wicked solutions" through bringing together the complex suite of service providers and program and policy developers to co-manage the responses to homelessness. Innovation outcomes from the process and strategic systems level, however, have been less than optimal and require the provision of a conceptual space to develop new initiatives, evaluate risks/rewards and devise implementation strategies. Indeed, the identified framework highlights that while government may lead strategic-level innovations, community organizations are active in developing innovation at the service and client level.

For the model of co-management to further develop, thrive and be adopted, there is a need for an adjustment in current practices and monitoring processes to encourage, adequately resource and make room for exploring, experimenting and correcting mistakes.

REFERENCES

Agranoff, R. 1991. Human services integration: Past and present challenges in public administration. *Public Administration Review* 51 (6): 533–542.

Anderson, I., Tulloch, D. 2000. *Pathways to Homelessness: A Review of the Research Evidence.* Edinburgh: Scottish Homes.

Australian Government, 2008. *Which Way Home? A New Approach to Homelessness.* Canberra: Green Paper.

Brandsen, T., and V. Pestoff. 2006. Co-production, the third sector and the delivery of public services. *Public Management Review* 8 (4): 493–501.

Brotsky, C. 2006. *Strategic Considerations in Creating and Operating Multi-Tenant Nonprofit Centers.* Presentation to the "Moving Forward" Conference, Madison and Milwaukee, Wisconsin, May 10–11, 2006.

Burt, M. 2009. *Widening Effects of the Corporation for Supportive Housing's System-Change Efforts in Los Angeles 2005–2008.* Washington DC: Urban Institute.

Burt, M., and S. Hall. 2008. *Major Recommendations: Summary Report of the Urban Institute's Assessment of the District of Columbia's Public Homelessness System.* Washington DC: Urban Institute.

Burt, M., C. Pearson, and A. Montgomery. (2005). *Strategies for Preventing Homelessness.* Washington, DC: Housing and Urban Development Office of Policy Development and Research.

Common Ground. 2009. *Our Mission is to end Homelessness.* http://www.commonground.org/.

Crane, M., A. M. Warnes, and R. Fu. 2006. Developing homelessness prevention practice: combining research evidence and professional knowledge. *Health and Social Care in the Community* 14 (2), pp.156–166.

Culhane, D., and S. Metraux. 2008. Rearranging the deck chairs or reallocating the lifeboats? Homelessness assistance and its alternatives. *Journal of the American Planning Association* 74 (1): 111–121.

Department of Communities. 2006. *Funding Information Paper. Responding to Homelessness—Service Hubs for Homeless People.* Brisbane.

Department of Communities. 2008 (February). *Service Integration Stocktake.* Senior Officers' Group on Homelessness. Brisbane.

Eardley, T. 2008. The impact of SAAP homelessness services on client self-reliance. *SPRC Newsletter,* 99 (July): 8–10.

Fine, M. 2001. The New South Wales demonstration projects on integrated community care. In M. P. Mandell, ed., *Getting Results Through Collaboration: Networks and Network Structures for Public Policy and Management.* Westport, CA: Quorum Books, pp. 26-219.

Fisher, K., G. Redmond, J. Tudball, L. Chenowith, and S. Robinson. 2007. *Service Needs of Residents in Private Residential Services.* Sydney: Social Policy Research Centre, University of New South Wales.

Gladwell, M. 2006. Homelessness. *New Yorker.* March 1, 2006.

Human Rights and Equal Opportunity Commission. 2008. *Homelessness is a Human Rights Issue.* Canberra: Author.

Keast, R., and K. Brown. 2006. Adjusting to new ways of working: Experiments in service delivery in the public sector. *Australian Journal of Public Administration* 65 (4): 41–53.

Keast, R., K. Brown, and M. Mandell. 2007. Getting the right mix: Unpacking integration meanings and strategies. *International Public Management Journal* 10 (1): 9–33.

Keast, R., and Waterhouse, J. 2006. Participatory evaluation: the missing component in the social change equation? *Strategic Change* 15 (1): 23–35.

Keast, R., M. Mandell, K. Brown, and G. Woolcock. 2004. Network structures: working differently and changing expectations. *Public Administration Review* 64 (3): 363–377.

Konrad, E. L. 1996. A multi-dimensional framework for conceptualising human services integration initiatives. In J. M. Marquart, and E. L. Konrad, eds. *Evaluating Initiatives to Integrate Human Services. New Directions for Evaluation.* San Francisco: Jossey–Bass.

Leutz, W. 1999. Five laws for integrating medical and social services. Lessons from the United States and the United Kingdom. *The Milbank Quarterly* 77 (1): 77–110.

Levitt, A., D. Culhane, J. DeGenova, P. O'Quinn, and J. Bainbridge. 2009. Health and social characteristics of homeless adults in Manhattan who were chronically or not chronically unsheltered. *Psychiatric Services* 60 (7): 978–981.

Mulgan, G. 2006. The process of social innovation. *Innovations* 1 (2): 145–162.

Mulgan, G., S. Tucker, R. Ali, and B. Saunders. 2007. Social Innovation: What it is, why it matters and how it can be accelerated. *Proceedings of the Skoll World Forum on Social Entrepreneurship*, March 27–29, 2007, Oxford, Said Business School, University of Oxford.

Osborne, S., and K. McLaughlin. 2004. The cross-cutting review of the voluntary sector: Where next for local government voluntary sector relationships? *Regional Studies* 38 (5): 573–82.

Osborne, S., and K. Brown. 2005. *Managing Change and Innovation in Public Service Organizations.* London: Routledge.

Peters, B. G. 1998. Managing horizontal government: the politics of coordination. *Public Administration* 76 (2): 295–311.

Pierre, N. 2007. *A Safer Haven: Innovations for Improving Social Housing in Canada.* Canadian Policy Research Networks (CPRN), Ontario.

Queensland Government. 2005. *Responding to Homelessness.* Brisbane.

Rhodes, R. A. W. 1997. *Understanding Governance: Policy Networks, Governance, Reflexivity and Accountability.* Buckingham: Open University Press.

Sereacki, M. M. 2007. *Fostering Better Integration and Partnerships for Housing in Canada.* Ontario: Canadian Policy Research Networks.

Tosi, A. 2005. Re-housing and social integration of homeless people: A case study from Milan. *Innovation*,11 (2): 184–203.

Waldfolgel, J. 1997. The new wave of service integration. *Social Service Review* 71 (3): 463–484.

Walker, R., E. Jeans, and R. Rowlands. 2002. Managing public service innovation: The experience of English housing associations. *Journal of Housing and Built Environment* 17 (2): 203–205.

Wolch, J. 1996. Community-based human service delivery. *Housing Policy Debate* 7 (4): 649–671.

Yin, R. K., 2003. *Case Study Research Design and Methods.* 3rd ed. London: Sage.

12 Co-Management in Urban Regeneration

New Perspectives on Transferable Collaborative Practice

Hans Schlappa

INTRODUCTION

Contemporary regeneration policy emphasizes the vertical as well as horizontal integration of key stakeholders in local development partnerships (LDPs) because this is considered to be of critical importance in achieving lasting socioeconomic improvements. Ensuring the integration of residents and third sector organizations (TSOs) is a persistent problem for LDPs, however, and has posed a wide range of challenges for policy and practice ever since national governments started to experiment with area-based approaches to urban regeneration in the 1980s (Department for Communities and Local Government, 2008; Wilks-Hegg, 2000; Carley et al., 2000; Diamond and Liddle, 2005). Over the past twenty years, European Union regional policy has also deployed a range of policy instruments to improve the integration of TSOs and residents in the regeneration process, with mixed results (Commission of the European Communities, 1999; 2007a; 2007c; 2008).

More recently, a number of national governments adopted the "Acquis Urban" accord, in that they confirm their commitment to European policy goals aimed at the integration of local communities in the regeneration process (Deutsch-Österreichisches URBAN-Netzwerk, 2005; Office of the Deputy Prime Minister, 2006). At local levels, there is a growing number of cities in the European Union working on the further development of the "Leipzig Charter" into a detailed performance assessment tool intended to improve their approaches toward the integration of residents, TSOs and businesses in the urban regeneration process (EuroCities & Deutsches Institut für Urbanistik, 2007; German Presidency of the European Council of Ministers, 2007; LC-Facil, 2010).

While local, national and European policy is likely to continue to promote the integration of community stakeholders, the practical experience of policy makers and regeneration practitioners shows that their engagement is fraught with difficulty. There is a substantial body of literature that points to the many failings of LDPs in their attempts to engage TSOs and to harness the many resources that one found in even the most disadvantaged of urban communities (for an overview, see Wilks-Hegg, 2003; Taylor et al., 2007; Balloch and Taylor, 2001). This literature provides important insights into the relationships between the controllers and users of funding within partnership contexts and also offers a significant amount of guidance on how to improve regeneration practice (see for example: Taylor, 2001; Lowndes and Sullivan, 2004; Whitehead, 2007). However, accounts of "what works" are by their very nature highly context specific, and while there are many examples that identify transferable regeneration policy and practice (Burton et al., 2004; Taylor et al., 2007; Wates, 2010; Royal Town Planning Institute, 2010), LDPs often find themselves "re-inventing the wheel" in their attempts to adapt approaches developed elsewhere to their local circumstances.

This problem is amplified in the cross-national transfer of policy and practice, where different national traditions and institutional structures present very significant barriers. Although overarching conceptual frameworks to support such efforts appear to be poorly developed (Hantrais, 2000; Hantrais and Mangen, 1996) the popularity of cross-national learning and exchange programs, such as URBACT (URBACT Secretariat, 2007; Commission of the European Communities, 2007b), demonstrates that there are many regeneration practitioners and policy makers in Europe alone who are undeterred by the challenges associated with comparing and transferring effective practice across countries.

One way of supporting the transfer of effective practice is to improve our understanding of the different sectoral and organizational characteristics of TSOs across the growing number of European Union member states (Kendall, 2009; Osborne, 2008) or to develop a conceptual focus on a particular kind of TSO, such as social enterprise (Evers and Laville, 2004; Borzaga and Defourny, 2001). This chapter suggests that viewing the integration of community stakeholders through the conceptual lens of co-management offers important advantages over existing comparative approaches toward the study of collaborative service design and delivery, because co-management provides a sharp focus on the practical actions that are directly related to the provision of a service. By focusing on the interactions between LDP staff and TSO workers, we are stripping away many of the contextual layers that make comparisons between different locations difficult. The interactions between program management and TSO staff naturally do not take place in a vacuum, and organizational context therefore needs to be taken into account in any comparative analysis. However, in contrast to other attempts aimed at identifying transferable policy and practice, which tend to focus on the institutional architecture established to create an integrated regeneration process, the application of the concept of co-production in its broadest sense (see Pestoff's chapter 2 in this volume) allows us to focus on behaviors, skills and competencies that underpin regeneration practice.

To illustrate the advantages of the co-production concept in comparative analysis and to develop a deeper understanding of the co-management process in regeneration contexts, this chapter analyses two cases where staff working for LDPs have produced new services in collaboration with workers from TSOs. These two cases are then contrasted with a case where the LDP placed a strong emphasis on contracting and commissioning procedures with limited scope for collaborative practice. The analysis shows that co-management can occur in very different institutional contexts, and that TSOs and LDPs can both derive significant benefits from co-managing the development and delivery of new services. In addition, a number of variables can be identified that support the co-management process, specifically in regeneration contexts. These include a high degree of organizational flexibility in participating organizations; workers who together share responsibility for the provision of a new service; and senior managers who are able to navigate regulatory, institutional and political barriers that stand in the way of collaborative cross-organizational working. A commissioning approach, in contrast, was found to have created a situation where the TSO considered the LDP and program management staff as a barrier to their creating new services.

The findings reported here are drawn from a cross-national doctoral study that explored the link between European Union funding and organizational change in TSOs (Schlappa, 2009). Out of the nine cases that were part of the study, three were chosen for analysis in this chapter because they provide the clearest contrast between co-management and commissioning approaches in urban regeneration. The data for the three case studies presented here were collected through eighteen semi-structured interviews. Interviewees included paid and unpaid workers of three TSOs, as well as the program managers and their support staff who were responsible for the delivery of the European Union-funded URBAN II programs in Bristol, Belfast and Berlin. Data were analyzed with NVivo using an open coding method and are presented anonymously.

TWO CASES OF CO-MANAGEMENT

The URBAN II program in Belfast had the objective to regenerate parts of North Belfast, which over decades had suffered disproportionately from sectarian violence, into a safe and viable urban community. The LDP was a third-sector-led partnership that brought together public agencies, TSOs, local politicians and local residents. Program management staff were employed by the TSO that serviced the partnership, and the accountable body for the European funding was Belfast City Council. In Bristol, the LDP was governed by a board led by young residents who lived or worked in the target area. The program had the objective to improve the local social and economic conditions by engaging young people in the regeneration process. Program management staff were employed by Bristol City Council, which was also the accountable body for the URBAN II funding.

Both case study organizations were small TSOs that relied extensively on unpaid workers and had a turnover of less than £150,000 per year; however, they had contrasting backgrounds and purposes. At the time the study was conducted, Bereavement Support was a campaigning organization in Belfast without formal institutional status or structures, and with a loosely organized network of supporters. Outdoor Pursuits for Young People in Bristol, in contrast, had been established for over 30 years and formed part of a national federation of TSOs. In both cases, the founders were actively engaged in their organizations and had approached their local URBAN II program for financial support.

Bereavement Support, Belfast

The founder of Bereavement Support was a father who had lost his son through suicide. He campaigned for several years, challenging public agencies to invest more in bereavement services and also personally provided support for others who had lost relatives through suicide. Over the years, the founder had developed a self-help network of volunteers and supporters in North Belfast. By the time the founder approached the URBAN II program for financial support, the campaign had achieved a high-profile status, and he struggled with a burgeoning workload that involved coordinating volunteers, supporting individuals, and taking advantage of lobbying opportunities, while holding down his paid job at the same time:

> I have to say, it is a struggle. I was out at seven yesterday morning and I was here until nine last night and I had no dinner, no lunch. . . . We have to be careful that we don't destroy ourselves. (Founder)

Instead of simply making the requested funding of £10,000 available to the project, the program manager seconded one of her outreach workers to assist the founder in the development of the service and an institutional structure that could support service provision. The grant was administered by the program management team and could be drawn down as and when required by the founder. Without delay, the outreach worker and the founder began to tackle a number of developments simultaneously and jointly. This included obtaining premises free of charge from a local housing association, organizing volunteers to renovate and manage the premises, organizing regular drop-in sessions organized by volunteers, developing a district-wide emergency support network based on two hundred volunteers, developing a formal organization and its registration with the Charity Commission and recruiting an administrator.

This development process was opportunistic in that there was no defined strategy and both founder and outreach worker drew on their respective networks and resources in public agencies and local communities to progress the project as best they could. Each took the lead on particular tasks they were well equipped to handle, and with the active support of the other partner, negotiated funding agreements with public agencies, recruited volunteers, coordinated services provided by other TSOs and spoke about their work at conferences. As a result, the organization grew rapidly and gained political support at the highest levels, but its success also put significant strains on the two actors. In addition, the recently created paid administrator post required extra support to deal with the burgeoning workload that resulted from the growing number of people offering as well as requesting support:

> This organization generates an awful lot of work. We really do a lot of good work and that hit me when the minister [for Health in Northern Ireland] made reference to us, saying that we are providing an important service in the community. (Outreach Worker)

> I think we've been doing alright the way we've been going, but we can't seriously organize and run an organization like this without money. We have one worker and that's it. I would like to see maybe another two people working in here. (Founder)

Its profile and access to decision makers created substantial opportunities to access public sector funding and to grow the organization as a public service provider, but the founder and outreach worker were adamant that they did not want to become a "contractor" for public agencies. They wanted to nurture the involvement of and accountability to local people instead:

> You can easily lose the community aspect; the more professional you become, the more distant you become. But as long as I and [the outreach worker] are here we will keep this as grass roots and as close to the community as we possibly can. (Founder)

> This project was never money driven. It was there because there was a need. . . . If this did become a money grabbing organization I wouldn't want to be part of it. (Outreach Worker)

While both outreach worker and founder worked very closely together on many tasks, drawing on their different skills and access to different resources, there were also areas where they would work largely independent from the other. For example, the founder was dealing with the restructuring of the governing body and led on all political and lobbying activities. Arrangements concerned with the leasing of the premises or the recruitment of the administrator, on the other hand, were made by the outreach worker in consultation with the founder. The manager of the URBAN II program was also involved in these developments, but not directly. In addition to acting as a banker for the grant that had been awarded, the program manager also provided access to individuals and networks that could assist Bemovement Support in the development of services while maintaining strategic accountability to political and institutional stakeholders for the use of program resources. There seemed to be a strong consensus among LDP members that the resources available should be used not only to create improvements and new services but also to support the development of organizational capacity among local TSOs to provide such services:

> So, if you are working in an area that has limited community capacity, you can't just give people some money and walk away. You have to maximize the organizations' chances of successful project delivery and to achieve that you have to give them some additional support. (Program Manager)

Outdoor Pursuits, Bristol

At the time of data collection, the organization had doubled the number of young people taking up its services as a result of engaging with the URBAN II program and provided weekly recreational and education activities for approximately 160 young people on a housing estate in South Bristol. The founder had made an application for URBAN II funding to employ an administrator with the intention of reducing the administrative burden for the 31 volunteer instructors working for Outdoor Pursuits. This was in part intended to increase the enjoyment they could derive from volunteering but also to help instructors obtain legally required certifications to enable them to deliver a wider range of outdoor activities, such as canoeing, mountain climbing, caving and more. The grant application was approved in principle by LDP on the condition that the program manager would first gauge whether the applicant needed additional support to realize the organization's aspirations. This proved to be the beginning of the co-management process:

> To be honest, if the Program manager had not wanted to help us develop our project, I would have had a grant of £10,000 a year to pay the administrator's wages for five years and that would have been it. But his seeking questions made us think, and the project just suddenly went from being this very narrow administrator post to being "wow, oh my God!" (Founder)

The founder and the program manager jointly developed a service model and business plan for a social enterprise that would provide certified training for instructors of other similar organizations in the city, offer organized outdoor activities for schools and youth clubs on a commercial basis, and create employment opportunities for some of the young people who were volunteering at Outdoor Pursuits. With a grant of £56,000 from URBAN II, the founder changed the organization in ways that increased the number of young people it served, diversified its activities, modernized its equipment and transport, created a subsidiary organization with a separate governing body and, at the same time, was able to employ the originally envisaged administrator:

> We have done a lot with the URBAN II money. It has enabled us to get that initial training, that initial bit of equipment and the great thing is, it becomes self-sustaining. It just carries on forever because the money that we are saving and the money that we are generating enable the project to continue." (Founder)

> Well, before URBAN II we had operated with two ropes and three harnesses and we could take a dozen kids. Now we take twenty kids climbing; everybody's got their own helmet, everybody has their own harness and it allows us to deliver a better activity to a lot more kids. (Volunteer Instructor)

While Outdoor Pursuits developed and improved its services very quickly, the program manager struggled to honor a number of commitments he and the LDP had entered into at the planning stage. At times this required "bending the rules" in order to create access for the TSO to the funding that was available:

> This was a very controversial project because they had to provide £50,000 of match funding from their own resources. But if you looked at their bank statements at the time, they didn't have £50,000. Theoretically, at the time we approved the project, we probably shouldn't have done so because the organization just simply didn't have the money in the bank. . . . It was an act of faith in some respects in the beginning. (Program Manager)

In addition, the local authority finance department refused to reimburse Outdoor Pursuits for a number of items that had been approved by the LDP as being eligible project expenditure, such as a new mini-bus, on the grounds that these approvals contravened financial regulations in some way. The situation became so protracted that the LDP requested the intervention from the Regional Government Office in order to achieve the release of the funding to Outdoor Pursuits:

> And there were some very major items of expenditure that the finance team just simply refused to pay for. This was the source of immense conflict. And URBAN II, for a while, gained a reputation of being not only a program that was very difficult to get money out of but also a very unreliable program. (Program Manager)

A CASE OF COMMISSIONING SERVICES

The case study organization, Youth Enterprise, was located in a neighborhood of Berlin that, following the unification of Germany, had suffered disproportionately from the collapse of the East German economy and the exodus of the local population. The URBAN II target area straddled two local authority districts, and each authority had a strong representation on the LDP that consisted almost entirely of public sector representatives. The LDP was chaired by a senior representative of the governmental department that coordinated economic regeneration initiatives across the city of Berlin and that was also the accountable body for the European funding. Program management staff worked for a private consulting firm specializing in the management of regeneration contracts. This firm had been contracted by the LDP through a competitive tendering process to manage the delivery of the program.

Youth Enterprise had supported vulnerable young people in the neighborhood for over thirty years and had its roots in the youth work of the local church. Following the unification of East and West Berlin, the organization acquired a range of residential properties that were refurbished through government-funded youth training schemes and then let out to young people in need. The annual turnover was £3.3 million, there were 130 staff and trainees and the organization maintained extensive contractual relationships with public agencies. Youth Enterprise became involved with URBAN II because its director had been invited by the LDP to put forward project ideas for inclusion in funding proposals by the city council in order to help secure EU resources for the socioeconomic regeneration of the neighborhood.

The director of Youth Enterprise was a founding member and had led the organization through a period of rapid growth during the years following the unification of East and West Berlin. This growth was mainly due to service delivery contracts with the local authority and other public agencies, which used Youth Enterprise extensively as a provider of services for vulnerable young adults in the district. Despite its close contacts with public agencies, the organization saw itself primarily as a mechanism through which local people were enabled to bring about change in their personal circumstances. In representing the interests of the local community, Youth Enterprise often challenged the decisions of public officials about the design or availability of services for vulnerable young people, which led to frequent and, at times, deep tensions:

> We are first and foremost servants of local residents, the interest of public agencies come second. This enrages the local authority and we are regularly in conflict with council officials and local politicians. (Director)

> It really is terrible. They are the complete opposite to us. For council officials it is not the human being that matters but the budget. (Board Member)

Youth Enterprise wanted to create a community center by using the URBAN II grant to refurbish a derelict building that had been donated to them by a private individual. They had to go through a lengthy competitive bidding process, which was administered by the program manager and controlled by the LDP, to secure £133,000 that represented a small proportion of the total project cost. Not only was the application process very demanding, there was also suspicion that the project selection and approval process was biased toward the interests of public agencies that used their influence on the LDP to secure funding for their own projects first:

> The URBAN Steering Committee gave preference to projects put forward by public agencies. . . . Very few third sector organizations were given a chance. (Project Officer)

> We began to have serious reservations about the URBAN application and considered pulling out. Our proposal was rejected three times and had to be re-written and re-submitted. In the end it took two people three months to write just one application! (Board Member)

Once Youth Enterprise had secured its funding, the program manager required detailed and frequent reports on project progress. This was very demanding for workers and contributed to the high levels of frustration among staff of Youth Enterprise, in part because they had not used European Union funding before but also because the program management team offered very little support in dealing with problems arising from the project implementation process. The program manager seemed primarily interested in ensuring that contractual obligations and agreed deadlines were met:

> I think that the amount of effort required to draw down URBAN II funding is crazy. (Board Member)

> The program manager shows no interest whatsoever in what we are trying to achieve here. They only show up when they have official delegations who want to see an integrated youth training project. (Project Officer)

Members of the LDP representing the two local authorities, on the other hand, saw no reason why their approach could be interpreted as unsupportive. Program management staff were not expected to provide additional support because TSOs had won funding for their project on the basis that they had the necessary capacity to deliver the service. Local authority staff also had to take a "strategic" approach toward ensuring the implementation of the regeneration program and did not perceive themselves as being able to become involved with the delivery of services. In their view, TSOs were contracted to deliver a specified project, and once they had entered into a legally binding agreement, it was up to TSOs to deal with any problems that might prevent them from fulfilling their contractual obligations:

> The borough defines the projects and we select suitable TSOs to deliver them. (Program Manager)

> Some TSOs thought that they would sail through the application process because they had a strong local presence. That was not the case. They had to secure URBAN funding through a competitive bidding process like everyone else. It was good to do it that way. It's the process that makes the decision. This process prevents you from following just a nice project idea and instead helps you to get the best deal for your money. (LDP member)

> I don't know in detail what their problem is. I can't get involved in all the URBAN projects. The question is, if they do have substantial problems what are they going to do about it? That's their problem, isn't it? (LDP member)

For the director of Youth Enterprise, the approach taken by the LDP and program management staff reflected a way of working with public agencies that he had become accustomed to. While funding from public agencies remained critically important to enable his organization achieve its mission, wherever possible he and his colleagues would try to minimize the influence of funders on their work. This created a situation where many services were produced in parallel to public agencies, rather than in collaboration with them:

> "I am glad when they don't get involved in our work. That always creates problems. We develop solutions with residents, not with public agencies." (Director)

DISCUSSION

The case studies presented here show that TSOs and LDPs can derive a range of benefits when service development and delivery is co-managed. The analysis also points to a number of preconditions that facilitate or hinder co-management in regeneration contexts. In the following section, the different benefits that LDPs and TSOs obtained through the co-management of services are identified and then compared to the challenges that were created through a commissioning approach toward program delivery. In addition, the discussion will focus on the different roles that were played by program management and TSO staff in creating some of the preconditions that appear to have supported co-management practice.

Benefits of Co-Management in Regeneration Contexts

The case studies point to a range of benefits arising for LDPs and TSOs that can be related to the co-management process. These include the development of new services based on local entrepreneurship, targeted service delivery in socially diverse neighborhoods and the active engagement of local residents in service development and design—all of which are strategic priorities for national and European regeneration policy. In addition, TSOs benefited from organizational changes that were brought about by the co-management process.

In the case of Bereavement Support, which had embryonic organizational structures, the co-management process contributed to the rapid development of organizational processes and structures that in turn facilitated the development and provision of a wide range of new services. In the case of Outdoor Pursuits, co-management changed long-established organizational processes and structures, including the establishment of a subsidiary social enterprise with a separate governing body and a rapid expansion of the range of activities young people could participate in. Both case studies show that organizational challenges resulting from these developments were regarded as positive developments by TSOs, enabling them to do more of the type of work they were created for and leaving them better placed to sustain their work in future. This suggests that organizational change resulting from co-management can enable TSOs to respond to challenges as well as opportunities in ways that strengthen their organizational capabilities and leave them better placed to provide their services in future.

Such findings are in contrast to much of the literature exploring the link between organizational change and the influx of public sector funding. Many such studies tend to conceptualize organizational change resulting from governmental funding as a problem for TSOs because change is seen as being externally imposed and as reflecting the interests of funders, rather than the needs of TSOs (Blackmore, 2004; Crack, Turner, and Heenan, 2006; Hanion, Rosenberg, and Clasby, 2007; Scott, 2001). While such concerns will frequently be justified, the argument advanced here is that organizational change resulting from governmental funding is not inevitably a negative process: TSOs can secure substantial organizational benefits for themselves if public sector funding is used to support co-productive processes.

Furthermore, the case studies suggest that co-management does not take place within the institutional structures created by regeneration partnerships. Rather than making great efforts to engage TSOs in structures and funding decision-making processes of the LDPs, the TSOs studied here integrated staff working on behalf of LDPs into their own organization and involved them in the planning and design of their new service. TSO workers then also pro-active and strategic important decisions about how the new service would change their organization. This involved decisions on new organizational structures, changes to governing bodies, employment of staff, development of volunteering programs, the acquisition of property and, ultimately, the provision of services that reflected their own values and were, at the same time, valued by the communities they served. It would appear, therefore, that co-management requires a high degree of organizational adaptability, including having the flexibility to make significant and quick adjustments to the way in that people, technology, processes and resources interact.

Pre-Conditions for Co-Management in Regeneration Contexts

The findings reported here point to the important role of program management staff as key actors who can trigger or prevent co-management. In encouraging a collaborative approach toward program delivery, program management staff took account of the organizational needs and capacities of the TSOs they were working with and provided support that was not mechanistic, that is, did not follow a particular predesigned procedure. Moreover, the findings suggest that the co-management of new services seems to be the opposite to "contracting out" and involves some sharing of responsibility for the success of the new service between funder and provider. Such "deep collaboration" (Huxham and Vangen, 2005) could be perceived as a form of capacity building, and there is much literature that analyses how TSOs can be supported in obtaining and using public sector funding (Her Majesty's Treasury, 2004; Barnes and Sullivan, 2002; Brown and Kalegaonka, 2002; Improvement and Development Agency, 2006).

However, the capacity building literature conceptualizes such interactions primarily as processes in that something is done *for* TSOs, for example, providing advice on how to obtain funding, how to manage projects or how to account for expenditure (Harris and Schlappa, 2007), and the shortcomings of such top-down approaches have been subject to extensive debate and criticism (Harrow, 2001; Macmillan, 2007; Shirlow and Murtagh, 2004; Taylor, 2000). It would appear, therefore, that co-management in regeneration contexts can be more effective than "capacity building," in part because staff from LDPs and TSOs take joint responsibility for the creation and delivery of new services.

An actor with very substantial influence over the co-management process was the regeneration program manager. The cases of Belfast and Bristol show how the regeneration program manager provided a buffer between the demands for compliance from public officials and the ability of TSOs to respond to them. In addition, he facilitated the provision of technical, financial and staffing support, enabling TSOs to design services that matched their aspirations to the opportunities they had, and at the same time minimizing the constraints and administrative burdens arising from EU funding conditions. While these actions are in themselves not particularly unusual, the case studies suggest that the boundaries between the roles of "controller" of EU funding and "provider" of an EU-funded service at times became blurred during the co-management process. The regeneration program manager or his staff worked at times "inside" TSOs and supported them in dealing with the challenges arising from the new services they were providing and, at the same time, were able to ensure that contractual requirements and program-level policies were adhered to.

The collaboration of individual officers who work for funders and providers of services clearly is pivotal in the co-management process, and their actions seem at least as important as the LDP structures through which resources are allocated and controlled. Unlike commissioning relationships, the co-management process seems to put TSOs in a relatively strong position vis-à-vis the LDP, primarily because they do not simply fulfill contractual obligations drawn up by the LDP but involve program management staff in the practical steps that lead to the provision of a service. Co-management therefore seems to require program management and TSO workers to engage on equal terms and in ways that do not follow a particular template of interventions but that instead reflect specific organizational contexts and capabilities. Such an approach is very different from the hierarchical commissioning of services where contractual obligations force TSOs to adhere to procedures, targets and service specifications set by the funder, regardless of their own preferences. The case of Youth Enterprise in Berlin shows the negative consequences of such hierarchical working practices. Here, the TSO tried to minimize the influence of the LDP on their work; a situation more akin to "parallel production" (Pestoff, 2006) than any aspect of co-production, co-management or co-governance.

The approach taken by the LDP in the delivery of Berlin's URBAN II program reflects findings from many earlier studies in that public agencies were criticized for dominating regeneration partnerships through hierarchical relationships characterized by a dialogue dominated by formal communications, a strong emphasis on binding agreements and poorly developed social relationships. Shaw and Allen (2006) are not alone in arguing that such constellations are ineffective in supporting the achievement of urban regeneration goals, undermining the mission of TSOs and stifling innovation, learning and change. Yet many regeneration initiatives continue to be structured and delivered in such a way, both in the United Kingdom and abroad (Whitehead, 2007; Davies, 2001; Atkinson, 2003; Marshall, 2005). It would seem obvious that commissioning approaches driven by the interests of public agencies are unlikely to tap into the resources of local communities; however, a strategic change of hierarchical governance arrangements may be required to encourage LDPs to engage more in the co-management and co-production rather than the commissioning of services. European Union regional policy and its financial instruments would appear to be well suited to support such a change in policy and governance of regeneration partnerships and in the future should perhaps focus more on co-management processes than on the institutional structures through which urban regeneration is facilitated.

While institutional, historical and cultural differences can play an important part in facilitating or hindering the co-management of services, the previous discussion suggests that these factors are unlikely to be the main variables that influence the co-management process. The LDPs in Belfast and Bristol were both operating close to local communities with control over strategy and policy resting largely with residents and TSOs, yet the structures used to deliver the regeneration program differed substantially between the two cities. The case study TSOs were also very different from each other with regard to their history, purpose and structure.

However, the actions taken by program management and TSO staff showed a number of similarities. These included each partner drawing freely on their own strengths and resources, a nonhierarchical approach to joint working between funder and provider and being able to deal efficiently with obstacles and barriers within their respective organizations to ensure progression of the initiative. Program management and TSO workers also took a holistic view of desired outcomes by looking beyond mere service provision and paying attention to how these services could be provided and how this might affect the provider. The allocation of funding to the TSO did not mark the handing over of responsibility for the provision of a new service from funder to provider; instead, it was the beginning of a process in that both actors were taking on a shared responsibility for the provision of a new service. In addition, we saw a high degree of organizational adaptability in the two case study organizations that provided the locus for the co-management process.

CONCLUSIONS

Focusing on the practical actions of individuals in the co-management of a service has a distinct advantage over other analytical frameworks rooted in institutional or policy analysis, because it provides a clear perspective on the benefits as well as challenges that result from the actions taken by funders and providers of services. Evidence of co-management could therefore become the benchmark for a deep form of integration of local communities in the regeneration process. Comparisons of "what works" would also become much easier and more effective, with the primary unit of analysis being the actions of the co-managers rather than the different policy and institutional structures in which they operate. Furthermore, identifying effective behaviors supports the transfer of good practice because behaviors can be learned, copied and adapted in ways that respond effectively to the institutional context in which they take place.

Another conclusion that can be drawn from the previous discussion is that LDPs have significant room to maneuver when it comes to working with TSOs and that regulations that govern EU funding do not appear to be an obstacle to the co-management of services. The level of integration of TSOs and local communities therefore appears to be less a consequence of EU regulations that govern EU funding and more a question of how these regulations are interpreted locally. Consequently, there are choices that LDPs, policy makers and regeneration practitioners have to make. They have to decide whether to co-manage services with TSOs or whether to use them as "service providers" commissioned by the LDP to do a job specified by the LDP. The latter approach is much criticized, yet appears to remain favored by public agencies, in part because it responds well to the fundamental characteristics of public institutions that have to ensure both accountability for and predictability of their actions (Bourgon, 2009). Ultimately, it may be easier for policy makers and practitioners to focus on the creation of spaces in which co-productive behaviors can unfold than to try to change deeply embedded institutional structures, especially as such collaborative spaces can be provided outside public institutions by TSOs themselves.

Partnerships are expected to overcome institutional inflexibilities by synthesizing features from different institutions to create inclusive and integrated regeneration processes. Perceiving LDPs as hybrid rather than ideal type organizational forms (Skelcher, 2004; Billis, 2010; Brandsen, Van de Donk, and Putters, 2005) and focusing on individuals who work across institutional boundaries (Sullivan and Skelcher, 2002; Breathnach, 2007) offers useful perspectives for the analysis of contemporary institutional contexts through which regeneration is facilitated. The focus on the interactions between funders and providers of services, which was adopted in this analysis, therefore reflects current theoretical and conceptual developments. Taking a behaviorist perspective in the analysis of the co-management process would consequently seem a promising route of further inquiry for the identification of effective and transferable collaborative practice in the provision of public services.

REFERENCES

Atkinson, R. 2003. Addressing urban social exclusion through community involvement in urban regeneration. In R. Imrie, M. Raco, eds. *Urban Renaissance? New Labour, Community AND Urban Policy*. Bristol, UK: Policy Press.

Balloch, S., and M. Taylor, eds. 2001. *Partnership Working: Policy and practice*. Bristol, UK: Policy Press.

Barnes, M., amd H. Sullivan. 2002. Building capacity for collaboration in English health action zones. In C. Glendinning, M. Powell, K. Rummery, eds. *Partnerships, New Labour and the Governance of Welfare*. Bristol, UK: Policy Press.

Billis, D., ed. 2010. *Hybrid Organisations and the Third Sector*. London: Palgrave.

Blackmore, A. 2004. *Standing Apart, Working Together: A Study on the Myths and Realities of Voluntary and Community Sector Independence*. London: National Council for Voluntary Organisations.

Borzaga, C., and J. Defourny, eds. 2001. *The Emergence of Social Enterprise*. London: Routledge.

Bourgon, J. 2009. New directions in public administration: Serving beyond the predictable. *Public Policy and Administration Journal* 23 (3): 309–330.

Brandsen, T., W. Van de Donk, and K. Putters. 2005. Griffins or chameleons? Hybridity as a permanent and inevitable characteristic of the third sector. *International Journal of Public Administration* 28 (9–10): 749–756.

Breathnach, C. 2007. *Engaging in Cross-Boundary Organisational Relationships: Challenges for Irish Nonprofit Organisations*. Dublin: Centre for Nonprofit Management, University of Dublin.

Brown, L. D., and A. Kalegaonka. 2002. Support organisations and the evolution of the NGO sector. *Nonprofit and Voluntary Sector Quarterly* 31 (2): 231–258.

Burton, P., et al., 2004. *What Works in Community Involvement in Area Based Initiatives: A Systematic Review of the Literature*. London: Home Office.

Carley, M., et al, 2000. *Regeneration in the 21st Century*. Bristol, UK: Policy Press.

Commission of the European Communities. 1999. *Sustainable Urban Development in the European Union: A Framework for Action*. Brussels: European Commission.

Commission of the European Communities. 2007a. *Growing Regions, Growing Europe: Fourth Report on Economic and Social Cohesion*. Luxemburg: Office for Official Publications of the European Communities.

Commission of the European Communities. 2007b. *The Urban Development Network Programme URBACT II: Final Operational Programme*. Brussels: European Commission.

Commission of the European Communities. 2007c. *The urban dimension in Community policies for the period 2007–2013*. Brussels: European Commission.

Commission of the European Communities. 2008. *Fostering the Urban Dimension: Analysis of the Operational Programmes Co-Financed by the European Regional Development Fund*. Brussels: European Commission.

Crack, S., S. Turner, and B. Heenan. 2006. The changing face of voluntary welfare provision in New Zealand. *Health and Place* 13(1): 188–204.

Davies, J. S. 2001. *Partnerships and Regimes: The Politics of Urban Regeneration in the UK*. Aldershot, UK: Ashgate.

Department for Communities and Local Government. 2008. *Transforming Places; Changing Lives: A Framework for Regeneration*. London: Author.

Deutsch-Österreichisches URBAN-Netzwerk. 2005. *Innovative Urban Development by Means of the "Acquis Urban."* Berlin: Deutsch-Österreichisches URBAN-Netzwerk.

Diamond, J., and J. Liddle. 2005. *Management of Regeneration*. London: Routledge.

EuroCities & Deutsches Institut für Urbanistik. 2007. *Leipzig Memo*. Leipzig: Proceedings of a conference organised jointly by Euro Cities and the Deutsches Institut für Urbanistic.

Evers, A., and J. L. Laville, eds. 2004. *The Third Sector in Europe*. Cheltenham, UK: Edward Elgar.

German Presidency of the European Council of Ministers. 2007. *Leipzig Charter on Sustainable European Cities*. Final draft May 2007. www.eukn.org/binaries/eukn/news/2007/5/leipzig-charter-final-draft-020507-en.pdf. Accessed February 28, 2008.

Hanion, N., M. Rosenberg, and R. Clasby. 2007. Offloading social care responsibilities: recent experiences of local voluntary organisations in a remote urban centre in British Columbia, Canada. *Health and Care in the Community* 15 (4): 343–351.

Hantrais, L. 2000. *Social Policy in the European Union*. Basingstoke, UK: Macmillan Press.

Hantrais, L., and S. Mangen, eds. 1996. *Cross-national Research Methods in the Social Sciences*. London: Pinter.

Harris, M., and H. Schlappa. 2007. "Hoovering up the money"? Delivering government-funded capacity building programmes to voluntary and community organisations. *Social Policy and Society* 7 (2): 135–146.

Harrow, J. 2001. Capacity building as a New Public Management tool: myth, magic or the main change. *Public Management Review* 3 (2): 209–230.

Her Majesty's Treasury, 2004. *The Compact: Working Together, Better Together*. London: Author.

Huxham, C., and S. Vangen. 2005. *Managing to Collaborate*. London: Routledge.

Improvement and Development Agency. 2006. *Capacity Building Toolkit*. www. idea-knowledge.gov.uk/idk. Accessed October 30, 2006.

Kendall, J., ed. 2009. *Handbook on Third Sector Policy in Europe*. London: Edward Elgar.

LC-Facil, 2010. *Implementing the Leipzig Charter: A Cities Perspective*. Paris: URBACT II.

Lowndes, V., and H. Sullivan. 2004. Like a horse and carriage or a fish on a bicycle? How well do local partnerships and public participation go together? *Local Government Studies* 30 (1): 51–73.

Macmillan, R. 2007. The unsettled state of third sector infrastructure. *Day Conference of the Voluntary Sector Studies Network*. Birmingham: VSSN.

Marshall, A. 2005. Europeanization at the urban level: Local actors, institutions and the dynamics of multi-level interaction. *Journal of European Public Policy* 12 (4): 668–686.

Office of the Deputy Prime Minister. 2006. *UK Presidency: European Union Ministerial Informal on Sustainable Communities*. London: Office of the Deputy Prime Minister.

Osborne, S. P., ed. 2008. *The Third Sector in Europe: Prospects and Challenges*. London: Routledge.

Pestoff, V. 2006. Citizens and co-production of welfare services: Childcare in eight European countries. *Public Management Review* 8 (4): 503–519.

Royal Town Planning Institute. 2010. *Regeneration Network*. www.rtpi.org.uk/regeneration_network. Accessed September 30, 2010.

Schlappa, H. 2009. Change in third sector organisations: The impact of European Union funding in cross-national perspective. In *Aston Business School*. Birmingham, UK: Aston University.

Scott, D. W. 2001. Contracting: The experience of service delivery agencies. In M. Harris, and C. Rochester, eds., *Voluntary Organisations and Social Policy in Britain: Perspectives on Change and Choice*. Basingstoke, UK: Palgrave, pp. 49–64.

Shaw, S., and J. B. Allen. 2006. "We actually trust the community." Examining the dynamics of a nonprofit funding relationship in New Zealand. *Voluntas* 17 (3): 211–220.

Shirlow, P., and B. Murtagh. 2004. Capacity-building, representation and intracommunity conflict. *Urban Studies* 41 (1): 57–70.

Skelcher, C. 2004. *Hybrids: Implications of New Corporate Forms for Public Service Performance*. Paper to the British Academy of Management Conference, Edinburgh.

Sullivan, H., and C. Skelcher. 2002. *Working Across Boundaries: Collaboration in Public Service Delivery*. Basingstoke, UK: Palgrave.

Taylor, M. 2000. Communities in the lead: Power, organisational capacity and social capital. *Urban Studies* 37 (5–6): 1019–1035.

Taylor, M. 2001. Partnership: Insiders and outsiders. In M. Harris, C. Rochester, eds., *Voluntary Organisations and Social Policy in Britain*. Basingstoke, UK: Palgrave, pp. 94–107.

Taylor, M., M. Wilson, D. Purdue, and P. Wilde. 2007. *Changing Neighbourhoods: Lessons from the JRF Neighbourhood Programme*. Bristol, UK: Policy Press.

URBACT Secretariat. 2007. *The URBACT Programme 2002–2006*. Paris: URBACT.

Wates, N. 2010. *Community Planning*. http://www.communityplanning.net: Accessed September 30, 2010.

Whitehead, M. 2007. The architecture of partnership: urban communities in the shadow of hierarchy. *Policy and Politics* 35 (1): 3–23.

Wilks-Hegg, S. 2000. *Mainstreaming Regeneration: A Review of Policy over the Last Thirty Years*. London: Local Government Association.

Wilks-Hegg, S. 2003. Economy, equity or empowerment? New Labour, communities and urban policy evaluation. In R. Imrie and M. Raco, eds., *Urban Renaissance? New Labour, Community and Urban Policy*. Bristol, UK: Policy Press.

13 'Don't Bite the Hand That Feeds You?'

On the Partnerships between Private Citizen Initiatives and Local Government

Karolien Dezeure and Filip De Rynck

INTRODUCTION: PARTICIPATION AND CO-MANAGEMENT

This chapter examines partnerships between Belgian citizen initiatives and local government in the realm of arrangements for local service delivery in Flanders. We address the following questions: How does local government cope with the private initiatives set up by groups of citizens in several policy domains over time? Do these arrangements evolve into governance in terms of co-management or partnerships? How are these arrangements perceived by the private initiatives from the perspective of their autonomy? To cope with those questions, we merge insights of two theoretical strands in the literature: literature on participation and literature on governance. Despite the undeniable link between the theories on local governance and participation, it seems like these two theorhetical strands of literature "do not talk to each other," notwithstanding combining the insights from both strands of theory could be very fruitful.

How could it be explained that two related sets of literature didn't meet thus far and why is this academic blindness only questioned in recent literature? First, until now, the participation literature was dominated by concepts related to "classical political participation" from a governmental viewpoint. Although some research in public administration and urban politics has focused exclusively on questions of how and why citizens participate in organizations and activities associated with the provision of public goods and services (Levine, 1984; Ostrom, 1996; Percy, 1984; Sharp, 1980; Marschall, 2004), this area of inquiry remains relatively untouched by participation scholars, who tend to study so-called mainstream political behavior, such as voting, contacting politicians and attending political meetings (Verlet and Reynaert, 2004).

These studies consider participation as a one-way process, where groups of citizens aim to influence the government. They focus on the question of how citizens can be involved in the policy-making cycle of government and not on the question of how government should be involved in citizen initiatives. The perspective of government is still the leading principle, and only in recent literature has this question been reversed: how can government make a better use of the power and the competencies of citizen initiatives? As the government view dominated, the last rung on Arnstein's well-known ladder of participation (citizens running their own business) was perceived as utopian, whereas nowadays witnessing the decline of representative democracy, the changing perception on participation explains the reversed ladder: how can government cope with, and make a better use of, autonomous citizen initiatives? How could policy making be based on citizen initiatives; how can representative politics build coalitions with citizens to tackle the societal problems?

Second, in the traditional participation literature based on the classic concept of the policy cycle of government, participation is considered part of what is the most important in that cycle: the policy formulation or the first stage in the policy cycle. This policy cycle, from agenda setting to evaluation of the effectiveness of policies, is certainly a formalistic version of reality (Van Humbeeck et al., 2004). Nowadays, researchers are aware of the fact that the stages in the cycle should be understood as elements of a more circular model of policy making, where implementation and policy formulation are interwoven. In terms of participation, our attention shifts to the phase of what is formally labeled "policy implementation." The question now becomes: which types of organizational design could promote strong or vital participative coalitions between government representatives and citizen initiatives?

This brings us to the second strand of literature, focusing on private initiatives by citizens in the theory on co-production. Ostrom (1996) defines co-production as the process through which inputs used to provide a good or service are contributed by individuals who are not in the same organization. The co-production approach assumes that service users and their communities can, and often should, be part of service planning and delivery. This has major implications for the democratic practices by locating citizens and communities more centrally in the policy-making process. Bovaird describes this relatively new and recent phenomenon, changing the structural character of policy making and service delivery in the United Kingdom:

> In recent years, there has been a radical reinterpretation of the role of "policy making" and "service delivery" in the public domain. No longer are these seen as "one way" processes. Policy is now seen as the negotiated outcome of many interacting policy systems, not simply the preserve of "policy planners" and "top decision makers." Delivery and management of services is no longer just the preserve of the professionals and the managers, users and other members of the community play a large role in shaping decisions and outcomes. (2007, 846)

This is also conceptualized as "network governance" (Marcussen and Torfing, 2003). The concept of "network governance" can be defined more empirically as: (1) a horizontal articulation of interdependent, but operationally autonomous actors; (2) who interact through negotiations, (3) transpiring within a regulative, normative, cognitive and imaginary framework, (4) that to a certain extent is self-regulating and (5) which contribute to the production of public purpose within a particular area (Marcussen and Torfing, 2003). Co-production at the site of service provision is nevertheless different from the mesolevel phenomenon of co-management, where the third sector participates, alongside other public and private actors, in managing the growing complexity of delivery of diverse publicly financed services, without any direct citizen or user participation (see Pestoff in this volume). As the focus of this chapter is on these voluntary organizations, the focus is on co-management. Later we use the concept of "local co-management arrangements" that include, the five basic elements of network governance embedded in the institutional context in our cases.

However, what seems, according to Bovaird, to be new in the Anglo-Saxon tradition of government and what seems to be new on the bridge of two strands of literature, has been one of the core characteristics of policy making and service delivery for decades already, especially in the Netherlands (Dekker, 2004) and in Belgium.[1] Private nonprofit organizations, set up by and governed by citizens delivering services in arrangements with government, have a longstanding tradition in Flanders. The regionalization of the country didn't change these systemic features of the policy system. Those arrangements developed in a complex institutional setting of formal and informal variables, one of which was the intense interaction and connectivity between the official representatives of the state (politicians and public administrators) and the representatives of the private organizations (members of the boards, professionals, users). The real functioning of those arrangements and the real impact on decision making and the nature of service delivery does not follow from the analysis of the formal components of those arrangements, but from the institutional contingencies in and around those arrangements. Patterns of interaction are one of those institutions. It is this last viewpoint that inspires the central theme of this chapter to shed light on the relationship over time between the local government and the private organizations.

In this chapter, the first section provides a historical overview of private initiatives embedded in the governance literature. The second section sets out the analytical grid with which to assess the co-management arrangements explaining its origins in the participation literature and discussing its more problematic aspects related to empirical testing. These two sections illustrate the theoretical tools used in the empirical research presented in the following sections. The third part of the article features an explorative analysis of the case selection, while the fourth conducts a detailed analysis.

Finally, the fifth and last part outlines the main empirical findings and indicates directions for further research.

HISTORICAL OVERVIEW

Private nonprofit organizations, set up and governed by citizens, have a strong and long-standing position in the Flemish society. These are groups of citizens in voluntary associations pursuing issues that supersede individual interests. To explain this situation of autonomous and strong private initiative, we have to go back to the nineteenth century, to the "nightwatchman"-state and the pillarization (*verzuiling*) of society and politics. In the absence of a strong state, citizens in trade unions, churches and cooperatives started to organize themselves and they established their own systems of solidarity, which includes offering services to their member-citizens: schools, health care and social security. Those initiatives grew and were stimulated along the lines of the ideological cleavages, leading to a pillarized society. Pillarization is the vertical segregation of various population groups along religious or political lines. It is the result of building of associations and linking existing organizations into blocs. In Flanders, there were three pillars along political lines. Catholic organizations definitely formed the most encompassing and homogenous pillar. Also the existence of a socialist and liberal pillar has rarely been contested, but these pillars were not so developed as the first one. The existence of these pillars stimulated the development of what would later be called the nonprofit sector. Pillars had their own hospitals, schools, associations, newspapers, media, women's and youth organizations, soccer clubs and more. Gradually, the state became, in the light of pacification between the pillars, more involved in these private initiatives by means of financial and material support.

However, the Belgian nonprofit sector as we know it today is, to great extent, a product of the unique welfare state model the country adopted in the immediate post-World War II period (1945). This model, a combination of the principle of subsidiarity and centralized public administration, facilitates cooperation between nonprofit organizations and government agencies to provide social welfare services, such as health care and education. By subsidiarity we refer to the idea that "the state" should not do what individuals or groups of individual organizations can do. As a consequence, there was a great autonomy for private initiatives. This short overview indicates that private action for public purposes, often publicly financed, has become accepted in Flanders as a normal "state" of affairs and is a central part of the political culture. In political practice this led to complex systems of regulation, financing, controlling and interwovenness between politicians (also as members of the pillars), public servants and private initiatives. Meanwhile, the private initiatives also evolved and their nature changed, in part due to the increased government interventions. One of the most important trends certainly is the professionalization of the management of those private initiatives, resulting, in some cases, in very large organizations. But despite the professionalization, today most members of the boards of those private initiatives are still volunteers.

For the purposes of this chapter, we define governance as societal, institutional and administrative processes that constrain, enable and prescribe the provision of public goods and the determination of public interest (Kooiman, 2003; Stoker, 2006). According to Munshi, good governance "signifies a participative manner of governing that functions in a responsible, accountable and transparent manner" (2004, 51). Also, other authors stress the importance of interaction between government and private organizations in their definition of good governance (Hirst, 2000). In broad terms government refers to the machinery of the state exercising coordination and steering through hierarchy, bureaucracy, laws, rules and regulation; while governance marks the movement of the state toward governing of society through networks based on interdependence, negotiation and trust of both public, private and third sector actors (Sorensen and Torfing, 2005).

Using this approach of "governance," the phenomenon of Flemish public-private arrangements in a vast array of types and in several policy domains could be labeled as "old governance." From the nineteenth century on, and especially since 1945, there has been an enormous increase of co-management arrangements, but of course those arrangements have been the subject of policy changes in general and in the Flemish region in particular. As a consequence, there has been a shift from "old governance" in which there was a great autonomy for private initiatives (subsidiarity) and a real "government at a distance" (sometimes even "governance without government") toward what could be labeled now as "new governance." The institutions in which those arrangements were embedded changed, due to the increased ambitions of a new regional government, due to the effects of professionalization (both of government and of private initiatives) and to the introduction of new policy instruments aiming at evaluating outcomes, outputs and customer satisfaction.

The changing institutionalization provokes fierce debates about the role of government and the autonomy of private initiatives, which according to those initiatives, puts them under severe pressure. "New governance" means that government uses those arrangements to realize policy objectives, using a set of instruments (negotiated agreements, contracts and indicators). The general feeling in the nonprofit spheres is that the impact of government has increased and that government actors tend to "contractualize" the private initiatives, introducing new types of control and steering, thereby reducing private initiative to the status and the role of "semi-public" service deliverers. This is the object of our research question in the case study part of this chapter.

A GRID FOR ANALYSIS: LOCAL CO-MANAGEMENT ARRANGEMENT

Recently, social scientists have attempted to grasp the relationship between government and private initiatives (Brandsen and Pestoff, 2006; Blakeley, 2010). We still lack a comprehensive empirical understanding of what really happens when the third sector is drawn into public service provision and how the relationship between government and the private organizations evolve. Bassoli (2010) introduces the concept of "local governance arrangements." According to his ideal-typical distinction, this concept integrates both network governance arrangements and participatory governance arrangements. The focus of a network governance arrangement is on the product, on a few organized interests. It is based on an ex ante selection of the partners in a closed structure. By contrast, the focus of a participatory governance arrangement is on the process, based on organized interests but also on citizens, and there is an ongoing selection of partners during the process.

There are many interests, and the structure is open for the analysis of a whole range of arrangements. Our focus is on local co-management arrangements (LCMAs) between local government, private initiatives and/ or nonorganized citizens. More specifically, the focus is on the mesolevel or on co-management (Pestoff, 2011), involving new forms or patterns of collaboration between local governments and third sector providers of publicly financed services. This comes close to the concept of "local governance arrangement" of Bassoli. But our approach is more based on institutional analysis aimed at describing the functioning of local arrangements from the bottom-up instead of categorizing them using some general features. We also try to focus on the process of interaction between local governments and citizen initiatives. Analyzing the nature of this interaction is necessary to describe the role of private initiatives in policy making and to measure the effect of the interactions in those arrangements on policy making. The conclusions on the open or closed structure of the arrangements should wait for the result of the analysis of the dynamics in the arrangements.

This dynamic approach results in a historical analysis of several case studies: different LCMAs are reconstructed over time with insights on the differences and similarities between several stages in their development. The case studies are based on extensive documentary analysis and on a series of in-depth, semi-structured, face-to-face interviews with key actors in the co-management field of the city of Ghent (public administrators, politicians and active citizens involved in the private organizations).[2] The importance of this type of research is twofold. First, a dynamic analysis on LCMAs is rather innovating. Most research investigates a local co-management process at a certain point in time and does not take into account the evolution and the dynamics of the relationship between the government and private actors.

Second, the purpose of this research design is to go beyond the official storytelling of the government or private initiatives (rules-in-form) by taking into account the effective rules-in-use (Lowndes, Pratchett, and Stoker, 2006). This will reveal something about both the formal and the informal side of the LCMA. Looking at the rules-in-use, the basic question is: how autonomous are these private initiatives in their relation to government? How can we describe the role of the government in these LCMAs? This is researched by means of a bottom-up analysis of the institutional factors of the arrangement. In theory, an LCMA consists of a negotiated *process*, steered by a set of *instruments* between a limited number of negotiating *actors*.

In the light of Belgium's federal structure, almost all LCMAs are under the steering of at least two governments. The Flemish government especially takes up a steering role, at least formally, vis-à-vis the local government and the private organizations. This is already one of the typical features of local arrangements: what is the impact of instruments used by the central government on the interaction of local government and local private initiatives?

To give an answer to the research questions, the focus is on the instruments and the control implemented by the local and Flemish government vis-à-vis the private initiative. The adoption and implementation of "old" and "new" policy instruments offers a useful analytical touchstone because governance theory argues that regulation is the quintessence of government (Jordan, Wurzel, and Zito, 2005). The focus on control is induced by the fact that the traditional ways of controlling the goals achieved by the private organizations has given way to experiment with a variety of innovations. Although none of these reforms have wholly replaced traditional regulation that emphasizes enforcement of rules by governmental agencies and penalties, the widespread interest in the new approaches is evidenced by the adoption by various governments of one or more of these innovations (management based systems, performance based approaches) (May, 2007).

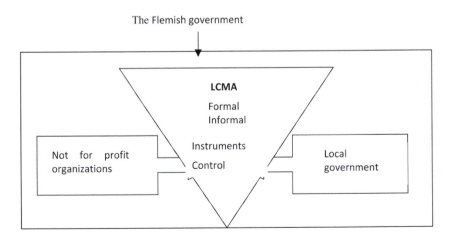

Figure 13.1 The Flemish governments and LCMAs.

CASE SELECTION AND METHODOLOGICAL CONCERNS

In research of this kind, the universe of possible cases is huge. Nonetheless, there are certain features that must be taken into account. To control for the variables influencing the LCMA, the cases are selected in one city of Flanders, Ghent. As a consequence, they share the same political, administrative and societal framework, and they concern the same territory. Ghent is the capital and biggest city of the East Flanders province. With almost 240,000 inhabitants, Ghent is Flanders's second largest city. Second, in the light of Belgium's federal structure, almost all LCMAs are under the steering of at least two governments. A diversity of cases seems to be by far the one best suited to grasp the relationship between the Flemish government and the local organizations.

Three cases have been selected for explorative analysis: one LCMA that is mostly funded (and thus probably mostly steered) by the local government (VZW Jong) and two LCMAs that are mostly funded by the Flemish government, although they are presented as co-management between local government and private initiatives: VZW Samenlevingsopbouw and VZW Intercultureel Netwerk Gent.

VZW Jong is mainly financed by the local government. Seventy-five percent of its funds come from Ghent, while 21 percent of their financial income is from the Flemish government and only 6 percent of its means stem from private gifts and funds. VZW Samenlevingsopbouw (organization for Community Development), on the contrary, is mainly subsidized by the Flemish government (60 percent), while 35 percent stems from the local government. In the 1960s and 1970s, VZW Samenlevingsopbouw represented an example of "old governance." This changed in 1983, due to the restructuring by the Flemish government. From 2000 on, also the city of Ghent started to intervene with VZW Samenlevingopbouw, by means of negotiated agreements. The same was true when we look at VZW ING, the Intercultural Network of Ghent. ING wants to encourage a dialogue with, and the integration of, migrants in Ghent. Due to a Flemish decree on minorities in 2001, several independent organizations working for ethnic minorities were "obliged" to work together ("forced marriage"). VZW ING is subsidized by 75 percent by the Flemish Government and by 20 percent from the local government.

EXPLORATIVE CASE ANALYSIS

As described earlier, historically in the Belgian nonprofit sector, multiple organizations representing the citizens were established and run independently from the government. However, nowadays this independence is under severe pressure. This is not only due to the professionalization of these private organizations, but also as a result of the increasing institu-tionalization. The majority of the organizations are financed by the gov-ernment in exchange for performing governmental tasks. The requirements for this are determined by means of negotiated agreements and contracts. As a consequence, some argue that these organizations have become part of the system, being "directed" by the Flemish or the local government (Hertogen and Debruyne, 2007; Cannoot, 2009). These negotiated agree-ments become, in effect, the rules-in-form for such private organizations. However, in reality, these organizations may function more autonomously than appears at first sight. In what follows, the three cases are presented and analyzed in this light.

VZW Jong

VZW Jong is an organization in the field of youth work. Youth work refers to every possible action from a private organization intentionally dedicated to young people and including active direct or indirect participation. Tradition-ally, youth work in Ghent was mainly in the hands of independent organiza-tions set up by individuals. A number of youth organizations were working in different districts and neighborhoods in Ghent. Despite informal contacts between them, they mainly worked independently from each other, trying to obtain government support in several ways (lobbying, informal contacts) for their own organization. As a consequence, there was an unclear structure, and the city government had to spend a lot of time and energy negotiat-ing and controlling each organization. Given this opacity, the city govern-ment decided that one contact organization was required to establish a more coherent and efficient youth policy. As a result, VZW Jong was established in 2002, grouping nine independent organizations. On the one hand, it was an explicit request from the city, but on the other hand, the organizations were aware of the advantages of this restructuring. The city acted as a "meta-governor" at that time; a governing body that distributes decision-making competence between multitudes of territorially and functionally defined self-governing actors (Kooiman, 1993; Sorensen, 2002).

In the beginning, the VZW operated as a network organization for nine youth organizations. VZW Jong functioned as the main contact organiza-tion and served as a bridge between the local government and these nine organizations. Its focus was on supporting provisions for youth workers and defending the interests of the member organizations. The network organization Jong was steered by the representatives of all the member organizations. Then, in 2005, there was a fusion between seven of the nine organizations,[3] together with three governmental youth organizations into one new hybrid structure: VZW Jong. This scale-up was explicitly requested and organized by the local government, acting as a meta-governor for the second time, for four reasons.

First, their aim was to achieve a more coordinated youth policy with one recognized conversation partner. Second, they could better divide the work and the competencies among the organizations. As such, they would be capable of giving answers to policy requests. Third, the efficiency of the organizations would increase due to the concentration of overhead and facilities. And fourth, it's more efficient for the local government to have one partner. Notably, the fusion came without any negotiation with any of the partners. Still, these organizations were not very resistant, as they were aware of the advantages coming along with this scale-up. They realized they did not have the capacity nor the means to implement projects on a citywide level. A scale-up could provide an answer to that missing link.

VZW Jong is mainly directed by the local government. However, several public and semi-public governments do intervene, directly (legislation) or indirectly (funding), with this private organization. There are many interacting public and private authority structures at work, influencing the functioning of this local private organization. It illuminates the entanglement between the local, Flemish, federal and even European levels of authority in this arrangement.

Since 2005, the city of Ghent has a negotiated agreement with VZW Jong. The goals that are stipulated in the agreement are a result of intense negotiations among the several stakeholders. The agreement makes clear that the local government considers VZW Jong a subcontractor, and a partner in implementing part of their youth policy. Furthermore, it lists a number of criteria, bargained and approved by the partners, to evaluate

Table 13.1 Entanglement between Different Levels of Authority

	Public government	Semi-public government	Particular sector	Citizens
European Level		European Social Fund (ESF)		
Federal level	Ministry of equal opportunities and migration policy		Fortis, Proximus	
Flemish level	Ministry of youth, Department of Youth, Ministry of interior governmental affairs	ESF-Agency Public Employment Service of Flanders (VDAB)		
Provincial level				
Local level	City council Youth Department Sport Department Department of work and economy Department of local safety and prevention	University of Ghent	VZW Jong	Volunteers Citizens youth

their performance by objective measures. The goals that each activity must achieve are expressed in quantitative terms: "VZW Jong should reach a number of youngsters. . . ." However, the way these goals should be achieved is the responsibility of the organization. This type of performance measurement is considered as an "objective assessment," which is apolitical in nature (Mintzberg, 1996). In theory, the system cannot afford a great deal of ambiguity or nuance.

Still, due to the "informal" contacts and networks between the sub-contractors and the public officials, the organization has a lot of "freedom" and "autonomy." There are multiple moments of institutionalized contacts that enable the partners to keep in touch in a free-and-easy way. To control the functioning of the VZW, the local government has set up a number of "structural working groups" consisting of local politicians and public officials who should control the working of the VZW. This strategic control focuses on how effectively the organization's strategies result in the attainment of goals. In addition to this, control of financial resources of the organization is in the hands of the local government. This LCMA can be characterized as "loose" instead of tight, free-flowing instead of controlled and interactive instead of sharply segmented. The local government is more a partner in the "network" of organizations, fashioned to work out problems as they arise and linked by informal channels of communication. This informal link is partly a result of the scale-up in 2005: three governmental youth organizations became part of the VZW Jong. A number of people working for and in the VZW used to be employed by the city and do retain their professional contacts. Both partners, the VZW Jong and the local government, express their satisfaction with the current situation. VZW Jong still has the feeling they are autonomous,

Table 13.2 Rules-in-Form and Rules-in-Use of VZW Jong

Rules-in-Form (de jure)	Instruments	Control
Flemish Government	-	-
Local Government	Negotiated agreement	Performance control
Rules-in-Use	Instruments	Control
Flemish Government	-	-
Local government	Negotiated agreement with strict output indicators, however, in case VZW Jong does not obtain those, it is not considered as a problem Daily contacts with public administrators, informal	Informal control Network government-organization The criteria are "negotiated and approved"

despite the fact that they should obtain their objectives stipulated in the negotiated agreement. However, the informal network of public officials, politicians and the professionals of the organizations facilitates their tasks, and the professionals of the VZW can use their influence in the network, which gives them strategic opportunities to influence political decisions supported by public servants.

Taking a closer look, LCMA reveals a more nuanced story. On paper, there is not much room for autonomy considering the negotiated agreement with strict criteria and the annual controls by the city council. In reality, however, due to the informal daily contacts, the autonomy of VZW Jong is higher than expected. In addition to this, the control on this LCMA is not that strict. As a consequence, the difference between the rules in form (de jure) and the rules in use (de facto) is rather big.

VZW ING (Intercultural Network Ghent)

VZW ING, on the contrary, describes a clear loss of independence and autonomy. The pressure of the government, and the Flemish government in particular, is rather striking according to them. VZW ING is a rather "young" and recent organization. It is established out of four independent smaller private organizations, each of them having their own specific target group (Turkish people, new immigrants, refugees). This merger resulted from the Flemish Decree toward ethno-cultural minorities (1998, 2001). Besides the fact that this Decree defined three basic components of the "minorities" policy in Flanders, it also added two features that are important for the LCMA VZW ING. The "minorities" decree recognizes and reorganizes the whole sector of regional, subregional and local integration centers, and establishes the possibility for regional funding for local public integration services.

As a consequence, a number of criteria are established to evaluate the working of ethnic cultural organizations. In addition to this, the Decree recognizes a "forum of organizations of ethno-cultural minorities" as an official spokespartner for the Flemish government. Except for the recognition of the forum, the Decree establishes different mechanisms for enabling ethno-cultural minorities to participate in the policy development process. Not only does the Flemish government put constraints on the ethno-cultural organizations, the decree also stipulates that the local government should safeguard these rules. Moreover, it obliges the local government to reach a negotiated agreement with the VZW ING. Although this framework seems to be quite constraining, several stakeholders (including VZW ING) stress the fact that the decree is a result of negotiations with the ministry's cabinet and the administration. Furthermore, the Decree provides a framework, but the detailed implementation is not determined.

In 2001, the Flemish government also imposed several requirements within the framework of the Quality Decree. In particular, they set out a number of instruments in order to measure and evaluate the results of community development. By means of a revision of the annual report of the organization, the Flemish government controls a number of criteria concerning quality. In reality, however, the control is not that harsh. The organizations are obliged to submit an annual report, still these reports are only checked on a number of criteria ("these are reports that no one ever reads"). In that sense, it cannot be said that the control of the Flemish government is severe. In addition to this, the Flemish government reached a negotiated agreement with VZW ING for the period 2009 to 2014. The agreement is based on negotiations between the VZW and the Flemish government, although both partners recognize the fact that the contents are mainly stipulated by the organization. By contrast, the control of the "Financial inspection of the Flemish Government" is rather strict. The organization should reach and document a number of stipulated objectives and the audit by the Flemish government is rather rigorous.

In this LCMA, the Flemish government at first sight can be seen as a machine dominated by rules, regulations and standards. When looking to the rules-in-use, however, it is clear that the superstructure plans and controls, while the organization only executes. However, in reality, there is some space left for the organization to bargain and negotiate with the Flemish government. The control, however, sheds another light on the "freedom

Table 13.3 Rules-in-Form and Rules-in-Use of VZW ING

Rules-in-Form	*Instruments*	*Control*
Flemish Government	Regulation (decree on minorities) constraining for the organization and for the local government	Audit
	Negotiated agreement with the organization	Strict financial control
	Quality decree	
Local Government	Negotiated agreement	Audit
Rules-in-Use	*Instruments*	*Control*
Flemish Government	Decree as a result of negotiation with the stakeholders	Audit—in fact only checking the annual report of the organization
	Negotiated agreement	Strict financial control
Local government	It evolved from a "one way agreement" to a negotiated agreement (government to governance)	In practice no audit but negotiation instead

and autonomy" of the organization. The emphasis on performance and, in particular the financial control, reinforces the conventional hierarchical control (Mintzberg, 1996). As a result of the Flemish decree, the local government also set up a negotiated contract with VZW ING. While in the beginning this negotiated agreement was fully determined by the city, it is now a result of intense negotiations. In case the organization does not meet its targets, a reasonable explanation is considered as "satisfactory." In contrast to the Flemish government, the local government is less strict concerning the control on the outputs and outcomes of the organization. In that sense, we can discover a shift from "government" to "network governance" at the local level in particular.

To sum up, this LCMA shows that nonprofit sector relations with government are multilayered and best understood as something comprised of the views obtained through each layer. It is clear that there is a huge difference between the relationship Flemish government-VZW ING and the relationship local government-VZW ING. Whereas in the latter we can speak of autonomy and freedom, it is not the case in the former.

VZW Samenlevingsopbouw ("Community Development")

The case of VZW Samenlevingopbouw is comparable to the case of VZW ING, despite the fact that the former is an organization with a longer history. The pioneers of Samenlevingsopbouw were involved in a number of initiatives under the title of "community development." Community development is the process of helping local residents, especially the deprived ones, to strengthen themselves. Given their critical standpoint with regard to society, the government, and more specifically the local authorities, saw them as an opposition. Yet, in the 1980s, many community workers were establishing local consultative platforms that, in consultation with the government and other partners, worked to provide appropriate facilities for rural areas. The pioneer phase saw the emergence of all sorts of initiatives. There were no strategic ways of working (Hautekeur, 2008). Many community workers were, in fact, doing what they thought they should do.

This changed in 1983, when the Flemish government imposed a fundamental restructuring of the whole community development sector. It subsidized one Flemish support institute that had to provide support for community development in Flanders and Brussels. Additionally, five provincial and three urban institutes for community development were established each being responsible for the community workers in their city or province. By means of this restructuring, the Flemish government would no longer subsidize neighborhood work, but rather support temporary projects to combat deprivation. Up until 1991, there was no suitable legislative basis for the recognition and subsidizing of the sector. To obtain subsidies, institutes and other bodies had to take account of the regulations set out of in the annual letter sent out by the ministry. Structural regulation only came with the decree of 1991 with regard to the recognition and funding of community development work (Hautekeur, 2008).

In 2001, the Flemish government also imposed all sorts of requirements within the framework of the Quality Decree. In particular, they set out a number of instruments in order to measure and evaluate the results of community development. They control it by means of a revision of the annual report of the organization. It is clear that the Flemish government is quite "steering" in this story. Due to the fundamental restructuring in 1983, the organization lost a lot of its autonomy, but the professionals still claim to be relatively "autonomous": they mention that they are "subsidized opposition," still being able to "play this role." However, qualitative analysis of the data indicates their fear for a loss of means and, as a consequence, a loss of employees. The nonpaid volunteers involved in the organization, however, mention something else: they complain about the lack of decisiveness of the organization and the fact that the organization is forced to undertake activities that are not their core business (e.g., only working in predefined projects and no right to criticize the government).

Besides the subsidies of the Flemish government, the regional institutes for community development work in Flanders can always call on additional financing from the local authorities. To this end, they reach a negotiated agreement in order to implement certain tasks, such as setting up participatory projects and organizing local people for a better dialogue with the city (Hautekeur, 2008). Also the local government in Ghent subsidizes VZW Samenlevingsopbouw. Besides a number of projects for which they should cooperate with the city, the local government also uses their expertise in city renewal programs. Moreover, the VZW has been given the task to organize the "participation" in these programs. It should support initiatives from and for (deprived) citizens. The negotiated agreement is a result of a formal and informal negotiation process, and VZW Samenlevingsopbouw experiences it positively.

However, as it was also the case for VZW ING, the contents of the negotiated agreements changed over time. Whereas in the beginning (1990–2002) it was more a global assignment "organization of participation," it is nowadays much narrower. It stipulates a number of goals and effects that the organization should obtain and their assignment has been "narrowed" down. However, controlling the achieved targets happens in a more informal way. Still, the local government stipulates that VZW Samenlevingsopbouw is not expected to get (critically) involved in the process of city renewal, their only task is to "organize the participation." It is clear that the local government is taking a leading role and that the VZW Samenlevingsopbouw is following. The city administration expects "loyalty and obedience" of VZW Samenlevingsopbouw and considers it a subcontractor or even an "extension of the city administration."

Table 13.4   Rules-in-Form and Rules-in-Use of VZW Samenlevingsopbouw

Rules-in-Form	Instruments	Control
Flemish Government	Legislation of 1983, 1991, 2001	-
Local Government	Negotiated agreement	Control on output indicators Criteria
Rules-in-Use	*Instruments*	*Control*
Flemish Government	Recent legislation (2001) is negotiated	-
Local government	Negotiated agreement is quite strict, the VZW has input but the local government decides	Control is rather strict Informal contacts

The autonomy of VZW Samenlevingsopbouw is rather restricted. Their goals, means and targets are strictly stipulated in the negotiated agreement. Despite the fact that there is room for negotiation, it is clear that the local government has a dominant role, steering the VZW in the direction they prefer.

CONCLUSION

This chapter examined partnerships between citizen initiatives and local government in the realm of arrangements for local service delivery in Flanders. We addressed the following questions: How does local government cope with the private initiatives set up by groups of citizens in several policy domains over time? Do these arrangements evolve into governance in terms of co-management or partnerships? How are those arrangements perceived by the private initiatives from the perspective of their autonomy? To deal with those questions, we merged insights of two theoretical strands of literature "that do not (yet) speak to each other": literature on participation and literature on local governance. By developing the concept of local co-management arrangement (LCMA) and by exploring it, the aim was to shed a light on the functioning of these LCMAs. This brings us to five conclusions that could be used for further research.

First, it is impossible to use the generalized concept of "the nonprofit" in their relation to the government. Although our analysis needs to be improved on the methodological level, the main conclusion is that each nonprofit organization has its own story and line of development over time, embedded in its own institutional setting, mixed with the different balance between rules-in-form and rules-in-use. Each LCMA is different on a number of variables and levels. Reaching a single conclusion about the autonomy of nonprofit organizations in relation to the government is hardly possible. Only taking the rules-in-form into consideration would lead to another configuration of the arrangement over, compared to than also bearing in mind the rules-in-use. By considering these two dimensions, the three presented LCMAs can be drawn on a continuum, putting VZW Jong on the one end (with much autonomy) and VZW Samenlevingsopbouw on the other end (with little autonomy).

Second, although it is not possible to fully grasp the relationship between NPOs and the local government, it is clear that a number of instruments are imposed on them to "control" and to "steer" them. It seems these organizations have lost a lot of their autonomy, although they do not necessarily perceive it that way. This might be due to the (informal) contacts with public officials and politicians, but also due to the fact that some very government-like instruments tend to be very governance-like in daily practice. There is no control on strict performance indicators; a quite strictly negotiated agreement is in reality the product of bargaining and has been influenced by the nonprofit professionals. There is an important difference between the rules-in-form and the rules-in-use in the three presented LCMAs.

Third, the real impact of the rules is the result of close interactions between local civil servants and local organizations. This is typical for the local level: people know each other, there are professional or other types of links between the key decision-makers. It is difficult for researchers to grasp the real impact of this close networking. However, the lines of influence are reciprocal: the nonprofit organization is more open to the representatives of the local government, but those politicians and public servants are also sensitive for the needs and demands of the nonprofit professionals. They often need the input and collaboration of those organizations to obtain their political goals and to deliver some services that are essential in the local community. If there is a loss of autonomy on behalf of the nonprofit, the same can be said of local government.

Fourth, public servants play an important role in the three presented LCMAs. Their role has been underdeveloped in the literature so far. The professionals of the organizations have their own ambitions and strategy; the board (consisting of volunteers) may have another perception of the role of the organization and the nature of the relationship with local government. Politicians and public servants are their "public" counterparts, although in reality the distinction between public and private actors is blurring. They seem to act on the boundary between public and private. But civil servants are the eyes and ears of local government, and their attitudes and the ways they interpret formal instruments determines the policy space of both nonprofit and government.

Fifth, there is a difference between the "governance regimes" in the multilayered arrangements. Nonprofit organizations have to cope with different regimes. There is no such thing as "government": there are more "governments" at stake. This gives the nonprofit organizations some strategic opportunities. And even on the same governmental level, several actors belonging to that level can act differently, as was the case, for instance, for the financial controller of LCMA ING.

NOTES

1. According to the John Hopkins comparative study on nonprofit organizations, the Belgian nonprofit sector is very large by international standards. The employment share of the nonprofit sector in the Netherlands, Belgium and Ireland is over 10 percent, clearly more than in the other Western European countries.
2. These explorative case studies are part of a doctoral study (Dezeure, forthcoming) that focuses on citizen participation in Flemish cities and the functioning of politicians and civil servants in local participation arrangements. For the purpose of this chapter, a secondary analysis of the case study data was carried out.
3. Two organizations did not participate in the merger, as they wanted to stay independent. However, today they are both subcontractors for VZW Jong. Their (financial) means are from the VZW, and they have to implement specific tasks and projects.

REFERENCES

Arnstein, S. 1969. A ladder of citizen participation. *Journal of the American Planning Association* 35 (4): 216–224.

Bassoli, M. 2010. Local governance arrangements and democratic outcomes (with some evidence from the Italian case). *Governance* 23 (3): 485–508.

Blakeley, G. 2010. Governing ourselves: Citizen participation and governance in Barcelona and Manchester. *International Journal of Urban and Regional Research* 34 (1): 130–145.

Bovaird, T. 2007. Beyond engagement and participation: User and community co-production of public services. *Public Administration Review* 67 (5): 846–860.

Brandsen, T., and V. Pestoff. 2006. Co-production, the third sector and the delivery of public services. *Public Management Review* 8 (4): 493–501.

Brandsen, T., V. Pestoff & B. Verschuere. 2011. Co-production as a maturing concept.

Cannoot, V. 2009. We zijn normatief. We willen een andere samenleving. Interview met Pascal Debruyne. *TiensTiens, de andere k(r)ant van Gent,* 3, pp. 24–30.

Dezeure, K. (forthcoming). Stedelijke participatie ontleed. Analyse aan de hand van de arrangementenbenadering. PhD-dissertation. Ghent University.

Dries, I., Larosse, J. and P. Van Humbeeck. 2005. Linking innovation policy and sustainable development in Flanders. In: OECD. *Governance of innovation systems: volume 3: case studies in cross-sectoral policy.* OECD Publishing. Pp. 245-270.

Hautekeur, G. 2008. Community development in Flanders. In R. Brake, U. Deller, eds., *Community development—A European Challenge.* Leverkusen Opladen: Barbra Budrich.

Hertogen, N., and P. Debruyne. 2007. Het middenveld verliest terrain. *TiensTiens, de andere k(r)ant van Gent,* 10.

Hirst, P. 2000. Democracy and governance. In J. Pierre, ed. *Debating Governance: Authority, Steering, and Democracy.* Oxford, UK: Oxford University Press.

Jordan, A., R. Wurzel, and A. Zito. 2005. The rise of "new" policy instruments in comparative perspective: has governance eclipsed government? *Political Studies* 53 (3): 477–496.

Kooiman, J. 1993. *Modern governance: New government-society interactions.* London: Sage.

Kooiman, J. 2003. *Governing as governance.* London: Sage.

Levine, C. 1984. Citizenship and service delivery: The promise of co-production. *Public Administration Review* 47 (March): 26–34.

Lowndes, V., L. Pratchett,and G. Stoker. 2006. Local political participation: The impact of rules-in-use. *Public Administration* 84 (3): 539–561.

Marschall, M. 2004. Citizen participation and the neighborhood context: A new look at the co-production of local public goods. *Political Research Quarterly* 57 (2): 231–244.

Marcussen, M., and J. Torfing. 2003. *Grasping Governance Networks.* Working Paper Series, Roskilde, Centre for Democratic Network Governance, 5.

May, P. 2007. Regulatory regimes and accountability. *Regulation & Governance* 1 (1): 8–26.

Mintzberg, H. 1996. Managing government, governing management. *Harvard Business Review* 74 (3): 75–83.

Munshi, S. 2004. Concern for good governance in comparative perspective. In S. Munshi, B. P. Abraham, eds., *Good Governance, Democratic Societies and Globalization.* London: Sage.

Ostrom, E. 1996. Crossing the great divide: Co-production, synergy, and development. *World Development* 24 (6): 1073–1087.

Percy, S. 1984. Citizen participation in the co-production of urban services. *Urban Affairs Quarterly,*19 (4): 431–446.

Sharp, E. 1980. Towards a new undertanding ofurban services and citizen participation: the co-production concept. *Midwest Review of Public Administration.* 14(June): 105-118.

Sorensen, E. 2002. Democratic theory and network governance. *Administrative Theory & Praxis* 24 (4): 693–720.

Sorensen, E. & J. Torfing. 2005. Network governance and post-liberal democracy. *Administrative Theory & Praxis.* 27,2, 197-237.

Sorensen, E. & J. Torfing. 2007. *Theoretical approaches to democratic governance.* Basingstoke: Palgrave Macmillan.

Stoker, G. 2006. 'Public Value Management: A new narrative for networked governance. *American Review of Public Administration.* 36,1: 41-57.

Verlet, D. & H. Reynaert. 2004. De participerende burger op lokaal vlak in Gent, Brugge en Antwerpen. *Burger, Bestuur en Beleid.* 3: 237-256.

14 Co-Producing Safety or Participative Window Dressing?

Regulation Partnerships in German Local Governance Arrangements

Matthias Freise

INTRODUCTION

Since the early 1990s, municipalities and counties in all German states (*Länder*) have been implementing a new wave of administrative reforms, partly in response to a budgetary squeeze, but also to make local governance more accessible to citizens (Wollmannn, 2000). In the words of Scharpf (1993), local governance reforms in Germany aim to realize the ambitious intention of increasing both input and output legitimacy at the same time and against a backdrop of financial and economic turbulence.[1]

These activities are in line with the new public management (NPM) debate, which has been dominating international discourse since the early 1980s (Holtkamp, Bogumil, and Kißler, 2006). Currently, many modernization projects are underway all over the country. In addition to the ongoing hierarchization of local administrative structures and a tendency toward privatization, the intensified implementation of policy networks is shaping the transformation of local governance in Germany. In this context, numerous municipalities are experimenting with the institutionalization of new cooperative steering tools, including co-production arrangements with third sector organizations and civil society groups (Holtkamp, 2007).

At first glance, co-production partnerships between public and civil society at the local level are nothing new. On the contrary, in Germany, such cooperation is supported and legally grounded in two central concepts of state action, neo-corporatism and subsidiarity (Zimmer et al., 2009). These dictums of societal organization have put civil society organizations in a privileged position in numerous policy fields. However, as in other European countries, until recently, Germany's local democracy was dominated by the principle of representative or indirect democracy. Doubtlessly, the increasing vitalization of citizen participation programs and policy networks in various forms is a more recent development in the context of the NPM debate (Holtkamp and Bogumil, 2007). Another new element is the adoption of these instruments in policy sectors that had previously been dominated by a strictly hierarchical administration structure. In contrast to business-oriented public-private partnerships, these networks aim principally at strengthening the input component of governance legitimacy, which focuses on the interconnection of political decisions with the authentic preferences of the citizens involved by means of participative procedures. Nevertheless, these networks also seek to increase output legitimacy, though to a lesser extent.

This also holds true for so-called regulation partnerships (*Ordnungspartnerschaften*). These are institutionalized, usually local, policy networks in which municipal police stations, local authorities, public institutions and civil society organizations build up network structures with the aim of developing strategies and instruments in the policy field of local law and order (Schümchen, 2006). In the context of this volume, these regulation partnerships could be classified as a mixture of the co-management and co-governance types of co-production (Brandsen and Pestoff, 2008, 5): third-sector organizations participate in the planning and delivery of public services, in this case, the improvement of local traffic safety.

They were first introduced by a few municipalities in the late 1990s, and now there are several hundred local regulation partnerships focusing on various security issues, such as youth crime, drug abuse, burglary, and graffiti prevention. Numerous glossy brochures published by municipalities or the interior ministries of the *Länder* have lavished praise on these partnerships, classifying them as "prime examples for the successful implementation of participative governance structures in local safety policy which have made communal decision making more responsive, more democratic and at the same time more efficient" (Innenministerium NRW, 2007,3). But how realistic is such an assessment?

The potential of regulation partnerships have rarely been analyzed in a systematic or comparative way, and when they have been, this has usually been initiated by the financers of the partnerships. This study will therefore analyze thirteen comprehensive case studies of communal regulation partnerships, focusing on one area, the issue of traffic safety in cities in North Rhine-Westphalia.[2] There are three dimensions to this study: (1) Can traffic safety regulation partnerships be characterized as instruments of cooperative local co-production? (2) Which strategies and methods have been developed by these traffic regulation partnerships? (3) Can regulation partnerships between municipal police departments and civil society organizations increase input and output legitimacy, or are they perhaps a form of cooperation that has been imposed from the top down, which serves the purpose of democratic "window dressing"?

This chapter is divided into three sections: the next section presents the current state of regulation partnerships as instruments of local governance in Germany, discusses the methods used and the case selection, and justifies our focus on the policy field of traffic safety. The following section presents the results of the comparative case analysis. The final section discusses the results in the perspective of the debate on the advantages and disadvantages of cooperative network governance.

LOCAL GOVERNANCE AND REGULATION PARTNERSHIPS

For a long time, the German police authorities ignored the fact that the subjectively perceived threat of crime often failed to reflect reality. Over the past fourteen years, criminality has not increased significantly. Quite the contrary, the numbers of most of the delinquencies listed in the official police statistics have been declining since 1996. At the same time, subjective perceptions of security have worsened considerably (Frevel, 2007).

Obviously, the fear of criminality in society increases particularly when the residential environment is influenced by an appearance of degeneration, dilapidation and disorder. The popular broken windows theory assumes that a neglected environment will result in further criminality and that is why it has to be maintained by municipal authorities as well as possible (Wilson and Kelling, 2004). To achieve this, two different police strategies were discussed in Germany. On the one hand, the "Zero Tolerance Strategy," originally developed in New York, prefers a heavily repressive approach to fighting and preventing crime. However, this model has not been widely accepted in Germany, because it shows that aggressive police action often increases fear of criminality rather than lowering it (Feltes, 2008).

On the other hand, there are police strategies that favor participative and cooperative approaches to crime prevention. Here, the German debate is oriented toward U.S. role models that fall under the label of "community policing" (Skogan and Hartnett, 2000). The German states, which are basically responsible for the police law, introduced such strategies in the early 1990s. The overall idea is to complement traditional crime fighting with prevention-oriented approaches based on the involvement of the "normal" citizen. These so called "Chicago approaches" are usually shaped by a reorganization of municipal police departments (Frevel, 2007).[3] Against this background, many local regulation partnerships and other criminal prevention boards have been introduced in recent years. They are examples of a new form of co-management and co-governance in a policy field that was previously characterized by a strictly hierarchical administrative organization.

Measures and Developments of Local Criminal Prevention in Germany

The legal framework for regulation partnerships varies from German state to state. However, in all states regulation partnerships are seen as preventive instruments for specific aspects of local safety, such as vandalism, reckless driving, drug abuse, aggressive begging and so on. Typical measures put in place by these partnerships would include information desks in the city, intensified presence of police officers around accident hot spots, urban development or special traffic training for students and senior citizens (Frevel, 2007).

From a governance perspective, regulation partnerships and other crime preventive boards can be classified as instruments of focal co-governance, but they are usually initiated from the top down. This means that the network is ruled by a dominant (focal) partner—usually the local police department—which steers the relationships within the network and controls the network's resources to a large extent. By contrast, the other partners in the network are rather poorly interconnected.[4] There is little or no information exchange between them besides the central coordination carried out by the focal partner. The strong position of the police in the network usually results in a hierarchical organization and governance, although regulation partnerships aim to strengthen cooperative elements (Holtkamp, Bogumil and Kißler, 2006).

The basic assumption of all regulation partnerships is that these networks can strengthen both the input and output legitimacy of local governance at the same time. On the one hand, they aim to enhance the efficiency of local governance by involving private and civil society actors in crime prevention based on the notion that in times of limited budgets, many problems cannot be solved using police measures alone. On the other hand, the involvement of local civil society aims to introduce some degree of co-determination into political and administrative decision making in what was formerly a strictly hierarchical field of local politics (Holtkamp, 2008).

The reorganization of municipal police procedures entered public perception for the first time in 1997, when a coordination committee of the German states formulated recommendations for local participative safety policies (Wurtzbacher, 2008). The networking of various institutional and noninstitutional actors in the field of local police policy was an entirely new element of municipal police procedures and was not introduced without controversy. Critics were concerned about a further deepening of the surveillance society and complained about the dubious legitimacy of the partners involved (Kant and Pütter, 1998; Van Elsbergen, 2004). Nevertheless, the use of participative elements of crime prevention has since gained momentum in the debate on the reform of local governance structures.

In 1998, the influential conference of the Ministers of the Interior of the sixteen German states decided to introduce cooperative forms of crime prevention in all German states, albeit in different forms. Because not all states document these local projects and measures, it is difficult to estimate the current number of regulation partnerships. However, in 2007, Schreiber counted 960 working regulation partnerships nationwide. Similarly, Wurtzbacher (2008) estimates 500 to 600 active regulation partnerships in the country.

In North Rhine-Westphalia, regulation partnerships were first introduced in 1998, when six major cities launched regulation partnerships (Frevel, 2007). Until now, the implementation of regulation partnerships is down to the free choice of the municipalities. However, the Ministry of the Interior of North Rhine-Westphalia promoted regulation partnerships at the local level with a number of incentives for the municipalities. For instance, the ministry published a comprehensive overview of the possible fields of application for regulation partnerships, including numerous examples of best practice, which range from networks against fecal street pollution by dogs to the prevention of drug-related crimes and fare dodging (Innenministerium NRW, 2007). Since 2003, the provincial government has also awarded the *"Landespreis Innere Sicherheit"* (Prize for Law and Order), which rewards successful regulation partnerships and other initiatives of cooperative network governance in this policy field.

However, encouragement from provincial government is not only based on altruistic motives. Regulation partnerships are a relatively cheap means of gaining additional resources for the municipal police authorities. Moreover, the focal structure of the networks maintains a dominant role for the police, and the partnerships enable provincial government to implement ideas and concepts aimed directly at the local level, thereby bypassing the city councils (Schierz, 2004). This impression is confirmed in some of the case studies mentioned in this chapter.

Evaluating Regulation Partnerships

The question of how regulation partnerships can be evaluated in a reasonable way is not beyond dispute. For many years, German municipalities did not evaluate their regulation partnerships in empirical terms and neither did social scientists. The few surveys investigating regulation partnerships were usually individual case studies. However, interest in these cooperative governance instruments has increased recently. Holtkamp, Bogumil and Kißler (2006) compiled the results of several qualitative and quantitative studies.

They noticed that the initiative for regulation of partnerships for the prevention of criminality has usually come from municipalities and only in a few cases from the local police authorities themselves. However, the latter usually function as the focal partner in the networks. Generally, local authorities, schools, business associations and free welfare associations are strongly represented in the networks, while the "normal" citizens or associations of concerned people involved, such as drug addicts or the homeless, are underrepresented.[5] The regulation partnerships are usually only partially funded through public subsidies, and in most cases approximately one-third of the budget is provided by outside private actors, such as through donations, sponsoring or in-kind contributions. The thematic focus of the analyzed regulation partnerships is usually on sensitive aspects of criminality, such as drugs or violence (see also Albrecht, 2002).

Frevel (2007) investigated regulation partnerships in five medium-size towns in North Rhine-Westphalia (Detmold, Gladbeck, Rheine, Troisdorf) and Lower Saxony (Emden). Like Steffen (2005), he came to the conclusion that there is no visible causal relationship between local safety policy and criminality. In many cases, the selection of the topic of the regulation partnerships and the measures put in place are more the result of political motives than empirical necessity. The structure, main focus and competences of the regulation partnerships differ sharply from city to city. He also shows that suspect groups of people are not involved in the boards. This leads to a highly asymmetric constellation of actors.

Van den Brink (2005) interviewed seven members of two regulation partnerships in two cities in North-Rhine Westphalia. He points out that regulation partnerships are often shaped by very diffuse constellations of interests. This requires a lengthy negotiation processes and a high degree of coordination by the police authorities. Finally, Wurtzbacher (2008) analyzed the political landscape of twelve criminal prevention boards in larger cities and conducted two case studies in Berlin and Stuttgart. He documents that improving the perceptions of safety is not usually the main focus of the boards. Often, they are interested in negotiating solutions for specific problems, such as dangerous intersections or traffic reduction in residential areas. He confirms that the involvement of citizens in the cities analyzed was usually low, and self-help groups were usually not incorporated. In only four of the twelve cities did Wurtzbacher find consistent attempts to build sustainable regulation partnerships.

The aim of this study is to explore whether these results also apply to regulation partnerships in the policy field of traffic safety in North Rhine-Westphalia. This is an interesting question because these boards do not focus on crime prevention, but rather on more technical questions involving city planning and traffic routing.

Method and Case Selection

Safety in traffic and accident prevention is the topic of several regulation partnerships in North Rhine-Westphalia, and the provincial government has identified these topics as particularly suitable for cooperative network governance (Innenministerium NRW, 2007). There are several reasons for this. First, local traffic policy is directly relevant to the day-to-day lives of many of the citizens: traffic calming, new one-way street routing, or the rearrangement of traffic lights are evident at the local level and frequently affect almost everybody. Vandalism in public transport facilities, alarming reports about serious traffic accidents in the local newspapers and the recruitment of wardens on school crossings are specifically local problems. In addition, the prevention of accidents and other forms of criminality in traffic can, in contrast to other local policy problems such as youth criminality or drug abuse, be tackled on a case-by-case basis. As noted in the following, although a speed limit can be the subject of serious political debates, the identification of problems in local traffic policy is usually based on accident statistics or intermunicipal comparative studies.

Local traffic policy in Germany is usually shaped by consensual rather than conflictual negotiations. Finally, local traffic policy is suitable for cooperative regulation partnerships because in addition to the "normal" citizen, a considerable number of associative interests are affected: merchants are interested in parking areas for their customers; insurance companies are interested in reducing damage rates; teachers, parents and pupils want safe routes to school and traffic organizations such as the German Car Driver Association (ADAC) or the German Bike Rider Association (ADFC) argue for improvements to infrastructure. Furthermore, public utility companies, local transport and traffic companies and the local chambers of industry and commerce are often members of traffic regulation partnerships. In addition, the topic is also of interest to the local media because it is publishable and easy to illustrate. In short, regulation partnerships that deal with issues relating to local traffic policy and accident prevention are meeting points for the "usual suspects" of local governance networks in Germany.

For this study, traffic regulation partnerships were selected because they are shaped by similar actors, similar measures and similar goals. In addition, the topic allows us to keep the numbers of case studies at a workable level. Altogether, thirteen individual case studies were carried out in the context of a university seminar at Münster University in 2009.[6] The selection of these cases was the result of intensive Internet research that analyzed the websites of all regulation partnerships in North Rhine-Westphalia. Afterward, each regulation partnership was studied by comprehensive, half-standardized interviews with the actors involved, and an analysis of further documents such as press articles and internal minutes was done. In all cases, the coordinator of the regulation partnership (usually a police officer of the local police authority) was interviewed. In most cases, a selection of further actors was carried out. In some cases, group interviews were conducted. The issues discussed at these interviews included the reasons for initiating regulation partnerships; the structures of the networks; aims, governance modes, strategies and instruments of the network; and their development, landmarks and interest coalitions within the regulation partnerships. Furthermore, the interviewees were asked for their personal satisfaction with the network and their estimation of its success.

RESULTS

The traffic regulation partnerships analyzed confirm some of the findings of the pioneer studies that were previously discussed. The initiative for the establishment of the networks was usually taken by municipalities, not by the local police authorities. Often the regulation partnerships were developed by the city council or (more frequently) by the mayor. In many town halls, regulation partnerships were (rightly) seen as relatively cheap measures for participation in local policy making. The introduction of a regulation partnership does not burden municipal budgets significantly. In the policy field of traffic in particular, most municipalities already have budgets for construction activities, road safety education and accident prevention available, so that the regulation partnerships entail no new expenses. In addition, regulation partnerships sometimes afford the opportunity of raising extra public or private funds for chronically indebted municipalities. In many of the investigated regulation partnerships, the partners were able to attract additional funding from the private sector. In particular, insurance companies show a clear preference for the topic of accident prevention as a field of activity for sponsorship and corporate social responsibility measures. In most of the cases investigated, the local media is involved in more than just reporting. Often, local publishing houses are members of the regulation partnerships and contribute significant services, such as the cheaper distribution of promotional material. Last but not least, funds are provided by the provincial government, which supports a nationwide network of regulation partnerships and finances the training of police officers for establishing cooperative policy networks. Overall, regulation partnerships are cheap steering tools for the treasurers of the municipalities, and they can sometimes promote the allocation of external resources.

By contrast, regulation partnerships with many participants often entail significant labor costs for the police authorities involved. The organization of the regulation partnerships was focally arranged in all the cases analyzed. Almost the entire flow of information within the network was controlled by the police officer responsible. It is thus understandable that the scope and density of the network activities are dependent to a high degree on the personnel engagement of the operational center in the local police stations. There was only one example where the regulation partnership was not coordinated by the police, but by the principal of an elementary school.

The interviews carried out for this study show that the coordinators of the regulation partnerships have some very different motives. In one case for instance, the police officer interviewed admitted frankly that the municipality wanted a regulation partnership, and he achieved this by labeling an already existing informal discussion group in his district as such. Other cases confirm that regulation partnerships, from the perspective of the police officers involved, often represent—to varying degrees—an additional and unwanted workload. In these cases, the renaming of already existing networks with other authorities, such as the highway agencies, schools or the town clerk's office, is a favored solution for keeping workloads manageable. These networks hardly live up to the idea of enhancing citizen participation by introducing policy networks. Rather, these forms of regulation partnerships have been set up to solve specific problems for which the interlocking of the police with other authorities seems useful. These regulation partnerships have not usually been institutionalized, and meetings have only been called on an ad hoc basis. Nevertheless, most of the municipalities proudly see these networks as "new forms of participative local governance."

However, the mode of operation of these "exemplary governance tools" may sometimes seem strange. For instance, one police officer characterized the following as the most important achievement of his traffic regulation partnership. Principals of local schools, teachers and parents, who were all protesting against private bus companies that were operating a chaotic bus service, were told to contact him directly. He admitted that most of the citizens probably did not know that the police department was presenting this offer as an ideal regulation partnership. In six of the case studies, regulation partnerships were closed shops under the aegis of a local police officer who was not intrinsically interested in the time-consuming work of supporting the network.

Conversely, the remaining case studies illustrate that traffic regulation partnerships functioned as instruments of co-production. This was particularly true of the big cities of North Rhine-Westphalia, where police departments have larger staff and can thus entrust the organizational tasks of the network to a police officer. Although this was an additional task in all the cities analyzed here, the officers were really interested in establishing effective network governance by involving actors from civil society in the regulation partnerships. In some of the traffic regulation partnerships analyzed, networks were developed with a remarkable size of thirty regulation partners, and there were even more who meet regularly on an institutionalized basis. Some of these regulation partnerships established subgroups that specialized in specific topics. The police invited a typical set of actors to participate in the network, besides the already mentioned local authorities, such as county courts, public utility companies, insurance companies, local merchant associations, the Technical Control Board (TÜV and Dekra) and civil society organizations, such as the ADAC and ADFC.

As Frevel's (2007) study of crime preventive boards and regulation partnerships has already shown, the local policy field of accident prevention and traffic safety is characterized by close cooperation between exclusive partners. All the traffic regulation partnerships analyzed are shaped by a clear expert orientation: the police are interested in cooperating with suitable partners and thus search for organizations that can guarantee this profile. Consequently, the organizations represented usually send traffic experts, such as lawyers, engineers and urban planners, to the network meetings. Interested citizens are usually very underrepresented or not represented at all in the regulation partnerships. However, some of the networks try to make citizen participation possible by functioning as a central contact point of contact for all questions related to local traffic policies. They consider suggestions from the citizens, comment on them and forward recommendations to the local authorities. As a result, local traffic regulation partnerships have close connections with associations and local authorities in their day-to-day work. In their self-perception, then, they also fulfill a voice function for citizens.

Surprisingly, the analysis of the case studies showed that the political parties represented on the municipal council were often not reflected in the regulation partnerships. This is remarkable because those boards were usually a stomping ground for local party activists. Although none of the interviews with party representatives included open rejection of the regulation partnerships, it became obvious that parties were very reluctant to accept the activities of those boards that had not been legitimized by elections. This is a typical outcome, already described by Holtkamp (2008). Over decades, German local politics have been shaped by a strongly representative system. The introduction of a rather consensus-oriented form of network governance challenges established modes of governance by reducing the influence of municipal boards and upgrading the position of the local administration, particularly the role of the mayor. Especially when a traffic regulation partnership involved on a subject that might be relevant for election campaigns, the classical problem concerning the compatibility of representative democracy and participative (or deliberative) democracy became very apparent, because the parties have to decide whether to follow the down-to-earth empirical expertise of a board or the assumed interests of their party stalwarts.

Basically, the case studies illustrate that the variety of co-production networks labeled as traffic regulation partnerships is very broad. They include simple informal discussion meetings arranged by various local authorities, small but institutionalized boards dealing with the specific problems of local traffic policy, as well as comprehensive networks with a broad spectrum of public, private and civil society actors. An important characteristic of the regulation partnerships that we analyzed was their thematic focus. In most cases, the partners agreed on jointly defined problems that were often the reason for the launch of the network. Examples included a poor position in the provincial accident statistics, reckless driving, the development of bicycle-friendly infrastructure, the traffic education of children and the designation of traffic-calming areas.

Generally, the case studies show that the actors involved were satisfied with their activities when the network agreed on a concrete problem that could be solved with the instruments available to the network. In comparison with the focus of other regulation partnerships, such as youth criminality or aggressive begging, it was obviously much easier to reach agreement in the policy field of local traffic. For instance, the fact that high numbers of traffic deaths need to be reduced is relatively uncontroversial compared to perceptions of graffiti. Traffic regulation partnerships thus often agree on an overarching goal, such as the reduction of accidents by a certain percentage or road reconstruction to eliminate accident hot spots. Conversely, participants of the regulation partnerships were not satisfied with their work when there was no clear aim of the network, or as one interviewee from a civil society organization put it, when the regulation partnership was "a discussion club for talking about the world and his brother."

The regulation partnerships that we analyzed typically included four types of instruments: (1) penalties for traffic violations, (2) the development of recommendations for construction measures, (3) traffic education and (4) public relations. These measures were not undertaken in the same way in all the case studies. Nevertheless, in all cases the development of more or less systematic expertise was the basis for the work carried out by the regulation partnerships. Some of the partnerships we analyzed were able to consult additional external opinions for their strategic development, while others characterized their problem definition as "gut decision on which all partners agreed on the basis of [their] everyday experience."

From a governance perspective, the instruments used for the joint development of strategies for the punishment of traffic violations and traffic supervision are particularly notable. This area of responsibility belonged solely to the police authorities. Now it has become an issue for negotiation between police and civil society actors. However, some of the police officers interviewed pointed out that they reserved the right of the final decision for themselves.

The development of recommendations for road construction and technical traffic regulations were an issue in half of the regulation partnerships that we studied. Typical recommendations concern one-way street regulations, the widening of bicycle lanes, traffic calming,[7] right-of-way regulations, traffic light calibrations or parking areas. In this context, the expertise orientation of the networks is clear: the negotiation process is usually shaped by an analysis of the empirical results of sciences of traffic. In just one case, there was a conflict between the participants when the majority of partners recommended the reduction of inner-city parking areas to resolve some accident hot spots, while the representatives of the merchant associations successfully blocked this proposal by lobbying the city council directly. This was, however, an exceptional case.

The softer measures of traffic education and public relations went undisputed in all the traffic regulation partnerships. In the context of traffic education, the networks identify specific target groups—such as young school pupils, senior citizens, migrants or cyclists—and cooperate with their respective organizations (schools, cyclist clubs, retirement homes, migrant associations). In recent years, the regulation partnerships have developed a number of very different measures, from yellow footsteps along school routes to cycling proficiency lessons for adult female migrants.

In the following sections, the impact of the co-production arrangements on input and output legitimacy is put to the test. The concept of legitimacy developed by Scharpf is therefore briefly introduced again.

Output Legitimacy of Regulation Partnerships

According to Scharpf (1993), a political system achieves output legitimacy when it is oriented toward the authentic preferences of the citizens, which are realized by efficient and effective measures. Input legitimacy, by contrast, can be obtained when political decisions are directly or indirectly related to the value orientation of their stakeholders, through procedures for controlling collective action or modes of participation, for example. Output legitimacy is thus more rewarding for social science research, because concrete policy outcomes are much easier to measure than the more diffuse demands that are made of the political system by citizens.

Trying to measure the output legitimacy of local regulation partnerships with limited resources is not an easy task, particularly because many of them do not specify concrete problems and goals for their work. Instead, they agree on abstract ideas, such as "the improvement of traffic safety in our city" or "improving consideration among road users." Such targets are very difficult to quantify. But even in cases where the participants in the regulation partnership have agreed on more or less concrete targets, such as the reduction of traffic deaths or the improvement of bicycle paths, an evaluation is difficult, usually requiring expensive traffic surveys that most regulation partnerships cannot afford. However, it became obvious that in most cases, the interviewed participants did not really intend to evaluate their work. In fact, just two of the thirteen regulation partnerships ordered traffic surveys, and even there, the methods used were questionable as one interview partner frankly admitted. According to him, the traffic analysis did indeed show the number of traffic accidents that involved cyclists had decreased since the regulation partnerships had started their work some years ago. However, the analysis did not explain whether this was a result of the concrete instruments used by the regulation partnership or a result of better weather with less black ice, for example. Almost none of the other traffic regulation partnerships agreed on concrete evaluation methods for their work.

But does this really show that the output legitimacy of the traffic regulation partnerships is lacking? Not necessarily, because output legitimacy is not always bound to quantifiable policy outcomes. In many policy fields, the perception of success is enough to increase the input legitimacy of a political system. For instance, many of the participants interviewed highlighted positive coverage in the local media as a major success for the traffic regulation partnerships and presented folders filled with articles concerning their work. Obviously, the policy field of local traffic policy has a high news value for local newspapers, especially given their participation in them.

Accordingly, the possibility of regulation partnerships does not necessarily depend on its quantifiable achievements in road safety. In fact, the subjective feeling (perception) of safety of the citizens is more relevant. As already seen at the beginning of this chapter, subjective and objective feelings of safety do not necessarily correspond. Apparently, in our case studies, the subjective feelings have improved because citizens have repeatedly read about safety innovations in the media. Particularly in the study at hand, most of the networks were very successful. In other words, increasing the output legitimacy of political systems can be achieved by an increasing perception of safety, even though there may not be any substantial improvement of concrete problems.

As such, criticism of regulation partnerships as mere discussion clubs or democratic "window dressing" in local politics is perhaps too limited. Most of the measures initiated by the regulation partnerships were not short-term prestige projects—even though the comparative study at hand was unable to evaluate the impact of the regulation partnerships on the real perceptions of the road safety of the citizens. Nevertheless, the case studies did find some evidence for the assumption that coverage of the issues in the local media is comprehensive and remarkably positive whenever the regulation partnerships seek their attention.

But even if traffic regulation partnerships are just closed shops made up of several local authorities and the police working together, output legitimacy can increase, although not from the perspective of participative democracy. Instead, it can be argued that from the perspective of new public management that local governance is shaped by the establishment of cross-governmental areas beyond the German traditional hierarchical bureaucracy model (Bogumil, 2002). In this respect, regulation partnerships gain legitimacy when they are able to establish efficient cooperation between different authorities. Our analysis of the case studies produced various results: while some regulation partnerships really tried to establish open governance networks, most were still bound to the traditional ideas of hierarchical local government. Sometimes, the organizational structure of the regulation partnerships was treated almost like a state secret. In these cases, the regulation partnerships provided good examples of cooperation, which was imposed at will by the involved authorities in the network. In those cases, neither output nor input legitimacy can be increased.

Input Legitimacy of Regulation Partnerships

Democratic governance promotes input legitimacy when it is based on accepted rules, on the one hand, and when decision making is connected to the authentic preferences of the citizens (e.g., as expressed through elections) and effective stakeholder participation, on the other. Depending on which strand of democratic theory is emphasized, the perspectives on the various components of input legitimacy will vary. The advocates of cooperative democracy call for the further use of participative instruments, while defenders of representative democracy respond by pointing out that most tested instruments of participative democracy have not proved successful in the past. On the contrary, many measures (including regulation partnerships or participative budgeting initiatives) fail to attract the citizens. The typical town dweller is not interested in more participation. In fact, she or he would be satisfied when allowed to elect the city council every four or five years (Holtkamp, Bogumil, and Kißler, 2006; Stortone, 2010). Some of the cases we studied here seem to confirm this criticism. For instance, one of the traffic regulation partnerships only existed on paper because the police officer in charge was no longer able to motivate the participants of the network to attend the network's meetings. Other police officers pointed out that they would like to involve more "normal" citizens in the network. However, despite their efforts to promote the network publicly, they had not been able to find interested citizens.

However, input legitimacy cannot only be achieved procedurally (e.g., through elections) or by stakeholder participation (e.g., through citizen participation). The involvement of expertise in the political decision-making process can also increase input legitimacy when the citizens accept the involved experts as qualified to contribute to the solutions of problems. This was evident in a number of the traffic regulation partnerships. As previously illustrated, associations of concerned citizens were not often involved in the networks. However, this was less important in the specific policy field of local traffic safety, because the topic is suitable for a technocratic treatment (e.g., by the orientation on surveys). To this extent, the involvement of experts in traffic regulation partnerships can promote input legitimacy provided that the regulation partnerships keep their work out of the normative day-to-day discussions of local party politics.

To summarize, it is possible to formulate the hypothesis that traffic regulation partnerships as expert boards can enhance input legitimacy when they focus on technocratic topics beyond the normative discussions of party politics. Furthermore, successful regulation partnerships depend on a consensual internal mode of operation and a committed focal actor who guides the network activities.

CONCLUSIONS AND POLICY RECOMMENDATIONS

As a first conclusion, and as already noted, many studies do not make favorable references to regulation partnerships in general. They are often classified as an exclusive and closed form of cooperation that usually involves local elites and to which "normal" citizens do not have access (for an overview of the criticism, see Wurtzbacher, 2008). The case studies carried out for this chapter only partly confirm this criticism. Around half of the traffic regulation partnerships were indeed "imposed" cooperation, in which the participants involved (in particular, the representatives of the local authorities) cooperated rather reluctantly. In these, the police officers involved are merely implementing hierarchical instructions in the bureaucratic manner. This procedure thus excludes effective network governance. At best, these kinds of regulation partnerships result in informal network structures that are not visible to the public, even though the municipalities may seek to present them as ideal forms of citizen participation on their websites. They seem to provide, then, a good example of how not to organize co-management between public authorities and third sector organizations. To a certain extent, these examples show that in some cases, co-management between public authorities and other organizations may be some kind of window dressing: there seems to be a kind de-coupling between the rhetoric of increased participation and involvement ("network governance") and the reality of how partnerships actually work.

Second, we can derive some policy recommendations from the comparative case study analysis. Regulation partnerships should not be enacted top-down by the mayor or the city council if there is no police officer available who wants to invest time and effort to organize and supervise the network. Where this is not the case, regulation partnerships are doomed to fail, because the focal coordinator of the network is central to the coordination and control of information for all network activities and thus also for the success of the regulation partnership. The outcome of the case studies shows that regulation partnerships can indeed be initiated by incentives from the top down. However, in cases where regulation partnerships are politically motivated, the output and input legitimacy of local politics cannot be expected to benefit.

Third, and in contrast to the rather discouraging results of the literature, this study also shows that the instrument of regulation partnerships may nevertheless be appropriate for the technical policy field of local traffic policy. When a specific topic was dealt with for which there is a consensual problem, definition, and for which a balance of representative and expert democracy is possible, regulation partnerships can achieve remarkable success. It remains a challenge for local governance research to focus on the frameworks under which regulation partnerships can be used as measures for co-management and co-governance type of co-production.

In sum, it seems that expanding co-management and co-governance could contribute to the further development of local democracy in Western countries when the various approaches to the concept succeed in realizing a substantial increase in citizen involvement and efficient governance at the same time. In other words, we could finish this chapter with a proposition that needs further inquiry: it seems to be the case that co-management can effectively yield an improved local democracy, but only when some conditions are fulfilled. First, there should be a specific societal problem that is recognized as such by most actors and citizens in the local society. These actors should also agree on the problem, solution and the desired effect. Second, the presence of a set of motivated actors and citizens that are willing (motivated) to address the problem is needed. Third, the presence of a "network-broker" is needed, who is able to bring together the relevant actors and to direct their heads in the same direction.

NOTES

1. According to Scharpf (1993) political systems have to ensure that their structures and processes are perceived as legitimate (input legitimacy) and at the

same time that the implementation of their regulation and their problem-solving capacity is effective (output legitimacy).
2. North Rhine-Westphalia is the most populous German state (former West Germany).
3. As a reaction to the "Zero Tolerance Model" of the New York Police Department, Chicago and several other American cities experimented successfully with Participative Prevention Models in the late 1980s. See Frevel, 2007.
4. For the concept of focal governance, see Oppen and Sack, 2008, 271–272.
5. The Free Welfare Associations are German umbrella organizations for NPOs, which play a privileged role in the production of person-based social services, such as nursing homes, welfare centers and child care facilities. The big five Free Welfare Associations are Caritas, Diakonia, German Red Cross, Arbeiterwohlfahrt and Parity.
6. I thank Daniel Becker, Peter Bednarz, Marine Beth, Jana Kiewit, Jowanna Lohmöller, Maren Meißner, Christoph Michel, Thomas Oeljeklaus, Florian-Fritz Riener, Annett Rößling, Annemarie Schlicksupp, Philippe Seidel and Anna Six for carrying out the lion's share of the case studies.
7. Traffic calming is used in residential zones: additional speed limits, speed ramps, etc.

REFERENCES

Albrecht, H.-J. 2002. Kriminologische Erfahrungen und kriminalpräventive Räte. In R. Prätorius, ed. 2002. *Wachsam und kooperativ? Der lokale Staat als Sicherheitsproduzent*. Baden-Baden: Nomos, pp. 22–40.

Bogumil, J. 2002. Kommunale Entscheidungsprozesse im Wandel. In J. Bogumil, ed. 2002. *Kommunale Entscheidungsprozesse im Wandel*. Opladen: Leske + Budrich, pp. 7–51.

Brandsen, T., and V. Pestoff. 2008. Co-production, the third sector and the delivery of public services: an introduction. In V. Pestoff, and T. Brandsen, eds., *Co-production. The Third Sector and the Delivery of Public Services*. London: Routledge, pp. 1–9.

Feltes, T. 2008. Null-Toleranz. In H.-J. Lange, M. Gasch, eds. *Kriminalpolitik*. Wiesbaden: VS Verlag für Sozialwissenschaften, pp. 231–249.

Frevel, B. 2007. Kooperative Sicherheitspolitik in Mittelstädten. In B. Frevel, ed. 2007. *Kooperative Sicherheitspolitik in Mittelstädten*. Frankfurt am Main: Verlag für Polizeiwissenschaft, pp. 13–212.

Holtkamp, L. 2007. Local governance. In A. Benz, ed. 2007. *Handbuch Governance*. Wiesbaden: VS Verlag für Sozialwissenschaften, pp. 366–377.

Holtkamp, L., and Bogumil, J. 2007. Bürgerkommune und Local Governance. In L. Schwalb, H. Walk, eds. *Local Governance–mehr Transparenz und Bürgernähe?* Wiesbaden: VS Verlag, pp. 231-250.

Holtkamp, L., J., Bogumil, and L. Kißler. 2006. *Kooperative Demokratie*. Frankfurt am Main: Campus.

Innenministerium des Landes Nordrhein-Westfalen. 2008. *Landespreis für Innere Sicherheit 2008*. Düsseldorf.

Kant, M., and N. Pütter. 1998. Sicherheit und Ordnung in den Städten. *Bürgerrechte & Polizei/CILIP* (59) 70–79.

Oberwittler, D. 2003. Die Entwicklung von Kriminalität und Kriminalitätsfurcht in Deutschland—Konsequenzen für die Kriminalitätsprävention. *Deutsche Zeitschrift für Kommunalwissenschaften* 42 (1): 31–52.

Oppen, M., and D. Sack. 2008. Governance und Performanz. Motive, Formen und Effekte lokaler Public Private Partnerships. In G. Schuppert and M. Zürn, Michael, ed. 2008. *Governance in einer sich wandelnden Welt.* Wiesbaden: VS Verlag für Sozialwissenschaften, pp. 259–281.

Pütter, N. 2002. Kommunale Politik als Kriminalpolitik—Über die Verwandlung des Politischen in der Präventionsgesellschaft. In R. Prätorius, ed. 2002. *Wachsam und kooperativ? Der lokale Staat als Sicherheitsproduzent.* Baden-Baden: Nomos, pp. 64–79.

Scharpf, F. 1993. Versuch über Demokratie im verhandelnden Staat. In R. Czada and M. Schmidt, ed. 1993. *Verhandlungsdemokratie, Interessenvermittlung, Regierbarkeit.* Opladen: Westdeutscher Verlag, pp. 25–50.

Schierz, S. 2004. Ordnungspartnerschaften in Nordrhein-Westfalen—Sicherheit und Ordnung werden erlebbar. In G. van Elsbergen, ed. 2004. *Wachen, kontrollieren, patrouillieren.* Wiesbaden: VS Verlag für Sozialwissenschaften, pp. 119–131.

Schümchen, W. 2006. Ordnungspartnerschaften. In H.-J. Lange, M. Gasch, eds. 2006. *Wörterbuch zur Inneren Sicherheit.* Wiesbaden: VS Verlag, pp. 207–209.

Skogan, W., Hartnett, S. 2000. *Community policing, Chicago style.* Oxford: Oxford University Press.

Steffen, W. 2005. Gremien kommunaler Kriminalprävention – Bestandsaufnahme und Perspektive. In: B. Bannenberg, M. Coester, E. Marks, eds. *Kommunale Kriminalprävention.* Mönchengladbach: Forum-Verlag Godesberg, pp. 155–167.

Stortone, S. 2010. Participatory budgeting: heading towards a civil democracy? In M. Freise, M. Pyykkönen, E. Vaidelyte, eds. 2010. *A Panacea for all Seasons? Civil Society and Governance in Europe.* Baden-Baden: Nomos, pp. 99–119.

Van den Brink, H. 2005. *Kommunale Kriminalprävention. Mehr Sicherheit in der Stadt?* Frankfurt am Main: Verlag für Polizeiwissenschaft.

Van Elsbergen, G. ed. 2004. *Wachen, kontrollieren, patrouillieren.* Wiesbaden: VS Verlag für Sozialwissenschaften.

Wilson, J., Kelling, G. 2004. Broken windows: the police and neighbourhood safety. In E. McLaughlin, ed. 2004. *Criminological perspectives.* London: Sage, pp. 400–412.

Wollmann, H. 2000. Local government systems: from historic divergence towards convergence? Great Britain, France and Germany as comparative cases in point. *Government and Policy,* 18(1), pp. 33–55.

Wurtzbacher, J. 2008. *Urbane Sicherheit und Partizipation.* Wiesbaden: VS Verlag für Sozialwissenschaften.

Zimmer, A. et al., 2009. Germany: on the social policy centrality of the Free Welfare Associations. In J. Kendall ed. 2009. *Handbook on Third Sector Policy in Europe. Multi-level Processes and Organised Civil Society.* Cheltenham: Edward Elgar, pp. 21–42.

15 The Potential of Nonprofit-Government Partnerships for Promoting Citizen Involvement

Ichiro Tsukamoto

INTRODUCTION

This chapter examines the potential of nonprofit government partnerships as a means of promoting citizen involvement as "co-production" at the local level in Japan. In recent years, an increasing amount of attention has been paid to the involvement of nonprofit organizations in the provision of public services and their partnerships with local government. In some cases, local citizens who were originally consumers of public services have set up nonprofit organizations and actually become the producers of services—in other words, "consumer-producers" (Parks et al. 1999)—in order to improve and control the quality of services. Such a system of provision can be regarded as "co-production" (Ostrom, 1996; Parks et al., 1999; Pestoff, 2006, 2008).

On the other hand, the potential for citizen involvement such as co-production can be constrained by contractual relationships with local governments. Such relationships occasionally bring to bear institutional pressures and organizational changes called "institutional isomorphic pressure" (DiMaggio and Powell, 1991) in nonprofit organizations. In fact, current public service reforms at the national and local levels have been driven by the more market-oriented new public management (NPM) regime through the introduction of contracting regimes and the "Designated Manager System." The latter is a newly introduced contracting regime in the field of management and service delivery of public facilities owned by local government. Under new contract regimes, nonprofit contractors tend to still suffer from the institutional pressures.

However, in our view, the potential to promote active civic participation in the production of public services is not necessarily diminished under contracting regimes, including the Designated Manager System (Tsukamoto and Nishimura, 2006; Tsukamoto, 2009). Particularly for community-based facilities that promote community and citizen activities, the transformation from local government management to other community-based forms of nonprofit organization management seems to improve the participative approach to delivering public services. Private contractors, including nonprofit organizations, can exercise more discretional power over the management of the facilities under the new contracting system than they could through traditional contractual relationships.

This chapter therefore looks at the potential to promote active civic participation and public service provision in the form of co-production. We conducted empirical research on a local nonprofit organization in Tokyo named Mirai Kodomo Land (MKL). This nonprofit organization was established by local citizens and is involved in the co-production and delivery of public services under a contractual relationship. We also examine what organizational or interorganizational factors limit the potential of co-production in Japan.

AN OVERVIEW OF JAPAN'S NONPROFIT SECTOR

The nonprofit sector in Japan has moved into a new phase since the late 1990s. This has been characterized by a radical increase in a new type of nonprofit organizations. The emergence of the new nonprofit movement has been influenced particularly by the growing public interest in voluntary activities after the Hanshin-Awaji Earthquake of 1995 and the enactment of the Law to Promote Specified Nonprofit Activities (the NPO Law) of 1998. The NPO law created a new category of incorporated organizations for nonprofit and voluntary activities and enabled civic groups to acquire a legal personality known as "the Specified Nonprofit Corporation" (NPO *hōjin*) (Pekkanen, 2003). An NPO hōjin is much easier to incorporate than traditional nonprofit corporations because less government regulation is involved. According to the statistics of the cabinet office, over 40,000 nonprofits with the legal status of NPO hōjin were active in the whole country at the end of June 2010. This figure shows the rapid growth of new type of nonprofits in the last twelve years since the enactment of the NPO Law.

Needless to say, Japan has a long history of nonprofit and community organizations. During the early Meiji Era, traditional nonprofit corporations known as "public interest corporations" were institutionalized with the enactment of the Civil Law of 1897. Public interest corporations known as *koueki hōjin* are further categorized into two types: *shadan hōjin* (incorporated association) and *zaidan hōjin* (incorporated foundation).[1] Subsequently, other types of nonprofit corporations, such as *shakai fukushi hōjin* (social welfare corporation), *gakkō hōjin* (the private school corporation), *shūkyō hōjin* (religious corporation) and others were institutionalized, each according to different laws. The total number of these traditional nonprofit organizations is currently estimated at over 200,000. After incorporation, they are required to follow strict regulations that are supervised by relevant authorities who also have discretionary powers. Thus, many civic and grassroots groups are reluctant to be incorporated in these traditional legal forms. Such reluctance, and the demand for a more civic-oriented nonprofit form, led to the enactment of the NPO Law.

THE EMERGENCE OF A NEW CONTRACTUAL REGIME

Focusing on the changing needs of governments, most local governments have been keen to contract out their services to local nonprofit organizations, especially the NPO hōjin type of nonprofits under the current local government reforms. Most local governments have sought greater collaboration, occasionally called "partnership," with local nonprofits to promote citizen involvement, improve local public services and solve local issues. Nikkei Shinbun (Nikkei Inc.), a major newspaper in Japan, conducted the postal survey in March 2008. Ninety-seven local authorities responded this survey, including 47 prefectures, 32 municipalities in which prefectural governments are located, and 18 ordinance-designated cities whose population is more than one million. According to the survey, the total number of partnership programs numbers 5,842 in 2008, representing an increase of around 7 percent compared to the figure in 2007.

In reality, most partnerships in public service provision take the form of contractual relationships. According to the national postal survey on nonprofit organizations (n = 951, of which 373 replied) conducted by the cabinet office in 2004, over 80 percent of partnership programs with local governments were based on contracts. According to the national postal survey of 894 local authorities conducted by the governmental research institute (Keizai Sangyo Kenkyujo, 2007) in 2006, 51 percent of local authorities have contracted out their services to nonprofit organizations, while 45.8 percent of local authorities have not. One hundred percent of prefectural governments (n = 28) and large cities' municipal governments (n = 32) have contracted out services to nonprofit organizations.

Furthermore, most local governments have outsourced the management functions of the public facilities that they own—such as museums, public halls, sports centers and volunteer support centers—to private nonprofits and businesses after the revision of "the Local Government Law" of 2003. Before the revision, the management function of these public facilities could not be delegated to private enterprises or nonprofit organizations, except to local government or private corporations founded with shares from governments. In terms of the management of all local public facilities, local government is legally obliged to leave these management functions to other corporations, known as "designated managers," or to retain direct management themselves after the enactment of the revised law. Local councils are required to stipulate the basic principle and designating procedure of the system in their ordinances. According to more recent government statistics which was based on a national survey conducted by Ministry of Internal Affairs and Communications in 2006(Izumi, 2008, 23), the designated manager systems had been introduced in 61,565 government facilities in Japan. In terms of allocation among different private and public corporations, just 11 percent of all facilities were contracted out to private companies—36.2 percent to traditional nonprofit corporation subject to tight government controls, 50 percent to government or governmental institutions, just 1.7 percent to NPO hōjin and 5.6 percent to other corporations. The progress of the new contracting system has been limited, then, and irrelevant to such new types of nonprofit organizations. However, in specific areas, in particular nonprofit intermediary organizations, the designated manager status is associated with survival.

Under this new contracting system based on the revised law, private contractors can receive more discretionary power to manage the facilities, although both the government and contractor sides share responsibility for the efficient, effective and accountable operation of facilities. For example, private contractors can receive fees for services as their own income if they have formal agreements with local government. In addition, the terms of these contracts tend to be relatively longer than traditional contracts, in which one-year contracts are usual. For example, the contractor can now sign a five-year contract with local government. This seems to be helpful for financial stability. In some cases the term can be ten years.

Certainly, this new system can be regarded as a financial retrenchment scheme. In addition, "ownership" and ultimate control remains in the hands of the local government. Many nonprofit organizations are keen to be engaged in managing government facilities to ensure their own survival. The activities of nonprofit contractors tend to become executors of government policy and are generally constrained by government regulations.

Nevertheless, devolution of the part of the government's control of the public facilities to nonprofit organizations seems to provide them with opportunities to promote more active civic participation in various public spheres jointly controlled by nonprofit and public sectors. In other words, such joint control of public facilities by government and civic organizations has the potential to create a new type of cooperation in the delivery of public services: co-production.

THE CONCEPTUAL FRAMEWORK: CO-PRODUCTION, CO-GOVERNANCE AND INSTITUTIONALIZATION

In this chapter, "co-production," "co-governance" and "institutionalization" are used as key concepts in the analysis, although the main focus is the aspect of co-production. Co-production and co-governance are central concepts for understanding the implications of changing modern governance. In the field of political science and public administration and in local economic circles, the difference and interdependence between these two concepts has been discussed. The concept of institutionalization has also received more and more attention by scholars of nonprofit organizations and public private partnerships, as well as neo-institutional organizational theorists. It seems to be difficult to find some relevance for the former two concepts. However, in our hypothesis, these three concepts—co-production, co-governance and institutionalization—should be considered as mutually related. In reality, the institutional aspects and specific interorganizational relations in service provision can constrain the actual form and function of co-governance and co-production. In addition to political perspectives, such as co-production and co-governance, then, an organizational perspective that focuses on institutional aspects such as institutionalization is essential if we are to understand the provision of complex modern public services. Three key concepts can be recognized as follows.

First, co-production is characteristic of much public service production in modern society. The concept of co-production, which means the involvement of citizens or consumers in the production of public services, has frequently been mentioned in many publications. For instance, co-production can be seen as the joint provision of public services by a public agency as well as by the service consumers (Levine, 1984). In other words, co-production involves "a mixing of the productive efforts of regular and consumer-producer" (Parks et al., 1999, 382) and can be considered as "one way that synergy between what a government does and what citizens do can occur" (Ostrom, 1996, 1079).

In more recent works, according to Pestoff (2006, 506), "co-production" implies citizen participation in the execution or implementation of public services. That is, co-production is characterized by a mix of activities carried out by both public service agents who are involved as professionals or "regular producers" and citizens whose production is based on the voluntary efforts of individuals or groups who contribute to the provision of public services. The work of Brandsen and Pestoff (2006) also notes that co-production focuses on policy implementation rather than policy formulation. By contrast, Cooper and Kathi view co-production as having two parts: the participation of citizens in the planning of services to be delivered as well as the delivery of those services (Cooper and Kathi, 2005, 47).

Further, while maintaining the basic consumer-co-producer idea, attention has been shifted to the organizational, as well as interorganizational, logics that underlie the concept (Manfredi and Maffei, 2008, 188). From the organizational perspective, co-production can be understood as "the involvement of different organizations in the production of services" (188, 190). As such, the concept of co-production still seems incomplete and confusing. The perspective of focusing on the policy formulation process and interorganizational or collaborative relationships is important. Nevertheless, in its analysis of co-production, this chapter focuses on the aspect of citizen involvement in order to distinguish co-production from other related concepts, such as co-governance and institutionalization. Hence, the more restricted use of the term is employed in this analysis: "an arrangement where citizens produce their own services, at least in part" (Brandsen and Pestoff, 2006, 497).

Second, changing modern governance can be characterized by a shift that can be described as "doing things together instead of doing them alone," either by the state or by the market (Kooiman, 1993). In other words, modern governance can be seen as "a mix of all kinds of governing efforts by all manner of socio-political actors, public as well as private" (Kooiman, 2003, 3). In reality, under the progress of public-private partnership (Osborne, 2000), the concept of the local governance has been radically changed. According to Rhodes, governance refers to self-organizing, interorganizational networks characterized by interdependence, resource exchange, rules of the game and significant autonomy from the state (Rhodes, 2000, 15). The concept of co-governance is related to this new governance perspective. Kickert and Koppenjan define the term co-governance as "negotiating government whereby opportunities for creating win-win situations by means of interactive strategies are explored and pursued" (Kickert and Koppenjan, 1997, 40–41). Focusing on the aspect of cooperation in the delivery of public services, Brandsen and Pestoff (2006, 5) consider co-governance as an arrangement in which the third sector participates in the planning and delivery of public services. From this perspective, the concept of co-governance focuses on policy formulation. This differentiates it from the concept of co-production, which focuses more on policy implementation.

Finally, institutionalization can be defined as "the process by which actions are repeated and given similar meaning by self and others" (Scott and Davis, 2007, 260). The frequently quoted term "institutional isomorphism" (DiMaggio and Powell, 1991) is useful when describing organizational changes that tend to be embedded within government-dominated institutional frameworks. DiMaggio and Powell identify three mechanisms through which institutional isomorphic change occurs: "coercive isomorphism," "mimetic isomorphism" and "normative isomorphism" (DiMaggio and Powell, 1991, 67).[2] In relation to the notion of "institutional isomorphism," they refer to the "organizational field" as

> those organizations that, in the aggregate, constitute a recognized area of institutional life: key suppliers, resource and product consumers, regulatory agencies, and other organizations that produce similar services or products. (DiMaggio and Powell, 1991, 64–65)

The mechanism that induces the isomorphism of structural features operates most strongly within delimited "organizational fields." The neo-institutional organization theorist's concept of "organizational field" is helpful in understanding the organizational context of the contractual relationship.

RESEARCH METHOD

The research goal of this chapter is to look at the potential to promote citizen participation and public service delivery through co-production. In terms of the research method used to reach this research goal, this study examines the results of a case study of a nonprofit organization delivering child care services and the data of a postal survey on national advanced cases of nonprofit organizations.

First, this study will look at the case of a nonprofit organization that is engaged in delivering child care. This nonprofit organization was set up by local citizens who were originally service consumers and now involves citizens in public service provision in partnership with local government. The organization can be regarded as being involved in both co-production and co-governance. We conducted semi-structured interviews with the representative (president) and directors in July 2006 and February 2009. This organization was incorporated with the legal status of NPO hōjin and was also active in managing public facilities and providing public services, based on its partnership and contractual relationship with local government.

Second, this study uses the findings of a postal survey on mature nonprofit organizations across the nation that are engaged in partnerships with local governments. This postal survey of nonprofit organizations was conducted in February 2008 by a research group based at Meiji University (Institute of Nonprofit and Public Management Studies, 2009). The sample included 287 nonprofit organizations in Japan (Open Research Center Project, 2005), of which 102 replied, a response rate of 35.5 percent. These 287 organizations were regarded as active partners by local governments and responded to the questionnaires in our previous postal survey on local authorities in 2004. For this reason, the respondents of this study can be regarded as representative mature partnerships. The analysis in this chapter is thus based on research findings from both qualitative and quantitative data from our previous surveys. Some questions in the postal survey are related to our main concepts of co-production, co-governance and institutionalization. In the case study, we also try to assess these concepts by focusing on the relationship between a local government and a nonprofit organization and internal relationships among members, service providers and users.

THE DATA FROM A POSTAL SURVEY:
PARTNERSHIP UNDER THE CONTRACT REGIME

This section examines the results of the national postal survey conducted by our university-based research group (Institute of Nonprofit and Public Management Studies, INPMS) in February 2008 in relation to this research agenda (Institute of Nonprofit and Public Management Studies, 2009). Concerning the level at which partnerships are carried out, we asked about the frequency of partnerships in the levels of public policy. The results showed that (N = 95), 93.7 percent of respondents were involved in the implementation process of public services, whereas, those involved in the policy formulation process made up only 13.7 percent of the total. In terms of other levels, the number involved in the "planning of the program" (for example, proposing new or renewed public service programs to local governments) was 69.5 percent (the other data were as follows: "program evaluation" 32.6 percent; "policy evaluation" 10.5 percent; "others" 7.4 percent; "no response" 3.2 percent).

To examine the form of the partnerships, we asked about the form of partnership with local government. The data (N = 95) shows that contractual relationships were dominant. Of respondents, 54.7 percent were engaged in partnerships in the form of contracts and 21.1 percent in the form of the newly introduced designated manager system (other data were as follows: "joint organizing local events" 17.9 percent, grants 17 .9 percent, "sponsorship without funding support" 16.8 percent, "no response" 3.2 percent and "others" 2.1 percent).

Turning to the perception of an equal relationship with local governments (N = 95), most respondents (57.9 percent) perceived their relationships as equal despite the fact that contractual relationships were dominant. (Other data were as follows: "not so equal" 14.7 percent, "no response" 14.7 percent, "not equal" 9.5 percent and "others" 3.2 percent.)

However, according to results of our question about the perception of a contractor on the local government side (N = 95), respondents from nonprofit organizations recognized some challenges for promoting partnership.

Table 15.1   Priorities for Promoting Partnerships (%) (N = 95)

better understanding of nonprofit organizations by local government employees	48.0
regular consultation or meeting with local government	39.2
increasing government budget for partnership programs	35.3
partnerships support division within local government	25.5
capacity building among employees of nonprofit organizations	25.5
ordinance (by-law) or guideline to promote partnership	24.5
increased government budget for building social infrastructure of nonprofit organizations	20.6
understanding of government by employees of nonprofit organizations	19.6
partnership program schemes proposed by nonprofit organization	17.6
contract based on equal partnership	16.7
partnership agreement	14.7
strengthening intermediary organizations	13.7
assessment of partnerships by third party agencies	12.7
no response	8.8
others	4.9

Of respondents, 53.7 percent (totaling percentages of both "perception" [37.9 percent] and "clear perception" [15.8 percent]) felt that they were only considered a "contractor" by local government (other data were as follows: "little perception" 30.5 percent, "no perception" 12.6 percent and "no response" 3.2 percent).

In addition, Table 15.1 shows that 48 percent of respondents view improving the understanding of NPOs by local government employees as a matter of priority, and 39.2 percent of respondents think that there should be more opportunities for regular consultation.

Interpreting this data, we can confirm some of the same findings of previous surveys (Tsukamoto and Nishimura, 2006). Namely, the sphere of most partnerships remains at the policy implementation level rather than the policy formulation level. In addition, most partnerships are involved through contract frameworks. The data seem to show that most nonprofit organizations benefit from equal relationships with local government partners. Yet, many nonprofit organizations feel that mutual understanding and opportunities for interactive negotiation should be enhanced.

In short, the potential for co-production characterized as civic participation in service delivery can be found from this data. Local government provides various opportunities for civic participation through nonprofit organizations as Table 15.1 shows. However, involvement in the sphere of co-governance viewed as "negotiating government" (Kickert and Koppenjan, 1997, 40–41) is viewed as underdeveloped even though many nonprofit organizations are seeking more interactive negotiation. In reality, 53.7 percent of respondents feel that they are only seen as a "contractor" by local government according to our survey.

CASE STUDY MIRAI KODOMO LAND (MKL): THE CASE OF A CHILD CARE FACILITY

Mirai Kodomo Land (MKL) is a nonprofit organization with the legal status of an NPO hōjin. MKL was established by local citizens in the Nerima Ward of Tokyo in April 2005. This nonprofit organization not only delivers child care services, but it also manages a child care facility. MKL employs over 50 paid staff and has 114 children enrolled. It is one of largest nursery schools in Nerima Ward. Its annual income amounted to 210 million yen (€1,400,000/US $2,625,000) in the fiscal year of 2006.

MKL is a unique NPO. It was set up by working parents who had previously left their children at the local child care facility, which was a public nursery school called "Tsutsuji Hoikuen." In 2004, the municipal government suddenly announced that the public nursery school would be privatized without any negotiation with the parents whose children were at the facility. The aim was cost reduction due to a tight fiscal situation. Parents protested against this privatization policy, because they were afraid that quality of care would deteriorate as the result of contracting out to a for-profit company and the loss of skilled care workers. Nonetheless, municipal government rejected the proposal for maintaining it as a public facility by the parents and began the contracting out procedure.

The parents group changed their strategy. They sought to win the contract thereby changing themselves from "service consumers" into "service producers." They set up a nonprofit organization that would act as the contractor. In the early process of contracting out, the requirement for entry into the competitive bidding procedure was restricted to providers who had already managed child care facilities. This made their entry impossible, but they negotiated with the municipal government to change this "unfair" requirement. The board of directors of MKL are mostly parents, including a lawyer, a business consultant, a professor and a local government official in other city. This meant that they had the expertise to negotiate with government officers. In the end, they succeeded in changing the requirement and they won the contract in December 2005. MKL, run as a user-founded NPO, continues to manage the child care facility and the high quality of child care is appreciated both by the local government and community.

In terms of its governance structure, the board is composed of nine directors, including five parents. It has twenty-five members who can participate in decision making at the annual general meeting, fourteen members are parents, three members are staff, five members are local citizens and other two are professional advisers. The governance structure shows the fact that MKL is a stakeholder-owned organization, a classic example of co-production.

Considering the case of MKL, it seems to be a successful case of citizen involvement and co-production although it has many issues to address. In fact, MKL is an organization managed by stakeholders including both service providers and users, based on a participative decision-making structure. In addition, its members have a strong incentive to control the quality of the child care services that they provide. They are thus not only consumers. In terms of co-governance, the organization seems underdeveloped. The municipal government does not necessarily pay much attention to equal relations with a nonprofit organization founded by local citizens. Nevertheless, relations were improved through the negotiation and dialogue process.

Turning to institutionalization, the organization has suffered from institutional pressures stemming from the contracting regime. First, the flexibility of the operation of its facility was restricted by the contract framework and government-imposed rules. For instance, the organization must seek permission from the local government before purchasing equipment valued over 20,000 yen (roughly €160/US$250). Second, the term of the contract is too short despite that fact that child care service providers need long-term relations with parents as service consumers in order to build trust and maintain the quality of their services. The term was previously one year, but it was later changed into a three-year-term contract. MKL viewed even three years as too short. To solve such issues, the political and institutional frameworks themselves need to change. Institutional pressure caused by a government-led contractual relationship seems to make the organization more bureaucratic. Because managers and workers tend to learn and take on bureaucratic behavior under the process of adapting rules set by a government. Such institutional isomorphism may constrain the potential for co-production.

On the other hand, they have also faced organizational change. The vital issue was that parents, in particular new users of the facility, tended to regard MKL as just an ordinary "service provider," or just another "regular producer" with themselves as its consumers. The professionalization that is essential to quality assurance seems to reinforce this tendency. If such a divide within stakeholders is allowed to grow, it can undermine the co-production spirit. In relation to this, Smith and Lipsky (1993) refer to the fact that the professionalization and specialization brought about by the contracting out process has an impact on nonprofit organizations. Government facilitates professionalization by making funds available, and professionalization plays key role in the competition for contracts; as a result, nonprofit organizations are required to hire professionals (104). They also consider workers in NPOs receiving government contracts to be agents of the government and new "street-level bureaucrats" (115–116). In this case, it may be difficult for them to maintain their identity as nonprofit organizations controlled by co-producers.

CONCLUSION

It is difficult to generalize the findings of our postal survey and case study because our findings are based on restricted samples. However, this study confirms the conclusions that previous studies have arrived at from a more theoretical perspective, focusing on co-production, co-governance and institutionalization.

Our postal survey and case study indicate that nonprofit organizations have the potential to incorporate citizen participation as co-production in the delivery of public services, even where there is a contractual relationship. In reality, most respondents perceived their relationships as equal, and the MKL was even able to influence the contracting out framework led by local government. As the postal survey shows, there are different forms of partnerships, and many local governments promote partnerships with local nonprofit organizations, thereby providing opportunities for citizen participation in the delivery of public services in different ways. This means that nonprofit organizations play a vital role in promoting citizen involvement in the field of local public services.

However, most partnerships are restricted to the sphere of policy implementation rather than policy formulation, as the results of the postal survey show. This is related to the reluctance of local governments to consult with nonprofit organizations on essential issues related to basic institutional and policy frameworks. It is certainly true that many local governments provide opportunities for citizens and NPO leaders to participate in many meetings, but local government always retains the upper hand. It seems difficult for nonprofit organizations to influence and change the basic policies and rules laid down by local government. In short, co-governance, characterized as interactive negotiation, has been slow to develop in nonprofit-government partnerships in Japan.

Such immature co-governance relates to the limitation of co-production, because the function of co-production seems to be constrained by the state of the "organizational field." If government power is excessively dominant in an organizational field, nonprofit organizations suffer from institutional isomorphism. The tendency toward coercive isomorphism caused by the contracting framework and normative isomorphism from professionalization can influence the co-production relationship. Specifically, more professionalized "consumer-producers" may assume bureaucratic methods, becoming just like "regular producers." As a result, the divide between citizen stakeholders can widen, thereby undermining co-production.

First, it is important to build and maintain "organizational identity as citizens"—that is, citizenship between stakeholders when nonprofit organizations aspire to co-production. As Smith and Lipsky mentioned, contracting regimes raise important questions about the nature of citizenship (1993). If citizenship as an organizational culture diminishes within nonprofit organizations, they may become nothing more than preferred contractors or service providers for governments.

Second, co-production requires not only organizational collaboration but also individual citizen participation in the planning and delivery of public services. Organizational participation without actual citizen participation based on democratic governance structures seems to promote isomorphism and undermine co-production.

Third, co-production requires the development of co-governance known as "negotiation government" (Kickert and Koppenjan, 1997, 40–41). As mentioned previously, co-production depends on interactive negotiation between nonprofit and government sides. To realize co-production in the delivery of public services, local governments should change their culture from a bureaucratic culture toward one that is more conducive to negotiation.

NOTES

1. In most recent years, public interest corporations have faced radical changes as a result of public administration reforms with the aim of clearly distinguishing between two different corporations , that is, those working for public benefit or not. Up to the end of 2008, existing public interest corporations were legally required to choose two different legal forms, public interest association/foundation with tax advantage or general association/ foundation with no or less tax advantage.

2. Coercive isomorphism stems from political influence and the problem of legitimacy. It results from both formal and informal pressures exerted on organizations by other organizations on which they are dependent and by cultural expectations in the society within which organizations function (DiMaggio and Powell, 1991, 67). Mimetic isomorphism results from standard responses to uncertainty (ibid.). Uncertainty is also powerful force that encourages imitation (DiMaggio and Powell, 1991, 69). Normative isomorphism is associated with professionalization (67).

REFERENCES

Brandsen, T., and V. Pestoff. 2006. Co-production, the third sector and the delivery of public services: An introduction. *Public Management Review* 8 (4): 493–501.

Cooper, T. L., Kathi, P. C. 2005. Neighborhood councils and city agencies: A model of collaborative co-production. *National Civic Review* 94 (1): 43–53.

DiMaggio, P. J., and W. W. Powell. 1991. The iron cage revisited: Institutional isomorphism and collective rationality in organizational fields. In W. W. Powell, P. J. DiMaggio, eds., *The New Institutionalism in Organizational Analysis.* Chicago: University of Chicago Press.

Institute of Nonprofit and Public Management Studies. 2009. *NPO Gyousei no kyoudo no jittai nikansutu chousa kenkyu 2007/2008* [The Research on NPO-Government Collaboration 2007/2008]. Tokyo: Institute of Nonprofit and Public Management Studies, Meiji University.

Izumi,K. 2008. Shitei Kanrisha Seido no Genjou. *Chihou Jichi Shokuin Kenshū* 89. [The State of Designated Managers. *Human Resource Development for Local Government* 89.]

Keizai Sangyo Kenkyuj, 2007. *NPO hōjin ankeito chousa kekka (Chihojichitai Chousa) 2007* [*The Research Report on the National Survey of the Specified Nonprofit Corporations(Survey on Local Authorities)*]. Tokyo: Research Institute of Economy, Trade and Industry [RIETI]. www.rieti.go.jp/jp/projects/npo/2006/1.pdf. Accessed April 16, 2011.

Kickert, W. J. M., and J. F. M. Koppenjan. 1997. Public management and network management: An overview. In W. J. M. Kickert, E.-H. Klijn, J. F. M. Koppenjan, eds., *Managing Complex Networks: Strategies for the Public Sector.* London: Sage.

Kooiman, J. 1993. *Modern Governance: New Government-Society Interactions.* London: Sage.

Kooiman, J. 2003. *Governing as Governance.* London: Sage.

Levine, C. H. 1984. Citizenship and service delivery: the promise of co-production. *Public Administration Review* 44 (March): 178–187.

Manfredi, F., and M. Maffei. 2008. Co-governance and co-production: from the social enterprise towards the public–private co-enterprise. In S. P. Osborne, ed., *The Third Sector in Europe: Prospects and Challenges.* London: Routledge.

McGinnis, M. D., ed. 1999. *Polycentricity and Local Public Economics: Readings from the Workshop in Political Theory and Policy Analysis.* Ann Arbor: University of Michigan Press.

Open Research Center Project, 2005. *Zenkoku Jichitai Ankeito Chousa Houkokusho.* [A National Survey on Collaborations between Local Government and Nonprofits in Japan.] Tokyo: Institute of Business Management, Meiji University.

Osborne, S. P. ed. 2000. *Public-Private Partnership.* London: Routledge.

Ostrom, E. 1996. Crossing the great divide: Co-production, synergy, and development. *World Development* 24 (6): 1073–1087.

Parks, R. B., P. C. Baker, L. Kiser, R. Oakerson, E. Ostrom, V. Ostrom, S. L. Percy, M. B. Vandivort, G. P. Whitaker, and R. Wilson, 1999. Consumers as coproducers of public services: some economics and institutional considerations. In M. D. McGinnis, ed., *Polycentricity and Local Public Economics: Readings from the Workshop in Political Theory and Policy Analysis*. Ann Arbor: University of Michigan Press.

Pekkanen, R. 2003. The politics of regulating the nonprofit sector. In S. P. Osborne, ed., *The Voluntary and Nonprofit Sector in Japan*. London: Routledge.

Pestoff, V. 2006. Citizens and co-Production of welfare services: childcare in eight European countries. *Public Management Review* 8 (4): 503–519.

Pestoff, V. 2008. Co-production, the third sector and functional representation in Sweden. In S. P. Osborne, ed., *The Third Sector in Europe: Prospects and Challenges*. London: Routledge.

Pestoff, V., and T. Brandsen, eds. 2008. *Co-production: The Third Sector and the Delivery of Public Services*. London: Routledge.

Rhodes, R. A. W. 1997. *Understanding Governance: Policy Networks, Governance, Reflexivity and Accountability*. Buckingham: Open University Press.

Scott, W.R., and G. F. Davis. 2007. *Organization and Organizing: Rational, Natural, and Open System Perspectives*. New Brunswick, NJ: Pearson Prentice Hall.

Smith, S. R., and M. Lipsky. 1993. *Nonprofits for Hire: The Welfare State in the Age of Contracting*. Cambridge, MA: Harvard University Press.

Tsukamoto, I. 2009. Institutionalization, Commercialization and Hybridization of Nonprofit Organizations under Public Service Reforms in Japan. *The Bulletin of Institute of Social Sciences, Meiji University* 31 (2): 1–22.

Tsukamoto, I., and M. Nishimura. 2006. The emergence of local nonprofit-government partnerships and the role of intermediary organizations in Japan: contractual relationship and the limits to co-governance. *Public Management Review* 8 (4): 567–581.

Tsukamoto, I., and M. Nishimura. 2007. *The State and the Strategic Partnerships of Local Intermediary Organizations in Japan: Between Contractual Relationships and the Co-governance*. Paper presented at the conference of the European Group of Public Administration (EGPA), Madrid, Spain, September 19–22, 2007.

Part IV
Effects of Co-Production

Service Quality,
Accountability and Democracy

16 Co-Production and Service Quality

A New Perspective for the Swedish Welfare State

Johan Vamstad

The Swedish welfare state is known for its vast public sector, high taxes and a state that actively intervenes to create economic equality. Sweden's path to become a universal welfare state with a high standard of living during the twentieth century was cleared by a continuously expanding public sector that developed, funded and provided social services for every Swedish citizen regardless of social class. The welfare state was built almost entirely by the public sector, and nonpublic service providers remain rare exceptions in most service areas today. How is the issue of service quality addressed in a system where all aspects of the services are cared for by the same public sector? There has traditionally been little competition between service providers, and freedom of choice has only recently become a political goal in the Swedish welfare state. The service quality has therefore been an issue for the public service providers themselves to develop, monitor and, if necessary, improve. Their method for doing so has been their knowledge and expertise as professional service providers. The service quality is guaranteed by the training and the accumulated experience of the professionals in areas such as health care, elderly care, schools, child care and so on. In fact, service quality has almost become synonymous with the level of professionalism in any given service area in Sweden.

What are the implications of this focus on professionalism for the concept of co-production? Co-production is here understood a system for service provision in which the users of the services also participate in the provision of them. The users are by definition not professional service providers, and their involvement is a challenge to service quality in its Swedish interpretation. There is, in spite of this, a service area in Sweden where a substantial level of co-production is found. This service area is child care, and the reasons for co-production in Swedish child care will be explored further in this chapter. Child care is therefore not only a good example but the only example in which to study the effects of co-production on service quality in Sweden. How has the unlikely occurrence of co-production in the Swedish welfare state affected service quality? This question will be explored with the help of data collected for a study of Swedish child care in

2007. The data have previously not been used to study service quality, and there are no other studies at this point that show the link between co-production and service quality in Sweden specifically. It is therefore important to look at theory and previous studies from other settings to get a better understanding of how this link might look. This is the purpose of the following section.

CO-PRODUCTION AND SERVICE QUALITY

Many of the theories and much of the previous research concern co-production in a broader perspective that includes its importance for society as a whole. Bovaird sees co-production as part of a more general development toward a form of public governance where the role of the government is radically reduced. The argument is that co-production is breaking the traditional top-down alignment of policy making and service delivery by introducing users in the production of the services (Bovaird, 2005). Co-production has also been seen as a source for revitalization of democracy in modern welfare states (Pestoff, 2008, 2009; Vamstad, 2007). The focus here will be exclusively on the link between co-production and service quality.

One of the most common arguments for why co-production benefits service quality has to do with communication. By involving the users in the production of services, the service provider achieves a direct channel of communication with the users. Hirschman famously differentiated between exit and voice functions in the relation between the providers and the users of goods or services. The exit function, which consists of the users leaving providers that do not meet their demands, is very rarely used in welfare services. The voice function, in which the user communicates dissatisfaction with the provider, is much more important. It is difficult to move a child from a familiar preschool to a new one, and it can also be quite difficult to actually find another preschool with available room for an additional child. Hirschman argues that situations like these necessitate the use of voice (2006). Voice is dependent on several things to be efficient. The users must have the opportunity to express their opinion about the service and they must have an adequate level of information about the service. The feedback must, in other words, go both ways for the quality of the service to be improved through voice. Co-production between users and service providers is a way to share information and make voice possible, which, as already mentioned, is important because exit is not a realistic option. Co-production therefore has a quite instrumental value for service quality.

The positive effect of co-production was shown in a study of British local authorities by Bovaird and Downe in 2006. Representatives for local authorities were asked what benefits of co-production they had experienced. Nearly 90 percent of the respondents said the co-production lead to services that are more responsive to the needs of the users (Bovaird and Downe, 2009, 6). Furthermore, the survey showed support for co-production leading to more informed decisions (86 percent), more accessible services (81 percent), higher quality services (79 percent), more "joined-up" services (76 percent) and better value of money for tax payers (59 percent) (ibid., 6). An especially interesting aspect of these positive results for co-production is that it makes no difference whether or not the co-production is being performed in a public or private organization. This is of outmost importance in Sweden, where the simple question of public or private can decide the political future of a political reform, because private services are considered a challenge to the Swedish welfare regime both by their protagonists and antagonists. It is also noteworthy that co-production is a method to reach many goals for public management that is not coming from the influential, market-oriented management literature originally intended for the private sector (Hartley, 2005). The success of co-production is dependent on both the type of service and the type of co-production. Bovaird shows how professionals and users can be involved in different degrees in both delivery and management, which creates a wide range of different combinations that are suitable for different circumstances (Bovaird, 2007).

The existing research in the area has also identified several problems with co-production in relation to service quality. One such problem is the issue of accountability (Bovaird and Downe, 2009). Who can the users hold accountable for a low service quality if they themselves are part of the production? This kind of co-option issues are a serious concern because they indicate that co-production performed the wrong way could be a way to facilitate low service quality rather than develop high service quality. Another often-cited problem with co-production is that certain people are more likely to gain influence from it than others (ibid.). The option to participate in the production of the services might be explored by people who already have a strong position in society, which could make already existing inequalities worse.

The success of co-production is likely to vary between different types of services. Co-production seems to be the most efficient in settings where the users are naturally involved, resourceful and generally "strong." There is, however, also research that suggests that co-production might be of special importance for traditionally "weak" groups, even if it does work less smoothly among these. Hyde and Davies have studied co-production in two different types of mental health care, and they show that whatever little communication that is established between patients and staff is very valuable because these two parties are especially distant from each other (2004). A rare Swedish study of co-production by individuals undergoing treatment for drug addiction, another "weak" group, reports good results in spite of great challenges (Meeuwisse, 2008). Similar results have been shown for co-production by minority groups that can otherwise be difficult to involve in community issues (McKenzie et al., 2008).

Another recognized problem with co-production is one that is of central importance in the case of Swedish child care. This is the opposition to co-production by professional staff who maintain that education, training and experience are more important than the perspective of the user (Bovaird, 2007). Pollitt and colleagues bring this up as an example of several problems with co-production by referring to previous findings that organizations can adapt to co-production with the exception of the top professionals that find it much harder to allow amateur users in the service production (Pollitt, Bouckaert, and Löffler, 2006). This finding about the top professionals indicates that the level of professionalism is important. The more professional a service provider is, the harder it is for them to allow co-production. This is an important aspect of co-production and professionals for understanding the Swedish case because it is, as we shall see, an unusually professionalized welfare state with unusually great resistance to co-production.

PROFESSIONALISM AND SERVICE QUALITY IN SWEDEN

The development of the Swedish welfare state and the social democratic welfare regime, of which it is the primary example, was and still is driven by the state. Whatever welfare services that existed in Sweden in the early twentieth century were to a large degree provided by charitable organizations that also provided moral guidance as to how the users of elder care, child care and so on should lead their lives. The expansion of the public services, that was initiated just before World War II and accelerated after it, was more than anything an attempt to create a universal availability of all necessary welfare services, which would preempt the need for private, charitable services. This expansion of the public sector was, in other words, not just a state initiative to meet the public demand of welfare services; it was also a way of making the whole of society more democratic, professional or in one word, modern. In Sweden, modernization, professionalization and the growth of the public sector are all aspects of the same pursuit of new, better society in an atmosphere of optimism that is typical for what Beck and Giddens call the modern era of the welfare states (Beck, 1992; Giddens, 1991).

The concept of service quality at this time entailed services provided to all by trained professionals employed in the public sector, without any moral strings attached. A text of this length is too short to fully explore the role of professionalism in the Swedish welfare state. Even a brief look at the philosophical influences on the early welfare state can, however, shed some light on why professionalism and service quality is considered to be so entwined in Sweden. Some of the most influential contributions to the rationale of the Swedish welfare during the first half of the twentieth century were the value nihilistic philosophy of the so-called Uppsala School

(Sigurdson, 2000). This school of thought, which is represented by scholars such as Hägerström, Hedenius and Lundstedt, argued that moral values and subjective opinions could be replaced by rational arguments and an objective truth (Cassirer, 2005; Hedenius, 2009).

Other scholars, such as Gunnar Myrdal and Alva Myrdal, also offered a pragmatic, rational and material view of how the welfare state and the society as a whole should work. The Myrdals also, in a very practical way, developed the tools to implement these ideas and are therefore sometimes said to have invented the Swedish type of social engineering (Sigurdson, 2000; Appelqvist and Andersson, 2005). What these public policy makers and many like them had in common was that they rejected subjective ideas of what the state should do and instead forwarded the claim that objectively correct public policies were possible through a process of secular, rational and deliberative policy making. For the most part, they also rejected the idea that the ambition of the state should simply be defined by the sum of its citizen's wishes and choices. The actions of the state should be guided by the higher understanding that comes from deliberative reasoning and not the sum of individual wishes. This could, in part, explain the skepticism toward market solutions and the confidence in state powers for societal development.

The deliberative aspect of Swedish policy making deserves special attention in this context. Even if an objective "right" was considered obtainable through reason, this did not imply that an "enlightened" political elite should rule. The rational, objective "good" would instead emerge from a deliberative process in which experts and organized interests reasoned in a corporatist process to reach a not only an objective but common "good". In short, what leading academics as well as politicians aimed to achieve during the early stages of the welfare state was a well-functioning and modern society where conservative moral values and metaphysical ideas of how society functions were replaced with rational and democratic problem solving (Hägerström, 2010).

A practical implication of this Swedish mix of welfare ideology was that trained professionals were favored over volunteering amateurs because their superior knowledge would bring the best possible service quality. In accordance with this philosophy, there is a "right" way of providing welfare services that can be obtained from research and education. Scientific findings about the best ways to provide social services were incorporated in public policies as well as the educations of future professional service providers and the level of education and share of educated staff became a very influential indicator of service quality in welfare services. The importance of professionalism based on academic education of the care givers varies somewhat between different welfare services in Sweden. Ahnlund shows, for instance, that such professionalism is valued very highly in general, but even more in elder care than in care for people with handicaps (2008). Practical experience and an ability to develop the service in dialogue with the service user is considered more important in care for the handicapped, possibly because this group can better voice their opinions than the elderly can or want to. Professionalism in the provision of welfare services is, of course, not uniquely Swedish. The level of professionalism is equally high in countries such as Germany or the Netherlands, where nonprofit facilities provide a large portion of the welfare services. What makes Sweden stand out in a comparison with other countries is the dominant role of the public sector, from the publically funded research to the political policy process to the actual provision of services by public service facilities.

Another aspect of the state as provider of service quality through professionalism is the issue of rights. There are very few instances in which the Swedish state could be held accountable in a court of law for violating the rights of the service user when providing social services. The relation between the citizen and the state is based on political and social rights rather than civil rights, using Marshall's famous typology (Marshall, 1950). Significant flaws in service quality in the welfare services are usually not addressed by individual users claiming their rights. There is one piece of legislation in particular that aims to protect the rights of handicapped people receiving care, but this is the only existing law that binds the public service providers in a legal relation to the users. The service quality is instead monitored by the municipalities themselves and on the national level by a few state agencies awarded the role of "control authority" over different areas. Many social services are, for instance, ultimately under the responsibility of the National Board of Health and Welfare. The rationale behind this is that a system based on a rational and even scientific approach to social issues is best suited to work out responses to flaws in service quality from within the existing system of professional service providers. Service quality is defined as professionalism, and the only ones who can evaluate the work of professionals are other professionals. There is, therefore, a direct link between professionalism and a kind of paternalism in Sweden.

Politicians are, generally speaking, not held responsible for the performance of the welfare services. Sweden has, together with Finland, the strongest separation between the political sphere and the public administration in the world (Petersson, 2000). A minister in the government cannot be held responsible for serious problems with service quality in Sweden, and the minister is also forbidden to intervene directly in the running of the public administration. There is a greater level of political accountability at the local level, but the performance of service providers seldom becomes a local political issue. The public administration can therefore work according to the laws and regulations provided by the elected representatives in a relative isolation from both individual citizens and politicians, both in social services at the local level and in service areas seen as a whole at the national level. This kind of autonomy from external influences is known among researchers studying organizational theory to be the source of a strong sense of identity as a professional that can lead to a canonization of the role as a professional (Johansson, 2007). This seems to be the case in Sweden. The autonomy and strength of the public administration has grown a culture of professionalism where role of the user is a passive one.

CO-PRODUCTION IN SWEDISH CHILD CARE

It is hard to see how co-production could fit into a welfare state model such as the Swedish model, even if its underlying philosophy as described here should be seen as guiding principles and not rules taken literally. Co-production by the users of services could be considered a step away from the professional view of what are the best practices to reach a high service quality. Involvement by untrained individuals as well as nonprofit organizations in social services is to a large degree limited to a complementary role, as for instance in elder care, where volunteers might walk and talk with the elderly but not assist the actual care giving (Dahlberg, 2004, 2005, 2006). Untrained individuals and nonprofit organizations are, in fact, considered in a somewhat similar manner, as sources of added value to the public services that cannot and should not take responsibility for the services themselves.

There are few examples of co-production in Sweden. There are some elements of co-production in elementary school education as well as care for the handicapped and people undergoing treatments for of drug addiction. Co-production in the public sector is rare, and it is in all cases very limited by the authority of the professional service providers. Child care therefore stands out in the Swedish welfare state as an area where co-production is more significant, not least of economic importance. Between 10 and 15 percent of all child care in Sweden is being provided by parent cooperatives that rely heavily on parent participation. Why is child care such an exception? There are several possible answers to this question.

The first parent cooperatives were initiated in the 1970s by parents who wanted to provide a pedagogy alternative to the services offered by the municipalities, which are the public sector institutions responsible for child care in Sweden (Pestoff, 1998). These early cooperatives were little more than odd curiosities in the otherwise almost homogenous child care area. Still, certain emerging problems in the child care area at this time could be interpreted as a lack of co-production. The results of a four-year public investigation of Swedish child care were published in 1972. The report described how the professionalization and centralization of the child care area had created a much greater distance between the municipal staff providing the child care and the politicians who decided over it (SOU 1972:26, 146–147). There was, in other words, a downside to the "rational" approach to child care with its large, efficient units staffed by trained professionals.

The report suggested reforms within the public sector to address these issues, it proposed, for instance, that the staff from child care facilities should attend the relevant meetings in the local political assembly (SOU 1972:26, 147). None of the more than 1,100 pages in the report even hinted at the possibility of greater user involvement or, for that matter, nonpublic alternatives to the public sector, which illustrates how far-fetched these ideas were in the Swedish public debate in the 1970s. There are, of course, good reasons for this. One of the political incentives for the investments in public child care in the postwar era was to increase participation in the labor market, especially that of women. The principle was, in other words, that both mothers and fathers should be able to work full time while professionals took care of their children, a principle that at that time might have made co-production seem counterproductive.

The parent cooperatives grew as a proportion of the Swedish child care during the second half of the 1980s, following a political reform in 1985 that allowed them to receive public funding. This was a highly controversial reform that was realized only after an intense and partly harsh debate within the ruling Social Democratic Party. Only the year before the reform, Swedish Minister of Finance Kjell-Olof Feldt was severely criticized by leading social democrats for even suggesting in an interview that cooperative preschools should receive public funding. The social democrats feared that this would expose the children to the assumed harsh realities of the private sector (Ahlqvist and Engqvist, 1984; Feldt, 1991). Prime Minister Olof Palme was among the politicians who considered all nonpublic preschools as market solutions directly or indirectly aimed at "making profits from children" and he warned famously in 1984 of creating "Kentucky Fried Children," a far from flattering reference to an American chain of fast food restaurants (Pettersson, 2001).

The reason that parent cooperatives were allowed public funding, in spite of these sentiments, was that the public sector could not keep up with demand for child care, particularly in new suburban areas (Pestoff, 1998). The Swedish public sector experienced a continuous growth from the end of World War II to the 1970s that was sustained by an equally substantial growth in the Swedish economy. With the economic downturn in the 1970s, the expansion of the public sector slowed down, and child care was one area in which the public sector had not yet managed to meet the full demand for services at that time (Von Bergmann-Winberg, 1987). An increase in public spending was not considered feasible in the mid-1980s, which opened for allowing parents to organize their child care themselves, with funding from the state. Co-production was thereby introduced in the Swedish welfare state primarily for financial reasons, even if the pedagogical innovations of the parent cooperatives were mentioned in the government's bill to the parliament (Regeringens Proposition 1984–85: 209). This is consistent with the Swedish welfare logic because service quality comes from professionalism and, indirectly, public sector spending. Co-production is therefore motivated as a compromise with quality when the full funding for public services is lacking.

THE EMPIRICAL STUDY OF SWEDISH CHILD CARE

The seemingly unlikely occurrence of co-production in the Swedish welfare state makes Swedish child care an interesting case. Has the co-production had any effect on the service quality in the parent cooperatives? This question has to this day been largely overlooked when discussing Swedish child care. If anything, the assumption still seems to be that co-production is harmful for the service quality because it might interfere with the work of the trained professionals. An empirical study of Swedish child care did, however, address the issue of co-production and its effect on service quality a few years ago, and its results indicated that co-production might be of greater and more positive importance than first thought (Vamstad, 2007).

The results of the research were published as early as December 2007, and then again in 2009, but these publications did not focus on the connection between co-production and service quality (Vamstad, 2007; Pestoff, 2009). The data, which have both qualitative and quantitative parts, have therefore not previously been used for this purpose. A total of 271 families and 116 members of preschool staff participated in the 2 separate survey studies, which gave a participation rate of 49.5 and 81.1 percent respectively. The quantitative material was complemented with 36 in-depth interviews, primarily with preschool managers. The data were collected in 6 different city wards in Stockholm and the town of Östersund, about 600 kilometers to the north of Stockholm. The six city wards represent different social settings, from the affluent inner city wards to the much more socially challenged suburbs southwest and northwest of the city. These city wards do not include any rural settings or any small towns. However, Östersund, a town of 58,000 inhabitants in the geographical center of Sweden, clearly does.

There are certain limitations and problems that come with studying cooperative child care as an example of co-production in Sweden. The parent cooperatives are interesting examples because they are a rare exception in the Swedish context but it should be mentioned that the users of cooperative services might also be an exceptional category of citizens. The users of parent cooperative child care are much more educated, better off financially and more often living in families with two parents than the average child care user (Vamstad, 2007). This could be seen as a reason why the experience of co-production in child care could not easily be transferred to other service areas with a more average set of users. It could also, to the contrary, be argued that the cooperative users today are an "avant-garde" type and that the cooperative services could attract more users if the information and the necessary resources were made available to them. This is a task that could involve the public sector if it considers co-production worthwhile to support. Much of the research on the subject brings up that already powerful users gain even more influence from co-production and more generally that co-production might not be best suited for marginalized groups in society, even though that issue is far from resolved (Bovaird and Downe, 2009, 30–31). It could also be that co-production is even more important for these marginalized groups because other, more complex, forms of participation and influence are even more unobtainable, as is suggested by the already mentioned Swedish study of patients undergoing treatment for drug addiction (Meeuwisse, 2008). Which is the case is difficult to say because there is still very little research on this issue in the Swedish context.

Another important issue to keep in mind when studying co-production in child care is the matter of size. The parent cooperative preschools are, generally speaking, much smaller than most municipal and for-profit facilities. This, and to a lesser degree the organizational form, could be an important determinant of service quality. This is a possibility that was suggested and further explored in the longer study from which the material is gathered (Vamstad, 2007). The importance of this possible, intermediary variable is difficult to estimate with any accuracy but preschools of all sizes in all organizational forms were included in the study and the correlation between preschools with co-production and preschools with a good service quality seem to hold, regardless of size, even if the strength of that correlation appears to vary. It is, however, not possible to give a statistical estimate of this strength because of the rather limited sample of preschools and the qualitative nature of some of the data.

The two main indicators of service quality were user experience and experiences of the staff working at the preschools. Simply measuring user satisfaction as an indicator of service quality is, of course, problematic because the users performing co-production to some extent evaluates themselves. The users of cooperative services are not just passive users but managers, providers and perhaps owners of their preschool, which clearly affect their perspective on service quality. The presentation of the results will instead include data on the extent of the co-production and how it is organized to analyze its implications for service quality. The user experience is contrasted with that of the staff, which will give a richer, two-sided description of how co-production affects service quality. All presented results in this chapter originate from this study unless stated otherwise.

PARENTS' CO-PRODUCTION IN SWEDISH CHILD CARE

The highly held principle of professionalism in the Swedish welfare state is present but less dominating in the area of child care compared to other welfare service areas, which is, of course, why co-production is more greatly accepted in child care. This is natural from a user perspective, as a parent, you might believe that you know how to look after your child even if you do not have the same three-year college education as the preschool teachers. The perspective of the preschool staff is, according to the in-depth interviews in this study, different. Throughout the interviews with the managers of municipal preschools the issue of their role as trained professionals reoccurs. Their main argument is that Swedish preschools are not just a place to keep children while their parents work. Swedish preschools are, at least to some degree, learning institutions with a pedagogical mission that requires a professional staff.

A second argument was that only a professional preschool teacher could identify the special needs of some children and adjust the activities accordingly. Some of the preschool managers especially warn against allowing parents a position of authority because this could create a conflict of roles. It is, put simply, difficult to act both in accordance with professional expertise and the wishes of amateurs. An example of a difficult situation brought up by one of the municipal preschool managers was that the staff might not as easily address family problems if the parents of the family in question are also their bosses. This description of the different roles of professionals and users are not unique for Swedish child care. Bovaird and Downe describe the need for both parties to take risks in order to allow co-production. The service user must trust the expertise of the professional staff, but the staff must also take the risk of trusting the behavior of the users (2009, 29). The locked positions described by the municipal preschool managers in this study illustrates well how great that risk is perceived by professionals in a welfare state with little tradition of co-production in either their service area or in any other service areas.

All parent cooperatives have trained staff that have undergone the same schooling as the staff in municipal preschools. The actual difference in the level of formal professionalism is therefore only slightly to the municipal preschool's advantage (Vamstad, 2007). The job description for the staff in cooperative and municipal preschools differ relatively little, but the former seem to have a slightly different approach to their relation with the parents. Professional staff at parent cooperatives describe how they, for better and worse, must invest a lot of time and energy into the communication with parents. To have to explain aspects of their daily work to the parents in laymen's terms is described by some as an unnecessary but unavoidable addition to the workload. Others describe the relation with the parents as one of "give and take," where both parties than gain knowledge in a dialogue and thus make better decisions for the children. The relation between the co-producing parents and the professional staff naturally varies from one preschool to another. It seems, however, that there also exist a general difference between municipal and parent cooperative preschools, which is significant because of the close association between service quality and professionalism in the Swedish context. Using Bovaird's distinction between management and production, one could say that the parent cooperatives all have a high level of parent participation in the management, while the extent of the participation in the actual service production varies from one preschool to the other (2007).

The most common practical arrangement at parent cooperative preschools is that the executive manager is a trained professional, while the board consists of a selection of parents that changes as their children leave the preschool or by some other type of periodic rotation. The managers are therefore a valuable source of continuity and know-how at the cooperative preschools. What is then the role of the parents in the co-production at the preschools? The level of involvement by the parents varies from strict management (although very unusual) to a co-production with a minimal need for hired staff. The typical parent cooperative is rather small, with one group (15–20) or two groups (30–40) of children and one to four full-time employees and possibly some part-time employees working in the kitchen or doing cleaning, laundry and so on. The parents can participate in the regular activities at the preschool, in more large-scale cleaning or repair efforts or both. As many as 94.6 percent of the users of parent cooperative child care claimed that they regularly did at least some cleaning and repairs in the survey study. This is the most common activity in the parents' co-production, and it is, in fact, possible that some of the remaining 5.4 percent of the respondents were board members at their preschools. Board members are often relieved of other duties because of the workload of being in the board.

Even more interesting is perhaps that 43.7 percent of the parents from the municipal preschools responded that they also participated in cleaning or repairs with some regularity. This would indicate that there is, in fact, some co-production taking place in the public sector. This interesting finding from the survey was addressed in the in-depth interviews with the preschool managers. As it turned out, almost all municipal preschools in the study had some sort of communal cleaning and repair day with involvement of the parents, once or twice a year. These are mainly social events where staff, children and parents get to meet and do something together, and several of the preschool managers were very clear that these activities were not "needed" in a strict operational sense. The survey study also reveals that only 4.7 percent of the parents consider these work efforts a source of influence in municipal services. Still, activities such as these show that the municipal preschools are not "closed" institutions and that interaction with the parents is considered important there.

The regularity of social events is, however, much lower at the municipal preschools compared with the parent cooperatives. Only 16.4 percent of the parents from municipal preschools responded that their preschools offered social activities "often or rather often," while 42.3 percent answered "never or seldom." In contrast, 63.2 percent of the parents from the parent cooperatives answered "often or rather often," while only 6.6 percent said "never or seldom." These social activities are not co-production per se, but they are a good estimate of the parent involvement in a more general sense. More specifically, social activities also offer an opportunity for communication between staff, parents and children.

Co-production, unlike strictly professional services, requires an even or relatively even distribution of information among the parties involved.

The interaction of staff, parents and children therefore has a great indirect value. The level of insight into the preschool was also measured by the survey study. As expected, the level of insight as experienced by the users was considerably higher in the parent cooperatives compared to the municipal preschools. Of the cooperative parents, 73.8 percent replied that they had "much" or "very much" insight, while only 25.3 percent of the municipal parents replied the same. Conversely, 8 percent of the municipal parents claimed to have "little," "rather little" or "very little" insight, while none of the cooperative parents gave any of these three replies.

The parents themselves with the help of professional hired staff manage the parent cooperatives. Most cooperatives have boards consisting of parents, as already mentioned. The study shows, however, that the work at the preschool itself can be seen as a source of influence. No less than 78.4 percent of the cooperative parents check off "work at preschool" as a source of influence in the survey study. This makes the work effort the second-most widespread source of influence after "meetings with power to decide" (79.7 percent). The most important source of influence for the parents in the municipal preschools are "informal talks" with the staff, which 75.6 percent of the users stated in the survey. Not surprisingly, the parents at the parent cooperatives estimate their influence as much higher than the parents at the municipal preschools.

USER PERSPECTIVES ON SERVICE QUALITY

User satisfaction with child care is very high for all forms of child care in Sweden. In fact, the preschools are among the most appreciated public institutions in Sweden according to the Swedish branch of the international Extended Performance System Index (EPSI). The Swedish preschools made 75.5 out of a hundred on the index, which can be compared to 65.6 for the average of 15 different municipal services (Extended Performance System Index, 2011). The preschools consistently score about 10 percentage points higher than the average over the ten documented years in the data and between five to ten percentage points higher than services as health care, universities and elementary schools (Extended Performance System Index, 2011).

This study could not find any significant differences in user satisfaction between the public and the parent cooperative forms of child care. At least not from the general question of whether or not the parents were satisfied. The slightly more specific question of whether or not the parents were satisfied with the staff at their preschool showed some interesting results. As many as 94.6 percent of the users of parent cooperatives were either "pleased" or "very pleased" with their staff, while 83.8 percent of the users of municipal child care replied the same. The two groups were of equal size and they had comparable response rates. The study showed, as has already been presented, that the co-production at parent cooperative preschools led to a more developed two-way communication between staff and parents. This management through dialogue could be one reason why parents at parent cooperatives value the preschool staff even higher than the parents at municipal preschools.

The questions that more clearly asked the respondents to consider alternatives to their current preschools also showed some interesting results. The survey asked if they had previous experience from another preschool and, if so, if they were more or less satisfied with their present preschool. The replies included both previous experiences with another child and instances where the same child was moved from one facility to another. The latter category is, however, very rare and very little exists of what Hirschman calls an "exit" option in Swedish child care (2006). One hundred and five families had previous experiences, and 77 of them were more satisfied now. This is not surprising, a reason for switching preschool can simply be that you are not satisfied with the one that you have. The patterns of satisfaction are, however, vastly different between the different forms of child care. The users of municipal child care are evenly split in the middle between those who are more and less satisfied with their present preschool, 48.5 percent are more satisfied and the remainder are less satisfied. The users of parent cooperatives are almost all more satisfied with their new preschool, 94.3 percent of them. This pattern becomes even clearer if one considers that 91 families had previous experience of a municipal preschool but only 21 of these picked another municipal preschool when they switched.

It should be mentioned that the clear preference for cooperative preschools is not a result of lower fees at the parent cooperatives. There is in Sweden a state-imposed ceiling on preschool fees that is set quite low, lower than the price level before its introduction in 2001. The municipalities cover all costs for the child care not covered by the fee, which means that about 90 percent of the total is paid by the public sector regardless of provider. All Swedish parents pay about the same because no preschool can offer child care at a cost that is even lower than the ceiling on the fees. This, in turn, means that there is no price competition between Swedish preschools, private or public. It is, however, in the preschools' interest to attract children and thereby receive public funding, which means that there is competition in service quality. When parents tend to favor parent cooperative over municipal preschools when switching, this says something about their perception of service quality.

Service quality is, as we have seen, closely associated with professionalism in Sweden. The look at how co-production works at cooperative preschools illustrates that there need not be a conflict of interest or conflict of perspectives between professional staff and co-producing parents. The co-production requires a greater effort in terms of communication from the staff, but this effort seems to provide valuable feedback, greater insight for parents and possibly a greater level of user satisfaction. There is therefore a link between co-production and service quality from the perspective of the users. It remains to be seen if this link holds when considering the data about the professional staff in the study.

STAFF PERSPECTIVE ON SERVICE QUALITY

The in-depth interviews with the managers of the municipal preschool touch on a reoccurring argument from the managers. They argued that "private" preschools could not supply good services for all children because they did not have the proper resources. One manager of a municipal preschool mentioned, for instance, that she could call in any of the twenty-five different experts in the municipal for a long range of special needs among the children. Another manager also argued that the nonpublic preschools could not provide services to children with special needs and thus discriminating against them and indirectly creating segregation between "strong" and "weak" groups in society. The most common argument was, however, that nonpublic preschools cut corners to save money for the owners, especially by not hiring enough staff or not replacing staff on leave. Staff density is not only one of the most common service quality measures in the data for this study but in the public debate as well. The ratio between the number of children and the number of staff members is often discussed as an indicator of service quality.

The official statistic reveals that the density of staff is slightly higher in the municipal preschools than in the nonpublic, which, in a manner typical for Swedish statistics in the area, includes both cooperative and for-profit child care (Skolverket, 2009b, 30). This study did not map staff density at the studied preschools, the official statistics already covers that information. It did, however, include the question of how the staff perceived staff density. The results are interesting because the parent cooperative staffs do not perceive the staff density as being worse than the municipal staff's perception of theirs. In fact, 90.9 percent of the staff at the parent cooperatives considers the staff density to be "good" and only 4.6 percent state that it is "bad." The corresponding figures for the municipal staffs are 76.1 percent and 13.1 percent, respectively. A reasonable explanation is, of course, that the users consider the staff density better at the parent cooperatives because of their co-production. The official statistics count the number of professional staff members as a measure of service quality because service quality is centered on professionalism in the Swedish context. The value of having parents co-producing certain aspects of the child care is not measured, but this study suggests that it might affect staff density positively.

Staff density might, in other words, not provide an argument for there being a higher service quality in municipal services. The municipalities are, however, large organizations with a large total number of preschool staff, while the parent cooperatives are typically small, single facilities with only a few hired members of staff. Does this mean that the municipalities have greater means of maintaining a stable staffing situation, for instance, when employees get ill or are home on maternity/paternity leave? This study looked into this issue by asking the preschool managers about their practices for filling vacancies at the preschool. As it turned out, the differences between the practices at parent cooperatives and municipal preschools were very small. All preschools, regardless of organizational form, had developed an improvised list of people to call in for short-term vacancies. Some of municipal preschools had arrangements with staffing firms, but these were used only rarely and only for long-term vacancies. One municipal preschool manager explained that using such firms was "a gamble" because you did not know if the person showing up would be competent enough to do the job. It also takes a lot of extra time to teach a new person all the routines at the preschool. The municipal preschools therefore used the same kind of list of familiar people to fill vacancies as the parent cooperatives. The most significant difference between the two forms of child care in this sense was that the parent cooperatives in many cases could avoid calling in substitute staff if the parents can step in and do an extra share of the work at times. The parents are familiar with the workplace, and the children are in most cases familiar with them. Most parent cooperatives even have a rotating schedule of parents to call in case of short-term staff shortages. This advantage can potentially be quite significant because there is a general shortage of preschool staff in Sweden.

Another aspect of bringing in parents as regular or substitute staff is that you get a more even distribution between mothers and fathers. Only three percent of the professional preschool teachers in Sweden are men (Skolverket, 2009a, 23). There are no statistics on the distribution of work between mothers and fathers in co-production at parent cooperatives, but it seems to be relatively even. Children at parent cooperatives therefore have a much greater chance of seeing both women and men during the day. The quality aspect of this fact can of course be debated, but an even distribution of men and women is certainly considered desirable in other public services in Sweden, as is evident from the recruiting policies of many public institutions. From the child's perspective meeting, both men and women at the preschool can resemble their home environment in many (but obviously not all) cases.

The quality of a service is usually measured in terms of how it appears when the user of the service consumes it. The quality of the service measured as it is being produced for the ones that produce it is usually overlooked but no less important. This study therefore looked into the issue of work environment as a measure of service quality. Two different types of work environment were considered, physical work environment and psychosocial work environment. The former refers to the preschool facilities, availability of lifts, tools and so on. The latter refers to the social interaction of the staff and the employees' feelings toward work. Both types of work environments are measured in a survey among the staff of the preschools in the study. Of the staff in the parent cooperatives, 79.5 percent responded that the physical work environment was "good" or "very good," while only 55.6 percent of the municipal staff replied the same. Conversely, 6.8 percent of the staff at the cooperatives considered the work environment "bad" or "very bad," while 22.2 percent of the staff at the municipal preschool entered those replies. It is in some ways surprising that the cooperatives, which are small preschools with limited resources, should score better than the large-scale municipal preschools on this variable. To renovate a house to improve the physical work environment can be very costly and probably too costly for a small, nonprofit preschool.

The survey study could not explain why the cooperatives did better in physical work environment, but a possible answer was suggested in the in-depth interviews. The staffs at the cooperatives are, as already described here, in a continuous dialogue with the parents at the preschool, and the parents are the members of the board that has to approve all significant investments in the physical work environment. The high level of communication at the cooperatives creates a mutual understanding of the importance of good work environment, which allows for problems being addressed swiftly and in cooperation. The managers of the municipal preschools have to compete for public funding or other resources, such as maintenance personnel, with many other public services. Another problem for the municipal services is that the politicians and high-ranking administrators with the authority to supply funding might not always have a full understanding of the work environment issues at hand.

The psychosocial work environment reveals even greater differences between the municipal and parent cooperative preschools. Of the staff at the parent cooperatives, 97.7 percent responded that the psychosocial work environment was either "good" or "very good," while only 71.2 percent of the staff at the municipal preschools did the same. Not a single member of staff at any of the cooperative preschools stated that the psychosocial work environment was either "bad" or "very bad," while 15.6 percent of the municipal employees did this. It is, in other words, clear that the staff at the cooperative preschools feels good about working there and that their psychosocial work environment is even better than their physical work environment. The same difference between the two types of work environments seems to exist at the municipal preschools. Table 16.1 is designed to illustrate de differences between the two types of work environment and the two forms of child care. All replies in the survey scored from one point for the "very bad" replies to seven for the "very good" replies. The means and the average difference between the types of work environment are thereafter calculated.

The parent cooperatives score better in both types of work environment, but the difference is greater for psychosocial work environment as seen from the vertical difference in the table. The difference between the two types of

Table 16.1   Two Types of Work Environment on a Scale of 1–7*

	Physical	Psychosocial	Difference	n
Municipal	4.5778	5	0.4222	(45)
Parent cooperative	5.1591	5.9773	0.8182	(44)
Difference**	0.5813	0.9773		

Source: Vamstad, 2007.
Note: *Means in table

work environment within the two forms of child care is also greater in the parent cooperatives, as seen from the horizontal difference in the table. The better psychosocial work environment could be explained by a number of factors. The cooperative preschools are smaller and, to quote a member of staff, "cozier" than the larger municipal preschools. The chain of authority is shorter and more informal, and the already described relationship with the parents might also be of importance. It is not possible to link the work environment directly to the existence of co-production since we do not know how much, if at all, it explains the better work environment at the parent cooperatives. What we can say is, at the very least, that co-production certainly does not seem to be a significant hindrance for a good work environment.

It seems, from a staff perspective, that the type of child care that practices co-production has several benefits with regard to service quality. The density of professional staff is slightly lower but less problematic thanks to co-producing parents, who can also step in during staff shortages. The findings about work environment were clearly in favor of co-production in spite of the lower degree of reliance on professional staff.

CONCLUSION

Sweden is an unlikely place to find co-production of social services. A strong tradition for professional services that are developed, funded and provided by the public sector has made the role of co-producing users seem like a compromise with service quality at best.

The results from the study of Swedish child care show that parent cooperative child care services have a better service quality in many regards, from both a user and staff perspective. Previous research has supported the theory that these positive effects of co-production on service quality come from the extensive, two-way communication between staff and users in the co-production. This study supports that theory in the case of Swedish child care, especially through the in-depth interviews with preschool managers. The study also illustrated that the preference of professionalism over co-production that characterizes the Swedish welfare state is clearly present in the child care sector. What makes child care interesting is, however, the twenty-five years of experience of co-production and that the co-producing preschools are not at all known for low service quality.

It is not clear to what extent these experiences in child care could tell us anything about how co-production might work in other service areas in Sweden. The history of Swedish child care is in some regards unique, especially in how cooperative preschools were allowed to receive public funding for a few years in the 1980s, when the for-profit ones still were not. This gave the cooperatives an advantage while they today compete, mostly unsuccessfully, on the same terms as big business. There are no other service areas with a comparable proportion of cooperatives, and no service areas where co-production is an important element in public or for-profit service provision. There is, of course, also the issue of the users of cooperative child care being disproportionally well-off compared to the average service user. It appears, as seen in the case of child care, that the establishment of co-production in the Swedish welfare provision is dependent on active support from the state, in terms of legislation and funding.

The results of this study are, of course, limited by the modest size of the data set. The results are, however, clear enough to suggest that there are no harmful effects of co-production on service quality. This is a bold enough conclusion and a new perspective for a system of welfare delivery so entirely reliant on the expertise of trained professionals for achieving service quality.

REFERENCES

Ahnlund, P. 2008. *Omsorg som Arbete—Om Utbildning, Arbetsmiljö och Relationer i Äldre och Handikappomsorgen.* Umeå, Norway: Umeå University.

Ahlqvist, B., and L. Engqvist. 1984. *Samtal med Feldt.* Stockholm: Tidens Förlag.

Appelqvist, Ö., and S. Andersson, ed. 2005. *The Essential Gunnar Myrdal.* New York: New Press.

Beck, U. 1992. *Risk society.* London: Sage.

Bovaird, T. 2005. Public governance: Balancing stakeholder power in a network society. *International Review of Administrative Sciences* 71 (2): 217–228.

Bovaird, T. 2007. Beyond engagement and participation: user and community co-production of public services. *Public Administration Review* 67 (5): 846–860.

Bovaird, T., and J. Downe. 2009. *Innovation in Public Engagement and Co-production of Services.* White Paper (policy paper).

Cassier, E. 2005. *Axel Hägerström.* Stockholm: Thales.

Dahlberg, L. 2004. *Welfare Relationships: Voluntary Organizations and Local Authorities Supporting Relatives of Older People.* Stockholm: Stockholm University Press.

Dahlberg, L. 2005. Interaction between voluntary and statutory social service provision in Sweden: A matter of welfare pluralism, substitution or complementary? *Social Policy and Administration* 39 (7): 740–763.

Dahlberg, L. 2006. The complementary norm: Service provision by the welfare state and voluntary organizations in Sweden. *Health and Social Care in the Community* 14 (4): 302–310.

Extended Performance System Index. 2011. Available at www.kvalitetsindex.se. 2011-09-28

Feldt, K.-O. 1991. *Alla Dessa Dagar.* Stockholm: Norstedts Förlag.

Giddens, A. 1991. *The Consequences of Modernity.* Stanford: Stanford University Press.

Hägerström, A. 2010. *Socialpolitiska Uppsatser.* Göteborg: Daidalos.

Hartley, J. 2005. Innovation in governance and public services: past and present. *Public Money and Management* 25 (1): 27–34.

Hedenius, I. 2009. *Tro och Vetande.* Malmö, Sweden: Fri Tanke Förlag.

Hirschman, A. O. 2006. *Sorti eller Protest.* Lund: Arkiv Förlag.

Hyde, P., and H. T. O. Davies. 2004. Service design, culture and performance: collusion and co-production in health care. *Human Relations* 57 (11): 1407–1426.

Johansson, R. 2007. *Vid Byråkratins Gräns: Om Handlingsfrihetens Organisatoriska Begränsningar.* Lund: Arkiv Förlag.

Marshall, T. H. 1950. *Citizenship and Social Class and other Essays.* Cambridge, UK: Cambridge University Press.

McKenzie, D., T. A. Whiu, D, Matahaere-Atariki, K. Goldsmith, and T. P. Kokiri. 2008. Co-Production in a Maori context. *Social Policy Journal of New Zealand* 33 (1): 32–46.

Meeuwisse, A. 2008. Organizational innovation in the Swedish welfare state. *Critical Social Policy* 28 (2): 187–210.

Osborne, S. 2006. The New Public Governance. *Public Management Review* 8 (3): 377–387.

Pestoff, V. 1998. *Beyond the Market and State.* Aldershot, UK: Ashgate.

Pestoff, V. 2008. *A Democratic Architecture for the Welfare State: Promoting Citizen Participation, the Third Sector and Co-Production.* London: Routledge.

Pestoff, V. 2009. Towards a paradigm of democratic participation: citizen participation and co-production of personal social services in Sweden. *Annals of Public and Cooperative Economics* 80 (2): 197–224.

Peterson, O. 2000. *Nordisk Politik.* Stockholm: Norstedts Juridik.

Pettersson, L.-O. 2001. *Från Rivstart till Stopplag: Privatiseringsvågen i Välfärden 1979–2001.* Stockholm: Agoras Förlag.

Pollitt, C., G. Bouckaert, and E. Löffler. 2006. *Making Quality Sustainable: Co-Design, Co-Decide, Co-Produce and Co-Evaluate.* Unpublished conference paper, 4QC Conference Tampere. Helsinki: Ministry of Finance.

Regeringens Proposition 1984/85:209, 1985. *Förskola För Alla Barn,* Stockholm: Riksdagstryck.

Sigurdson, O. 2000. *Den Lyckliga Filosofin: Etik och Politik hos Hägerström, Tingsten, Makarna Myrdal och Hedenius.* Stockholm: Symposion Förlag.

Skolverket, 2009a. *Beskrivande data 2009—föreskoleverksamhet, skolbarnomsorg, skola och vuxenutbildning.* Stockholm: Skolverket.

Skolverket, 2009b. *Skolverkets lägesbedömning 2009—förskoleverksamhet, skolbarnomsorg, skola och vuxenutbildning.* Stockholm: Skolverket.

SOU 1972:26, 1972. *Betänkande Angivet av 1968 års Barnstugeutredning Del Ett.* Stockholm: Allmänna Förlaget.

Tritter, J. Q., and A. McCallum. 2006. The snakes and ladders of user involvement. *Health Policy,* 76(2): 156–168.

Vamstad, J. 2007. *Governing Welfare: The Third Sector and the Challenges to the Swedish Welfare State.* Östersund: Mid-Sweden University.

Von Bergmann-Winberg, M.-L. 1987. *Wohlfahrt, Lebensniveau und Lebenweise im Deutsch-Deutschen Vergleich.* Helsinki: Swedish School of Economics and Business Administration.

17 Co-Production

An Alternative to the Partial Privatization Processes in Italy and Norway

Andrea Calabrò

INTRODUCTION AND MOTIVATION

Market reforms such as privatization are often put in place with the aim of improving economic efficiency, reducing the role of the state and increasing the degree of private sector competition. These reforms are expected to have a positive effect on the local economy (Megginson and Jeffry, 2001). However, the measure of the success of privatization is often very narrow (Kikeri and Nellis, 2001). In fact, concerns have been raised in many cases about the privatization process in terms of the effective provision/production of services and accountability to citizens. Moreover, in many countries (e.g., Italy and Norway), public service providers are still controlled by the state, and there is therefore a situation that we could call partial privatization. We can talk of partial privatization when two characteristics are satisfied:

- restructuring actions are undertaken by the state in order to create joint stock companies that are supposed to produce and/or provide public services more efficiently
- after formal privatization has taken place (the restructuring of the public sector apparatus according to business-style guidelines), there is no substantial market competition, meaning that the situation is effectively a state monopoly

This chapter emphasizes the attributes and limits of the privatization process and examines the debates surrounding it. It suggests that co-production may be a reasonable alternative to the privatization of public goods and services. There are many reasons for the failure of privatization (e.g., corruption, lack of accountability and unethical behavior on the part of public officers). Focusing on public services and the governance systems of goods providers (Bjorvatn and Soreide, 2005) may shed new light on the actual involvement of citizens in the production/provision of public services. Therefore, by considering what role citizens have after the privatization of public services, we should be able to understand how co-production practices may help to overcome the ethical concerns that arise from cases of incomplete privatization.

Related to this debate, the study looks at whether privatizing public sector activities could improve or undermine new public management (NPM) reforms. We start, then, by noting that privatization is an important element of market reform programs, which are expected to improve economic efficiency by reducing the role of the state in the economy. However, some countries in Europe have only recently begun to privatize or have halted the process without having achieved a situation of effective market competition, meaning that they may be considered examples of partial privatization. The primary aim of this chapter is to reveal the impact of privatization on the system of accountability for public service providers and discuss how co-production may address accountability issues in favor of the public interest. The primary research questions are as follows: what are the main characteristics of the privatization processes in Italy and Norway? Are public service providers' governance systems able to grant public value to citizens? How can co-production be introduced in order to avoid accountability gaps?

The chapter makes several contributions to the debate on privatization, the governance systems of public service providers, accountability and co-production. First, we show clearly how the accountability of public service providers is negatively affected by cases of incomplete privatization in Italy and Norway.

Second, we show that a valid alternative to privatization may exist (Pestoff, 1992, 2008). Co-production is often cited as a reasonable alternative to public service privatization, and this chapter identifies specific areas in which a co-production approach could be used in the public interest.

The rest of the chapter is organized as follows: in section two, the main characteristics of privatization are discussed from different theoretical perspectives. In section three, the focus is on corruption and conflicts of interest in relation to privatization. The methods are described in section four. Section five summarizes the main results. The discussion, findings and future research directions are presented in the final sections.

THE PRIVATIZATION PROCESS FROM
VARIOUS THEORETICAL PERSPECTIVES

The privatization process is designed to shift functions and responsibilities, in whole and in part, from the government to the private sector. It has been applied to state industries in the manufacturing, public utilities, transport and telecommunications sectors (Millward, 2005). The privatization process has been a fundamental tool in the re-organization of the national states. Indeed, it has turned the so-called state-owned firms into more market-oriented entities.

However, cracks have recently appeared and in view of the weaknesses of new public management (NPM), the need for a new way of thinking of public management practice has begun to be addressed. Many studies have sought to address those weakness, and the public value approach is attracting particular attention (Bozeman, 2002; Hefetz and Warner, 2004; Smith, Anderson, and Teicher, 2004; Hartley, 2005; Stoker, 2006). A new paradigm on government activity, policy making and service delivery may be emerging that will have important implications for public managers. This approach also sheds new light on the privatization process. Authors are starting to look at the negative effects of privatization processes that have often resulted in partial privatization with no improvement in public service values for citizens. They are seeking to address the main shortcomings of these partial processes, which may give rise to ethical problems arising from conflicts of interests between the various actors involved (Groot and Budding, 2008). Additionally, there is increasing concern about the impact of NPM reforms on the ethics of public officials (Maesschalck, 2004).

Authors from the U.S. have expressed their concerns about the ethical consequences of NPM innovations, such as privatization, and argued for re-regulation (Frederickson, 1999). Some other authors have argued in favor of what has been labeled the new public service (NPS) (Denhardt and Denhardt, 2000). NPS is seen as an alternative to the dichotomy of old public administration and NPM. NPS includes new mechanisms in which the primary role of the public official is to help citizens, focusing on citizens' interests rather than attempting to control or steer society. In contrast to NPM, NPS also recognizes that the relationship between government and its citizens is not the same as that which exists in the business sector between a firm and its customers. Therefore, the privatization process is seen as a market-based mechanism that is inappropriate in some contexts, partly due to the ethical problems that arise from its use. According to NPS, therefore, the privatization process is seen as far from perfect, but the emphasis is more on ethical issues relating to the behavior of public officials rather than on that process directly.

The most serious concerns with privatization, as it has so often been practiced, are, then, unethical forms of behavior, conflicts of interests and accountability problems. Indeed, in cases of partial privatization, managers of firms that are still state-owned are often political appointees, and their employees are given a status equivalent to that of civil servants. As such, the impact of their actions seems to be related directly to the citizens. Unethical behavior may potentially lead to damage to the public interest of citizens. Moreover, the recent scandals in the public sector have led us to reflect on the importance of ethical systems that avoid conflicts of interest and possible unethical behavior in the public services. The importance of renewing the ethical system and its introduction into the governance structure of public service providers is thus crucial. It is also important to appreciate that public sector employees can face conflicts of interest, especially when personal goals are not consistent with maximizing the benefits for citizens. Given the large number of partial privatization processes, it is important to understand what exactly constitutes a conflict of interest, and how it may be avoided in public service providers. This aspect becomes more critical in these firms because of the involvement of the public interest and of citizens.

A reasonable alternative (Pestoff, 1992, 2008) to privatization is presented by the new public governance (NPG) perspective (Osborne, 2006). This perspective includes many modes of governance (e.g., joined-up governance, network governance, co-production and cooperation). These are viewed as alternatives to privatization in public service provision; it seems that they might also be able to alleviate many of the previously described issues (corruption, conflicts of interest, and unethical behavior).

This becomes particularly important for public service providers that are still state-owned. Indeed, in many countries around the world, there are companies that are partially or completely state-owned. These are often known as state-owned companies (SOCs). In those cases, business-style practices must be adopted while bearing in mind the public interest and value, and using the right tools to ensure effective accountability and citizen involvement.

A significant shift is taking place in attitudes toward ethical standards and, subsequently, in unethical behavior in public services (Hondeghem, 1998; Van Wart and Berman, 1999; Organisation for Economic Co-Operation and Development, 2000; Bovens, Schillemans, and 't Hart, 2008). There is a feeling that something must change in public sector organizations. The importance of citizens' interests and the need to focus on public value are leading us to consider the accountability system that each public organization should adopt and the various ways of improving citizen co-production in public services.

These problems can partly be solved through expanding the role of participatory citizenship in the governance of complex areas, such as public service delivery (Klijn, 2008). This discussion has pointed out how the privatization process has assumed different meanings in relation to different perspectives (NPM, NPS and NPG). What also seems to be the case is that when there is partial privatization, deregulation in public service delivery and a process of reorganization, the form and the power of the governing bodies are constantly in flux. This poses some questions: Is the accountability system able to keep up with these developments? Would moving from an NPM approach to an NPS or NPG approach better address the previously mentioned issues and ensure that the public interest of citizens is upheld? Could the implementation of co-production practices be the solution to the lack of accountability generated by these partial privatization processes?

CO-PRODUCTION: A REASONABLE ALTERNATIVE TO PRIVATIZATION AND TO ITS NEGATIVE EFFECTS

What does co-production mean? And how can co-production be a reasonable alternative to partial privatization processes? Definitions of co-production range from "the mix of public service agents and citizens who contribute to the provision of public services" to "a partnership between citizens and public service providers" (Pestoff, 2008). Co-production is therefore a partnership between citizens and public services to achieve a valued outcome. Such partnerships empower citizens to contribute more of their own resources and have greater control over service decisions and resources. Co-production should be central to governments' agendas for improving public services because there is emerging evidence of its impact on outcomes and value of money, its potential economic and social value and its popularity.

Much of the thinking that informs the concept of co-production has emerged as an approach to service and outcomes development that locates citizens alongside traditional service providers as necessary, expert and generative co-participants and co-partners (Ostrom, 1996; Alford, 1998; Bovaird, 2007). Alford (1998) notes the opportunities that were missed in the mid-1980s when governments turned away from the idea of system-wide co-production in favor of more market-orientated approaches, such as privatization. Indeed, a recent study measuring citizen voice and privatization found that governments engaging in higher levels of privatization focused more on technical efficiency measures while they overlooked the voice of the citizen (Hefetz and Warner, 2004). From the perspective of the co-production of public goods and services, it should be possible to overcome the ethical and accountability concerns that are often associated with the partial privatization of public services. This alternative strategy involves developing structures in which user organizations have a substantial input into managerial decisions, the organization of production and service delivery through an enhanced system of collective bargaining.

However, it seems important to underline that rather than simply replicating specific co-production practices, accelerating co-production relies on some more structural changes to the following aspects: budgets with more control passed down to individual users and frontline professionals, support for civic society and mutual assistance, performance regimes and professional training and culture. Co-production thus seems to be essential to meeting a number of these challenges, for neither governments nor citizens have access to all the resources necessary to solve these problems on their own.

Effective partnerships among citizens and public actors are based on four clear values: everyone has something to contribute, reciprocity is central, social relationships matter and social contributions (rather than financial contributions) are encouraged. Such partnerships empower citizens to contribute their own resources and allow them greater control over public resources to achieve certain outcomes. In turn, this may be useful to avoid the lack of information and accountability that characterize the governance systems of many public service providers and to monitor the behavior of the main actors involved in the decision-making process. It remains to be seen whether co-production will characterize more mainstream public services in the future. This study suggests that:

- co-production may improve outcomes more than privatization practices
- citizens may be more active partners (the public wants to be more involved when public services relate directly to them and their family)
- the value that citizens can contribute is significant
- co-production often improves value for money (the economic benefits of co-production approaches outweigh the costs)

If we are to bring co-production into the mainstream, we propose that we should not primarily spread specific programs, but rather change the nature of budgeting, relationships with civil society, performance management and professional cultures. It thus seems important to allow:

- *choice and control,* which give citizens greater control over resources
- *peer support,* which empowers citizens to support one another with new rights for groups of service users
- *incentivize partnerships* through performance management
- *professional culture,* which ensures that professionals value citizen contributions by involving more service users in professional training, staff recruitment and inspection, as well as support local leaders to drive a change in culture

These recommendations would need to be part of wider reforms to empower citizens, foster a new professionalism and provide a more strategic role for government, particularly in terms of giving citizens better information, involving citizens more directly in policy making and commissioning for long-term outcomes and better public services.

METHODS

The methodology adopted in this chapter is a cross-country case study that was conducted by comparing the Italian and Norwegian privatization processes and the accountability and ethical systems. The cross-country case study was chosen because it has been widely used in prior public sector studies (e.g., Christensen and Lægreid, 2001; Argento et al., 2010) as a useful tool to define common trends and differences in national contexts. Moreover, this methodology is particularly suitable for answering "how" and "why" questions and is ideal for generating and building theory in an area where little data or theory exists (Yin, 2003).

The study has been conducted to analyze the accountability and the ethical systems of public service providers in Italy and Norway. The content analysis methodology has been widely used in literature, particularly in corporate social disclosure studies (Parker and Saal, 2003). Content analysis objectively and quantitatively examines written or oral communication to make inferences about the values, meanings or understandings that are being conveyed (Holst, 1981; Riffe, Lacy, and Fico, 1998). This method was chosen as it is able to analyze explicit (manifest content) as well as implicit (latent content) statements in texts (Krippendorff, 1980). This methodology is particularly suitable in our study because it is useful for the objective, systematic, quantitative and reliable study of published information (ibid.) but also to measure comparative positions and trends in reporting (Guthrie and Parker, 1990). In sum, while analyzing the privatization processes and the ethical and accountability issues that were derived from the study, we used an inductive research approach (Stenbacka, 2001). This was done to uncover relevant information and explore the possibility of conducting such a case study comparing Italy and Norway. On the other hand, a deductive research approach (Rice and Ezzy, 1999) was used when searching for the necessary literature and finding a research gap that the other researchers had failed to develop.

The study focuses on public service providers in Norway and Italy. Two groups of public service providers—one from Italy and one from Norway—were selected. Our analysis included twenty-six services providers from Italy, and twenty-two from Norway. All of these are owned by a ministry. The twenty-six Italian public service providers are owned (totally or in part) by the Italian Ministry of Economy and Finance (MEF). Here we found four companies that were less than 50 percent state/MEF-owned, three others with less than 100 percent state-ownership, while the remaining 17 were 100 percent state-owned. (See Table 17.1 in the Appendix of this chapter for details.)

Our focus is on the public service companies owned by the Italian MEF in 2008. As in many other developed countries, the MEF is still an influential shareholder in several privatized companies where it lacks total control, such as ENI (21.1 + 17.36 percent), ENEL (20.3 + 9.99 percent), Finmeccanica (33.7 percent) and Alitalia (49.9 percent). Furthermore, it still has full ownership of FS, the railway system operator in Italy, and the RAI (Italian Radio Television) broadcasting company. The MEF owns public group of companies that are active in the delivery of public services, and it therefore determines their system of governance. Planning and control functions are carried out by the MEF, and these also influence the governance structure of public service companies. The MEF's state-owned companies have no sector-specific policy objectives. This demonstrates how the rationalization and restructuring of the state apparatus is still in progress and that further actions are needed in Italy to achieve a better organizational structure of MEF's SOCs.

In the Norwegian case, twenty-two companies operating mainly in the service sector were selected for our study (see Table 17.2 in the Appendix). Unlike in Italy, where all twenty-six state-owned companies are owned by the MEF, in Norway they are owned by several different ministries, including the Ministries of Transport and Communications, Trade and Industry, Petroleum and Energy, Justice and the Police, Labour and Social Inclusion,

Health and Care Services, Foreign Affairs, Culture and Church Affairs, Education and Research, and Agriculture and Food. The Norwegian situation is rather unique in this sense. Indeed, at present, the various ministries hold full or part ownership interests in eighty companies. These companies can be divided into four categories, based on the objective of the state's ownership, according to the Norwegian Ministry of Trade and Industry (2008). They are:

1. companies with commercial objectives
2. companies with commercial objectives and ensuring head office functions remaining in Norway
3. companies with commercial and other specific, defined objectives
4. companies with sectoral policy objectives

One of the main purposes of the ownership management of the companies in the first three categories is to maximize the value of the state's shares and contribute to the positive industrial development of the companies. Most of the companies where the main objective of state ownership is commercial are managed by the Ownership Department of the Ministry of Trade and Industry.[1]

State ownership in the other companies where one of the main objectives is commercial (category 3) are managed by various ministries: the Ministry of Local Government and Regional Development, the Ministry of Agriculture and Food, the Ministry of Petroleum and Energy and the Ministry of Transport and Communications. Companies with specific sectoral policy objectives (category 4) include companies where the main objectives of state ownership are not purely commercial in nature. For these companies, sector-policy and social objectives are the main objective of state ownership.

These companies are managed by the individual ministries responsible for sector policy in the various areas. For example, state ownership in Statnett SF and Statskog SF is managed by the Ministry of Petroleum and Energy and the Ministry of Agriculture and Food, respectively. The objectives that form the basis for state ownership in companies with sector-policy objectives are, for example, the provision of safe, environmentally friendly air traffic services everywhere in Norway (Avinor AS), the regulation of the sale of beverages containing alcohol (AS Vinmonopolet) and the provision of good and equal specialist health services for everyone who needs them (the regional health authorities). Even if the sector-policy companies do not have primarily commercial objectives, commercial results and the efficient use of resources are still key issues for these companies (Norwegian Ministry of Trade and Industry, 2008). In this study, we therefore only focus on the companies included in the category 4, "companies with sectoral policy objectives in Norway." In Norway, state ownership ranges from 53.4 percent to 100 percent, but only three of these twenty-two SOCs are less than 100 percent state-owned.

THE ETHICAL STRUCTURE

Recently, the relevance of ethical concerns has encouraged initiatives aimed at restoring confidence and maintaining integrity in businesses (Bozeman, 2009). Among public service providers in particular, well-defined ethical structures can help prevent corruption, conflicts of interest and unethical forms of behavior. The adoption of a code of ethics is thus a natural first step toward improving the ethical culture in today's public sector.

The term "code of ethics" is defined as a set of written standards that are designed to deter wrongdoing and promote honest and ethical conduct, including the ethical handling of actual or apparent conflicts of interest between personal and professional relationships; full, fair, accurate, timely and understandable disclosure in reports and documents; compliance with the relevant governmental laws, rules and regulations; prompt internal reporting in the case of violations of the code to an appropriate person or person identified in the code; and accountability for adherence to the code (Securities and Exchange Commission, 2003).

Mandatory codes of ethics began to be introduced in Italy for public service providers in 2001 (Law 231/2001). This was the result of changes in the system of public administration, and it reflected the effort of newly defined universally applicable ethical values. The new codes outline the values and ethical principles that should guide public officials in their professional activities. Tithe Norwegian Code of Practice for Corporate Governance, by contrast, stipulates that the board of directors in state-owned companies should adopt ethical guidelines for the company. In Norway, there is no a law that requires the adoption of codes of ethics. Generally, it can be said that Norwegian citizens have broad trust and confidence in public services. This confidence has always been considerable, and it is rooted in the basic values of the welfare state (Organisation for Economic Co-Operation and Development, 2005).

To investigate ethical and accountability issues, we analyzed the content of the codes of ethics of the public service companies selected for study. The first step in this process of analysis was to identify the documents to be analyzed and the units of analysis (Krippendorff, 1980). The choice of documents that provide the source data for content analysis depends on their availability, accessibility and relevance. In our cases, codes of ethics were generally found in the Corporate Governance section of company websites. Codes of ethics were collected in English or in the local language. This process yielded thirty-three codes of ethics (twenty-two from Italy and eleven from Norway), which we explored using content analysis based on the current version of the codes. The content analysis helped to identify existing and potential ethical concerns faced by these companies in the Italian and Norwegian contexts. To carry out the content analysis, we first compared several studies of the content analysis in different countries (Bondy, Matten, and Moon, 2004; O'Dwyer and Madden, 2006). We looked for indications of how corruption and conflicts of interest were avoided through ethical principles, values, norms and rules of conduct.

Despite the new Italian regulations, some of the public service providers that we analyzed have not disclosed their code of ethics on their website. In the twenty-six companies owned by the MEF, twenty-two disclosed their codes of ethics (84.7 percent). Among the twenty-two Norwegian companies, eleven disclosed their codes of ethics on the website (50 percent), the lower percentage of disclosure in Norway was due to the absence of a law that requires the code to be displayed, contrary to the situation in Italy.

The results of our content analysis are reported in a fashion that underlines the main topics dealt with in the codes. However, before turning to the topics analyzed in the codes, it would be of interest to explore several formal aspects: the title, extension, date and scope of application. Concerning the title of the document, in the Italian case, most companies simply use the denomination "Code of Conduct of X" (38.46 percent), "Standards of Ethics and Conduct" (23.07 percent), "Ethical Standards" (15.38 percent), "Code of Ethics" (7.6 percent). In few cases, there are indications (even if incomplete) of codes implementation realized by communication and disclosure actions.

In the Norwegian case, most companies use the denomination "Ethical Guidelines for X" (80.0 percent), while others report the denomination "Code of Conduct of X" (20.0 percent). The average length of the codes is approximately fourteen pages for the Italian cases, although some were as long as twenty-three or thirty pages. This is quite different from the length of the Norwegian codes of ethics. They are, on average, approximately five pages. However, in Norway there are both longer and shorter codes, ranging from twelve pages and just one page.

Regarding the date, in Italy most codes were drawn up and took effect four or five years ago (36.6 percent from 2001 to 2003, 45.5 percent from 2004 to 2006, and 17.9 percent from 2007 to 2008). In the case of Norway, most companies do not indicate the date of implementation of the codes. Only 25 percent indicate a date of implementation between 2005 and 2009. In addition, the main issues discussed in ethical codes concern employees and customers, emphasizing the ethical impact that managers, directors and partially public officials' behavior may have on these groups.

Turning to the content of the codes, in the Italian case codes are mainly imperative, stating a guide for the standards of conduct that firms would like their actors to follow. The structure of the codes usually contains two sections: the first section states the values and basic principles encouraged by the company, while the second section translates these principles into certain standards of conduct for the actors in their internal and external relationships. In the case of Norway, the codes do not follow any clear structure, but they list several guidelines that give the company, its employees and partners guidance and support in the daily duties and decision-making processes.

Going deeper in the analysis, in the Italian case, 45.4 percent of the codes analyzed lack a clear statement of their values and principles, while 36.4

percent lack indications of detailed norms of conduct. Tools for promotion and sensitization to the importance of the public interest and value are only present in 18.2 percent of cases. In the Norwegian case, the situation is very different. There is no clear statement of their values and principles in 85.0 percent of cases. Indications regarding norms of conduct and the importance of the public interest and value are totally absent.

The Italian codes are usually made up of provisions that cover the following areas: the use of public resources for personal benefit (31 percent), the definition of the target group to which the code is addressed to (23.6 percent), the duties to the public as opposed to private interests (22.8 percent), the definition of behavior or conduct that constitutes a violation of the code (13.6 percent), the statement of preventing conflict of interests (9 percent) and the sanctions applicable in case of violations (0 percent).

As mentioned, in the case of Norway, the guidelines contained in the codes consist of broad principles that can be classified as follows: openness (85 percent), referring to the degree of transparency of the firm in relation to its various stakeholders; professional independence (75 percent), which can be seen in the context of loyalty and neutrality; loyalty (55 percent), referring to the use of public resources for personal benefit; general provisions (30 percent), indicating that employees will be managed according to general ethics, business ethics and management ethical values and norms.

From the analysis of all the codes (Italy and Norway), it seems that many codes are characterized by the general nature of their contents, which tend to express themselves in terms of advice ("ought," "should" or "may") rather than obligation ("must"). Many codes are also ambiguous or unclear. The main ethical concerns in the companies we analyzed were related to the absence of information about conflicts of interest disclosure. Moreover, none of the codes analyzed have been characterized by a formulation process that includes consultation with citizens or their representatives. These are probably the major shortcomings to emerge from the analysis.

Ethical aspects seem critical in the governance system of public service providers in both Italy and Norway. Accountability, transparency, openness, the duties of public officials, sanctions, complex relationships between actors, the public interest and values are all key aspects. It seems that the codes of ethics analyzed are not binding, but simply suggest guidelines. In this sense, they are quite similar to a code of practice. The analysis shows clearly that the introduction of ethical issues is at an early stage in both countries and that more emphasis on ethical and accountability issues is urgently needed.

DISCUSSION AND FINDINGS

The Italian privatization process has been characterized by a "stop-go" dynamic. In fact, despite one of the largest privatization programs in the world in the 1990s, many Italian public service companies are still state-owned, and the current degree of market competition is not effective. In Norway, by contrast, privatization took place later, reflecting the reluctance of the Norwegian government to privatize until 1990s, when a number of reforms were also implemented (Christensen, 2003). Despite the different motivations and contexts in the two countries, what emerges is that the current situation in both countries has resulted in a partial privatization process and public service companies that are state-owned.

The motivations and the pressure toward the privatization were different in the two countries. Indeed, in Italy the privatization process was motivated by the need to address the inefficiency and ineffectiveness of public ownership (Saraceno, 1981; Cafferata, 1995; Bognetti and Robotti, 2007). In Norway, given the strong financial position of the state, fiscal improvement considerations were not a main driver of privatization—the economic situation was healthy and the public apparatus functioned well (Christensen and Lægreid, 2009).

Today, both countries are characterized by situations in which the ministries continue to be the major owners of service providers, but in the case of Italy, the MEF is the main owner, suggesting a concentration of power and strategic direction. In Norway, on the other hand, several ministries are involved in the governance of the SOCs, a pattern derived from the historical *agencification* (Christensen, 2003) of the Norwegian public sector. Moreover, although the role of ministerial governance has developed differently in the two countries, a common pattern exists in relation to ethical and accountability problems. The content analysis of the codes of ethics from both countries reveals that in spite of the contextual and historical differences in the development of the privatization process, there is a clear lack of accountability and of implementation on the codes of ethics, and of transparency in both the analyzed countries.

This study argues that co-production can be a reasonable alternative to privatization. The need for accountability, transparency and citizen involvement in the production/provision of public services and goods in SOCs is particularly important to avoid unethical forms of behavior and to increase public value and interest. Ethical issues arising from conflicts of interest for public officials may be one reason for the failure of privatization.

In order to verify whether the codes of ethics really aim to achieve these objectives, a content analysis of codes of ethics of thirty-three Italian and Norwegian SOCs operating mainly in the service sector was carried out. The results suggest that greater emphasis on accountability system is urgently needed. A greater focus on citizens' public value and interest is also necessary (Bozeman, 2009). Our results show that action to implement ethical and accountable procedures are sporadic and unstructured and were only recently introduced in both countries. The lack of accountability is the main weakness of the governance systems of the ministry or ministries and the public service providers involved. The lack of evidence of any real efficiency associated with the privatization process and the decline in accountability produced by restructuring and downsizing public services is thus evident (Bozeman, 2007).

More stringent requirements relating to transparency and public disclosure are needed to avoid unethical behavior. Public service firms should therefore be more open about dilemmas relating to conflicts of interest and accountability. In addition, many problems still refer to how the fundamental values of public service organizations have been undermined by this partial privatization process (Lawton, 1998).

Governmental reforms are necessary in order to introduce market principles and outsource public goods and services. But in a modern representative democracy, the public sector can be described as a circle of principal-agent relationships (Strom, 2003). Public accountability is an essential precondition for the democratic process to work, because it provides citizens and their representatives with the information they need to judge the propriety and effectiveness of government.

The findings of this study suggest that it is necessary to define and evaluate public services and public service organizations in greater detail. Clear channels of communication between government and citizens are becoming fundamental. New modes of governance that are more citizen-oriented will be a step in that direction (Klijn, 2008; Pestoff, 2008). The attention is now on NPG (Osborne, 2006), with its emphasis on partnership, networking (Klijn, 2008) and lateral modes of organization, rather than the vertical command and control forms that typify NPM (Newman, 2001). NPG also takes a more pragmatic view of public services that can be delivered publicly and privately. A more general concept of public governance (Osborne, 2006) often therefore incorporates administration, stakeholder pluralism, management within networks and legitimacy (Frederickson, 1999). These new modes of governance may help to address the accountability deficit in the governance of Italian and Norwegian public services structures. The analysis shows that accountability tools are often introduced through pilot projects, or to build support for more inclusive and transparent governance incrementally (Bovens, Schillemans, and 't Hart, 2008).

The lack of accountability has been a major concern, particularly with regard to the privatization process (Braithwaite, 2006). Mandatory codes of ethics are not enough, but they provide a good starting point. However, other means are surely needed to promote ethical behaviors in public services. Greater levels of citizen participation through a bottom-up process may complete the complex process of building codes with shared vision, values and interests. Public service providers have many stakeholders and are particularly visible to citizens. Issues of legitimacy and citizen involvement are growing in importance, and the use of codes of ethics may help to legitimize the actions of public officials, ensuring that their effects fall within the norms of society.

CONCLUSIONS AND FUTURE RESEARCH DIRECTIONS

Ethics and accountability have become ever more prominent in the debate on governance in recent decades. There is a perception that standards in public life are in decline, and existing ethical structures have not been well implemented. This raises questions about the costs of misconduct by those who are entrusted with upholding the public interest. This chapter has shown that the perception of a fall in public standards is linked to the shifting role of the state, which is undergoing enormous changes.

This chapter has shown that privatization was a starting point in the improvement of public services, but this process has now resulted in public service providers still being owned (totally or partly) by the state, often in the absence of effective market competition. The most relevant issue that arises from cases of partial privatization process relates to ethics and accountability to the citizens. The implementation of an effective ethical structure is necessary. To this end, a code of ethics represents an important tool. In order to verify the effectiveness of ethical structures in the Italian and Norwegian state-owned companies that providing public services and goods, their codes of ethics were explored using content analysis. The results led us to some interesting conclusions. Regardless of the contextual and historical differences in which the privatization process has developed in the two countries, better implementation of ethical structures is urgently needed. Indeed, it emerged that public service providers and their owners are under pressure to implement reforms, and the alternative offered by co-production could be a reasonable and effective way of including the citizens in the production and/or provision of public services. This may help to overcome the critical issues related to the use of privatization and business-style methods. However, it is important to note that co-production involves different dimensions (economic, social, political and service-specific participation) and, if it is to be considered a reasonable alternative to partial privatization, further analyses and elaborations are needed.

The results and findings of this study suggest that although the Italian and the Norwegian contexts have been characterized by different drivers toward privatization, and the companies still owned by the government (through its ministry in the case of Italy and its ministries in the case of Norway) have introduced codes of ethics, actions to implement ethical and accountable procedures remain sporadic, unstructured and have only recently been introduced in both countries. The lack of accountability is the main weakness of the governance structure of these companies. This study therefore contributes to the ongoing debate on privatization and, in particular, on the ethical concerns related to partial privatization processes.

The cross-country comparison allowed us to define common trends in the privatization process of two European countries. The comparison between the Norwegian and the Italian privatization processes has highlighted that despite many political, institutional and cultural differences between the two countries, partial privatization has been the outcome in both cases. New models have recently been proposed that challenge NPM (see Osborne, 2006) and new paradigms for government activity, policy making and service delivery are emerging—such as NPG (Osborne, 2009) and NPS (Denhardt and Denhardt, 2000)—which could have significant implications for public service managers, as alternatives to both traditional public administration and NPM. They are based on the idea that the relationship between the government and its citizens is not the same as that between a private-sector business and its customers.

In particular, the NPG perspective includes many modes of governance, such as joined-up governance, network governance, cooperation and co-production. Co-production indicates the importance of the changing relationship between citizens and state, and it seems a reasonable alternative to the partial privatization of public services. Indeed, by developing new ways for citizens to participate in the production and/or provision of public services, it will be possible to support a new theory of public administration that is more appropriate for citizens living in democratic societies. In this sense, NPG offers co-production as a valid alternative to privatization, because it relies on citizens actively participating in the governance of the services that they depend on in their daily lives and it is characterized by a combination of public service agents and citizens who contribute to the provision of public services. Given the limits of the privatization processes in Italy and Norway to date, conflicts of interest and corruption require greater public sector accountability. Public accountability is an essential precondition for the democratic process to work, because it provides citizens and their representatives with the information needed to judge the propriety and effectiveness of government.

By identifying and investigating these aspects, the chapter explicitly fills the gap in the literature that has called for more studies that focus on ethical and accountability concerns (Bozeman, 2007) in relation to privatization. Moreover, developing ways to produce public services that include citizens as key actors in the overall process may help to overcome some of the accountability and ethical gaps that characterize the current situation in many countries (including Italy and Norway). This can only be done by facilitating citizens to participate in that process (co-production) through appropriate incentives and by enhancing their involvement and engagement vis-à-vis other actors (service providers and local communities). In this way, it may be possible to overcome many of the ethical and accountability problems that characterize the relationship between service providers and citizens/users today.

NOTES

1. Over the past few years several SOCs have been transferred to the Ministry of Trade and Industry. This ministry is now in the process of becoming a more specialized ownership ministry.

APPENDIX

Table 17.1   Companies Owned by the MEF in Italy (2008)

Company	Ministry	%
Alitalia	MEF	49.9%
Enel	MEF	21.1%[1]
Eni	MEF	20.3%[2]
Finmeccanica	MEF	33.7%
Anas	MEF	100.0%
Arcus	MEF	100.0%
CDP	MEF	70.0%
Cinecittà Holding	MEF	100.0%
Coni Servizi	MEF	100.0%
Consap	MEF	100.0%
Consip	MEF	100.0%
Enav	MEF	100.0%
Eur	MEF	90.0%
Ferrovie dello Stato	MEF	100.0%
Fintecna	MEF	100.0%
GSE	MEF	100.0%
IPZS	MEF	100.0%
Italia Lavoro	MEF	100.0%
Poste Italiane	MEF	65.0%[3]
RAI	MEF	99.6%
Sace	MEF	100.0%
Sicot	MEF	100.0%
Sogesid	MEF	100.0%
Sogin	MEF	100.0%
Sviluppo Italia	MEF	100.0%

Source: Calabrò, 2010.
1. DP also holds 17.36% in Enel.
2. CDP also holds 9.99% in Eni.
3. CDP also holds 35.0% in Poste Italiane.

Table 17.2 Companies with Sectoral Policy Objectives in Norway

Company	Ministry	%
Avinor AS	Ministry of Transport and Communications	100.0%
Bjørnøen AS	Ministry of Trade and Industry	100.0%
Enova SF	Ministry of Petroleum and Energy	100.0%
Gassco AS	Ministry of Petroleum and Energy	100.0%
Gassnova SF	Ministry of Petroleum and Energy	100.0%
Innovasjon Norge	Ministry of Trade and Industry	100.0%
Itas amb AS	Ministry of Justice and Ministry of Labour and Social Inclusion	53.4%
Kings Bay AS	Ministry of Trade and Industry	100.0%
KITH	Ministry of Health and Care Services/ Ministry of Labour and Social Inclusion	80.5%
Norfund	Ministry of Foreign Affairs	100.0%
Norsk Eiendomsinformasjon AS	Ministry of Justice and the Police	100.0%
Norsk Rikskringkasting AS	Ministry of Culture and Church Affairs	100.0%
Norsk samfunnsvit- enskapelig datatjeneste AS	Ministry of Education and Research	100.0%
Norsk Tipping AS	Ministry of Culture and Church Affairs	100.0%
Petoro AS	Ministry of Petroleum and Energy	100.0%
Simula Research Laboratory AS	Ministry of Education and Research	80.0%
SIVA SF	Ministry of Trade and Industry	100.0%
Statnett SF	Ministry of Petroleum and Energy	100.0%
Statskog SF	Ministry of Agriculture and Food	100.0%
UNINETT AS	Ministry of Education and Research	100.0%
Universitetssenteret på Svalbard AS	Ministry of Education and Research	100.0%
AS Vinmonopolet	Ministry of Health and Care Services	100.0%

Source: Calabrò, 2010.

REFERENCES

Alford, J. 1998. A public management road less travelled: Clients as co-producers of public services. *Australian Journal of Public Administration* 57 (4): 128–137.

Argento, D., G. Grossi, T. Tagesson, and S. O. Collin. 2010. The "externalisation" of local public service delivery: Experience in Italy and Sweden. *International Journal of Public Policy* 5 (1): 41–56.

Bjorvatn, K., and T. Soreide. 2005. Corruption and privatization. *European Journal of Political Economy* 21 (1): 903–914.

Bognetti, G., and L. Robotti. 2007. The provision of local public services through mixed enterprises: The Italian case. *Annals of Public and Cooperative Economics*, 78(3): 415–437.

Bondy K., D. Matten, and J. Moon. 2004. The adoption of voluntary codes of conduct in MNCs: A three-country comparative study. *Business and Society Review*, 109(4): 449–477.

Bovaird, T. 2007. Beyond engagement and participation: User and community co-production of public services. *Public Administration Review* 67 (5): 846–860.

Bovens, M., T. Schillemans, and P. 't Hart. 2008. Does public accountability work? An assessment tool. *Public Administration* 86 (1): 225–242.

Bozeman, B. 2002. Public-value failure: when efficient markets may not do. *Public Administration Review* 62 (2): 145–161.

Bozeman, B. 2007. *Public Values and Public Interest: Counterbalancing Economic Individualism.* Washington DC: Georgetown University Press.

Bozeman, B. 2009. Public values theory: Three big questions. *International Journal of Public Policy* 4 (5): 369–375.

Braithwaite, J. 2006. Accountability and responsibility through restorative justice. In M. Dowdle, ed., *Public Accountability: Designs, Dilemmas and Experiences.* Cambridge, UK: Cambridge University Press.

Cafferata, R. 1995. Italian state owned holdings, privatization and the single market. *Annals of Public and Cooperative Economics* 66 (4): 401–429.

Calabrò, A. 2010. *Governance Structures & Mechanisms in Public Service Organizations. Theories, Evidence and Future Directions.* Rome: University of Rome Tor Vergata, Department of Business Studies, Ph.D. Dissertation.

Christensen, T. 2003. Narratives of Norwegian governance: elaborating the strong state tradition. *Public Administration* 81 (1): 163–190.

Christensen, T., and P. Lægreid. 2001. New Public Management: Undermining political control? In T. Christensen, and P. Lægreid, eds., *New Public Management. The Transformation of Ideas and Practice.* Aldershot, UK: Ashgate, pp. 93–120.

Christensen, T., and P. Lægreid. 2009. Public management reform in Norway: Reluctance and tensions. In G. Shaun, and W. Joe, eds., *International Handbook of Public Management Reform.* Cheltenham, UK: Edward Elgar.

Denhardt, R. B., and J. V. Denhardt. 2000. The New Public Service: Serving rather than steering. *Public Administration Review* 60 (6): 549–559.

Frederickson, H. G. 1999. Public ethics and the new managerialism. *Public Integrity* 1 (3): 265–278.

Groot, T., and T. Budding. 2008. New Public Management's current issues and future prospects. *Financial Accountability and Management* 24 (1): 1–13.

Guthrie, J., and L. Parker. 1990. Corporate social disclosure practice: A comparative international analysis. *Advances in Public Interest Accounting* 3 (1): 159–173.

Hartley, J. 2005. Innovation in governance and public services: past and present. *Public Money and Management* 25 (1): 27–34.

Hefetz, A., and M. Warner. 2004. Privatization and its reverse: explaining the dynamics of the government contracting process. *Journal of Public Administration Research and Theory* 14 (2): 171–190.

Holst, O. 1981. *Content Analysis for the Social Sciences and Humanities.* London: Addison-Wesley.

Hondeghem, A. 1998. *Ethics and Accountability in a context of Governance and New Public Management.* Amsterdam: IOS Press.

Kikeri, S., and J. Nellis. 2001. *Privatisation in Competitive Sectors: The Record so Far' in mimeo, Private Sector Advisory Services.* Washington DC: World Bank.

Klijn, E. H. 2008. Governance and governance networks in Europe. *Public Management Review* 10 (4): 505–525.

Krippendorff, K. 1980. *Content Analysis: An Introduction to Its Methodology.* London: Sage.

Lawton, A. 1998. *Ethical Management for the Public Services.* Buckingham: Open University Press.

Maesschalck, J. 2004. The impact of New Public Management reforms on public servants' ethics: toward a theory. *Public Administration* 82 (2): 465–489.

Megginson, W. L., and M. N. Jeffry. 2001. From state to market: A survey of empirical studies on privatization. *Journal of Economic Literature* 2 (1): 321–389.

Millward, R. 2005. *Private and Public Enterprise in Europe. Energy, Telecommunications and Transport 1830–1990.* Cambridge, UK: Cambridge University Press.

Newman, J. 2001. *Modernising Governance: New Labour, Policy and Society.* London: Sage.

Norwegian Ministry of Trade and Industry. 2008. *The State Ownership Report 2008,* www.ownershipreport.net.

Organisation for Economic Co-Operation and Development. 2000. *Privatisation, Competition and Regulation.* Paris: Centre for Co-operation with Non-Members.

Organisation for Economic Co-Operation and Development. 2005. *Managing Conflict of Interest in the Public Sector: A Toolkit.* Paris: Centre for Co-operation with Non-Members.

O'Dwyer, B., and G. Madden. 2006. Ethical codes of conduct in Irish companies: a survey of code content and enforcement procedures. *Journal of Business Ethics* 63 (3): 217–236.

Osborne, S. P. 2006. The new public governance? *Public Management Review* 8 (3): 377–387.

Osborne, S. P. 2009. Delivering public services: are we asking the right questions? *Public Money and Management* 29 (1): 5–7.

Ostrom, E. 1996. Crossing the great divide: co-production, synergy, and development. *World Development,* 24 (6): 1073–1087.

Parker, D., and D. Saal. 2003. *International Handbook on Privatization.* Cheltenham, UK: Edward Elgar.

Pestoff, V. 1992. Cooperative social services: an alternative to privatization. *Journal of Consumer Policy* 15 (1): 21–45.

Pestoff, V. 2008. Citizens as co-producers of welfare services: Childcare in eight European countries. *Public Management Review* 8 (4): 503–520.

Rice, P. L., and D. Ezzy. 1999. *Qualitative Research Methods: A Health Focus.* Oxford, UK: Oxford University Press.

Riffe, D., S. Lacy, and F. Fico. 1998. *Analyzing Media Messages Using Quantitative Content Analysis in Research.* London: Lawrence Erlbaum Associates.

Saraceno, P. 1981. Il sistema delle partecipazioni statali. *Economia e politica industriale,* 29(1): 35–71.

Securities and Exchange Commission. 2003. *Final Rule: Disclosure Required by Sections 406 and 407 of the Sarbanes Oxley Act of 2002.* Release Nos. 33–8177, 34–47235.

Smith, R. F. I., E. Anderson, and J. Teicher. 2004. Toward Public Value? *Australian Journal of Public Administration* 63 (4): 14–15.

Stenbacka, C. 2001. Qualitative research requires quality concepts of its own. *Management Decision* 39 (7): 551–555.

Stoker, G. 2006. Public value management: A new narrative for networked governance? *American Review of Public Administration* 36 (1): 41–57.

Strom, K. 2003. Parliamentary democracy and delegation. In K. Strom, W. Müller, and T. Bergman, eds., *Delegation and Accountability in Parliamentary Democracies*. Oxford, UK: Oxford University Press, pp. 55–109.

Van Wart, M., and E. M. Berman. 1999. Contemporary public sector productivity values. *Public Productivity and Management Review* 22 (3): 326–348.

Yin, R. K. 2003. *Applications of Case Study Research*. Thousand Oaks, CA: Sage.

18 The Challenges of Co-Management for Public Accountability

Lessons from Flemish Child Care

Diederik Vancoppenolle
and Bram Verschuere

INTRODUCTION

Numerous scholars (Gormley and Balla, 2004; Brandsen and Pestoff, 2006; Defourny and Pestoff, 2008; Heinrich, 2008; Pestoff and Brandsen, 2010; Macmillan, 2010) have argued that public services are increasingly being delivered by third sector organizations. The new public management (NPM) belief that service provision by nongovernmental actors may be more efficient, effective and customer-oriented compared to public service provision by governmental actors might have intensified this trend. But even in countries where nonprofit organizations traditionally have played a major role in delivering public services, the extent, the context and nature of the involvement of nonprofit organizations in service provision—further named co-management (Brandsen and Pestoff, 2006)—have been changing as a result of societal evolutions and public service reforms (Osborne, 2006; Pestoff and Brandsen, 2009).[1] Nowadays, nonprofit organizations often face a quasi-market environment (Bode, 2006; Kumar and Brandsen, 2008) in which commercial organizations also operate. Next, the nature of the relations between government and third parties seems to have changed due to the increased focus on efficiency and effectiveness. Kumar (1997) talks about the contracting state, in which the state becomes a purchaser with private providers; Anheier (2005) mentions purchase-of-services contracts; Smith and Grønbjerg (2006) mention the rise of result-oriented and contractual relations between "funder" and "fundee;" Pestoff and Brandsen state that "long term relationships based on trust have been replaced by short-term, contract-based relationships, changing the nature of the government-third sector partnership" (2009, 2).

Various implications of these evolutions in co-management have already been described and analyzed.[2] Some studies focused on the changes for the steering government that had to replace its governing activities by a kind of governance (see Ouchi, 1991; Heinrich and Lynn 2000; Paquet, 2001; Hodges, 2005), others pointed at the consequences of co-management for service delivery and for the nonprofit organizations (see for instance, Brandsen and Van Hout, 2006; Smith and Grønbjerg, 2006; Macmillan, 2010). A particularly interesting strand of the literature discusses the consequences of co-management for the notion of public accountability. Several scholars (Guttman and Willner, 1976; Salomon, 1989; Stone, 1995; Gilmour and Jensen, 1998; Mulgan, 2002; Hodge and Coghill, 2004; Kennedy, 2006) have warned for the implications of the contracting out trend in public administration, while others have been studying the rise of new accountability relations and mechanisms, either replacing or complementing the traditional vertical accountability relation with more horizontal mechanisms (see for instance, Kumar, 2003; Bovens, 2005; Oude Vrielink et al., 2009). However, it is surprising to state that the empirical basis of this research strand is rather poor, as also Hodge and Coghill (2004) and Pestoff (2010) have argued.[3] A lot of claims about the impact of co-management for public accountability were made, but only few studies (see for instance, Hodge and Coghill, 2004) tried to verify their validity. Is co-management really threatening (the traditional form of) public accountability? Have traditional accountability mechanisms been complemented or changed by new mechanisms? In what way are new patterns of service provision by public, nonprofit and/or for-profit organizations challenging public accountability?

In order to fill this gap in the literature, this chapter will address these questions by making an in-depth case study of service provision practices in Flemish child care. We chose this case as nonprofit organizations provide the largest share of child care places in Flanders, as they increasingly operate in a quasi-market environment where commercial for-profit organizations also offer a lot of child care services. Public accountability in this field was recently challenged by two studies, one about the practices of subsidized service providers and one about the search process of parents.

The chapter is structured as follows. First, we define the concept of public accountability and analyze the challenges that—according to several scholars—are posed by the evolutions in co-management in order to refine our research questions. Second, we present the complicated organization of the service provision field in Flemish child care and analyze the main accountability relations and mechanisms. Third, we describe two undesired practices that were recently observed in the child care service provision. Fourth, we question to what extent these disadvantages for (some) users are related to dysfunctional/inadequate accountability relations between the actors involved in service provision. We conclude with a summary of our empirical findings, and with raising some issues for further debate about the challenges of the involvement of public and private actors in service delivery, which go beyond our particular case.

PUBLIC ACCOUNTABILITY AND THE CHALLENGES OF CO-MANAGEMENT

Several authors (see for instance, Core, 1993; Mulgan and Uhr, 2001; Bovens, 2005; Kooiman and Jentoft, 2009) have tried to define public accountability.

Accountability is about the fact that an actor feels an obligation to explain and to justify his or her conduct to some significant other (Bovens, 2005), it is "a relationship in which one party, the holder of accountability, has the right to seek information about, to investigate and to scrutinize the actions of another party, the giver of accountability" (Mulgan, 2002, 3). Public accountability, however, is far more difficult to define, as the public sector is notable for the extensiveness of its accountability demands.

In its most simple form, public accountability is exercised by voters when they are called on to determine who holds the office as the government of the day (Mulgan and Uhr, 2001, 154). This basic—constitutional—form of public accountability can be further operationalized as a series of hierarchical accountability relationships between several actors.

> Citizens transfer their sovereignty to political representatives who, in turn confide their trust in a Cabinet. Cabinet ministers delegate or mandate most of their powers to more or less independent agencies and public bodies. The agencies and civil servants at the end of the line spend billions of taxpayers money and use their discretionary power to grant permits and benefits. At the end of the line of accountability relations stand the citizens who judge the performance of the government and can sanction their political representatives by voting the rascals out. Each of these principals in the chain of delegation wants to control the exercise of the transferred powers by holding the agents to account. (Bovens, 2005, 192)

Given the size and nature of the public sector reforms that were undertaken during the last few decades, this basic model came under severe pressure. The ministerial accountability was challenged by NPM reforms toward more autonomous agencies (Glynn and Perkins, 1997; Bovens, 2005), but the privatization and the contracting out of public services toward private for-profit or nonprofit organizations complicated accountability far more (Gilmour and Jensen, 1998). Guttman and Willner (1976) spoke about the *"invisible bureaucracy"* of private, for-profit, and nonprofit firms that contracted with the government to deliver public services, Salamon (1989) even stated that the U.S. welfare state was not run by the state at all, but by a host of nongovernmental "third parties." Questions arose if the acts of these private actors were still public (Kennedy, 2001). "Political efforts to keep government responsible and accountable—politically, fiscally and constitutionally—depend on the ability to identify government and to recognize when the state has acted" (Kennedy, 2006, 68). A second point of concern was that the complex chain of (contractual) relations might complicate efforts to make the third parties and the government more accountable. "How many links can be added in a chain of funding and authority (between the source and the use of funds) before public purpose and accountability are lost?" (Heinrich, 2008, 2). Who has to account for what practices in a chain of relations?

However, over time, other forms of accountability developed. Bovens (2005), for instance, saw an urge in many Western democracies for more direct and explicit accountability relations between public agencies on the one hand and clients, citizens and civil society on the other and discerned a trend toward a more diversified and pluralistic set of accountability relationships, including the establishment of ombudsmen, auditors and independent inspectors. Kjær (2004, 55) argued that the traditional vertical political relations and interactions had to be supplemented with lateral relations and interactions among institutions, professionals and users, who become politically integrated into, and made publicly accountable for, the common and public concerns. Mulgan (2002, 6–7) stated that the central (ministerial) accountability channel often is supplemented by a number of other accountability mechanisms, including the accountability of public servants directly to parliamentary committees, to independent accountability agencies, such as the auditor-general, the ombudsman, tribunals and the courts, to citizens via complaints and appeal procedures.

Moreover, the NPM—at least partly—strengthened some accountability relations by its focus on results and value for money. Scholars such as Smith and Grønbjerg argued that the increasing predominance of performance contracts and fee-for-service reimbursement policies meant that government "has even more powerful tools by which to control nonprofits, although not in as bureaucratic a fashion as under traditional purchase-of-service agreements" (2006, 227). Kennedy (2006) stated that the contracting out obscured, but did not alter the fact that government is choosing, directing and paying for those services. "The government funder still enjoys varying degrees of control over admission criteria, service delivery and discharge decisions for clients of the contracted services" (Anheier, 2005, 287).

Given the multiplicity of accountability demands and relations, we use the definition of Mulgan and Uhr (2001) that public accountability includes "a range of accountability practices, covering all types of accountability, which for important reasons of democratic legitimacy are acted out in public with the aim of generating a public record of performance open to community examination and debate" (Mulgan and Uhr, 2001, 154). Studying public accountability in a situation of co-management thus requires an analysis of a complex set of accountability relationships between different actors. As it would be difficult to study all relations and mechanisms in one chapter, we chose to limit our analysis to those relations/practices that are challenged the most by the involvement of third parties (nonprofit organizations and commercial for-profit companies): (1) the relation between users and the service providers, (2) the relation between service providers and the public service organization that is "contracting out" the public services (hereafter called "oversight authority") and (3) the relation between the user and the oversight authority. Each of them will be considered briefly in this chapter.

First, we will question how individual service providers can be held accountable, vis-à-vis the users/clients, for their service provision. The key issue for the users of the service (or their representatives) is to have sufficient access to services of good quality at a reasonable cost. In an ideal scenario, users can go to court whenever their needs are unsatisfactory addressed by service providers. In many instances, however, users of service provision have few opportunities to hold the organization accountable. This means that, in terms of Leat (1988), accountability will often be at most "explanatory" and "responsive," by which the organization explains and gives account to the clients or the users for what they are doing (explanatory accountability), or by which the organization takes into account the views of the clients after having consulted these clients in one or another way (responsive accountability). There is also, in normal circumstances, no room for sanctioning in the relationship between organization and client. The only options that users usually have are to complain to the organization or to the oversight authority, or to quit the service provider in case. However, neither strategy is without risk, as both may impair the good relationship between service provider and client, especially for relational goods (Van de Donk, 2008). Thus, the client may end up without any service at all. This is especially risky in a field where the demand for services is larger than the supply.

Whenever state, nonprofit and for-profit organizations are providing public service, other accountability problems may arise as the characteristics of the accountability relation may differ between different kinds of service providers. Public, nonprofit and commercial organizations may all have, to a certain extent, different bottom lines (Eikenberry and Kluver, 2004). We might, for example, expect that commercial service providers will be driven by a profit motive, besides their motivation to deliver good services to the clients. This may result, for instance, in a higher selectivity in their admission policies. So, commercial providers may deliberately focus on clients with higher financial status, while underprivileged parts of society will be underrepresented. But, in subsidized organizations the reverse may hold true. In terms of accountability toward clients, we can, therefore, expect that nonprofit and public providers will pay less attention to the demands of their shareholders to make a financial surplus, compared to commercial organizations. We also might expect that public service providers will pay more attention to the interest of the government.

Next, we can also question how individual public service providers can be steered and held accountable by the regulatory authorities. The key stake for the oversight authorities, besides the quality of service provision, is the compliance of the service provider with the requirements of the policy framework. This is all the more the case in an environment that is heavily regulated and subsidized by governmental means. Oversight authorities that subsidize service providers hold them accountable for the correct provision of services by their organization, with attention to regulations that apply in the sector. Here, we can expect a difference in accountability between those organizations that are heavily subsidized and those that are less subsidized. In return for subsidies, the oversight authorities will expect compliance with the governmental policy in terms of quality of service provision and accessibility to the service for citizens. We therefore might expect public and subsidized non-profit service providers to place greater focus on the demands of the oversight authorities than unsubsidized commercial service providers.

A final accountability relation exists between the oversight authorities and the citizen/clients of the service provision. Although the oversight agency does not deliver any service by itself, it often will be considered as the responsible authority by users, many of whom are not aware of the administrative details of the service provision network. Many users may expect an oversight authority to solve service delivery problems, either by intervening in the activities of private actors or by redrawing the structures and rules of the service provision network. Users may see the oversight authority as a neutral partner. This relationship can be characterized by several mechanisms and instruments that illustrate the responsiveness of the oversight agency toward the citizen/client of the public service. Through annual reports, for example, oversight authorities may inform clients about their activities. Another instrument is the installation of a complaint procedure, in which government is willing to address complaints and to give feedback about interventions, or to compensate for undesired outcomes or faults that were made under their responsibility.

The strongest form of accountability of government toward its citizens is to guarantee the protection of basic rights or to guarantee the existence of basic public service delivery. In many policy fields, basic rights for citizens are defined by (constitutional) law, such as the right for education, decent living conditions and public safety. Such basic rights imply that government is responsible for sufficient and qualitative service provision in all these fields. This includes the organization of an educational system, the organization of a welfare system that guarantees decent living conditions for every citizen, and the organization of a police and army force to guarantee and enforce safety in society. This can either be pursued by direct governmental service provision (e.g., army and police), or by service provision by third parties, one that is subsidized and regulated by government or its agencies (e.g., the welfare system in many Western countries). A system of basic rights or basic services substantially strengthens the position of the user, as the user can claim service provision as a legally defined right (Verschuere, 2006). This implies that users can directly hold the oversight authority accountable for not fulfilling their basic needs.

Having considered the implications that the co-management of service provision practices can pose on public accountability, we now turn to our case analysis to explore if co-management really is challenging public accountability in practice. We will focus on two questions in particular:

1. Is co-management really weakening the accountability relation between private service providers and oversight authority or is this relation perhaps being strengthened by the use of other accountability mechanisms?
2. Is public accountability challenged by the fact that public services are simultaneously delivered by organizations of different types (public, nonprofit and for-profit)?

In order to study this in practice, we have chosen the provision of child care in Flanders as an illustration of these accountability relations.

THE ORGANIZATION OF FLEMISH CHILD CARE

A Heterogeneous Field of Service Providers

Child care policy belongs to the authority of the Flemish Minister for Welfare, assisted by the public agency *Kind en Gezin*. *Kind en Gezin* does not deliver any child care service itself; it only regulates, subsidizes and controls child care services organized by private organizations or local governments. It offers information about the service provision landscape and the child care providers to parents, but it does not provide detailed guidance to parents who are searching a place in care for their children. The child care service provision landscape in Flanders is heterogeneous, as it covers organizations of different types and labels. There is a variety of actors or organizations in the Flemish child care field that can either be viewed from a sectoral, financial or supervision perspective, as seen in Table 18.1. This contributes to the complexity of the situation, particularly for parents who are trying to make sense of the difference between providers and to choose the right one for their child or children.

First, there are three main sectors involved in child care delivery in Flanders. Child care can be provided by either *local government*, by *private nonprofit* organizations (often embedded in religious or ideological networks), or by *private for-profit* organizations (commercial initiatives). As seen in Table 18.1, each of the three sectors represents more than 20 percent of the total number of places available in Flanders. The nonprofit sector has the largest share (50 percent), and the commercial sector is more important than the public sector (29 percent vs. 21 percent of the total share). The child care field in Flanders is thus a typical example of co-management of public service provision between different sectors (Brandsen and Pestoff 2006). Moreover, providers can either be subsidized or nonsubsidized.

The table also shows that most of the nonprofit providers are subsidized, implying that the Flemish child care field is a typical example of a government subsidized field in which the nonprofit sector is a heavily government funded sector (Anheier, 2005; Salamon and Anheier, 1998). Second, there

Table 18.1   Number of Places per Sector and per Type in Flemish Child Care

| | Recognized and subsidized child care | | Supervised non-subsidized child care | | |
	Day centers	Family care	Day centers	Family care	Total places per sector (%)
Nonprofit	8,958	21,766	3,913	-	34,637 (50%)
Profit (commercial)	-	-	13,390	6,859	20,249 (29%)
Public (local govt)	4,481	8,913	1,153	-	14,547 (21%)
Total places per type (%)	13,439	30,679	18,456	6,859	69,433 (100%)
	44,118 (64%)		25,315 (36%)		

is also a difference between *residential* care, on the one hand, and *family type* care at the home of the care provider, on the other hand. Most places (54 percent) are of the family care type that is often provided by subsidized family care services.

Last but not least, there is the difference between *recognized and subsidized* child care providers, on the one hand, and *supervised but not subsidized* child care providers, on the other hand. The first receive governmental subsidies for their personnel and for equipment, while the latter have to finance their personnel cost and other expenses (equipment such as beds, furniture and toys) with their own means. Only public and nonprofit organizations can be recognized and subsidized. All commercial care providers are supervised, but not subsidized. However, given scarce governmental resources, some public and nonprofit organizations also set up their own supervised care provision, without any public subsidies. Table 18.1 shows that in 2007, about two-third of the child care supply was delivered by recognized and subsidized child care providers, while 36 percent of the providers was supervised but not subsidized.

The difference between subsidized and supervised care providers does matter for children and parents, as it *may* lead to differences in quality, because supervised care providers are less heavily regulated by the government with regard to the qualifications of their personnel. Also the parental fee *may* vary between service providers of different types. Supervised child care providers are free to determine the parental fees, while subsidized child care providers are obliged to calculate an individual parental contribution based on the taxable income of the parents.

Next, there *may* also be differences concerning accessibility, because supervised child care providers can determine their own admission criteria, while subsidized child care providers are legally bound by strict admission rules. The latter may not discriminate families or children based on cultural, sexual, racial, ethnical or religious grounds, and they have to apply the legal priority criteria whenever they have to choose between different requests. According to these rules, subsidized day centers and family care services are obliged to give prior admission to the following groups: working parents who cannot—due to their jobs—take care of their children during the day, children for whom it would be good for social or pedagogical reasons to stay in a formal care setting outside the family, children of parents with the lowest income and children of single parents. Within these boundaries, subsidized child care providers may include other criteria or may give priority to one or another of these priority rules, as there is no hierarchy established between them.

Kind en Gezin pays subsidies, according to the number of places it has recognized for a child care provider. To get the right amount of subsidies, subsidized child care providers have to give information to *Kind en Gezin* about the number and kind of care moments, the total amount of parental contributions they received, and the names and age category of every member of their personnel. It is important to note they do not have to pass on names of children, nor private information about the financial or relational situation of the parents. However, the fact that *Kind en Gezin* does not ask this kind of information does not mean that these aspects are not controlled. Rather, they are controlled by a distinct Inspection Agency of the Flemish government. Child care providers are inspected once every five years by means of onsite visits when the inspectors examine if the child care provider is fulfilling all of the legal requirements with regard to the employment of qualified personnel, the permanent supervision of the children, the number of children in relation to the present staff, and so on. The inspectors also assess the child care provider's information policy, and will ask them, when necessary, to improve their service quality and practice. If they fail to do this, *Kind en Gezin* can withdraw their recognition as a subsidized provider.

Taken altogether, the service provision field in Flemish child care is characterized by a certain level of complexity, in particular for parents. Families are confronted with a vast diversity of care providers (either group or family care), organized by public, nonprofit or commercial organizations, sometimes subsidized, sometimes only supervised. There is no public body to support or help parents in their search for a child care place, because the public agency *Kind en Gezin* does not offer any direct service of that kind to parents.

Accountability Relations and Mechanisms in Flemish Child Care

In the description of the service provision field already some accountability relations and mechanisms were mentioned, but we will now analyze them in more detail in this section. Figure 18.1 depicts the amount and types of accountability relations that exist in Flemish child care.

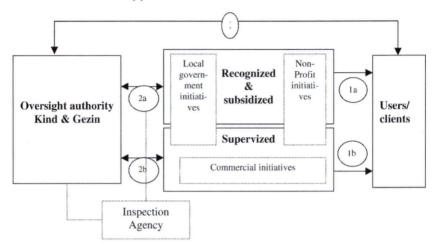

Figure 18.1   Current accountability relations in Flemish child care.

The accountability relation between *users and service providers* (1) is characterized by the fact that a difference exists between the accountability of subsidized (1a) and supervised (1b) organizations. Users sign agreements with each type of service provider, but subsidized organizations are more strictly bound by legal regulations than commercial for-profit providers, implying that public accountability should be better guaranteed by subsidized service providers. Obliged by the regulations of the Flemish government (*Kind en Gezin*), subsidized organizations, for instance, should inform parents about their accessibility policy, have to apply a quality policy, calculate and collect the parental fees according to the legal requirements and inform parents about their internal organization, work methods and procedures.

As there are two types of organizations (subsidized vs. supervised care providers), there are also two accountability relations between the *oversight agency* and *the service providers* (2a + 2b). Both types of service providers have to account for other aspects, and both types are (partly) controlled on a different basis. However, it is important to mention that the decision to recognize and subsidize or to supervise service providers does not imply that real contracts have been signed between the oversight agency and the service providers. Once they fulfill the basic conditions, service providers are authorized to deliver child care for a fixed amount of places, and they are expected to fulfill all the legal requirements. However, no output steering is explicitly foreseen for subsidized organizations, although the amount of the subsidy will be decreased if service providers fail to use of the assigned number of places.

The public accountability of service providers is controlled by *Kind en Gezin* based on the information they receive directly from the service providers themselves. But this information is mainly used to calculate the amount of the subsidies. Also, the information they receive from the Inspection Agency plays an indirect role. The Inspection Agency checks to what extent the service provider is following the legal requirements and is applying all the elaborated procedures. Inspections are held on a regular basis—once in five years—to control each organization, but they can also occur on an ad hoc basis whenever *Kind en Gezin* receives complaints from parents or other stakeholders. The Inspection Agency merely records its comments and observations, but it is up to *Kind en Gezin* to judge the service provider and to decide on the continuation or withdrawal of certificates of supervision and subsidies.

The accountability relation between *oversight authority and the users* (3) is characterized by the presence of a complaint procedure. Citizens/users can complain to *Kind en Gezin* about its work, but also about the practices and services of subsidized and supervised organizations. *Kind en Gezin* maintains an internal service that analyzes the complaints and decides on the cause of them after having heard the involved actors. Eventually, a complaint about a service provider in child care can lead to a visit by the Inspection Agency, which can result in a sanction of the service provider by *Kind en Gezin*. For instance, when service providers miscalculated the parental fee, *Kind en Gezin* can oblige them to reimburse fees. If an organization did not follow the legal requirements with regard to safety rules or the presence of (qualified) personnel, *Kind en Gezin* can withdraw the recognition or the certificate of supervision, making it more difficult if not impossible for an organization to continue their child care services.

FLEMISH CHILD CARE: DYSFUNCTIONAL SERVICE PROVISION?

This overview of the accountability relations in Flemish child care provides the background for our study of how accountability works in practice. We will focus on one important aspect, namely the functioning of waiting lists for places in child care. To do so, we draw on two recent studies that scrutinized the service provision system in Flemish child care. One study investigated the parents' search process; the other analyzed the admission policies of subsidized care providers. Both studies show that child care in Flanders has become dysfunctional because the interests of the users are not safeguarded, which naturally raises important questions of public accountability.

The Search Process of Parents

In 2007, *Kind en Gezin* commissioned a study about the potential problems facing parents when they look for a place in Flemish child care services (Market Analysis and Synthesis, 2007a).[4] The study provides some interesting findings about the start, the intensity and the result of the search process of parents, and about parents' satisfaction with the search process. Sixty-one percent of the families start to look for a place at least ten months before the preferred start of the child care. Families do not restrict their search process to single care provider. On average, each of the questioned families contacts thirteen care providers during the search process. The data show that 20 percent ended with a problematic child care situation. Half of those families that found a place continue to look for another place (with another provider), as the place they found does not completely fit their preferences. The other half of the families did not find a place at all for their child. These families may be confronted with considerable problems, as the parents can no longer fully commit to their job, have to change their work schedule or have to turn down a job or training offer. However, this does not mean that the remaining 80 percent of the parents had an easy search process. About 66 percent state that their search process was difficult or very difficult. Of course these findings are subjective appreciations by the parents, but the fact that their dissatisfaction is so large that it cannot be neglected. The study further showed that there are significant differences in the outcome of the search process for families with a different socioeconomic composition, cultural and educational background. Single-parent families, parents without a full time job and/or parents who do not have Belgian nationality do not find a place as easily as their counterpart families. It is remarkable because these are two of the "excluded" groups that should have prior admission to subsidized care providers, according to the legal priority rules (see admission rules discussed earlier in this chapter).

The Admission Policy of Recognized and Subsidized Child Care Providers

In a second study, the admission policies of subsidized child care providers were analyzed (Market Analysis and Synthesis, 2007b). All subsidized child care providers were sent a written questionnaire. Eighty-nine percent of them completed the questionnaire. The results are rather surprising, as they show that many subsidized child care providers do not fully follow the legal priority rules. A first important finding is that 54 percent of the day care centers refuse a request whenever the request for care does not correspond with a certain minimum number of days. In reality, 73 percent of all day centers expect, as a minimum, the presence of the child for at least 3.5 half days per week. Other important reasons to refuse requests are that "the child is too old" (35 percent), "neither of the parents is working or studying" (19 percent) or "neither of the parents lives in the community" (16 percent). These data indicate that child care providers use additional admission criteria to determine which requests will be taken into consideration and which ones will not. Although it is not forbidden to refuse requests on condition that the decision is not based on discriminatory grounds, these practices at least are questionable. As such, the additional admission criteria applied by child care providers may conflict with the legal priority rules. It may therefore not be surprising that the application of their own admission rules excludes several groups of families, such as families who deliberately decide to take care for their own children for at least two days a week, or families who need formal day care for only one or two days a week. Thus, it is very difficult to obtain part-time child care today in Flanders.

Second, in the study, the care providers had to assess the degree to which a criterion does matter in their decision to give priority to one or another request for child care. Table 18.2 shows the mean scores the providers attribute on a 7-point Likert scale concerning the importance of priority criteria they apply in their admission policy ("1" is "this criterion does not play an important role," "7" means "this criterion does play an important role"). In the table, the priority criteria are ranked with a decreasing order of attributed importance (according to the providers). (Criteria in bold are the legal priority criteria.) We observe that the subsidized child care providers ignore the legal priority rules, at least in part. They often prefer priority criteria other than the legal ones. Giving priority to families who already have a child in the day center or family care service turned out to be the most important priority rule applied by child care providers. This may seem reasonable from a pedagogical and practical perspective, but the criterion conflicts with the legal priority rules. The fact that the chronological criterion of when parents applied (the third criterion in Table 18.2) is so often applied by care providers implies that parents who legally should get priority can only do so if they submitted their request first. Given the nature of the care needs of some of these groups, it is clear that families who have to cope with a crisis or parents who need formal child care to follow job training will be disadvantaged compared to other groups.

Third, to apply the priority rules of their own admission policy, most (but not all) subsidized child care providers work with waiting lists. However, of

Table 18.2   Priority Criteria Applied by Subsidized Care Providers

Criterion	Mean score
Parents already have a child in our care service	6.68
Parent(s) do work in our care service	5.86
Parents applied prior to other parents	5.70
There is a crisis in the family	5.37
Parents had a child in our care provider some time ago	4.79
Parents have a job or are studying	4.66
Parent does not have a partner	4.60
Family has a low income	3.57

all care providers who use a waiting list, only 30 percent of the care providers write down the details of the families on the waiting list. In most cases, only the expected date of birth, the desired start of the care period and the number of care days per week are indicated on the waiting list. This implies that even if the subsidized child care providers would have been willing to apply the legal rules, most of the care providers would not be able to do so, due to a lack of relevant information. A lot of care providers use the chronological criterion, giving the place to the parents who apply first for admission. But the study illustrates that at least some of the care providers apply another (additional) chronology criterion. Whenever a place is available, some care providers offer the place to the parents who contacted them first after the place became available. As a matter of fact, most child care providers (56 percent) seem to expect that parents should take the initiative to contact the care provider on a regular basis to check their chances for a place. Waiting lists thus do not function as absolute rankings that install a fully transparent priority system for families with a registered care need. There are subjective elements—additional to the priority rules—that determine whose care needs will be satisfied first.

DYSFUNCTIONAL SERVICE PROVISION: THE RESULT OF FRAGMENTED ACCOUNTABILITY RELATIONS?

The problems in service delivery that have been documented above can not only be explained by a shortage in child care places. In our opinion, they are also and to a large extent caused by a subtle combination of several dysfunctional or nonexistent accountability relations between the many actors in the field of Flemish child care.

Failing Accountability Relations between Individual Service Providers and Users?

In Flemish child care, users are in a weak position, mainly due to the shortage of child care places. In particular, the demand for subsidized group care places is high, as these places are (in general) the cheapest and best quality places. Parents who find a place in the supervised sector, often tried already to get a subsidized place. All this implies that there is hardly any choice between child care providers, and that users are clearly not in a position to use the exit strategy whenever they are not satisfied with the child care. This leads to a situation in which child care providers *may* not feel really accountable to families looking for a child care place. In many cases, the needs and interests of the provider may determine the admission policy, not the requests by parents, nor the legal criteria. Moreover, child care providers can be expected to attach more importance to relations with other actors/stakeholders than parents looking for a place, like their relationship with parents who already have a child in the day center or family care service or with their personnel. Under such circumstances there is a real risk that the accountability toward (new) clients gets the lowest priority. Next, one can hardly say that the admission policies of most child care providers are transparent. Although child care providers are legally obliged to inform parents about their admission policy and procedures, the research results show that the practice in reality does not correspond to the rhetoric of the written procedures. In particular, the fact that the ranking on the waiting lists is often neglected and that the available place is offered to the first parent who calls are the best examples of the complete lack of transparency and accountability toward the potential users.

Failing Accountability Relations between Service Provider and Oversight Authority

The fact that subsidized child care providers do not respect several legal preconditions also reflects a hampered accountability relation between care providers and the oversight authority. This situation is partly caused by poorly designed instruments and procedures for control, which is the responsibility of the public agency *Kind en Gezin*. First, *Kind en Gezin* requests too little information about the admission policy and procedures of child care providers and/or does not hold them accountable for the poor accessibility for some of the priority groups. Second, the application of the procedures is never controlled, although some elements can be checked easily by the inspectors (e.g., the fact that the waiting lists do not contain any information about the family situation). One could also question whether the infrequency and possible consequences of the inspections visits can be considered as sufficiently important by the child care providers to provoke them to respect the legal priority rules.

Nevertheless, the reasons behind the undesired practices may also point to important shortcomings, or even contradictions, in the legal priority rules. This becomes obvious when we analyze the admission criteria that service providers tend to apply. First, the fact that child care providers give priority to children that attend child care for a sufficient amount of days in a week (at least 3.5 days) seems to illustrate that the child care providers prioritize their own interests. Indeed, for both administrative and financial reasons, it is advantageous for child care providers to have a lot of full-time children to care for. For administrative reasons, the fewer children, the fewer files, the fewer parental contributions have to be calculated and the easier the occupational planning. For financial reasons, it is obvious that the chance to lose subsidies due to an insufficient utilization of the subsidies will be low when most children are inscribed on a (nearly) full-time basis. Moreover, the employment of the staff will be more efficient when the size of the groups is stable on a daily basis. Thus, from the point of view of the providers, there seems to be a trade-off between two kinds of priority rules, as they are expected to attain a high occupation rate to enhance the efficiency of the governmental policy, while they should also ensure that children of families with a reduced or less predictable need for child care are admitted. Also, it is not unimportant that a stable composition of the groups is preferable for small children compared to a situation where they have to face the coming and going of other children who attend their group one day a week, or who only come for a short period each day.

Furthermore, the responsiveness of child care providers towards families looking for a place conflicts with their commitment toward families who already have a child with the child care provider. The fact that parents might have to take their children to several different child care providers before going to work conflicts clearly with other public goals of the child care policy, such as supporting families, to facilitate the work-life balance. However, we should be careful to consider ignoring the legal priority rule by giving prior access to brothers or sisters as a violation of their public responsibility and accountability. Thus, the fact that child care providers do not always respect the existing regulations does not automatically imply that they are neglecting the interests of the clients.

While the de facto inclusion of these two additional admission criteria by child care providers (priority for brothers and sisters, and priority for children that stay for more days per week) might perhaps be interpreted as more or less in line with governmental policy, other criteria applied by the providers clearly seem to be not in line. The observation, for example, that public child care provision, organized by local government, in some cases gives priority to admit their own citizens conflicts with the priority rules set by the Flemish government, although many public service providers are subsidized by Flemish means. The same holds true for providers giving priority to the children of their own personnel.

Failing Accountability Relationship between the Oversight Authority and the Clients

Kind en Gezin has developed several mechanisms to inform clients about their services. They have annual reports and a very informative website, providing a lot of tips for young parents looking for a place. There is also a well-functioning complaint procedure. Whenever parents are dissatisfied with the services of a provider that is supervised or subsidized by *Kind en Gezin*, they can complain to them. *Kind en Gezin* then examines the facts of the complaint and can order an inspection of the service provider, analyzing the validity of the complaint. This complaint procedure can result in a withdrawal of the supervision or the recognition of the service provider. For parents, however, it is very delicate, if not useless, to complain about the admission policy of a particular service provider. First, a complaint may threaten their chances to obtain a child care place. Second, *Kind en Gezin* cannot urge service providers to accept children, because service providers have a lot of discretion in applying the priority rules, making it difficult to point at, or control, irregularities. As long as child care is not a basic right or basic service, such as education or public transport, users can not urge *Kind en Gezin* to provide a child care place whenever they do not find one.

But, in addition to the failing accountability relations previously mentioned, the study about the search process of parents shows that there are also accountability relations lacking in the current service provision landscape. As a matter of fact, public accountability should not only be seen as a one-to-one relation between oversight authority, service provider and user, but it depends also on the cooperation between service providers and on the accountability of the *network* of service providers toward users and toward the oversight authority.

Failing Accountability Relations between the Network of Providers and the Clients

As Flemish child care is delivered by rather autonomous service providers of different sectors, operating in a rather competitive (quasi-market) environment, collaboration between service providers is not very evident. Although they all are forced to participate in a local advisory council on child care, it seems that most service providers are working on their own and do not share nor pass on information about children, families and their care needs to each other. The fact that supervised service providers compete with subsidized initiatives and that commercial and public initiatives seem to have specific (and conflicting) rationales to set up child care services seems to be additional hurdles for cooperation. This lack of cooperation clearly explains to a large extent the difficult search process parents have to face.

Although child care providers are not required to cooperate with other providers, it is clear that users would benefit greatly from collaboration of that kind. The search process for child care would be less frustrating and less time consuming if parents only had to contact a single organization for a place in child care, instead of contacting many. Moreover, child care providers would also profit from such cooperation, because the amount of intakes and administrative files would decrease. Furthermore, a unique contact point would reduce the size of the waiting lists, because there is a lot of double registration, as most children are inscribed on the waiting lists of several providers. This would also make it easier for child care providers to apply their admission criteria. Nevertheless, there is a real risk that individual child care providers are not interested in more cooperation on their own initiative, or for the sake of the users. That would require a shared feeling of responsibility toward the potential users. Hurdles to this may be that care providers do not see themselves as delivering a public service, or the fact that the service delivery field is too heterogeneous to develop a common understanding. But developing a culture of shared responsibility might also require some demands or incentives by the oversight authority.

Failing Accountability Relations between the Network of Providers and the Oversight Authority

Incentives by the oversight authority for greater cooperation between providers are few, because the relationship between the oversight authority and the network of providers is nonexistent. *Kind en Gezin* does not structurally direct the network of child care providers and does not hold them responsible for setting up any form of cooperation that would ameliorate the transparency, efficiency and/or accessibility of the child care supply. Nor does *Kind en Gezin* stimulate any form of collaboration within the bilateral relationship it has with every child care provider. However, it should be mentioned that *Kind en Gezin* did try to foster this type of cooperation between 2007 and 2009 by means of experimental subsidies for so called "Centers for child care projects." However, this kind of network-steering received very little political and financial support once the experiment ended. This can be explained by the fact that these experiments demonstrated that some characteristics of the child care service delivery field itself hinder fruitful collaboration. First, the fact that there is competition between child care providers complicates any collaboration between subsidized and nonsubsidized child care providers. There is, for example, a lot of distrust and anxiety that a unique contact point where parents could apply for child care would threaten the influx of children to commercial care providers. Second, the fact that local governments themselves are a major provider hinders cooperation because they are both a player and a referee at the same time (Verschuere and De Rynck, 2009).

CONCLUSION

We were interested in public accountability, but the empirical basis of such research is rather weak. So, we explored the consequences of co-management for the notion of public accountability by reviewing an in-depth case study of the Flemish child care sector. In the final section, we will discuss the main results of our study, starting with some general observations. Next, we will answer the two questions that formed the basis for our explorative study:

1. Does co-management really weaken the accountability relation between private service providers and oversight authority or is it, perhaps, being strengthened by the use of other accountability mechanisms?
2. Is public accountability challenged by the fact that public services simultaneously are delivered by different types of organizations (public, nonprofit and for-profit)?

General Observations

At first, our study showed that co-management indeed has a lot of consequences and implications for the actors and stakeholders involved: the users or clients of the service provision, the service providing organizations, and the government as a regulator and director of the public services (Ouchi, 1991; Heinrich and Lynn, 2000). For users, the presence of private actors alongside public service providers enhances their freedom of choice, but it may also impair the transparency and the accessibility of the public services. For service providers, their autonomy with regards to the price, quality and accessibility of the services is challenged by the fact that public and private service providers have to operate in the same field, with or without a cooperative relation or in competition with each other. For government, developing relationships with private nonprofit and for-profit organizations requires other instruments and capacities compared to steering public services (Verhoest, Vervloet, and Bouckaert, 2003; Loffler, 2009). It implies at least that governments need to take into account the interests and practices of the private parties when they are elaborating rules and procedures. But the design of right steering and accountability relations is far more challenging. Private parties have to be given a certain degree of autonomy, but—at the same time—their autonomy should be restricted and/or controlled to safeguard the public character of their services.

Next, our analysis confirms that public accountability is a complex concept to study, as it involves a multiplicity of accountability relations between several different actors (i.e., parents, child care providers, inspectors and oversight authorities). The way all these relations are set up and function is important, and the quality of these relationships determines the performance of the public policy and service delivery, as we argue in the previous paragraphs.

Challenges of Co-Management for Public Accountability

Two recent studies illustrated that the interests of the users were not adequately safeguarded in the co-management field of Flemish child care, raising serious questions of public accountability. Contrary to scholars like Heinrich (2008), we did not find that the involvement of third parties lead to a complete loss of public accountability. We share the opinion of Kennedy (2006) that co-management may obscure, but does not suppress the public accountability.

> Where a regulatory scheme substantially limits the options available to the private entity, where it prescribes the goals and limits the acceptable methods for achieving them, the state should bear responsibility for the results. (Kennedy, 2006, 74)

In fact, we think that co-management requires even more public accountability mechanisms, rather than less.

> When the relationship between government and citizen becomes more complex than that between a mere commodity or service provider and its customers, more than market place efficiency is required to hold the government and its proxies and surrogates accountable for their exercise of authority on behalf of the state. (Gilmour and Jensen, 1998, 247)

Nevertheless, our study showed that the undesired policy outcomes were to a large extent caused by a subtle combination of several dysfunctional and non-existent accountability relations between the many actors in the field of Flemish child care. In particular, the accountability relation between the oversight authority and the service providers did not function adequately. Although several scholars have argued that this is the logical consequence of involving private actors in service delivery, we are convinced that this accountability relation is not dysfunctional by definition. It could have functioning better if *Kind en Gezin* required more information from the service providers and if the frequency and intensity of the inspections were increased.

Even if the co-management practices in Flemish child care are not a prototype of the contracting out trend, the government was still able to weigh heavily on service outcomes as it sets the rules to become recognized, supervised and/or subsidized. But our analysis showed that it was apparently not enough to translate accountability relationships in legal requirements. It seems a bit contradictory in times of governance, but the public accountability could have been strengthened if the vertical-hierarchical steering relation would have been tighter, if the rules were made more explicit and if the oversight authority monitored providers more frequently and if it controlled the degree to which the delivered services corresponded to public goals. Or like Taylor stated (1996), "purchasers should not take accountability to users for granted, but need to ensure that appropriate mechanisms are in place."

But co-management did not only challenge the accountability of the oversight authority and/or the relation between the service provider and the oversight authority. It also challenged the accountability of the service providers toward their own public. Moreover, our study showed that "public" accountability is an ambiguous notion, as there might be conflicts between different public accountabilities. Some service providers were willing to break the legal rules to satisfy the needs of their users. It appeared that they felt more accountable to their public than to the public government that subsidized them.

Finally, our study showed that it is not sufficient to strengthen the accountability relations of individual private service providers to increase overall public accountability. We learned from the child care case that oversight authorities need to pay greater attention to the accountability of the service provision network to enhance the transparency of the network and to guarantee the necessary cooperation between different service providers. Public-private service provision networks do challenge the steering role of oversight authorities, often requiring a two-level steering of the service provision field: a direct steering of individual service providers and the network, and/or market steering of the whole service provision field (in a community or region). Therefore, accountability relationships should be established between the network of service providers on the one hand, and the user and oversight authority, on the other hand (see relations 3 and 4 in Figure 18.2).

The involvement of for-profit actors in service delivery may complicate this kind of network steering, but our case analysis shows that it may be necessary to promote this extra level of steering. This implies that the oversight authority should function as a pivotal actor in the public-private service provision network, and must realize the effective "governance" of this network (see Loffler, 2009), directing/regulating the relations between the service providers and between the network of service providers and the users.

As long as the regulatory agency, *Kind en Gezin*, fails to act as a real network manager or market regulator (and hence gives incentives to individual or groups of care providers to cooperate), holding the network of care providers accountable, multiple overlapping waiting lists will continue to exist. In addition, search processes for parents will remain difficult, and the transparency (for users) of the field will remain limited. In the role as network manager, *Kind en Gezin* should at least require some consolidated information about the free places in the environment and information about the length of the waiting lists from the network of care providers. This attention to the challenges of provider networks for accountability is not new. Several scholars have already pointed at the relevance of the accountability of networks (see for instance, Kooiman and Jentoft, 2009),

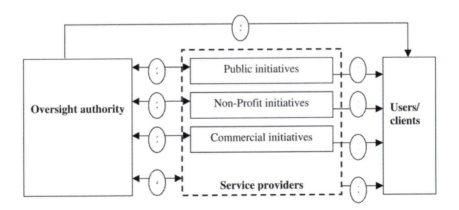

Figure 18.2   Accountability relationships in co-management situations.

but the challenges become increasingly important as the use of co-management develops further. This also means that if co-management is to function smoothly, the oversight authority must do something more than just hold individual service providers accountable. It must also actively promote greater network collaboration between all providers of publicly financed and/or regulated services in a given sector.

NOTES

1. Co-management refers to an arrangement in which third sector organizations produce services in collaboration with the state. (Brandsen and Pestoff, 2006, 497).
2. Sometimes labeled as third party government (Anheier, 2005) or third party governance (Heinrich, 2008).
3. "There has been much assertion, but too little examination of the evidence thus far" (Hodge and Coghill, 2004, 5). "Little attention has been devoted to the implications of co-management for public accountability" (Pestoff, 2010, 2).
4. The research comprised a qualitative study consisting of telephone interviews with a sample of 1,400 parents.

REFERENCES

Anheier, H. 2005. *Nonprofit Organizations. Theory, Management, Policy.* London: Routledge.
Bode, I. 2006. Co-governance within networks and the nonprofit-for profit-divide. A cross-cultural perspective on the evolution of domiciliary elderly care. *Public Management Review* 8 (4): 551–566.
Bovens, M. 2005. Public accountability. In E. Ferlie, L. Lynn, L. and C. Pollitt, eds., *The Oxford Handbook of Public Management.* Oxford, UK: Oxford University Press, pp. 182–208.
Bradach, J. L., and R. G. Eccles. 1991. Price, authority and trust: From ideal types to plural forms. In G. Thompson, R. Levacevic, J. Mitchell, eds., *Markets, Hierarchies and Networks: The Coordination of Social Life.* London: Sage.
Brandsen, T., and V. Pestoff. 2006. Co-production, the third sector and the delivery of public services: An introduction. *Public Management Review* 8 (4): 591–596.
Brandsen, T., and E. Van Hout. 2006. Co-management in public service networks: The organizational effects. *Public Management Review* 8 (4): 537–549.
Core, P. 1993. Accountability in the public sector. In J. Guthrie, ed., *Australian public service: pathways to change in the 1990's.* North Sydney: IRR Conferences Pty. 48–53.
Defourny, J., and V. Pestoff. 2008. *Images and Concepts of the Third Sector in Europe.* Working Paper no.08/02, EMES European Research Network.
Eikenberry, A. M., and J. D. Kluver. 2004. *The Marketization of the Nonprofit Sector: Civil Society at Risk?* Oxford, UK: Blackwell.
Gilmour, R., and L. Jensen. 1998. Reinventing government accountability: Public functions, privatization and the meaning of state action. *Public Affairs Review* 58 (3): 247–258.

Glynn, J., Perkins, D. 1997. Control and accountability in the NHS market: a practical proposition or logical impossibility? International Journal of Public Sector Management, 10 (1/2): 62–75

Gormley, T., and S. Balla. 2004. *Bureaucracy and Democracy. Accountability and Performance.* Washington DC: CQ Press.

Guttman, D., and B. Willner. 1976. *The Shadow Government.* New York: Pantheon Books.

Heinrich, C. 2008. A state of agents? Third-party governance and implications for human services and their delivery. *Fast Focus,* 1.

Heinrich, C., and L. Lynn. 2000. *Governance and Performance: New Perspectives.* Washington DC: Georgetown University Press.

Hodge, G., and K. Coghill. 2004. *Governing the Privatized State: The Accountability Challenge.* Working paper 57/04. Melbourne: Monash University, Department of Management.

Hodges, R. (Ed). 2005. *Governance and the public sector.* Cheltenham, UK; Northampton, MA : Edward Elgar Pub.

Huxham, C. 2000. The challenge of collaborative governance. *Public Management* 2 (3): 337–357.

Kennedy, S. 2001. When is private public? State action in the era of privatization and public-private partnerships. *George Mason University Civil Rights Law Journal* 11 (2): 203–223.

Kennedy, S. 2006. Holding "governance" accountable. Third-party government in a limited state. *The Independent Review* 11 (1): 67–77.

Kjær, A. 2004. *Governance.* Cambridge, UK: Polity Press.

Kooiman, J., Jentoft, S. 2009. Meta-Governance: Values, Norms and Principles, and the making of hard choices. *Public Administration.* 87 (4): 818-836.

Kumar, S. 1997. Accountability in a contracting state. *Findings, Social Policy Research 112* York: Rowntree Foundation.

Kumar, S. 2003. *Accountability: A Qualitative Study of Relationships between the Public Sector, the Voluntary Sector and the Users of Health and Welfare Services in the Context of the Purchase of Service Contracting*: Birmingham: University of Ashton.

Kumar, S., and T. Brandsen. 2008. *Governance Models in Quasi-Markets: New Institutional Arrangements.* Paper for the Conference of the International Society for Third Sector Research, July 9–12, 2008, Barcelona.

Leat, D. 1988. *The Voluntary Sector and Accountability.* London: National Council for Voluntary Organisation.

Löffler, E. 2009. Public governance in a network society. In T. Bovaird, and E. Loffler, eds., *Public Management and Governance.* London: Routledge.

Macmillan, R. 2010. *The Third Sector Delivering Public Services: An Evidence Review.* Working paper 20. Third sector Research Center.

Market Analysis and Synthesis. 2007a. *Analyse van het Zoekproces van Ouders naar een Voorschoolse Kinderopvangplaats.* Brussels: Eindrapport in opdracht van Kind en Gezin.

Market Analysis and Synthesis. 2007b. *Onderzoek naar het Gehanteerde Opnamebeleid van Erkende Kinderdagverblijven en Diensten voor Onthaalouders.* Brussels: Eindrapport in opdracht van Kind en Gezin.

Mulgan, R. 2002. *Accountability Issues in the New Model of Governance.* Paper for the political science program seminar, RSSS, April 2002.

Mulgan, R., and J. Uhr. 2001. Accountability and governance. In G. Davis, and P. Weller, eds., *Are You Being Served? State, Citizens and Governance.* St. Leonards, New South Wales, Australia, pp. 152–174.

Osborne, S. 2006. The new public governance? *Public Management Review* 8 (3): 377–387.

Ouchi, W. 1991. Markets, bureaucracies and clans. In G. Thompson, R. Levacevic, and J. Mitchell, eds., *Markets, Hierarchies and Networks: The Coordination of Social life*. London: Sage, pp. 246–255.

Oude Vrielink, M., T. Schillemans, T. Brandsen, and E. Van Hout. 2009. Horizontale verantwoording in de praktijk: een empirisch onderzoek in de sectoren wonen, zorg en onderwijs. *Bestuurskunde* 18 (4): 80–91.

Paquet, G. 2001. The new governance, subsidiarity and the strategic state. In *Governance in the 21st Century*. Paris: Organisation for Economic Co-Operation and Development, pp. 183–215.

Parker, L., and G. Gould. 1999. *Changing Public Accountability: Critiquing New Directions*. Accounting Forum 23 (2): 109–135.

Pestoff, V. 2006. Citizens and co-production of welfare services: childcare in eight European countries. *Public Management Review* 8 (4): 503–520.

Pestoff, V. 2010. Social accounting and public management: accountability for the public good. In S. P. Osborne, and A. Ball, eds., *Social Accounting and Public Management: Accountability for the Public Good*. London: Routledge.

Pestoff, V., and T. Brandsen,. 2010. Public governance and the third sector: Opportunities for co-production and innovation? In S. P. Osborne, *The New Public Governance? Emerging Perspectives on the Theory and Practice of Public governance*. London: Routledge, pp. 223–236.

Pollitt, C., and G. Bouckaert. 2000. *Public Management Reform: A Comparative Analysis*. Oxford, UK: Oxford University Press.

Prentice, S. 2006. Childcare, co-production and the third sector in Canada. *Public Management Review* 8 (4): 521–536.

Salamon, L. 1989. *Beyond Privatization: The Tools of Government Action*. Washington DC: Urban Institute.

Salamon, L., & Anheier, H. 1998. Social origins of civil society: Explaining the nonprofit sector cross-nationally. *Voluntas*, 9 (3): 213-248.

Schillemans, T. 2007. *Verantwoording in de Schaduw van de Macht. Horizontale Verantwoording bij Zelfstandige Bestuursorganen*. The Hague: Lemma.

Smith, S., and K. Grønbjerg. 2006. Scope and theory of government-nonprofit relations. in W. Powell, R. Steinberg, eds. *The Nonprofit Sector. A Research Handbook*. New Haven, CT: Yale University Press.

Stewart, J. 1984. The role of information in public accountability. In A. Hopwood, and C. Tomkins, eds., *Issues in Public Sector Accounting*. Oxford, UK: Philillan.

Stone, B. 1995. Administrative accountability in the Westminster democracies: towards a new conceptual framework. *Governance* 8 (4): 505–526.

Taylor, M. 1996. Between Public and Private: Accountability in Voluntary Organizations. *Policy & Politics*, 24 (1): 57-72

Van de Donk, W. 2008. *Maatschappelijk Besturen: Sector of Idee*. Cahier School voor Social Profit Management.

Verhoest, K., D. Vervloet, and G. Bouckaert. 2003. *Overheid, Markt of Nonprofit?* Gent: Academia Press.

Verschuere, B. 2006. *Autonomy and Control in Arm's Length Public Agencies: Exploring the Determinants of Policy Autonomy*. Doctoral dissertation. Leuven, Belgium: Catholic University Leuven.

Verschuere, B, and F. De Rynck. 2009. Regie zonder macht, besturen zonder kracht? Samenwerking tussen lokale besturen en de private sector. *Res Publica* 51 (3): 351–376.

Woodhouse, D. 1994. *Ministers and Parliament: Accountability in Theory and Practice*. Oxford, UK: Clarendon Press.

19 New Public Governance, Co-Production and Third Sector Social Services in Europe

Crowding In and Crowding Out

Victor Pestoff

INTRODUCTION

In recent decades, changes in the public sector itself were brought to the fore by various scholars to better understand the role of citizens and the third sector in the provision of public services. First, Vincent Ostrom challenged the dominant perspective of unitary provision of most public services and developed an alternative version of responsible government and democratic administration (1973). Following this, Elinor Ostrom, and her colleagues analyzed the role of citizens in the provision of public services in terms of co-production (Parks et al., 1981). More recently, several other prominent scholars of public administration and management joined the discussion. Hartley (2005) identified and analyzed three approaches to the public sector itself in the postwar period and their implications for policy makers, managers and citizens. These three approaches are traditional public administration, new public management (NPM), and networked governance. Osborne viewed NPM as a transitory stage in the evolution toward new public governance (2006 and 2010); Bovaird argued for a radical reinterpretation of policy making and service delivery in the public domain, resulting in public governance (2007); while Denhardt and Denhardt (2008) promote new public service as serving citizens rather than steering them. Common to all of these newer perspectives on public services is a central role attributed to greater citizen participation, co-production and third sector provision of public services.

This chapter focuses on co-production, particularly of social services, and also addresses the questions about the changing relationship between the third sector and the state in Europe. Can different perspectives on these changes be captured by different approaches to the study of public administration and management? What role is attributed to citizen participation and third sector provision of public services by traditional public administration, NPM and new public governance? What does comparative empirical evidence from preschool services in Europe say about co-production of social services? This chapter proposes to explore these questions.

The second chapter of this book explored several crucial conceptual issues related to co-production. Various definitions of co-production were considered and a generic one, stemming from the early writings of Elinor Ostrom and her colleagues was adopted. It focuses on the mix of activities that both public service agents and citizens contribute to the provision of public services. The former are involved as professionals or "regular producers," while "citizen production" is based on voluntary efforts by individuals or groups to enhance the quality and/or quantity of services they use (Parks et al., 1981). Chapter 2 also considered the relevance of different levels of analysis and distinguished between co-production, co-management and co-governance. It pursued our inquiry into the relations between the professional staff and their clients and noted that they can be interdependent, supplementary or complementary.

Chapter 2 then distinguished between co-production by the clients themselves and their family members. It noted that both the facility and salience of the service provided to the individual and/or their family were important for better understanding why citizens become involved in co-producing social services. It was argued that enduring social services have a greater salience than non-enduring services, given the impact such services have on their life and life chances, as well as that of their family and loved ones. Then it briefly explored differences between collective action in general and collective interaction in small self-help groups. It illustrated the necessity to engage in collective action in order to get access to better quality child care services in Sweden in the 1970s and to get access to any child care at all in many new suburban areas in the 1980s. It then turned our attention to whether co-production only comprises individual acts, collective action or both, and found several examples of a mixed pattern of involvement in the co-production of publicly funded social services both in different sectors and nations. Thus, it ended with an expanded definition of co-production for the social services that includes both individual and collective participation, both beneficiary and family member participation, and both public and third sector provision of social services, given that the latter receives substantial public funding.

PUBLIC ADMINISTRATION REGIMES AND CO-PRODUCTION

We need to inquire how changes in the nature of the public sector itself and different public administration and management regimes might impact on the relationship between the third sector and public sector in general. More specifically, how do different relationships between the government and its citizens impact on the role of the third sector as a provider of social services? The Ostroms sketched the development and growth of the study of public administration in the United States, including such foreground figures as Woodrow Wilson, Herbert Simon, the public choice school and more (Ostrom and Ostrom, 1999). They propose a new perspective on the study of public administration and argue that if the traditional principles of public administration are inapplicable, then we must develop a new theory of public administration that is more appropriate for citizens living in democratic societies. They conclude that perhaps a system of public administration composed of a variety of multiorganizational arrangements that is highly dependent on mobilizing clientele support would come reasonably close to a public administration with a high level of performance in advancing the public welfare (1999, 48).

Calabrò (2010) documents the growth in recent years of academic interest in "networked governance" and "public governance" in a review of journals on public administration and management between 1970 and 2009. Hartley (2005) identified and analyzed three approaches to the public sector in the postwar period for their implications for policy makers, managers and citizens. She spells out the various dimensions, similarities and differences of these three public sector paradigms (i.e., traditional public administration, NPM and networked governance). The first two paradigms are familiar, while the third is based on evidence of emerging patterns of governance and service delivery, which can be called "citizen-centered governance" or networked governance. In particular, the actors include hierarchies and public servants in the first paradigm; markets, purchasers and providers and clients and contractors in the second; and networks, partnerships and civil leadership in the latter. Key social benefits associated with each of them are public good in the former, public choice in the second and public value in the latter (ibid., 28).

Each paradigm or public administration regime may be linked to a particular ideology and historical period. However, they can also be seen as competing, according to Hartley, because they co-exist as "layered realities" for politicians and managers (ibid., 29) and in academic and public discourse. The role of citizens in the respective paradigms is either as clients, with little say about services; customers, with some limited choice in the scope and content of services; or as co-producers, who can play a more direct role in the provision of services. Hartley argues that as the United Kingdom moves to networked governance, the role of the state becomes to steer action within complex social systems rather than to control it solely through hierarchies or market mechanisms.

Bovaird argues that the emergence of governance as a key concept in the public domain is relatively recent, and he traces the evolution of the concept in public administration. He suggests that "governance" provides a set of balancing mechanisms in a network society, although it is still a contested concept, both in theory and in practice (2007, 217). By the end of the 1990s, various concerns about corporate governance, local governance and network society had crystallized into a wider focus on "public governance," which he defines as "the ways in which stakeholders interact with each other in order to influence the outcomes of public policies" (ibid., 220).

Co-production becomes a key concept and the importance attributed to it by public governance has two major implications for public administration. First, it seriously questions the relevance of the basic assumptions of NPM that service delivery can be separated from service design, because service users now play key roles in both service design and delivery. Second, service users and professionals develop a mutual and interdependent relationship in which both parties take risks and need to trust each other (ibid., 222).

Osborne (2006 and 2010) argues that NPM has actually been a transitory stage in the evolution from traditional public administration (PA) to what he calls new public governance (NPG). He agrees that public administration and management (PAM) has gone through three dominant stages or modes: a longer preeminent one of PA until the late 1970s or early 1980s; a second mode of NPM, until the start of the twenty-first century; and an emergent third one, NPG since then. The time of NPM has thus been a relatively brief and transitory one between the statist and bureaucratic tradition of PA and the embryonic one of NPG (Osborne, 2006; Osborne, 2010).

Hierarchy is the key governance mechanism for PA, with a focus on vertical line management to insure accountability for the use of public money. By contrast, NPM is a child of neoclassical economics and particularly of rational/public choice theory. It has an emphasis on implementation by independent service units, ideally in competition with each other, and a focus on economy and efficiency. Finally, NPG is firmly rooted within organizational sociology and network theory, and it acknowledges the increasingly fragmented and uncertain nature of public management in the twenty-first century. "It posits both a *plural state* where multiple interdependent actors contribute to the delivery of public services and a *pluralist* state, where multiple processes inform the public policy making system" (Osborne, 2006, 384).

Moreover, Bovaird (2007) argues that there has been a radical reinterpretation of the role of policy making and service delivery in the public domain. Policy making is no longer seen as a purely top-down process but rather as negotiation among many interacting policy systems. Similarly, services are no longer simply delivered by professional and managerial staff in public agencies, but they are co-produced by users and communities. He presents a conceptual framework for understanding the emerging role of user and community co-production. Traditional conceptions of service planning and management are, therefore, outdated and need to be revised to account for co-production as an integrating mechanism and an incentive for resource mobilization—a potential that is still greatly underestimated (ibid.).

Finally, Denhardt and Denhardt (2008) argue that the theoretical framework for new public service (NPS) gives full priority to democracy, citizenship and service in the public interest. It offers an important and viable alternative to both the traditional and the now-dominant managerialist model of public management. They suggest that public administration should begin with the recognition that an engaged and enlightened citizenship is crucial to democratic governance. Accordingly, public interest transcends the aggregation of individual self-interest. From this perspective, the role of government is to bring people "to the table" and to serve citizens in a manner that recognizes the multiple and complex layers of responsibility, ethics and accountability in a democratic system (ibid., 198–199).

Due to the conceptual similarity between these authors, I will employ the term new public governance for a regime or paradigm that emphasizes greater citizen engagement in and co-production of public services and greater third sector provision of the same. However, co-production in the context of multipurpose, multi-stakeholder networks raises some crucial democratic issues that have important implications for public service reforms.

CO-PRODUCTION: POWER AND INFLUENCE IN CLIENT RELATIONS WITH THE PUBLIC SECTOR

Consumer and client power and influence are often treated as self-evident and unproblematic. It is often assumed that consumers obtain power and influence on the market in modern societies by their purchase of goods and services. Equally, it is often assumed that clients obtain power and influence on the public sector in democratic societies through their voice and vote. Power and influence are there just for the taking; all that is required are rational consumers and active citizens. Thus, power and influence are not considered as "zero-sum" or relational phenomena. So more power and influence to consumers and clients is not conceived as meaning less power and influence for private businessmen and/or public bureaucrats. Both the hidden hand of the market and the political accountability of the public sector ensure that power and influence are readily available to consumers and clients. However, such interpretations stifle serious efforts to analyze consumer and client power and how to increase their influence on markets or in public services.

Moreover, power and influence are often seen as opposite sides of the coin. There is, however, an important difference between the two, as noted in the following. Here we will briefly present three different representations of citizen power, two of which focus specifically on client power vis-à-vis the public sector. Arnstein (1969) proposed a "ladder of citizen participation" that is comprised of eight rungs, ranging from manipulation to citizen control. Likert (1959) suggests different categories of worker power in four types of employers, ranging from "exploitative authoritative" to "participative groups." Pestoff (1998), extrapolating on Likert's model, introduced different categories of client power in four types of public sector services, ranging from administrative authoritative to citizens as co-producers. We will look closer at each of them.

Arnstein asks, what is citizen participation? Her answer is simply that it

> is a categorical term for citizen power. It is the redistribution of power that enables the have-not citizens, presently excluded from the political and economic processes, to be deliberately included in the future. It is the strategy by which the have-nots join in determining how information is shared, goals and policies are set, tax resources are allocated, programs are operated and benefits like contracts and patronage are parceled out. (1969, 216)

She discusses participation and nonparticipation and proposes a typology of eight *levels* of participation to help analyze this. For illustrative purposes, she arranges the eight types as a ladder, with each rung corresponding to the extent of citizens' power in determining the end product or service. The bottom rungs of the ladder are (1) *Manipulation* and (2) *Therapy*, which describe levels of "non-participation" that some see as a substitute for genuine participation. Their real objective is not to enable people to participate in planning or running programs, but rather to "educate" or "cure" the participants. The next rungs are (3) *Informing* and (4) *Consultation*, which reach the level of "tokenism" that allow citizens to hear and to have a voice; however, they lack the power to insure that their views will be *heeded*. They remain "window dressing," according to her. Rung (5), *Placation*, is simply a higher level tokenism, because the ground rules allow for citizens to provide advice, but the public sector retains the power to decide (ibid., 217). Further up the ladder, there are levels of citizen power with increasing degrees of decision making. Citizens can enter into a (6) *Partnership,* where power is shared in planning and decision making, through such structures as joint policy boards, planning communities and such. According to her, they work best when there is an independent organized power base in the community or third sector to which the citizens' leaders are held accountable, and when they can pay their own leaders and hire their own experts. At the topmost rungs are, (7) *Delegated Power* and (8) *Citizen Control,* where citizens obtain the majority of decision-making seats, or full-managerial power (ibid., 217), as seen in some contemporary European social services.

However, power is related to structural attributes of the market, like the number of actors on the demand and supply side, their resource specificity and convertibility, the asymmetry of knowledge between suppliers and buyers of goods and services and the existence of "externalities" (Sjöstrand, 1993, 40–44). Individual consumers or clients can influence the quality of the goods or services of a particular producer or provider without having power in the market or on public services. The influence they have may be sharply constrained by the power of structural attributes of the market or of public policy making. Thus, having influence and having power are not synonymous from a consumer and client perspective.

Likert's discussion of the system of organizations and the involvement of employees in decision making is relevant to understand client influence on public services. Likert classifies firms into four basic types on the basis of their system of labor relations, and he develops four corresponding models of employee involvement in decision making. *Exploitative authoritative* organizations do not permit any employee influence at all on firm decision making; *benevolent authoritative* organizations don't permit employee involvement in decision making, but they do nevertheless occasionally consult them on some work-related issues. *Consultative* organizations normally consult employees on important matters, but they are not, however, directly involved in decision making; and finally, *participative group* organizations fully involve employees in all decisions related to their work (Likert, 1959). The latter category would probably be best represented in the real world by employee ownership in worker cooperatives or social enterprises.

In a similar fashion, it is possible to study systems of organizations providing public services in terms of the varying degrees of client influence, from those with the least to those with the greatest client influence on the public services provided. Authoritative bureaucratic public agencies allow for no direct client influence or involvement in decision making, and, thus, they demonstrate the typical client/bureaucrat pattern of a clear top-down relationship found in many public services. The growth of benevolent bureaucracy in public services occasionally involves clients in consultation, although they are not given any influence on decisions made by the agency. This may include facilitating client complaints and suggestions for improvement, the use of client questionnaires and focus groups to evaluate service quality. Consultative bureaucracies go a step further in consulting their clients by establishing consultative mechanisms for involving "consumer" representatives on consultative boards, or in some well-defined projects. The citizens as co-producers category has the potential to provide the clearest model for client power and influence. Social service provision throughout Europe is beginning to involve greater client participation, as seen in the growing reliance on various self-help groups, social service enterprises and the contracting out of social services to cooperatives and various nonprofit organizations (NPOs).

Moreover, much of political science research and the discourse on democratic theory focus on influencing elective, democratic institutions and/or concerns their representativeness. Unfortunately, they continue to ignore the growing importance of civil servants and their routine decisions that impinge both directly and indirectly on the daily life of citizens. They also pay little attention to possibilities for citizens to influence such decisions. However, there is a growing interest among political scientists in democratic or participative governance (Schmitter, 2002). Some proponents favor greater openness and citizen participation in deliberations at various levels and in various forms before binding decisions are reached (Fung, 2004). Others argue the benefits of greater citizen participation in the provision of public goods and services (Ostrom, 1999, Pestoff, 2008). While these ideas about greater citizen participation may seem to represent different approaches to participative governance, they are not necessarily opposed to each other. In fact, it could be argued that they are complementary approaches to a common goal, or perhaps the opposite sides of the same coin. In particular, it can be argued that deliberative democracy is found at the input side of the political system, while participative democracy is located at the output side. Greater citizen participation on one side could perhaps promote greater participation on the other.

Easton (1965, 1996) distinguished between the input and output sides of the political system. Citizens make demands and give support on the input side of the political system, while they are subject to public decisions and receive goods and services on the output side. However, given the rapid growth of "framework laws" in most European countries, many of the details concerning the delivery of public goods and services are no longer decided by parliament or local councils, but rather by the public agencies responsible for implementing these laws and regulating or providing such services. This implies that the input side of democratic systems has also lost some relevance or importance in comparison with the output side of the policy-making process. Thus, a night-watchman state that only provided defense, courts and police for its inhabitants has long since been replaced by a welfare state providing multiple and complex services to many, if not most, citizens. Moreover, in most postmodern societies, citizens have become highly dependent on the state and local governments for the provision of many goods and services.

The cradle-to-grave services provided by many European welfare states also requires large bureaucracies and extensive public services for their delivery. This also means that the output side of the political system now greatly overshadows the input side in size, number of employees, financing and importance for everyday matters for many, if not most, citizens. At the same time, the growth of "framework laws" has blurred the distinction between the input and output sides of the political system, and it becomes more difficult to know where one begins and the other ends.

Citizen participation can also be analyzed at various levels or stages in the provision of public services. Thus, it is possible to distinguish between individual or group participation in the *co-production* of public services, at the site of service delivery; and *co-management* that is based on the participation of nonprofit organizations and for-profit firms in managing local public service delivery; while the participation of both public and private actors in the *co-governance* of public policy allows them to determine a specific policy. Thus, from this perspective, both co-production and co-management are found on the output side of the political system, while co-governance is located on the input side. Needless to say, there is a degree of blurring here too, because the same actors or groups of citizens can participate at different levels of the political system or different stages of the political process.

CO-PRODUCTION: BREACHING THE "GLASS CEILING"

The empirical materials briefly reviewed in this chapter come from two separate studies reported elsewhere: a comparative multiple case study of family policy and alternative provision of preschool services in promoting social cohesion in several European countries and a comparative survey study of public, private for-profit, parent cooperative and worker cooperative preschool services in Sweden. They permit a discussion of the political value added by third sector provision of social services. Some third sector providers can facilitate greater citizen participation and thereby help to breach the "glass ceiling" found in public and for-profit social services. This will be discussed in greater detail later in the chapter.

Co-Production: Two Comparative Studies of Parents' Participation in Preschool Services

Turning briefly to two comparative studies of parent participation in preschool services in Europe, the first is the TSFEPS Project that permitted us to examine the relationship between parent participation in the provision and governance of preschool services in eight EU countries (Pestoff, 2006, 2008, 2009).[1] We found different levels of parent participation in different countries and in different forms of provision (i.e., public, private for-profit and third sector preschool services). The highest levels of parent participation were found in third sector providers, such as parent associations in France, parent initiatives in Germany, and parent cooperatives in Sweden (ibid.). We also noted different kinds of parent participation (i.e., economic, political, social and service specific). Economic participation involves contributing time and materials to the running or maintenance of a facility; political participation means being involved in discussions and decision making: while social participation implies planning and contributing to various social events, such as the winter holiday party, spring party and so on. Service specific participation can range from the management and maintenance of a facility, or replacing the staff in case of sickness or when they attend a specialized course, to actually working on a regular basis in the child care facility. All four kinds of participation were readily evident in third sector providers of preschool services, while both economic and political participation were highly restricted in municipal and private for-profit services. Moreover, we observed variations in the patterns of participation between countries. Parents participated actively in the provision of third sector preschool services at the site of delivery in France, Germany and Sweden, but only in the first two countries in their governance at the local or regional levels, and not in the latter one (ibid.).

The second is a study of the Swedish welfare state that focuses on the politics of diversity, parent participation and service quality in preschool services (Vamstad, 2007). It compared parent and worker co-ops, municipal services and small, for-profit firms providing preschool services in Ostersund and Stockholm. This study not only confirms the existence of the four dimensions of co-production noted earlier in the TSFEPS study; but it also underlines clear differences between various providers concerning the importance attributed to these dimensions of co-production. Vamstad's study demonstrates that parent co-ops promote much greater parent participation than the other three types of preschool service providers, in terms of economic, social, political and service-specific participation. This comes as no great surprise, because the essence of the parent cooperative model is parent participation.

However, his study also shows that neither public nor private for-profit services allow for more than marginal or ad hoc participation by parents in the preschool services. For example, parents may be welcome to make spontaneous suggestions when leaving their child in the morning or picking her or him up in the evening from a municipal or small private for-profit preschool facility. They may also be welcome to contribute time and effort to a social event. Also discussion groups or "Influence Councils" can be found at some municipal preschool services in Sweden, but they provide parents with very limited influence. More substantial participation in economic or political terms can only be achieved when parents organize themselves collectively to obtain better quality or different kinds of preschool services than either the state or market can provide.

Thus, parent co-ops in Sweden promote all four kinds of user participation: economic, social, political and complementary. They provide parents with unique possibilities for active participation in the management and running of their child's or children's preschool facility and for unique opportunities to become active co-producers of high-quality preschool services for their own and others' children. It is also clear that other forms of preschool services allow for some limited avenues of co-production in publicly financed preschool services, but parents' possibilities for influencing the management of such services remain rather limited.

However, participation doesn't always translate into influence. So different types of service providers may or may not promote greater client and/or staff influence in the provision and governance of social services. Therefore, Vamstad asked parents and staff at the child care facilities he studied how much influence they currently had and whether they wanted more. Respondents to the question about their current influence could choose between seven alternatives ranging from "very little" and "little" at the low end to "large" and "very large" at the high end. By contrast, answers to the question about wanting more influence had simple "yes/no" answers. The results presented here only use some of the information about the current level of influence. Only the most frequent categories at the high end of the scale of influence are included in the two tables in this chapter. Table 19.1 reports parents' influence and their desire for more, while Table 19.2 expresses the staff's influence and its desire for more.

Table 19.1   Perceived and Desired User Influence, by Type of Child Care Provider

Provider/Perceived Influence:	Much*	av.**	(n)	Want more
Parent co-op child care	88.7	5.6	(107)	13.2
Worker co-op child care	50.0	4.6	(48)	28.3
Municipal child care	44.9	4.4	(89)	37.3
Small for-profit firm child care	12.5	3.6	(24)	58.3

Source: Adapted from Tables 8.6 and 8.8 in Vamstad, 2007.
Notes: *Combines three categories: "rather large", "large" and "very large". **average score, based on a scale ranging from 1 to 7, where low scores mean little influence.

Parent influence is greatest in parent co-ops and least in small, for-profit firms. This is an expected result, and nearly nine of ten parents in parent co-ops claim much influence. However, this is twice as many as in municipal services. Half of the parents in worker co-ops also claim much influence, which is also greater than the proportion in municipal child care. Finally, only one of eight parents claims much influence in small, for-profit firms. The differences in influence between types of providers appear substantial.

Turning to their desire for more influence, again we find the expected pattern of answers, which inversely reflect how much influence they currently experience. Very few parents in parent co-ops want more influence, while nearly three of five do so in small, for-profit firms. In between these two types are the worker co-ops, where more than one of four wants more influence and municipal child care where more than one of three does so. With as many as one-third of the parents wanting more influence in municipal child care, a solid base exists for increased parent representation in decision making. Thus, it is not merely a question of selective choice between various providers, where the more interested parents choose the more demanding, participative forms of child care, while the more passive ones choose less demanding forms. There appear to be widespread expectations of being able to participate in important decisions concerning their daughter's or son's child care among parents in all types of providers. Perhaps this reflects the spread of the norm of participation from parent co-ops to all publicly financed welfare services, regardless of the provider. Moreover, the Swedish reform known as "Councils of Influence" in municipal preschools would benefit greatly by involving many more of these motivated parents, if it were possible to offer them meaningful opportunities to influence decisions. Similarly, worker co-ops would gain greater legitimacy and trust if they could find ways to involve more parents in a meaningful fashion.

Shifting to the staff of child care facilities, there were many more who answered that they had much influence, but with some notable differences in the distribution of the frequencies, so both the "large" and "very large" categories are included separately in Table 19.2. Again the logically expected pattern of influence can clearly be noted here, where the staff in worker co-ops claims the most influence and the staff in municipal facilities claims the least influence. Nearly nine of ten staff members claim large or very large influence in worker co-op child care, while only a third does so in municipal facilities. Nearly three of five members of staff claim much influence in parent co-ops, while half of them do so in small, for-profit firms. Again, the proportion of the staff desiring more influence inversely reflects those claiming much influence. Few want more influence in either the worker or parent co-ops, while the opposite is true of the staff in the other two types of child care providers. Nearly three of five want more influence in municipal child care, and three of four do so in small, for-profit firms. Thus, there appears to be significant room for greater staff influence in both the latter types of child care. Greater staff influence could also contribute to improving the work environment in both these two types of child care providers (Pestoff, 2000).

However, one interesting detail is the relatively low proportion of staff in parent co-ops wanting more influence. It is almost identical with that found for the staff in worker co-ops. In spite of differences in "ownership," the striking similarity in the proportion of staff expressing a desire for more influence suggests that there must already be such a high degree of collaboration between the staff and parents in parent co-ops as to eliminate the need for more influence. It seems important to explore this matter closer in future research on third sector social services.

Thus, we found that neither the state nor market allows for more than marginal or ad hoc participation or influence by parents in the child care services. More substantial participation in economic or political terms can only be achieved when parents organize themselves collectively to obtain better quality or different kinds of child care services than either the state or market can provide. In addition, worker co-ops seem to provide parents

Table 19.2   Perceived and Desired Staff Influence, by Type of Child Care Provider

Provider/Perceived Influence:	Large	Very Large	av.*	(n)	Want more
Worker co-op child care	16.7	72.2	6.4	(18)	16.7
Parent co-op child care	34.1	22.7	5.7	(44)	16.3
Small for-profit firm child care	37.5	12.5	5.4	(8)	75.0
Municipal child care	23.9	10.9	4.8	(46)	57.8

Source: adapted from Tables 8.7 and 8.8 in Vamstad, 2007.
Note: *average score, based on a scale ranging from 1 to 7, where low scores mean little influence.

with greater influence than either municipal child care or small, private, for-profit firms can. In addition, the staff at worker co-ops obtains maximum influence, resulting in more democratic work places. But the staff at parent co-ops does not express a desire for more influence. Thus, both the parent and worker co-ops appear to maximize staff influence compared to municipal and small, for-profit firms, while parent co-ops also maximize user influence.

Third Sector Co-production: Breaching the "Glass Ceiling"?

Co-production not only implies different relations between public authorities and citizens, it also facilitates different levels of citizen participation in the provision of public services. However, participation also depends on the institutional setting or form of provision (i.e., who provides the services). Citizen participation in public service provision can be distinguished along two main dimensions. For the sake of simplicity, only three categories or levels will be considered here, but there can, in fact, be greater differences between them. The first dimension relates to the intensity of relations between the provider and clients of public services. Here, the intensity of relations between public authorities and citizens can either be sporadic and distant, intermittent and/or short-term or it can involve intensive and/or enduring welfare relations. In the former, citizen participation in providing public services involves only distant contacts via the telephone, postal services or e-mail, while in the latter it means direct, daily and repeated face-to-face interaction between providers and citizens over a longer period of time. For example, citizen participation in crime prevention or a neighborhood watch, filing their tax forms or filling in postal codes normally only involves sporadic or indirect contacts between the citizens and authorities. Face-to-face interactions for a short duration or intermittent contacts are characteristic of participation in public job training courses or maintenance programs for public housing that involve resident participation in some aspects (Alford, 2002). By contrast, citizen participation in the management and maintenance of publicly financed preschool or elementary school services involves repeated long-term contacts. This places them in the position of being active subjects in the provision of such services, not merely the passive objects of public policy (Pestoff, 2006, 2008, 2009). Here they can both influence the development and help decide about the future of the services provided. The same is true of other enduring social services.

Similarly, the level of citizen participation in the provision of public services can either be low, medium or high. By combining these two dimensions, we can derive a three-by-three table with nine cells. However, not all of them are readily evident in the real world or found in the literature on co-production. Moreover, an additional or third dimension needs to be included and made explicit—the degree of civil society involvement in the provision of public services. This clearly reflects the form of citizen participation (i.e., organized collective action, individual or group participation and individual or group compliance). (Consult Pestoff, 2008 for details.)

In general, we can expect to find a trend where increasing intensity of relations between public authorities and citizens in the provision of public services leads to increased citizen participation. Sporadic and distant relations imply low participation levels, while enduring social services will result in greater participation. However, when it comes to providing intensive and/or enduring welfare services, two distinct patterns can be found in the literature. First, a high level of citizen participation is noted for third sector provision, because it is based on collective action and direct citizen participation. Parent associations or co-op preschool services in France, Germany and Sweden illustrates this. Second, more limited citizen participation is noted for public provision of enduring social services. It usually focuses on public interactions with individual citizens and/or user councils. Citizens are allowed to participate sporadically or in a limited ad hoc fashion, like parents contributing to the social events in municipal preschool services. But, they are seldom given the opportunity to play a major role in, to take charge of, the service provision or given decision-making rights or responsibility for the economy of the service provision.

This creates a "glass ceiling" for citizen participation in public services that limits citizens to playing a more passive role as service users who can perhaps make some demands on the public sector, but who have little influence, make few, if any, decisions and take little responsibility for implementing public policy. Thus, it might be possible to speak of two types of co-production: co-production "heavy" and co-production "light." The space allotted to citizens in the latter is too restricted to make participation very meaningful or democratic. Co-production "heavy" is only possible when citizens are engaged in organized collective groups where they can reasonably achieve some semblance of direct democratic control over the provision of publicly financed services via democratic decision making as a member of such service organizations. A similar argument can be made concerning user participation in for-profit firms providing welfare services.

We also note that service delivery takes quite different forms in preschool services. Most preschool services studied here fall into the top-down category in terms of style of service provision. There are few possibilities for parents to directly influence decision making in such services. This normally includes both municipal preschool services and for-profit firms providing preschool services. Perhaps this is logical from the perspective of municipal governments. They are, after all, representative institutions, chosen by the voters in elections every fourth or fifth year. They might consider direct client or user participation in the running of public services for a particular group, such as parents, as a threat both to the representative democracy that they institutionalize as well as to their own power. It could also be argued that direct participation for a particular group, such as parents, would provide the latter with a "veto right" or a "second vote" at the service level. There may also be professional resistance to parent involvement and participation, including some misunderstanding about the extent of such client involvement and responsibilities (i.e., whether it concerns core or complementary activities).

The logic of direct user participation is also foreign to private for-profit providers. Exit, rather than voice, provides the medium of communication in markets, where parents are seen as consumers. So this logic also curtails most types of direct user participation. Only the parent cooperative services clearly fall into the bottom-up category that facilitates co-production "heavy." Here we find the clearest examples of new public governance, where parents are directly involved in the running of their daughter's or son's preschool center in terms of being responsible for the maintenance, management and such of the preschool facility. They also participate in the decision making of the facility, as members and "owners" of the facility. However, both these comparative studies of preschool services also illustrate the co-existence of several different layers of public administration regimes in the same sector and country, as Hartley and Denhardt and Denhardt suggested. In Sweden, for example, most preschool services are provided by municipalities in a traditional top-down public administrative fashion, which may facilitate co-production "light." Private, for-profit preschool services seem inspired by ideas of greater consumer choice related to NPM.

It should, however, be clearly noted that not all third sector organizations can automatically be equated with greater client participation. Whether or not they are depends primarily on their own internal decision-making rules. Many nonprofit organizations are not governed in a fashion that promotes the participation of either their volunteers or clients. Most charities and foundations are run by a board of executives that are appointed by key stakeholders, rather than elected by their members or clients. Very few such organizations can be found among providers of preschool services in Sweden. However, social enterprises in Europe usually include representatives of most or all major stakeholder groups in their internal decision-making structures, and they are often governed as multi-stakeholder organizations. In fact, participation by key stakeholders and democratic decision-making structures are two of the core social criteria applied by the European EMES Research Network to define and delimit social enterprises (see note 1).

SUMMARY AND CONCLUSIONS:
CROWDING IN AND CROWDING OUT?

In sum, after introducing the distinction between traditional public administration, new public management and new public governance, we explored two comparative studies of parent participation in child care in Europe. We found that there are four kinds or dimensions of parent participation in the provision of public financed social services. They are economic, political, social and service-specific participation. In the Swedish study, parent participation was clearly greatest on all four of these dimensions in parent co-op preschool services. Then the influence of both parents and the staff was compared in four types of service providers: parent co-ops, worker co-ops, municipal services and small, private, for-profit firms in Sweden. Both the parents and staff of parent and worker co-ops claim more influence than those of either the municipal services or for-profit firms. Thus, we concluded that neither the state nor market allow for more than marginal or ad hoc participation by parents in the preschool services. More substantial participation in economic or political terms can only be achieved when parents organize themselves collectively to obtain better quality or different kinds of preschool services than either the state or market can provide. In addition, worker co-ops seem to provide parents with greater influence than either municipal preschool services or small, private, for-profit firms can do, and the staff at worker co-ops obtains maximum influence, resulting in more democratic workplaces.

Both public services and small, for-profit firms demonstrate the existence of a "glass ceiling" for the participation of citizens as clients of enduring welfare services. Evidence also suggests similar limits for staff participation in the public and private for-profit forms of providing enduring social services. Only social enterprises such as the small consumer and worker co-ops appear to develop the necessary mechanisms to breach these limits by empowering the clients and/or staff with democratic rights and influence.

Thus, co-production is a core aspect of new public governance and implies greater citizen participation in and third sector provision of public services. Third sector provision of public services can, in turn, promote greater citizen participation as well as user and staff influence. Third sector provision of social services helps to breach the "glass ceiling" for citizen participation that otherwise exists in public and for-profit services. These findings can contribute to the development of a policy that promotes democratic governance (Pestoff, 2008) and empowered citizenship (Fung, 2004). However, it is important to emphasize the interface between the government, citizens and the third sector and to note that co-production normally takes place in a political context. An individual's cost-benefit analysis and the decision to cooperate with voluntary efforts are conditioned by the structure of political institutions and the facilitation provided by politicians. Centralized or highly standardized service delivery tends to make articulation of demands more costly for citizens and to inhibit governmental responsiveness, while citizen participation seems to fare better in decentralized and less standardized service delivery (Ostrom, 1999).

There are important differences between empty rituals and real influence. There is a substantial risk in promoting more citizen participation and co-production in the provision of public services. It can initially result in broad citizen support and enthusiasms, but if the promise of greater citizen influence remains hollow, if it appears merely to be window dressing, or even worse only manipulation, then it may turn into frustration, cynicism and withdrawal from public pursuits. Empirical research discussed from parent participation in child care in Europe shows that there is in fact a glass ceiling in participation. Therefore, it is possible to distinguish between "co-production heavy" in third sector services and "co-production light" in public and for-profit services. However, not everyone may be willing and able to engage in "co-production heavy" at the outset. Some citizens may need more time to develop their political resources and skills before they are willing to assume more responsibility. While the difference between levels of participation may appear controversial, and greater citizen participation may cause some tensions with the professional public service providers, this is to be expected in political processes. Nor will citizens be willing to engage in co-production in many types of public service. Citizens are not like a jack-in-the-box, just waiting for someone to push a button or latch to release their potential engagement in co-production. They will pick and choose when and where to participate according to their own preferences. The importance or salience of a particular service to them or their loved ones will help to trigger their willingness to participate. In addition, the facility or hurdles that they meet when they attempt to participate will serve to encourage or discourage them to participate in co-production.

The way in which the third sector can deliver services and have an impact on society is both related to the global forces of marketization and privatization, on one hand, and the experimentation with new forms of citizen participation, co-production and collective solutions to social problems, on the other. In Europe, many welfare states experienced extensive change starting in the early 1980s and will likely face even greater changes in the next ten to twenty years in terms of providing welfare services. The growing division between financing and delivery of welfare services is becoming more apparent. Ideological clashes over the future of the welfare state began with the appearance of neoliberalism and new public management. At the same time, alternative provision of welfare services was marginal in some countries, usually only found in specialized niches. However, by the first years of the twenty-first century, it had grown considerably, with a varying mix of for-profit firms and third sector providers in different social services areas and countries.

A continued public monopoly of the provision of welfare services seems therefore highly unlikely or ruled out by domestic political circumstances in most European countries. Thus, there appears to be two starkly different scenarios or trajectories for the future of the welfare state in Europe: either rampant privatization, with accelerated NPM, or the growth of new public governance, with greater welfare pluralism and more co-production. The latter scenario would include a major role for the third sector and social economy as an alternative to both public and private for-profit providers of welfare services. These two alternatives are sketched in Figure 19.1.

A public administration regime can "crowd out" certain behaviors and "crowd in" others in the population. For example, a welfare reform policy inspired by NPM that emphasizes economically rational individuals who maximize their utilities and provides them with material incentives to change their behavior tends to play down values of reciprocity and solidarity, collective action, co-production and third sector provision of welfare services. By contrast, one that emphasizes mutual benefit and reciprocity will promote public services that are "truly owned by the citizens they serve and the staff on whose service and innovation they rely" (HM Government, 2010).

Moreover, one-sided emphasis by many European governments either on the state maintaining most responsibility for providing social services or turning most of them over to the market will hamper the development of co-production and democratic governance. The state can "crowd out" certain behaviors and "crowd in" others in the population. A favorable regime and favorable legislation are necessary for promoting greater co-production and third sector provision of welfare services. Only co-production and greater welfare pluralism can promote new public governance and more democratic governance of social services.

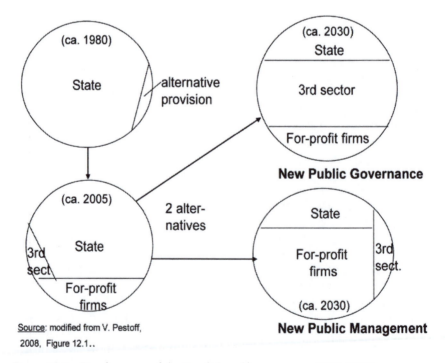

Source: modified from V. Pestoff, 2008, Figure 12.1..

Figure 19.1   Development of the Swedish welfare state, ca. 1980–2030.

NOTES

1. The TSFEPS Project, Changing Family Structures and Social Policy: Child-care Services as Sources of Social Cohesion, took place in eight European countries between 2002 to 2004. They were: Belgium, Bulgaria, England, France, Germany, Italy, Spain and Sweden. See www.emes.net for more details and the country reports.

REFERENCES

Alford, J. 2002. Why do Public Sector Clients Co-Produce? Towards a Contingency Theory; *Administration & Society*, v. 34(1): 32-56.

Arnstein, S. R. 1969. Ladder of Citizen Participation. *Journal of the American Institute of Planners* 35 (1): 216–226.

Bovaird, T. 2007. Beyond engagement and participation: user and community co-production of public services. *Public Administration Review* 67 (5): 846–860.

Brandsen, T., and V. Pestoff. 2008. Co-production, the third sector and the delivery of public services: an introduction. In V. Pestoff, andT. Brandsen, eds. *Co-production. The Third Sector and the Delivery of Public Services*. London: Routledge.

Calabrò, A. 2010. *Governance Structures and Mechanisms in Public Service Organizations. Theories, Evidence and Future Directions*. Doctoral dissertation. Rome: University of Rome Tor Vergata, School of Business Studies.

Denhardt, J. V., and R. B. Denhardt. 2008. *The New Public Service. Serving, not Steering*. London: M. E. Sharpe.

Easton, D., 1965. *A Systems Analysis of Political Life*. New York J. Wiley & Sons.

Fung, A. 2004. *Empowered Participation. Reinventing Urban Democracy*. Princeton, NJ: Princeton University Press.

Hartley, J. 2005. Innovation in governance and public services: past and present. *Public Money & Management* 25 (1): 27–34.

Her Majesty's Government. March 31, 2010. *Mutual Benefit: Giving People Power over Public Services*. Cabinet Office.

Likert, R. 1959. *New Patterns of Management*. New York: McGraw-Hill.

Osborne, S.P. 2006. The New Public Governance. *Public Management Review* 8 (3): 377–387.

Osborne, S.P., ed. 2010. *The New Public Governance? Emerging Perspectives on the Theory and Practice of Public Governance*. London: Routledge.

Ostrom, E. 1999. Crossing the great divide: Co-production, synergy, and development. In M. D. McGinnis, ed. *Polycentric Governance and Development. Readings from the Workshop in Political Theory and Policy Analysis*: Ann Arbor: University of Michigan Press, Ch. 15.

Ostrom, E. 2000. Collective action and the evolution of social norms. *Journal of Economic Perspectives* 14 (3): 137–158.

Ostrom, V. 1973. *The Intellectual Crisis in American Public Administration*. Tuscaloosa: University of Alabama Press.

Ostrom, V., Ostrom, E. 1999. Public choice: a different approach to the study of public administration. In M. D. McGinnis, ed. *Polycentric Governance and Institutions. Readings from the Workshop in Political Theory and Policy Analysis*. Ann Arbor: University of Michigan Press, pp. 34–55.

Parks, R. B., P. C. Baker, L. Kiser, R. Oakerson, E. Ostrom, V. Ostrom, S. L. Percy, M. B. Vandivort, G. P. Whitaker, and R. Wilson. 1981. Consumers as co-producers of public services: Some economic and institutional considerations. *Policy Studies Journal* 9 (7): 1001–1011.

Pestoff, V. 1998. *Beyond the Market and State: Civil Democracy and Social Enterprises in a Welfare Society.* Aldershot, UK: Ashgate.

Pestoff, V. 2006. Citizens as co-producers of welfare services: Preschool services in eight European countries. *Public Management Review* 8 (4): 503–520.

Pestoff, V. 2008. *A Democratic Architecture for the Welfare State: Promoting Citizen Participation, the Third Sector and Co-Production.* London: Routledge.

Pestoff, V. 2009. Towards a paradigm of democratic participation: Citizen participation and co-production of personal social services in Sweden. *Annals of Public and Cooperative Economics* 80 (2): 197–224.

Schmitter, P. C., 2002. Participation in Governance Arrangements: Is there any reason to expect it will achieve "Sustainable and Innovative Policies in a Multi-Level Context?", in Grote, J. R. & B. Gbikpi (eds), 2002. *Participatory Governance. Political and Social Implications,* Leske + Budrick, Opladen

Sjöstrand, S.-E. 1993. *On the Rational behind Irrational Institutions.* Stockholm: School of Economics, EFI.

Vamstad, J. 2007. *Governing Welfare: The Third Sector and the Challenges to the Swedish Welfare State.* Doctoral dissertation. Östersund: Mid-Sweden University.

20 Conclusion
Taking Research on Co-Production a Step Further

Taco Brandsen, Bram Verschuere and Victor Pestoff

OVERVIEW

In earlier work, it was suggested that "future research [on co-production] could conceptualize the different types of functions more systematically and assess them on a cross-sectoral and/or cross-national basis" (Pestoff, Osborne and Brandsen, 2006, 594). We took up the challenge and defined the questions presented in the introduction to this volume:

- *Conceptual issues*: What is the nature of co-production, and what different conceptualizations exist, especially in the context of public management?
- *Empirical issues*: How does co-production work in public service delivery in practice? Is it as successful or mundane as some of its proponents have claimed? Given that we know how it works in practice: can co-production contribute to improved quality in the public services?
- *Comparative issues*: How does the practice of co-production differ between countries and sectors?
- *Methodological issues*: What methods and theoretical approaches are most suitable for the examination of the topic?

In the concluding chapter of this volume, we will address each of these issues. Doing justice to the sheer volume and diversity of empirical data in this volume is a tall order. Therefore, we encourage readers to regard these conclusions as a starting point for further reflection, rather than an exhaustive analysis.

CO-PRODUCTION AS A MULTILEVEL CONCEPT

Co-production can exist at different levels of analysis. For example, we can discern between the level of individual users, of groups of users and of organizations: individuals and groups of users influencing services that are delivered to them versus organizations working together with other organizations in public service delivery (what we referred to as "co-management"). This is more than a minor difference, because depending on where co-production is situated, the meaning of the debate and the added value of the concept vary markedly.

At the individual or group level, co-production is one of several mechanisms that can be used to increase the influence of citizens over the services that are delivered to them (the most common alternatives being consumerism or representative democracy). Examples in this volume include the housing cooperatives examined by Brandsen and Helderman, in which tenants participate in the maintenance and construction of the built environment in which they live. Vamstad describes parent cooperatives in child care that develop in a dialogue between users and staff while they co-produce the services together. How such involvement of users potentially affects the nature and quality of services is discussed in this chapter.

At the organizational level, co-production is less about citizens and professionals than about the relationship between different types of organizations; particularly, between state and private nonprofit (third sector) organizations. Tsukamoto (in this volume) discusses the involvement of private non-profit organizations in the provision of public services in partnership with local governments. Vancoppenolle and Verschuere look at how organizational fields are shaped in which service providers of different types (public agencies, private NPOs and commercial organizations) offer the same public service. As regards the dynamics of the relationships between the organizations, the findings are similar to those of more general studies of networks and public-private partnerships.

There are two respects in which the findings have a specific added value. The first is that they focus on the role of private nonprofits, whereas most studies in public management research tend to look at interagency relationships or partnerships with the business sector. Schlappa in this volume shows how private nonprofits may be involved as real "co-managers" of urban reorganization projects, rather than as mere contractors without a voice in decision making. The findings of this volume also show changes in the internal dynamics of the organizations involved. As we will note later in this chapter, there is evidence both of institutional isomorphism and of hybridization.

The involvement of people and organizations in producing public goods and services is essential in defining the concept of co-production. Most chapters in this volume take this definition as the starting point. Some authors broaden the concept and discuss issues that go further than the pure production of public goods and services. Vaillancourt discusses the way private nonprofits ("the third sector") are involved in producing public policies. He therefore coins the term "co-construction" of policies. Ackerman (this volume) discusses co-governance, meaning the extent to which the "state" invites "society" in shaping policies that affect society, thereby attempting greater accountability. The case of participatory budgeting in Porto Alegre, for example, is a clear and well-known example of this "co-governance."

CHANGES IN THE STRUCTURE OF SERVICE DELIVERY

Interestingly, two seemingly contradictory developments seem to be at work in the case studies of co-production described in this volume. On the one hand, co-production appears to encourage diversity; on the other, there are instances of growing homogeneity. It depends, of course, on the institutional background in which co-production emerges.

The rise of co-production can, in some cases, contribute to fragmentation in the provision of public services. This is particularly the case where it allows users to carve their own pockets of service provision within a landscape dominated by a relatively small number of established providers (see Brandsen and Helderman in this volume). It is visible, for instance, in the area of housing, where small, scattered cooperatives sit alongside huge providers of social housing. It is, of course, also the case among digital communities, where fragmentation is endemic (see Meijer in this volume).

At the same time, there are tendencies toward isomorphism, where private organizations come into the public sphere and become entangled in local or national administrative practices. For instance, Dezeure and De Rynck in this volume found that Flemish organized citizen initiatives that cooperate with government for delivering public services tend to "change" over time, as does their relation with government: the many repeated interactions between organization and government bring both actors closer to each other, lead to some loss of autonomy, increase the interdependence between organization and government, and in some cases, organized citizen initiatives become "governmental instruments" to some extent. This echoes earlier findings of the effects of nonprofit involvement in the implementation of state policy (e.g., the well-known study by Smith and Lipsky, 1993). Co-production has made nonprofit organizations, at least in the context of public services, increasingly hard to categorize. As a result of their involvement in public service delivery and the contracting out and performance measurement that followed it, the traditional boundaries between market, state and third sector have been breaking down to the point where a class of indeterminate organizational hybrids has emerged (Evers, 2005; Brandsen, Van de Donk, and Putters, 2005). It means that the third sector organizations have taken on more characteristics of state organizations (e.g., in terms of formalization) and of market organizations (e.g., maximizing their income, but without maximizing their profit). Although no organization can be regarded as "pure," many organizations now reach the point where the ideal types, state, market or third sector, no longer help us to truly understand them.

EFFECTS ON THE NATURE OF SERVICE DELIVERY

Co-production also affects the nature of public service delivery. On the positive side, co-production can contribute to greater satisfaction of users to services. This has always been claimed, somehow, in a normative sense, by proponents of NPG (new public governance). As a feature of NPG, co-production is an alternative to traditional public administration ("bureaucracies") and markets and private businesses (new public management). As is argued in the chapters of Pestoff and Calabrò, public service delivery in close cooperation with citizens and the voluntary (third) sector has the promise of delivering better public services in the eyes of the beholder: the key stakeholder of public services(i.e., the citizens). While often stated, there is now actually some evidence that co-production may lead to better quality service delivery.

Greater involvement of users in service delivery can lead to higher levels of satisfaction due to greater "moral ownership" and tailoring of services to personal needs. Broadly speaking, it allows some of the benefits of market consumerism into the realm of public services. Vamstad found that co-operative child care in Sweden offers "better quality" compared to professionalized municipal child care, in the eyes of both clients and staff. According to Vamstad, co-production seems a promising method to reach the goals for public management that are not coming from the market-oriented literature originally intended for the private sector. Also Calabrò proposes co-production as an alternative to privatization of public services. It is argued that many privatizations of the 1980s and 1990s have only been "partial": privatization of public services formerly delivered by the state, but without introducing real market competition for these services. These partial privatization processes can be detrimental for the accountability of the service providers toward the citizens/clients. Therefore, co-production is proposed as an alternative: by developing new ways for citizens to participate in the production and provision of public services, a new relationship between citizen and state can be developed that is based on trust, true ethical standards and accountability. In particular, the chapters by Calabrò and Vancoppenolle and Verschuere discuss the impact of co-production and co-management on accountability of public services.

Similarly, it has been argued that co-production encourages active commitment by users. That appears to depend on the manner of their involvement. Small-scale initiatives appear more capable of motivating people than large institutionalized ones. However, this does not necessarily mean that only small organizations can be successful at it. The question is, rather, how citizen participation is organized within those structures. Vamstad and Pestoff discuss such issues in this volume.

However, there are of course also drawbacks. To begin with, co-production can strengthen insider-outsider dynamics when this type of service provision is only accessible to specific social groups, either because these groups actively guard their own borders or because there are institutional mechanisms that discourage certain groups from engaging. This is shown in the chapter by Brandsen and Helderman: there is a gap between the rhetoric of housing cooperatives (on paper, anyone can join at a relatively low cost), and the reality (cooperatives are in practice rather closed systems). Another related issue—"who is involved in co-production"—is still suffering from a lack of systematic evidence: we do not know much on the background of those involved in co-production, and the cases are indeed conflicting. Some suggest that the phenomenon is (like so many others) biased in favor of the middle classes, while in others it is cross-cutting.

A second potential drawback of co-production is that the issue of "accountability" may be problematic: who can the users hold accountable when the users themselves are part of the production process? In the case of co-management, where third sector organizations and public agencies (government) simultaneously deliver public services, there may also be an "obscured" public accountability, as the chapter by Vancoppenolle and Verschuere shows. They show that in a complex field with many service delivery agents of different types (public, private, NPO and commercial), as is the case with Flemish child care, the many relationships between these agents, and between agents and oversight authorities, may lead to loss of accountability between these actors. This, in turn, may lead to undesired policy outcomes and the observation that the interests of the users of child care are not fully safeguarded.

A third potential problem is the opposition of professional staff to have "non-professional" users involved: professionals may contend that education and experience are more important than user involvement. If not considered seriously, these concerns may result in co-production offering lower quality of services, instead of equal or better quality service delivery. Vamstad discusses this in his chapter in this volume.

At a higher level of analysis, the potential fragmentation of service provision associated with some forms of co-production can lead to a less efficient use of public resources. The methods used by researchers in this field (see the next section) tend to highlight case-specific quality improvements, but there is little evidence of the potential costs of co-production at higher levels of aggregation, and the effect of the fact that resources are "scaled-down." However, ignoring the potential benefit of user involvement also implies certain losses or costs.

COMPARATIVE ISSUES

At a general level, the collection of chapters in this volume is comparative in itself. It shows that co-production can be observed in a wide range of policy fields. Only to name some examples: Brandsen and Helderman discuss housing policy; Vancoppenolle and Verschuere, and Vamstad, discuss child care; and Schlappa discusses urban regeneration projects. It also shows that co-production is an international phenomenon. We collected contributions that discuss co-production in European, North American, Asian and Australian contexts.

When looking at the work of individual researchers reflected in the separate chapters, we observe diversity in the levels of "comparativeness." Some chapters deal with one policy field in one country, for example: Brandsen and Helderman on German housing cooperatives, Vancoppenolle and Verschuere on child care in Flanders, Freise on local regulation partnerships in the field of public safety in Germany, Tsukamoto presents a case study of co-production in Japan and Vamstad on child care in Sweden. The latter chapter is comparative, in the sense that it compares two different types of organizations delivering the same service: municipal (governmental) child care and cooperative (co-produced) childcare.

Other chapters compare different fields or sectors within one country. Dezeure and De Rynck reflect on three cases in which nonprofits are in a local co-management arrangement with the local government in the city of Ghent, Flanders/Belgium: youth policy, intercultural policy and community development. In another chapter, by Schlappa, one field is discussed for different countries: urban regeneration is compared between a German city (Berlin), a Northern Irish city (Belfast), and a British city (Bristol).

Some chapters compare co-production between different countries and between different sectors. Calabrò has compared Italian and Norwegian systems of public service delivery, using case studies of organizations from different policy fields. The importance of his contribution lies in the finding that similar results can be observed in different politico-administrative systems: the drawbacks of public service delivery that is only partially privatized are remarkably similar in both countries. Pestoff discusses a comparative multiple case study of family policy and preschool services in eight European countries. And Ackerman discusses co-governance by looking at four case studies in which different policy issues are discussed in four different countries: Brazil (participatory budgeting), Mexico (organizing elections), the United States (policing and education) and India (anticorruption).

On the whole, the research in the field has moved on. Whereas previous work was dominated by single case studies, there is now much more comparative work. Yet it is also evident that the nature of the comparisons is so different that it limits the cumulative effect of the research.

METHODOLOGICAL ISSUES

Most of the research presented here is case study based. Only a few references are made to data collected in a large N setting, through surveys and so forth. Vamstad's chapter is one exception. This of course limits the scope of the findings and should be compensated for in future research. If we could measure co-production in a large N setting, we could test hypotheses and theorize the determinants and effects of co-production, for example, trying to measure and compare the level and intensity of co-production in different settings.

Furthermore, most authors use qualitative data. Perhaps this is not surprising, given the ongoing conceptual debates on what "co-production" actually means. Conceptual clarity is a first prerequisite in order to be able to operationalize the concept of "co-production" for reasons of quantitative measurement. Some authors have tried to quantify their data. Calabrò, for example, has measured the number of public service providers that apply codes of conduct in public service provision, and how issues such as corruption and interest conflicts are avoided through the use of such codes and rules. This is, however, a measurement of a possible effect of co-production (ethical behavior and accountability while delivering public services), and not a measurement of (the presence of) "co-production" itself. Vamstad has surveyed clients and staff of Swedish child care facilities and asked how clients and staff perceive service quality in facilities of different types. This, too, is a measurement of an effect of co-production (service quality), and not co-production itself.

Another issue is that the units of analysis differ markedly. Some authors discuss policy initiatives and/or reforms aimed at stimulating co-production or third sector (Vaillancourt), either central or local governmental initiatives. Others discuss partnerships between organizations in policy fields (e.g., Schlappa, Dezeure and De Rynck, Vancoppenolle and Verschuere, and Freise). In these chapters, the focus is rather on how co-production works in practice. Yet others take organizations as the focal point of their analysis (Calabrò, Vamstad, Tsukamoto, Helderman and Brandsen). In these chapters, organizational functioning and effects of organizations are discussed.

All in all, the research on co-production is a rich one. Notwithstanding the criticism that can and should be leveled against current research, significant steps forward have been made over the past few years. However, the debate would benefit from greater methodological diversity (specifically, more quantitative comparative work) and yet further conceptual clarification.

IN PARTING

The aim of this volume has been to collect recent research findings on the co-production in the context of new public governance, with the aim of showing the state of the art on the topic. We believe that, at least to some extent, this ambition has been achieved. Our overview shows, we believe, that the debate has advanced considerably over the past few years. There is more evidence for dynamics, benefits and drawbacks that had previously

388   *Taco Brandsen, Bram Verschuere and Victor Pestoff*

been defined only theoretically. Furthermore, more of the research is comparative in nature, which we regard as an improvement in the quality of the work. We have also signalled that there is still much room for improvement. Particularly, conceptual confusion remains a problem and the methodological diversity is still limited.

On the whole, there may be grounds for satisfaction, but not for complacency. There is still much work to be done. And would we want it any other way?

REFERENCES

Brandsen, T., W. Van de Donk, and K. Putters. 2005. Griffins or chameleons? Hybridity as a permanent and inevitable characteristic of the third sector. *International Journal of Public Administration* 28 (9–10): 749–765.

Evers, A. 2005. Mixed welfare systems and hybrid organizations: Changes in the governance and provision of social services. *International Journal of Public Administration* 28 (9/10): 737–748.

Pestoff, V., S. Osborne, and T. Brandsen. 2006. Patterns of co-production in public services: Some concluding thoughts. *Public Management Review* 8 (4): 591–595.

Smith, S. R., and M. Lipsky. 1993. *Nonprofits for Hire: The Welfare State in the Age of Contracting.* Cambridge, MA: Harvard University Press.

Contributors

John M. Ackerman is Professor at the Institute of Legal Research of the National Autonomous University of Mexico (UNAM) and Vice President of the International Association of Administrative Law. He received his M.A. and Ph.D. in Political Sociology from the University of California, Santa Cruz and is an expert in the topics of corruption control, election law, transparency, accountability, independent agencies and citizen participation. He is Editor-in-Chief of the *Mexican Law Review*. Some of his most important scholarly publications include: "The Global Explosion of Freedom of Information Laws," *Administrative Law Review* (58:1, 2006), and "Co-Governance for Accountability, " *World Development* (32:3, 2004). He has also published the results of his research with *The World Bank, Gestión y Política Pública, Instituto Federal de Acceso a la Información Pública, Auditoría Superior de la Federación, Boletín Mexicano de Derecho Comparado, Perfiles Latinoamericanos, Revista Quórum*, as well as in numerous edited volumes.

Tony Bovaird is Professor of Public Management and Policy at INLOGOV and the Third Sector Research Centre, University of Birmingham, UK. He worked in the UK Civil Service, Aston and Bristol Business Schools before rejoining INLOGOV in 2006. He focuses on public sector reform strategy, performance management and policy evaluation. He recently led UK team researching user and community co-production of public services in five European countries. Co-editor of *Public Management and Governance* (2nd ed., London: Routledge, 2009).

Taco Brandsen is Associate Professor in Public Management at the Nijmegen School of Management, Radboud University Nijmegen, the Netherlands. His current research focuses on public management reform, civil society and partnerships. His latest books, together with Victor Pestoff (eds), are *Co-Production. The Third Sector and the Delivery of Public Services* (2008 & 2009), London & New York: Routledge and together with Paul Decker and Adalbert Evers (eds) is *Civicness in the Governance and Delivery of Social Services* (2010) Baden-Baden: Nomos.

Kerry Brown holds the Mulpha Chair in Tourism Asset Management and is a professor in the School of Tourism and Hospitality Management at Southern Cross University, Gold Coast, Australia, where she is also Director of the Research Centre for Tourism, Leisure and Work. Her main fields of research are public management and employment relations. Other principal research foci are collaboration, networks and industry clusters; capability, strategy, management and policy for infrastructure and asset management; work-life balance and negotiation, and employment relations. She has co-authored two books and published over 50 articles in scholarly journals.

Edgar S. Cahn is the creator of *Time Dollar* and founder of *TimeBanks USA*, as well as the co-founder of the National Legal Services Program and the Antioch School Law (now the University of the District of Columbia School of Law). He is the author of *No More Throw Away People: The Co-Production Imperative, Time Dollars, Our Brother's Keeper: The Indian in White America* and *Hunger USA*.

Andrea Calabro is European PhD in Governance and Management, Temporary Professor at "Magna Graecia" University of Catanzaro (Italy) and Research Fellow at University of Rome "Tor Vergata" (Italy). He is secretary for the EURAM Corporate Governance Special Interest Group (SIG). His main focus is on Public Governance. During the last years he has developed research on: governance mechanisms in Public Service Organizations, Local Public Utilities and Co-production. He has published papers in international journals such as International Journal of Public Administration, Journal of Management and Governance, Journal of Business Ethics, etc. His last book is *Governance Structures and Mechanisms in Public Service Organizations*, published with Springer in Contributions to Management Science.

Filip De Rynck is full professor in public administration at the University College of Ghent (Belgium), member of the University Ghent Association. He worked as a practitioner in local government and the non-profit sector for many years before returning to the academic world. His Ph.D. was about policy networks in regional development (1995, KULeuven). His research is focused on local government, policy networks, e-government, intergovernmental relations and citizen participation. He presided several official advisory committees for the Flemish government and is actively involved in programmes for urban policy.

Karolien Dezeure is full-time researcher at the Faculty of Business and Public Administration of the University College Ghent, Belgium. Her research focuses on local government and citizen participation. She is involved in several boards and urban projects concerning community participation.

Adalbert Evers is Professor for Comparative Health and Social Policy at the Justus-Liebig-University in Giessen / Germany. Fields of research, teaching and publications are: Social policy and personal social services, the third sector and civil society, governance and civic engagement. His latest books are *The Third Sector in Europe* (ed. with Laville, Jean-Louis; 2004 Edward Elgar); *Civicness in the Governance and Delivery of Social Services* (ed. with Brandsen, Taco and Dekker, Paul); *Third Sector Organizations Facing Turbulent Environments. Sports, Culture and Social Services in Five European Countries* (ed. with Zimmer, Annette), at Nomos.

Benjamin Ewert studied Political Science at the Philipps-University Marburg and the Charles University Prague. Since 2007 he is a research assistant at the professorship for Comparative Health and Social Policy at the Justus-Liebig-University Giessen. He worked as an administrator within the European Network of Excellence 'Civil Society and New Forms of Governance' (CINEFOGO) and is currently employed as a junior researcher within the EU-project (7th framework) 'Welfare Innovations at the Local Level in Favour of Cohesion' (WILCO).

Matthias Freise is Senior Research Fellow at the Department for Political Science at Münster University, Germany. Previously, he was the supervisor of the research group "European Civil Society and Multilevel Governance" at Münster University. His research interests include civil society theory, third sector research, European multilevel governance, and interest representation. His latest book is *A Panacea for all Seasons? Civil Society and Governance in Europe*, edited together with Mikka Pyykkönen and Eglė Vaidelytė (2010) at Nomos: Baden-Baden.

Christine Gray is Chief Executive Officer, TimeBanks USA. For ten years, she led development of new approaches to TimeBanking and Co-Production for systems change, and development of all TBUSA training and support materials. She co-teaches a course in System Change in the LLM program of the University of the District of Columbia School of Law. Prior to her work at TimeBanks USA, Christine was a community activist and leader in Agoura Hills, California, where she was engaged in a grass-roots movement for the community's cityhood. Her doctoral dissertation (UCLA 2011) focuses on the political status of American Indian tribes from 1763 to 1978, with special emphasis on their achievement of self-determination and self-governance in the later years of the twentieth century.

Jan-Kees Helderman is assistant professor at the Department of Public Administration and Political Science, Radboud University Nijmegen, the Netherlands. He studied Spatial Planning at the University of Nijmegen and he has worked at the Erasmus University Rotterdam where he obtained his Ph.D. His doctoral thesis *"Bringing the Market back in? Institutional Complementarity & Hierarchy in Dutch Housing and Health Care"* (Rotterdam, 2007) won the G.A. van Poelje award for the best doctoral dissertation in Dutch and Flemish public administration. He is specialized in comparative institutional analyses of welfare state reforms, more specifically, on housing and health care policy. He was member of the Health Reform Evaluation Advisory Panel of the British Department of Health and he regularly advises the Dutch Government and Dutch housing associations on issues concerning housing policy and related governance issues.

Robyn Keast is an associate professor in the area of public management, and social and technical innovation management in the School of Management, Queensland University of Technology (QUT), Brisbane, Australia. She received her PhD from QUT in 2003 and has researched and widely published in the areas of networks, collaboration, public management and innovation policy.

Elke Löffler is Chief Executive of Governance International, with more than fifteen years of professional experience in training of civil servants, facilitating participatory events, undertaking international consultancies, writing government reports and undertaking evidence-based research for public agencies. Her expertise is in service improvement, quality and performance management, citizen involvement in the commissioning, design, delivery and evaluation of public services, personalisation of public services, outcome assessment, partnership working and local governance. Co-editor of *Public Management and Governance* (2nd ed., London: Routledge, 2009).

Myrna Mandell is Professor Emeritus at California State University, Northridge, and an Adjunct Faculty at Southern Cross University in New South Wales, Australia. Her work includes articles and chapters on a number of different facets of networks, including: how to organize and manage networks, performance measures for networks, citizen participation in networks and leadership in networks. She is currently involved in compiling a book on building theories of networks. She has recently been a keynote speaker at a major international conference, has done seminars and projects as a visiting professor in Switzerland, has presented a number of papers and is a convenor on a number of panels at various international conferences. She is also the co-author of a booklet specifically for practitioners in the non-profit sector on best practices for networks.

Albert Meijer is an associate professor in Public Administration at Utrecht University in the Netherlands. His research focuses on new forms of governance in an information age. He has published extensively on technology and governance in journals such as Public Management Review, Information Polity and Government Information Quarterly. His latest books are *ICTs, Citizens and Governance: After the Hype* (2009, IOS Press, edited with KeesBoersma and Pieter Wagenaar) and *Migration and the New Technological Borders of Europe* (2011, Palgrave Macmillan, edited with HuubDijstelbloem).

Glen Murphy is currently a lecturer within the School of Management with teaching responsibilities within the Brisbane Graduate School of Business (BGSB) in the areas of Strategic Analysis. Glen's research interests are currently concentrated around improving data quality and data management within organizations; and Strategic decision making in technical and complex environments. Previous roles have included a post-doctoral research fellowship with the CRC Centre for Integrated Engineering Asset Management (CIEAM) at the Queensland University of Technology, Brisbane, Australia.

Victor Pestoff is Professor Emeritus in Political Science and currently Guest Professor at the Institute for Civil Society Studies at Ersta Skondal University College in Stockholm, Sweden. He has over 35 years of research on the Third Sector, its role in public policy and providing social services. His latest books are *A Democratic Architecture for the Welfare State* (2009), and together with Taco Brandsen (eds) *Co-Production. The Third Sector and the Delivery of Public Services* (2008 & 2009), both at Routledge: London & New York.

David O. Porter is Professor Emeritus in Business Administration at the University of Alaska Fairbanks, USA. Since retirement he has returned to his research on interorganizational program implementation and network structures. He served over 25 years as an executive in state government and universities. In addition to the University of Alaska he held faculty appointments at the Wayne State University in Detroit, University of California Riverside, the George Washington University in Washington D.C., the University of Texas at Austin and California State University San Bernardino. He was Research Fellow at the International Institute of Mangement, Science Center Berlin 1977–79.

Hans Schlappa is senior lecturer in strategic management at the business school of Hertfordshire University, UK. He has managed and researched public services over the past 20 years and undertaken a wide range of studies concerned with third sector organisations. His current research projects are concerned with the socio-economic regeneration of European cities, the provision of older people's services and graduate internships in third sector organisations.

Ichiro Tsukamoto is Professor of Public Management at the School of Business Administration, Meiji University, in Tokyo, Japan, where he specializes in public management, public private partnerships and social enterprises. He is the co-author of "Local Non-Profit -Government Partnerships in Japan" (*Public Management Review*, 8(4), 2006), *Social Enterprise: A Global Comparison* (Janelle A. Kerlin ed.) and "Comparative Study Between Japan and the UK on Shifting the Third Sector-Government Relationships" (*International Journal of Public & Private Healthcare Management and Economics*,1 (1), 2011).

Yves Vaillancourt holds a Ph.D. in political science. He is 'professeurassocié' at the School of Social Work of the University of Quebec in Montreal (UQAM). He is a member of LAREPPS, a research unit on social policy and of CRISES, a research center on social innovations. In the last 20 years, he has been publishing extensively on the contribution of the third sector (or the social and solidarity economy) in the development of social policy and social housing. His latest paper published is with Christian Jetté in *Voluntas* (March 2011): " Social Economy and Home Care Services in Quebec: Co-Production or Co-Construction? ". He is a member of GESQ (Grouped'économiesolidaire du Québec).

Johan Vamstad is a full-time researcher in Political Science at the Institute for Civil Society Studies at ErstaSköndal University College in Stockholm, Sweden. He has previously performed research and teaching at the Department of Social Science at Mid-Sweden University and at the Department of Political Science at Lund University. His research mainly concerns civil society and welfare states and he is currently performing research on Swedish freedom of choice reforms".

Diederik Vancoppenolle is Assistant Professor at the Faculty of Business and Public Administration of University College Ghent, Belgium. He studies welfare policies as well as policy roles of civil servants and ministerial advisers. He published in West-European Politics, Public policy and administration, the Journal of Social Research & Policy and Res Publica and wrote several book chapters about ministerial advisers, the policy work of civil servants and child care policies.

Bram Verschuere is Assistant Professor at the Faculty of Business and Public Administration of University College Ghent (Ghent University Association), Belgium. His main research and teaching interests are in public management, public sector organization, state-nonprofit relationships, and welfare policy. His latest books are *Autonomy and control of state* *agencies: comparing states and agencies* (Palgrave McMillan Ltd., 2010, with KoenVerhoest, Paul Roness, Kristin Rubecksen and MuirisMcCarthaigh), and *Re-thinking the state: critical perspectives on the citizen, politics and government in the 21st century* (Kluwer, 2009, with Filip De Rynck and Ellen Wayenberg).

Jennifer Waterhouse is a senior lecturer in the area of human resource management and employment relations in the Newcastle Business School, University of Newcastle, Australia. She received her PhD from the Queensland University of Technology, Australia, in 2003 and has researched and widely published in the areas of human resource management, public management and policy.

Index